I0819329

RAILROADS PAST AND PRESENT

INDIANA UNIVERSITY PRESS

H. Roger Grant and Thomas Hoback, editors

THE RAILROAD PHOTOGRAPHY OF
LUCIUS BEEBE AND CHARLES CLEGG

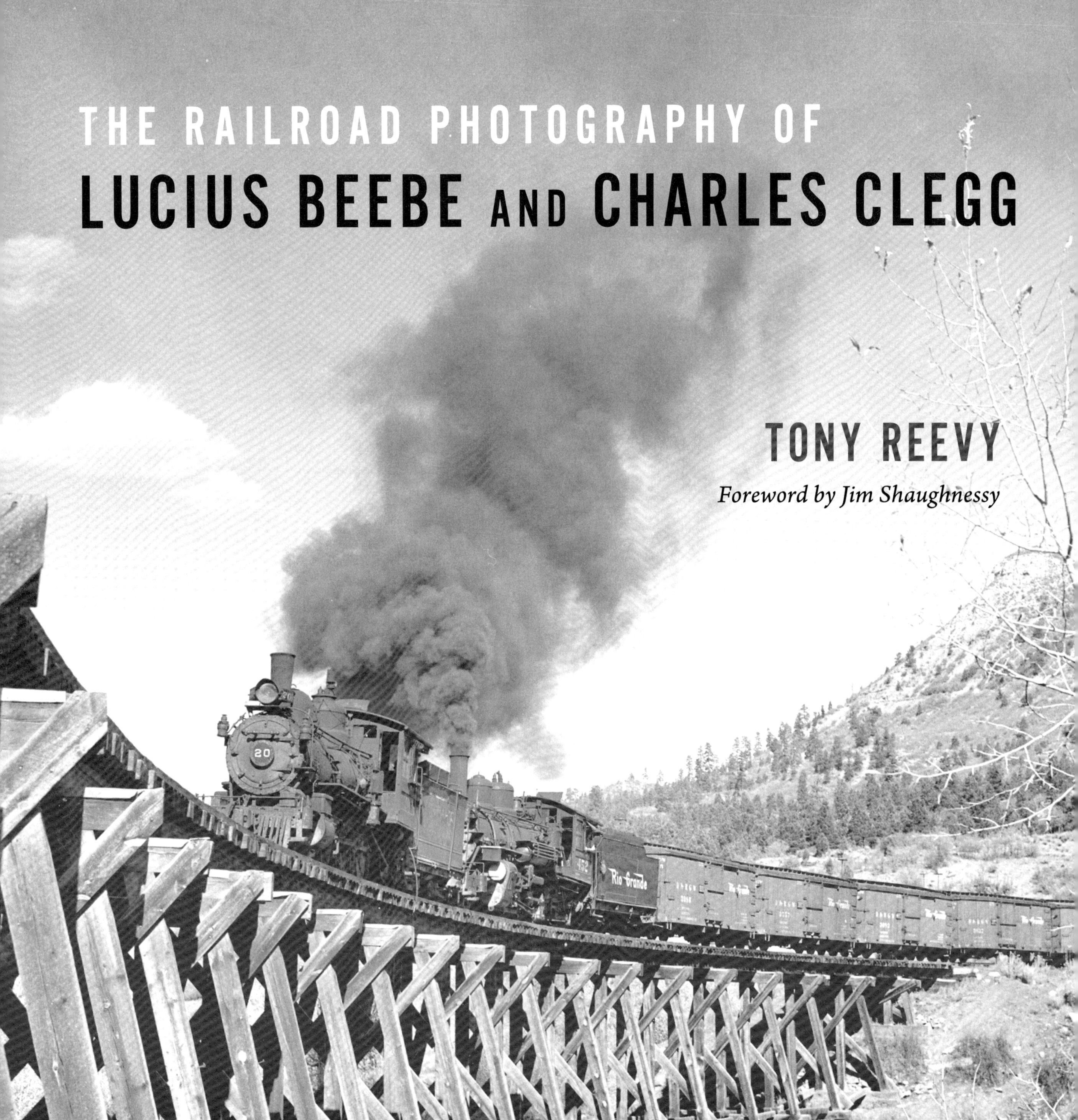

THE RAILROAD PHOTOGRAPHY OF LUCIUS BEEBE AND CHARLES CLEGG

TONY REEVY

Foreword by Jim Shaughnessy

This book is a publication of

Indiana University Press
Office of Scholarly Publishing
Herman B Wells Library 350
1320 East 10th Street
Bloomington, Indiana 47405 USA

iupress.indiana.edu

The paper used in this publication meets the minimum requirements of the American National Standard for Information Sciences—Permanence of Paper for Printed Library Materials, ANSI Z39.48-1992.

Manufactured in the United States of America

Library of Congress Cataloging-in-Publication Data

Names: Reevy, Tony, author. | Shaughnessy, Jim, writer of foreword.
Title: The railroad photography of Lucius Beebe and Charles Clegg / Tony Reevy ; foreword by Jim Shaughnessy.
Description: Bloomington, Indiana : Indiana University Press, 2018. | Series: Railroads past and present | Includes bibliographical references and index.
Identifiers: LCCN 2018019393 (print) | LCCN 2018021016 (ebook) | ISBN 9780253036681 (e-book) | ISBN 9780253036674 (cl : alk. paper)
Subjects: LCSH: Photography of railroads—United States. | Railroads—United States—Pictorial works. | Beebe, Lucius, 1902-1966. | Clegg, Charles, 1916-1979.
Classification: LCC TR715 (ebook) | LCC TR715 .R44 2018 (print) | DDC 779/.9385—dc23
LC record available at https://lccn.loc.gov/2018019393

2 3 4 5 23 22 21 20 19

TO LINDLEY AND IAN

and

In memoriam,

JIM SHAUGHNESSY

1933–2018

Jim, who wrote the foreword for this book, passed away just as it went to press. He was a pioneer of railroad-subject photography, and a friend to many. He will be missed.

CONTENTS

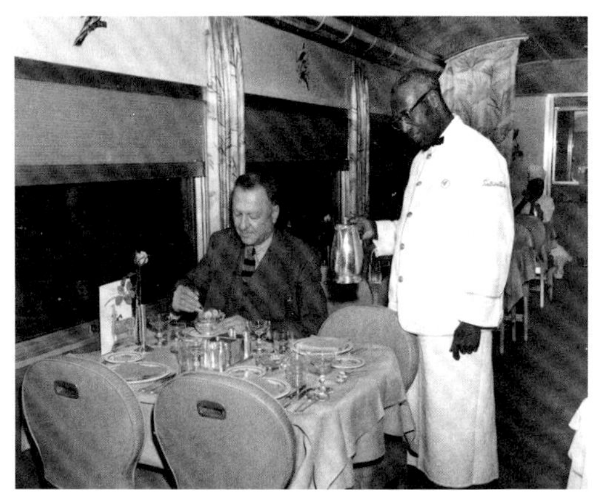

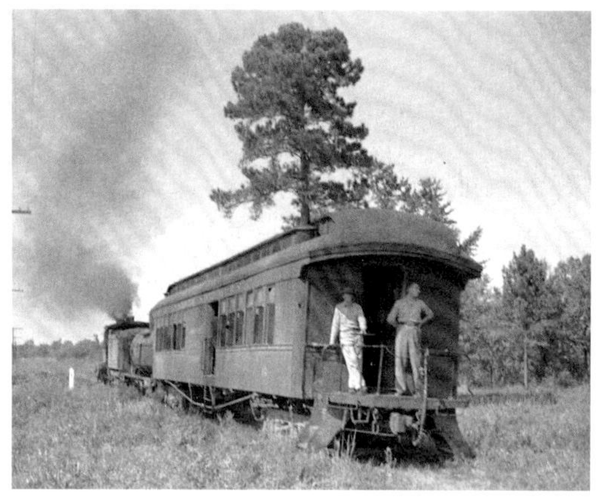

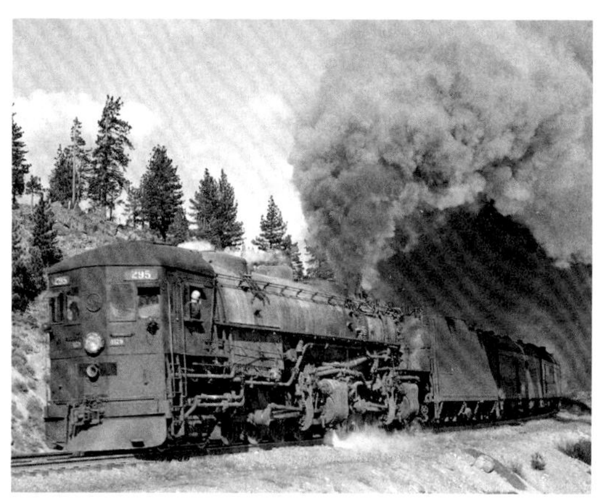

Preface *ix*
Acknowledgments *xi*
Foreword by Jim Shaughnessy *xiii*

The Railroad Photography of Lucius Beebe and Charles Clegg 2

1 The Three-Quarters Shot 23

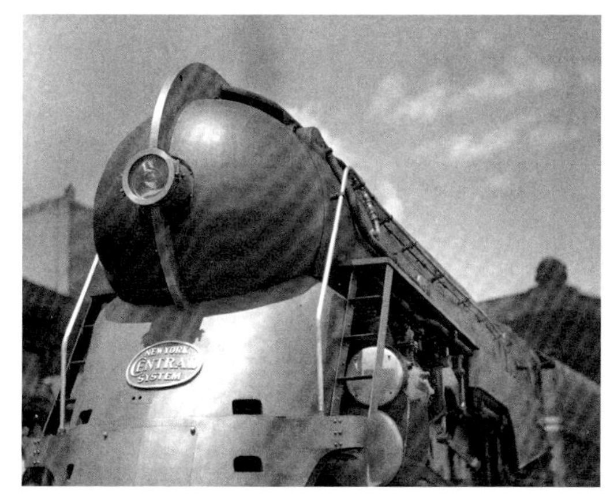

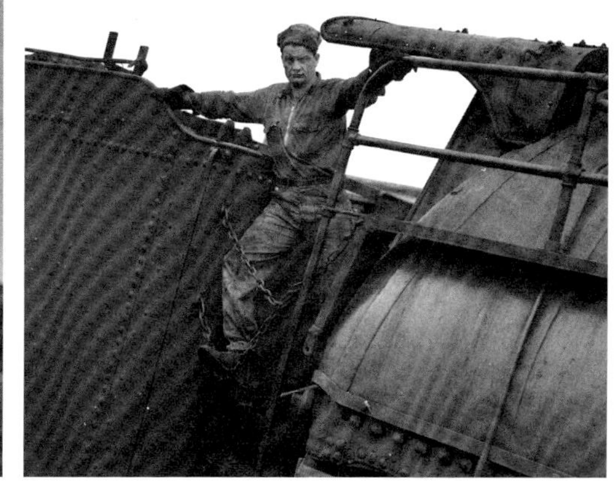

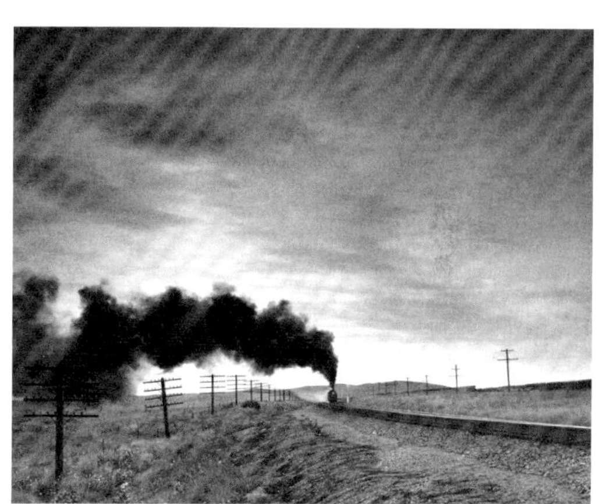

2
A Modernist View of the American Railroad 65

3
Railroaders 95

4
The Railroad in Its Environment 129

Appendix: Technical Details of the Photography 177
Notes 179
Chronological Bibliography of the Books of Lucius Beebe 185
Bibliography of Other Works 187
Index 191

PREFACE

I am often asked how I got interested in trains. One of the reasons has to do with my late father, a voracious collector of records and used books. He had little or no interest in railroads, but somewhere along the line, he bought a used copy of a book called *Highball*. The author was a man with the curious and, to a four-year-old, unpronounceable name of Lucius Beebe. I loved the book and remember spending many hours looking at it while lying on our living room floor. Dad finally gave me the book; I still have it.

I am by no means alone in having been introduced to railroad photography and writing by Lucius Beebe. In John Gruber's pamphlet, *Focus on Rails*, noted photographer Ted Benson mentions "devoting hours to back issues of *Trains* and the Beebe books" as a teenager.[1] Benson went on to say that he decided to pursue photojournalism as a career after "the momentous afternoon in 1962 when I came home from the public library with Lucius Beebe's *Age of Steam* under my arm."[2] Similarly, in Richard Steinheimer's *Backwoods Railroads of the West*, Steinheimer mentions that one of the reasons he got interested in trains was "stimulation from the gift of two fine photo books at this stage, namely Lucius Beebe's *High Iron* and *Highball*—books in which he threw out a great challenge to photographers to capture the sights of steam before the eclipse."[3]

In fact, Beebe developed the railroad picture book as we know it today. Therefore, Beebe's first such work, *High Iron: A Book of Trains*, published in 1938, marks an epochal date in the social history of American railroads. As famed *Trains* editor David P. Morgan put it in his obituary for Beebe, "Thus emerged the man who would enthrall the largest book audience in railroading for more than a quarter century."[4]

Who was this man with the curious name, and how did he come to originate a form that has been emulated by George Abdill, E. P. Alexander, Don Ball, Jeff Brouws, Arthur Dubin, O. Winston Link, David Plowden, H. Reid, Jim Shaughnessy, and many others? That is the question explored in the introduction to this book. In the four portfolios that follow, Lucius Beebe's photographs and the images taken by his creative and life partner, Charles Clegg, are profiled.

Beebe and Clegg inspired legions of railroad photographers and authors, and their life together helped establish a place for gay couples in our society. In addition, Beebe chronicled New York during Prohibition and the Great Depression, helping document and popularize café society. And Beebe's writing helped establish a greater appreciation for fine dining and travel in the United States. These creative and idiosyncratic men have been out of print, even marginalized, for too long. As we recover from the Great Recession and grapple with divisive issues such as same-sex marriage, it is time to rediscover them and their world.

ACKNOWLEDGMENTS

First, many thanks to my editor at Indiana University Press, Ashley Runyon; to her predecessor, Sarah Jacobi; and to Assistant Acquisitions Editor Peggy Solic. This book would not have been possible without their interest, their support, and their faith in my work. Thank you also to Jennifer Crane and Nancy Lightfoot.

The introduction is based on my article, "Writers of the Rail: Mixed Legacy," by Tony Reevy and Dan Cupper, from *Railroad History*, which won the 2006 David P. Morgan Article Award from the Railway and Locomotive Historical Society. I thank the then editor of *Railroad History*, Mark Reutter, and those I interviewed for the article: the late Arthur Dubin, Cornelius Hauck, the late Dick Kindig, Jim Shaughnessy, and John H. White Jr. Thank you also to Jim Shaughnessy, for contributing his wonderful foreword to this book.

This book and the article that preceded it would not have been possible without the help of the staff of the California State Railroad Museum and its library. Ellen Halteman, Cara Randall, Kathryn Santos, and Craig Castleton all provided invaluable assistance. Thank you also to the museum for permission to reproduce the images in this book and the article that preceded it.

Many thanks also to the staffs of the university libraries of the University of North Carolina at Chapel Hill, the Mid-Continent Railway Historical Society, and the Smithsonian Institution for assistance with this work.

Photography books represent a significant financial commitment. The University Research Council of my home institution at the time, the University of North Carolina at Chapel Hill, funded the scanning costs for the images in *The Railroad Photography of Lucius Beebe and Charles Clegg*, and my research in 2015 at the California State Railroad Museum was made possible by a 2014 John H. White Jr. Research Fellowship from the Railway and Locomotive Historical Society. A 2017 Overton Fellowship Prize from the Lexington Group in Transportation History funded the use fees for the images. Funding for the book was also generously provided by Tom Hoback and Rob Krebs.

As always, Jeff Brouws helped show me the way, and my family—Caroline, Lindley, and Ian—showed patience, understanding, and interest as I struggled to engage with Charles Clegg and, especially, Lucius Beebe. Creative and groundbreaking authors and photographers, they are challenging to read and difficult in many ways, from today's perspective, to understand.

FOREWORD

BY JIM SHAUGHNESSY

Lucius Beebe is widely considered to be the father of the railroad photo book as we know it today.

Lucius Morris Beebe was born in Wakefield, Massachusetts, north of Boston, on December 9, 1902, to a well-to-do family that traced its wealth back to the manufacturing of horse saddles for the Union Army during the Civil War. He attended two prep schools and Yale University and was expelled from all three because his style of pranks was not parallel with the school's administrators. He did, finally, graduate from Harvard University and went into the newspaper business, becoming a society editor—an opportunity no doubt related to his knowledge and contacts originating through his family's position. On even routine news coverage assignments, he might show up at the scene of a house fire wearing a top hat and opera cape. Lucius was one of a kind! He became very popular and well known as the society editor of the *New York Herald Tribune*, covering high-society splendor from just after Prohibition ended into the 1940s.

In addition to his high-society involvements, Lucius Beebe had always had a hidden interest in the Old West and railroads. When challenged to take railroad photographs, he went out, bought a four-by-five-inch Super D Graflex camera, put on his leather boots and Stetson hat, and went trackside.

Train photography at the time, the 1930s, was mostly perfectly posed images of locomotives only—with no other railroad items such as stations, water tanks, bridges, roundhouses, and so on. Very few railroad images showed locomotives in action. Beebe's early work mostly involved the front, three-quarter-angle action shot, or wedge. This involved the train roaring toward the camera with a great plume of smoke or steam rising and the cars strung out in the distance. Beebe was known to visit train crews, pass out a few good cigars, and request that they have the locomotive emit heavy smoke at a specific location on the line ahead, where, of course, he would be located, camera ready. His first railroad book, *High Iron,* was published in 1938 and featured Lucius's own wedge format images rushing past his camera. The captions for these images were enhanced by his colorful Victorian verbiage—like describing the locomotive being "under a pillar of cloud" or appearing to resemble "the burning of Rome."

In 1940, Lucius meet Charles Clegg, a young photographer who also had an interest in railroads, and the two went on to be lifelong partners in life and business. By 1948, Lucius's interest in reporting on high-society doings on the New York scene diminished. He gave up the top hat and tuxedo for a black Stetson, gold watch and chain, brocade vest, and leather boots. The American West had been a longtime passion, and he and Clegg moved to Virginia City, Nevada, a still-glowing ember from the heat of the Old West. There they bought a weather-beaten old gold miner's mansion and a faltering weekly newspaper, the *Territorial Enterprise.* The newspaper gained a nationwide following under their ownership, driven by Lucius's provocative coverage of and comments on local and national news. Finally, Beebe and Clegg bought a Victorian-appointed private railroad car and named it the *Gold Coast*. They used it extensively, traveling all across the American landscape gathering railroad photos.

Their projects all went well, and the pair bought a replacement for the *Gold Coast* from the Pullman Company and named it the *Virginia City*. They hired a Hollywood set designer to decorate the interior in a lavish red-and-gold, over-the-top Baroque style. The car featured marble-topped tables, a working fireplace, Venetian glass chandeliers, and a gold-leaf ceiling. To the uninformed observer, the car could possibly appear to be decorated in a style more like Nuevo Bordello. This was probably the most lavish private car ever to ride North American rails, and it certainly met Lucius's comment that "I want only the best of everything, and there's so little of that."[5]

Lucius went on to author about forty books, more than half of them about railroads, and most of them coauthored with Charles Clegg. Lucius was never a historian or technical fact gatherer and was criticized by some railroad history experts. But his mission was not to document technical details; it was to convey the excitement, thrill, and romance of train travel.

Lucius's photography improved with time, possibly under the influence of suggestions from Clegg. His technical quality was always good, but later in his career he looked more carefully at composition and subject, and included more railroad structures and working railroaders in his scenes. He also included more images from other photographers in his books, which helped to broaden the visual variety of his later volumes. His intention was to give the reader a taste of the thrill and satisfaction offered when traveling and being served in high-quality surroundings.

As the 1960s dawned, Beebe and Clegg sold their Virginia City newspaper. They purchased a mansion in Hillsborough, California, a few miles south of San Francisco, where they spent part of the year. There Beebe wrote about one railroad book a year until his sudden death in February 1966. The last several books were devoted to luxury passenger cars and trains, Lucius's lifelong passion.

We can thank Lucius Beebe for photos and prose that lifted the image of the speeding limiteds off the printed page and into our hearts. He was truly the father of the railroad photo book.

Jim Shaughnessy
Troy, New York, October 2017

THE RAILROAD PHOTOGRAPHY OF
LUCIUS BEEBE AND CHARLES CLEGG

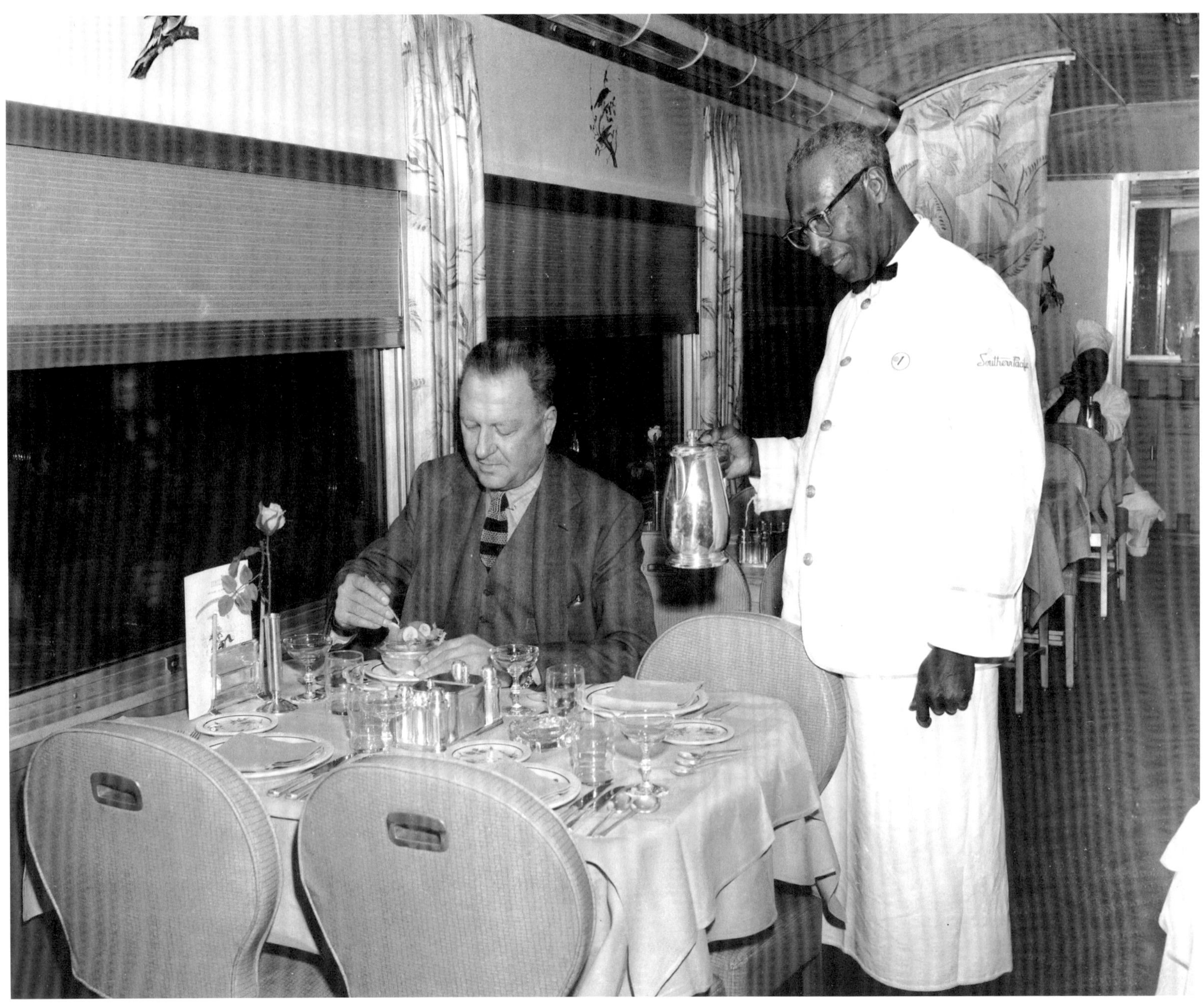

Lucius Beebe enjoying a meal in a Southern Pacific dining car. Photographer unknown. Beebe-Clegg negative 4002.

Courtesy of the California State Railroad Museum.

THE RAILROAD PHOTOGRAPHY OF LUCIUS BEEBE AND CHARLES CLEGG

AN AFFLUENT AND RIOTOUS NEW ENGLAND UPBRINGING

Lucius Morris Beebe was born in 1902 in Wakefield, Massachusetts, a suburb of Boston.[1] He came from a family of wealth; his father, Junius Beebe, headed a leather business and was involved with banks, a gas company, and a chemical company. The family also owned apple orchards in the state of Washington. Beebe had three siblings: an older sister, Lucia; an older brother, Junius Oliver Beebe; and another brother named Junius, Junius Merrick Beebe, who was born before the surviving Junius, but died at the age of one.

Junius Beebe served as a director of the Tidewater Railroad, which gave him access to its business car *Dixie*.[2] He was also involved with the Piney River & Paint Creek Railroad. As Y. Jean Stephens, a critic of Lucius Beebe's work, pointed out, Beebe was very proud of this part of his father's career. Stephens said, "Perhaps this aspect of his father's life—rather than the dime novels to which he [Lucius] ascribed a crucial role—determined the son's desire to have his own private railroad car someday."[3] Beebe's connection, through his father, to the luxurious aspects of railroading helped kindle a lifelong interest in and love of railroads.

Beebe's family came to what is now the United States in 1650 but achieved wealth producing leather, then a war material, for the Union during the Civil War. When Beebe bought a Rolls Royce in later life, he told the staff of his newspaper, the *Territorial Enterprise*, "My new automobile was not purchased with profits made from the publication of this newspaper. It's money my grandfather made selling saddles to the Union Army."[4]

Beebe's family was historically patrician, on both sides. His mother, Eleanor Harriet Merrick, was the granddaughter of Smith Gray, a Harvard professor. According to Wolcott Gibbs, by 1750, Beebe's ancestors "were men of property in the Galsworthian sense and warmly Tory in their sympathies."[5]

Beebe attended the North Ward School in Wakefield and ran through two prep schools, St. Marks and Berkshire, from which he was expelled for dynamiting and drinking incidents, respectively, before finally graduating from the Roxbury School. He then attended Yale, starting in 1921 in the class of 1925, but low academic performance led to Beebe's dropping out for a year and reentering in the class of 1926. Beebe's grades were not improved by the study atmosphere in his room, which was equipped with a roulette wheel, a hidden bar, and Picasso drawings. A college prank led to his expulsion from Yale in the middle of his sophomore year[6]: Beebe impersonated a professor from Yale Divinity School while attending a local theater and then threw an empty liquor bottle on stage. The professor, a valiant supporter of Prohibition, was not amused—and neither was Beebe's dean nor the president of Yale.

Beebe spent a year working for a newspaper, the *Boston Telegram*, and then entered Harvard in the class of 1927. He graduated in 1927.[7] Beebe remained at Harvard to work on a master's degree with Dr. John Livingston Lowes but was suspended in December 1928 for assaulting a fellow student. Beebe had published a pirated edition of lines by Edwin Arlington Robinson—Beebe was an authority on Robinson—and the student told Robinson about the transgression. Beebe assaulted his university colleague and reportedly put him in the hospital.

Viewed from today's remove, Beebe's record in prep school and college is a startling example of the privilege accorded to wealth and to white men at the time. The fact that Beebe could gain admission to these prep schools and universities given his record reflects his family's wealth and, therefore, power.

Beebe's record as a student also reflects a more innocent age. He was known as the local dynamiter in Wakefield and viewed blowing up outhouses as a prank. In today's post-9/11 society, incidents like this are treated a bit more harshly.

AN UNLIKELY REPORTER

With his college career ended by his suspension from Harvard, Beebe worked for another newspaper, the *Boston Transcript*, and then, in 1929, moved to New York City to work for one of its great newspapers, the *New York Herald Tribune*. He started work at the paper as a city staff reporter, covering news events such as fires, meetings, and petty crimes.

The *New York Herald Tribune* position advanced Beebe's bon vivant lifestyle, his later move to Nevada and California, and his interest in the Virginia & Truckee Railroad. The paper was owned by the Mills family, the descendants of Darius Ogden Mills, a wealthy West Coast mining and banking leader. At the time, Ogden Reid, Mills's grandson, headed the *New York Herald Tribune*, and another of Mills's grandsons, Ogden Mills, was using his fortune to keep the Virginia & Truckee Railroad in operation.[8] A fascinating character, Ogden Mills served as the secretary of the treasury for a time and also co-owned the equine hero of the Great Depression, "Seabiscuit."

Beebe was, at least in terms of his writing skills and style, an unlikely reporter. Beebe's prose was arch, and his writing style was old-fashioned even for its day, reflecting the influences of his family, prep schools, the New England environment, and Yale and Harvard. Beebe also paid too little attention to what nonfiction writers call "fact-checking." Some would even say that Beebe had disdain for the close use of factual information. These weaknesses in Beebe's writing seem to have been well recognized by the time Beebe joined the *New York Herald Tribune* in 1929. As Wolcott Gibbs said in 1937, before Beebe's first railroad book was released, "It can never be said that Mr. Beebe was much of a reporter. He had an apathy about facts which verged closely on actual dislike, and the tangled wildwood of his prose was poorly adapted to describing small fires and negligible thefts."[9]

Writing about Beebe's works, David P. Morgan said, "If date and digit accuracy was not his forte, let it be appended that he was without equal when it came to placing in print the actual emotion of an event such as Promontory or an incident such as the dance in Virginia & Truckee's stone enginehouse."[10]

Beebe's later writing, as seen in his railroad-subject books, reflects his work as a reporter. When asked if Beebe's day job influenced his writing, retired Smithsonian executive and distinguished railroad historian John White stated, "Sure it did. As a reporter, he learned to write very quickly and not worry about details too much—to not work on things draft after draft."[11] Railroad historian Cornelius Hauck said, "Reporters tend to learn to do things in a hurry and aren't very careful. Beebe, I think, tended to be impatient anyway, and had a short temper, and that shows up in his writing. He didn't want to bother with getting facts straight. He was looking for the feeling of railroading."[12]

After his two-year *New York Herald Tribune* apprenticeship as a city reporter, Beebe moved to the drama department as an understudy critic. Beebe's other assignments for the *New York Herald Tribune* included, according to Beebe's self-authored obituary, ship-news reporter, Sunday op-ed page editor, and feature writer.[13]

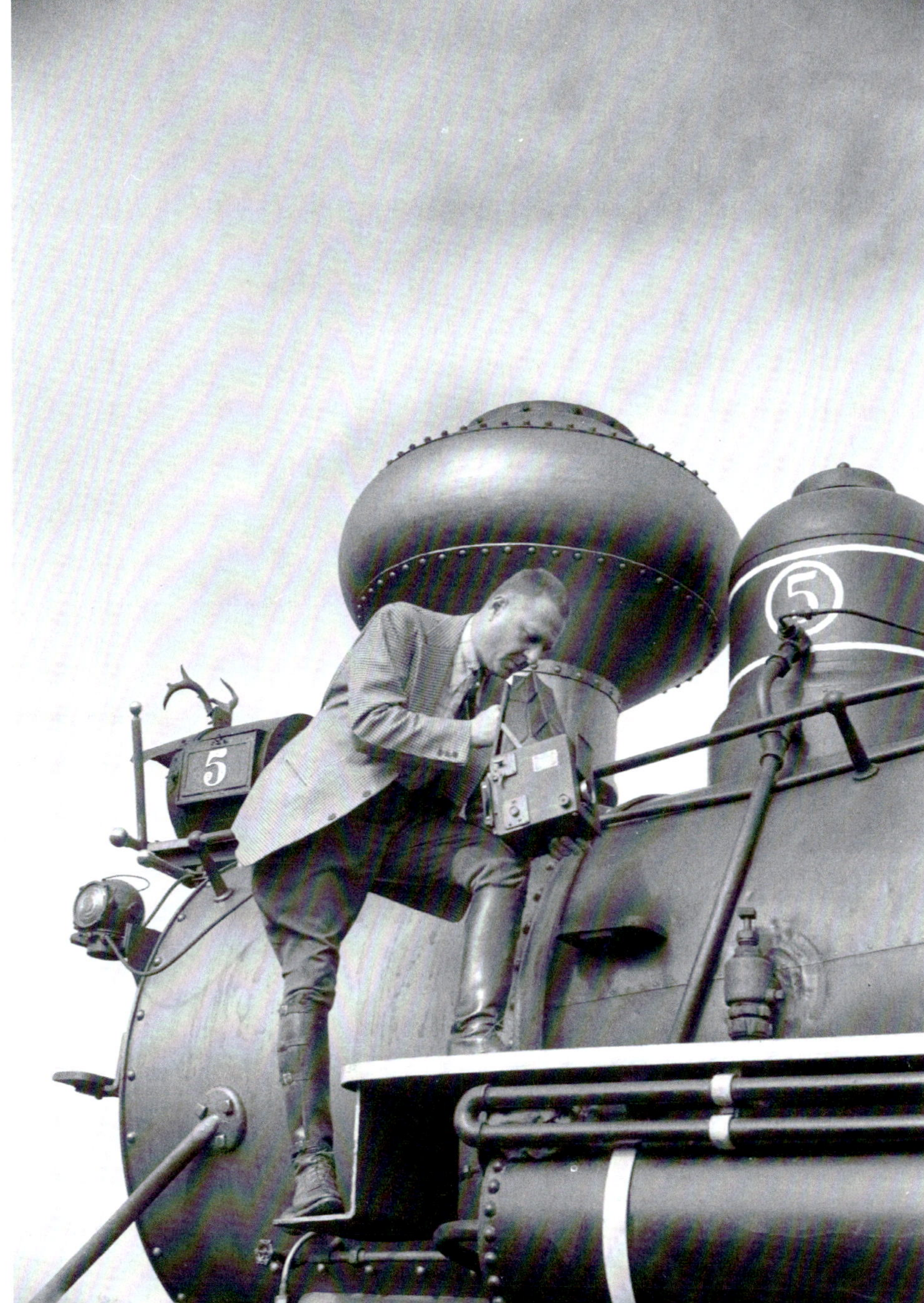

Lucius Beebe with camera on a Live Oak, Perry & Gulf Railroad steam locomotive. Attributed to Charles Clegg. Beebe-Clegg negative 2400.

Courtesy of the California State Railroad Museum.

A subject that fit Lucius Beebe's writing skills better was about to come his way. New York's café society was about to find its chronicler.

CAFÉ SOCIETY AND "THIS NEW YORK"

During the summer of 1933, Harry Stanton, the manager of the Herald-Tribune Syndicate, developed the idea for a new column—a written chronicle of New York's café society. He selected the *New York Herald Tribune*'s imposing and outrageous understudy drama critic, Lucius Beebe, to write the column. It premiered outside of New York in 1933 as "So This Is New York!" and "New York Speaking." When the column came to the *New York Herald Tribune* itself in 1934, it was renamed "This New York."[14] It would run in the newspaper for a decade.

Beebe is often credited with originating the term *café society* in his "This New York" columns.[15] Café society could not have existed without Prohibition. The widespread flaunting of the law prohibiting alcoholic drinks in the United States at the time led to the popularity of mixed drinks. Prohibition also created speakeasies, which were the direct ancestors of the clubs Beebe and his confreres visited during the "This New York" period of his career, such as El Morocco, the Stork Club, and the 21 Club.

The Great Depression also played a role in creating café society by decreasing societal respect for old families, such as the Vanderbilts in New York. In many cases it also radically diminished the wealth and, therefore, the power held by these families. This allowed the figures that surrounded Beebe—such as actor Clifton Webb, torch singer Libby Holman, and society photographer Jerome Zerbe—a place on the societal stage. The so-called four hundred figures of wealth in New York were, to some extent, supplanted by the five hundred members (the number according to Beebe) of café society.

Beebe would be known in later life for his penchant for private railroad cars, Rolls Royces, and his St. Bernard, T-Bone Towser. During his café society years, he was often recognized as one of the best-dressed men in the United States. He posed in fashion shows, was often depicted in fashion magazines, and endorsed a number of products. When profiled in the *New Yorker* in 1937, he owned forty suits.[16] His fame as a well-dressed man, in a style influenced by Edwardian grandee Berry Wall, was such that he was featured in full formal day attire on the cover of *Life* with the title "Lucius Beebe Sets a Style."[17]

Beebe is largely forgotten today, except by American railfans, but his fame at the time—derived largely from his role as the "This New York" columnist—was real and widespread. "Luscious Lucius," as he was often called— a nickname coined by Walter Winchell—was mentioned in Lorenz Hart's lyrics for "Zip" from *Pal Joey* and in Cole Porter's "Panama Hattie." "Mister Beebe" from the 1944 musical *Carolina Blues* was a tribute to Beebe in dance. His dress code inspired the costuming for fictional characters such as the well-groomed New York columnist and murderer Waldo Lydecker in *Laura*, played by the actor Clifton Webb.[18]

THE MID-1930S AND JEROME ZERBE

During the early "This New York" years, Beebe was involved with society photographer Jerome Zerbe.[19] Zerbe's photography, which seems dated now, was innovative for the time and was a profound influence on Beebe when he also became a photographer.

Often described as the first paparazzi photographer and also remembered as the probable inventor of the vodka martini, Zerbe was born in Euclid, Ohio, in 1904. Like Beebe, Zerbe came from wealth; his father was president of the Ohio and Pennsylvania Coal Company. Zerbe spent most of his childhood in Cleveland, Ohio, and attended Salisbury School, a prep school in Salisbury, Connecticut. His prep school career was interrupted by a bout with tuberculosis. Amazingly, given the prognosis for TB patients at the time, he was cured of the disease.[20]

Like Beebe, Zerbe attended Yale, starting in 1924 in the class of 1928. And, like Beebe, Zerbe was well known on campus for his flagrant violations of Prohibition. After graduation, Zerbe spent time in Hollywood drawing portraits of society figures and then lived in Paris for several years beginning in 1929. After the Great Depression diminished his family's income, Zerbe returned to Cleveland and established himself as a local society photographer, working for a new local magazine, *Parade*. Like Beebe, Zerbe was an innovator; he is credited with creating the figure of the paparazzi photographer. He "changed the rules for Cleveland," and then New York and the United States, by using his social position to attend closed events and take candid photographs of the guests.[21]

Parade soon went out of business, and Zerbe, who was already a freelance photographer for a New York–based magazine, *Town and Country,* soon moved to the city. He almost immediately found jobs at both the Rainbow Room and El Morocco. John Perona of El Morocco eventually hired Zerbe as the house photographer at the club. Zerbe worked there from 1933 to 1938. Zerbe and Beebe apparently met at El Morocco and became a couple. The reason for and exact timing of their breakup is unknown, but their relationship clearly ended by no later than 1941, when Lucius Beebe met Charles Clegg.[22] Zerbe served in the navy as a photographer during World War II, acting as the official photographer for Admiral Chester Nimitz for a time. He then returned to New York and resumed his role as a noted society photographer. Later in life, he also became known as an architectural photographer. Zerbe's best-known work, the book *Happy Times,* was published in 1973. Zerbe's health began to fail in 1974, and he died in 1988.[23] His collection, formerly owned by Frederick R. Koch, is available to scholars at the Beinecke Rare Book and Manuscript Library, Yale University.[24]

In his introduction to Zerbe's *People on Parade,* Beebe said of Zerbe, "Mostly, like Mr. Robinson's Richard Corey, people glitter as they walk through the pages of this album and you will probably find yourself among them. If you don't the chances are Mr. Zerbe has heard that you once chilled your claret or saw a play the second night. His code is a rigid one."[25]

Beebe had many other interesting and noted friends. Beebe's articles and books of the period often included photos by Ivan Dmitri (Levon West), a modernist photographer and artist who is nearly forgotten today despite his importance in popularizing and advancing color photography. During the 1930s, Beebe was also close to and "adored" Libby Holman, the torch singer and accused murderer of her famous husband, tobacco heir Z. Smith Reynolds.[26]

THE CALL OF THE IRON HORSE

Beebe's career as an author of railroad-subject books began sometime between 1934 and 1938, when a contact at his publisher, Elizabeth Haskell of D. Appleton-Century, suggested that Beebe write a popular illustrated book on railroading.[27] According to the 1937 Wolcott Gibbs profile, Beebe was already seen as "an authority on railroading" by then and had appeared at a 1936 exposition in Cleveland "driving Moguls and ancient Mason-built diamond-stackers."[28] In 1938, Beebe served as railroad consultant for Cecil B. DeMille's *Union Pacific,* an epic highlighting construction of the first transcontinental railway.[29]

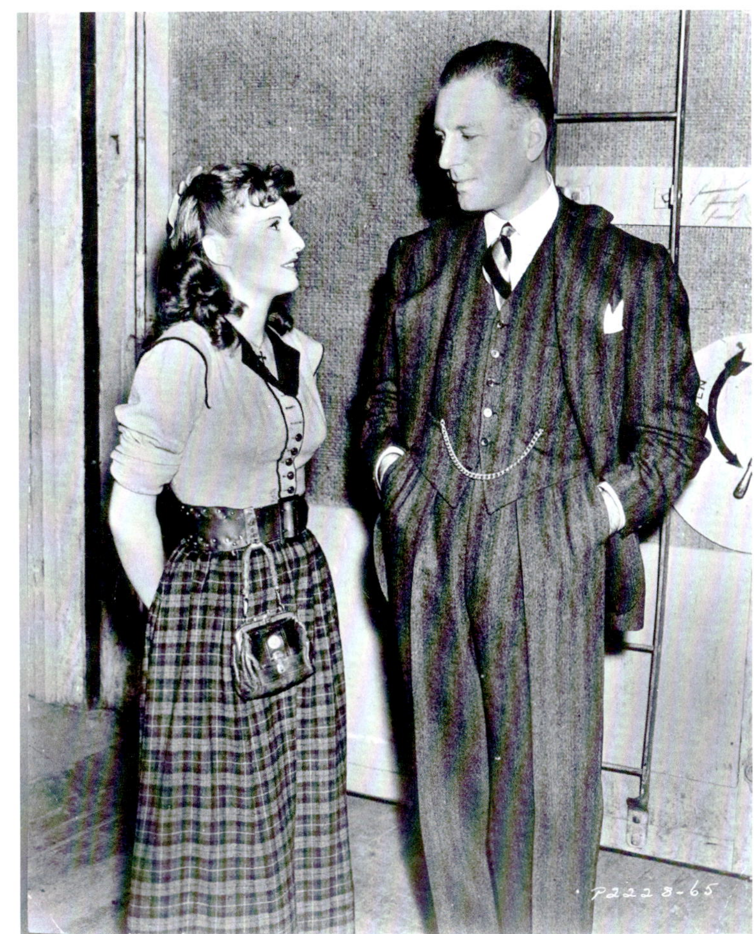

Lucius Beebe with actress Barbara Stanwyck, probably during the filming of *Union Pacific* (1939). Photographer unknown. California State Railroad Museum negative 26568.

Courtesy of the California State Railroad Museum.

Beebe at first declined Haskell's commission because of the poor quality of the railroad photographs available at the time. Haskell then suggested he take the photos for the book himself. In a leap of faith, Beebe, who had no training as a photographer, purchased a four-by-five-inch Graflex camera, traveled extensively taking railroad-subject photographs, and completed the assignment.[30] The book that resulted, *High Iron*, was published by D. Appleton-Century in 1938. Beebe spent his weekends and vacations for two years on preparing the book, traveling thirty-five thousand miles in the process. Like the later *Mixed Train Daily*, *High Iron*'s quality reflects the depth of Beebe's commitment to the book.[31]

High Iron has no real antecedents in the history of US book publishing. Robert Selph Henry's *Trains*, a very different book first published in 1934, is the only obvious book-length influence on *High Iron*.[32] *High Iron* is distinguished from *Trains* by its idiosyncratic approach to content, by better illustrations—Henry, a railroad industry executive, mostly used posed, often stilted, railroad publicity photographs—and by a clean design that placed one or two photos on a page. *High Iron*'s real antecedents were not books but the promotional photo albums and postcard series issued by railroads beginning in the late nineteenth century and by similar items produced as souvenirs by news agencies and other entities.

High Iron was an important innovation in publishing. The railroad pictorial album, or railroad picture book, is a medium that has given pleasure to millions, has gotten many young people interested in railroads, and has been published in many forms since *High Iron*.

The book caught those who viewed Beebe as the priest of café society by surprise. A "Transport" column in *Time* in 1938 presents a remarkable view of the period reaction to Beebe's *High Iron*, as well as a review of the book. "To his café-society circle," the reviewer said, "he [Beebe] is an overdressed young man who devotes himself to proper vintages and a perfumed nostalgia for the good old days. That so soigné a soul as Lucius Beebe should ride a hobby as undandified as railroading is as unlooked-for as red wine with fish." The article went on to term *High Iron* "A delight for railroad buffs"—as indeed it was and is. It also described Beebe as "wonderstruck in the vast trainshed at St. Louis," as well as at Cleveland and Omaha, and in a "disused roundhouse" discovering a "Taunton-built eight-wheeler."[33] Beebe's championship of railroads as a hobby certainly broadened the avocation's appeal.

Beebe's fame led to Hollywood consulting engagements and junkets. His first visit to his later home, Virginia City, Nevada, was to attend the premiere of a genre western, *Virginia City*. If Beebe didn't know artist Sheldon Pennoyer, a later influence on his photography, before this time, they definitely met at the premiere.[34]

MEETING HIS LIFE PARTNER, CHARLES CLEGG

In 1941, Beebe met a much younger man, photographer and department store clerk Charles "Chuck" Clegg. Clegg became his partner—in writing, photography, and life—for the rest of his days.[35] Like many other aspects of Beebe's story, their meeting was a larger-than-life episode. They met at Evalyn Walsh McLean's Washington, DC, mansion, "Friendship," where they were houseguests and shared a bathroom. Clegg had come to the party as the guest of J. Edgar Hoover, director of the Federal Bureau of Investigation.[36] When Clegg first noticed Beebe, Beebe was wearing McLean's Hope Diamond as a joke. When Clegg next saw him, Beebe was passed out in the bathtub in their common bathroom, covered with blood, and clutching a broken china pig. Clegg woke Beebe, cleaned him and the bathroom, put him to bed, and then went to bed himself. Clegg then set himself and "Friendship" on fire by falling asleep while smoking in bed.[37]

Like Beebe's earlier partner, Zerbe, Clegg came from an affluent Ohio background. Born in Youngstown, Ohio, in 1916, Clegg came from a family of mill owners. His mother, Ruth Standish, was a Lord & Taylor fashion illustrator who met Clegg's father, Charles Clegg Sr., while the elder Clegg was a student at Brown University. Ruth Standish's New England lineage was even more distinguished than Beebe's; she was a descendant of Puritan notable Myles Standish.

Clegg was the first of three children; he had a brother, Mike, and a much younger sister, Ann.[38] Clegg was fascinated by radio, photography, and trains. Clegg's parents divorced when he was a child. When Clegg turned twenty-one, he was living with his mother and grandfather, Granville Searcy Standish, in Rhode Island. On his twenty-first birthday, his grandfather asked him to move out. Clegg then moved in with his father in Washington, DC, and took a job at Garfinckel's Department Store. He later moved to New York City and worked as a floor manager for Arnold Constable & Company.[39] After moving to New York City, he studied photography with J. Ghislain Lootens.[40] Clegg volunteered for the navy reserve the day after the Japanese attack on Pearl Harbor, December 7, 1941.[41]

Like Beebe and Zerbe, Beebe and Clegg were fairly open about the nature of their relationship for the time. In fact, Beebe is credited with first using the word *partner* in print to refer to an LGBTQ romantic partner.[42] Prominent railfans, reporters, and members of café society considered Beebe and Clegg a couple. Cornelius Hauck; railroad photographer and historian Dick Kindig; John White Jr.; and railroad historian, architect, and author Arthur Dubin all knew Beebe, and all thought of Beebe and Clegg in this light. White said, "People suspected it, but it wasn't a topic that was talked about. Homosexuals were thought to be perverts; rarely was it openly accepted then. There were lots of jokes and snide comments about Beebe. However, he was not effeminate at all—he was very masculine. Beebe could afford to be independent—if people did not want to socialize with him, too bad."[43]

In "Boardwalk Bons Vivants," published in 1992, more than twenty years after the gay liberation movement in the United States found its genesis in the Stonewall riots of 1969, Andria Daley broke new ground by discussing the Beebe-Clegg relationship openly in print. She quotes the co-owner of Virginia City's Sazerac Saloon as saying, "We never thought about them being a gay couple. The town wasn't too fussed about them. . . . Virginia City was such a tolerant town then. . . . There were many of those who espoused the bohemian lifestyle, writers and artists, and that's the way it was."[44]

This article is the first known outright mention of Beebe's intimate relationship with Clegg, but there were many earlier hints. For example, Gibbs's 1937 profile of Beebe, written before Beebe met Clegg, said, "He has always been a bachelor—his friends would be a little startled if he ever married."[45] Today, we no longer need to shield gay and lesbian relationships with such coded language, and, in fact, many today would admire Beebe and Clegg for their commitment to each other under what must have been difficult circumstances.

The closest Beebe came to recognizing the nature of his relationship with Clegg in print appears in the delightful chapter "One-Man U.S.O." in Beebe's café society postmortem, *Snoot If You Must*. Beebe described Clegg as having an "even temper and kindness of disposition." When Clegg is finally called for duty in the navy during World War II, Beebe says, "Then silence. Or comparatively since I sniffed while shaving because I liked my roomy and felt like hell to see him going away."[46]

A DIFFICULT LIFESTYLE FOR THE TIMES—AND THE CHALLENGES IT CREATED

Beebe's lifestyle, which included club-going, drinking, and same-sex relationships, created difficulties for him and for his partner, Clegg. One of the challenges was Beebe's family, who had a low regard for his lifestyle, especially his drinking.[47] According to Gibbs, for example, Beebe's father, "with the exception of a little claret at Christmas, had never allowed liquor to be served in his house."[48] Period sources of course do not mention his relationships with men, but they likely caused difficulties with his family as well. A source who knew Beebe personally feels it likely that it was the disapproval Beebe faced from his family and from others around him that led to his assuming a façade, both in his public persona and in his writing, and that eventually led him to move to the western United States.[49]

What of Beebe's façade, the public persona? It is important for understanding more than his personal life in that it obviously affected his writing. He famously adopted a faux–Gilded Age writing style, which became increasingly affected as he aged. Uncharacteristic for a man of his time, this style was clearly seen as part of a public mask. Gibbs, very early in Beebe's career as a writer, said, "it is even rather hard to tell to what extent Mr. Beebe's present icy façade is actually part of the building and to what extent it is simply a false front run up for the benefit of a world which has not, in the whole, been as respectful as he had once hoped."[50]

In terms of assessing Beebe's personality, this book is late in coming. Beebe died over fifty years ago, so there are few people living who knew him and perhaps no one left alive who knew him well. John White, who worked at the Smithsonian Institution during Beebe's lifetime, met him several times and assisted him with photos for book projects. White said,

> *He was a very large man, flamboyant looking, and, when I first saw him, wearing a trench coat and a western-style hat. I got the sense that he was an actor, and he put on a big show—friendly, charming, telling stories.*
>
> *I got the sense that this was a cover, though, and that Beebe was troubled in many ways. My impression was that his personal life was not all he wanted it to be. He was, I think, seen as an oddball, but he knew everybody and was often recognized as the best-dressed man in the country—when that still meant something.*[51]

White also commented, in a later interview, "Beebe knew society disapproved of him. Society wanted him to be normal; to have a wife and kids. Beebe was very bluff and hearty in conversation, but he was also a melancholy, reflective man who wanted to hide his inner self." The late Arthur Dubin, who knew Beebe well, said, "For me the one word that describes Lucius is kindness. He was a very kind person—but he built up a wall around himself."[52]

WORLD WAR II, THE END OF "THIS NEW YORK," *MIXED TRAIN DAILY*, AND THE MOVE WEST

Just after Beebe and Clegg met, the United States joined the Allied side in World War II after the Japanese attack on Pearl Harbor. In "One-Man U.S.O.," Beebe describes Clegg's patriotism as he immediately volunteered as a radio technician in the US Navy. Clegg was stationed in New York; Stillwater, Oklahoma; San Francisco; and Washington, DC, before being called to shipboard service.[53] Meanwhile, Beebe's column, "This New York," seemed thin and frivolous in newspapers largely devoted to war news and was discontinued in 1944. Beebe remained with the *New York Herald Tribune* and would until 1950.

After Clegg returned from the war in 1944, Beebe and Clegg started work on their first book together, *Highball* (published 1945), and began traveling the United States collecting photographs and stories that would form their joint masterpiece *Mixed Train Daily*.[54] They did so under the spell of Archie Robertson's 1945 book, *Slow Train to Yesterday*, which proved to be a major influence on *Mixed Train Daily*.[55] By the time *Mixed Train Daily* was released in 1947, Beebe and Clegg had spent several years on it.[56] Their wealth allowed them to travel widely while researching the book, which presented a nationwide view of the short line railroad in the United States.

In an article discussing the book, Beebe stated that the turn away from the then standard railroad-subject three-quarters shot to a broader photographic view in *Mixed Train Daily* was deliberate:

> *Because we [Clegg and Beebe] were anxious that Mixed Train Daily should become an item of authentic Americana and a picture record of an even now fast disappearing aspect of national existence, the short line railroad and its operations and motive power, we at the same time became convinced that more than the simple ponderables of cars, locomotives, and installations, should be our pictorial concern. We aimed to include backgrounds and atmospheric incidentals which would suggest the countryside in which each little railroad had its being, and action shots in the depots and yards of remote farlands which would depict its social and economic function.*[57]

This manifesto is a clear path to the groundbreaking railroad-subject photography that followed.

When it was released, Beebe and Clegg's promotion of *Mixed Train Daily* was brilliant. Finding that legendary engineer Casey Jones did not have a proper grave marker, Beebe and Clegg unveiled a headstone for his grave in Jackson, Tennessee. In photos of the event, Jones's widow, Jane Brady Jones, and his fireman, Sim Webb, look on as Beebe and Clegg dedicate the marker.[58] The book release party for *Mixed Train Daily* was held aboard a chartered train on the famed Maryland & Pennsylvania Railroad, the "Ma and Pa." *Life* covered the event, including the music, cigars, champagne, punch, and caviar.[59]

Beebe was an astute businessman, managing his and Clegg's writing career closely. In a letter to another writer, who proposed a book on Mexican and Central American railroads, Beebe said, "My own experience with railroad pictures and literature leads me to believe that there are fans and a market for any sort of railroad material whatsoever, but I believe that your estimate of the potential sale of a book on Mexican and Central American roads is optimistic to the point of fantasy." Beebe went on to detail the

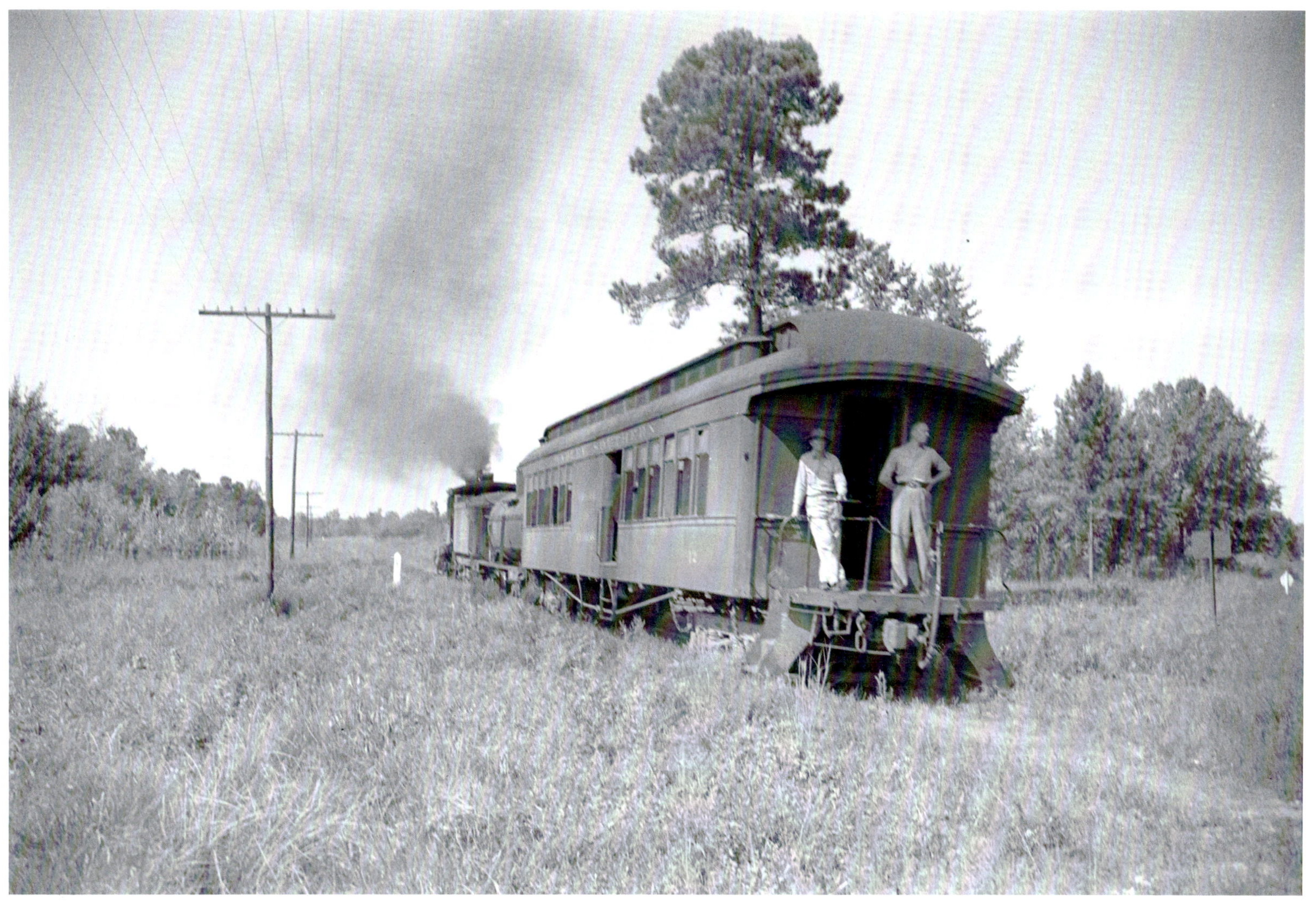

Lucius Beebe (*right*) on the platform of a Wadley Southern Railway combine (note that this is a segregated Jim Crow coach). Attributed to Charles Clegg. Beebe-Clegg negative 911.

Courtesy of the California State Railroad Museum.

sales of *Mixed Train Daily*, several of his other books, and books by Stewart Holbrook and Ed (Edward) Hungerford. In closing, Beebe said, "I do not wish to seem unenthusiastic about your plan because I know the powerful urgency of a specialized field of endeavor and exclusive information for any author. Simply I believe your economic structure is all wrong."[60]

In a long letter to his then publisher Grahame Hardy, Beebe, apparently referring to the book *Virginia and Truckee: A Story of Virginia City and Comstock Times*, discussed the strategies involved in producing special, as well as trade, editions of books. Beebe went on to discuss why he and Clegg picked the Virginia & Truckee and San Francisco cable cars as subjects for books:

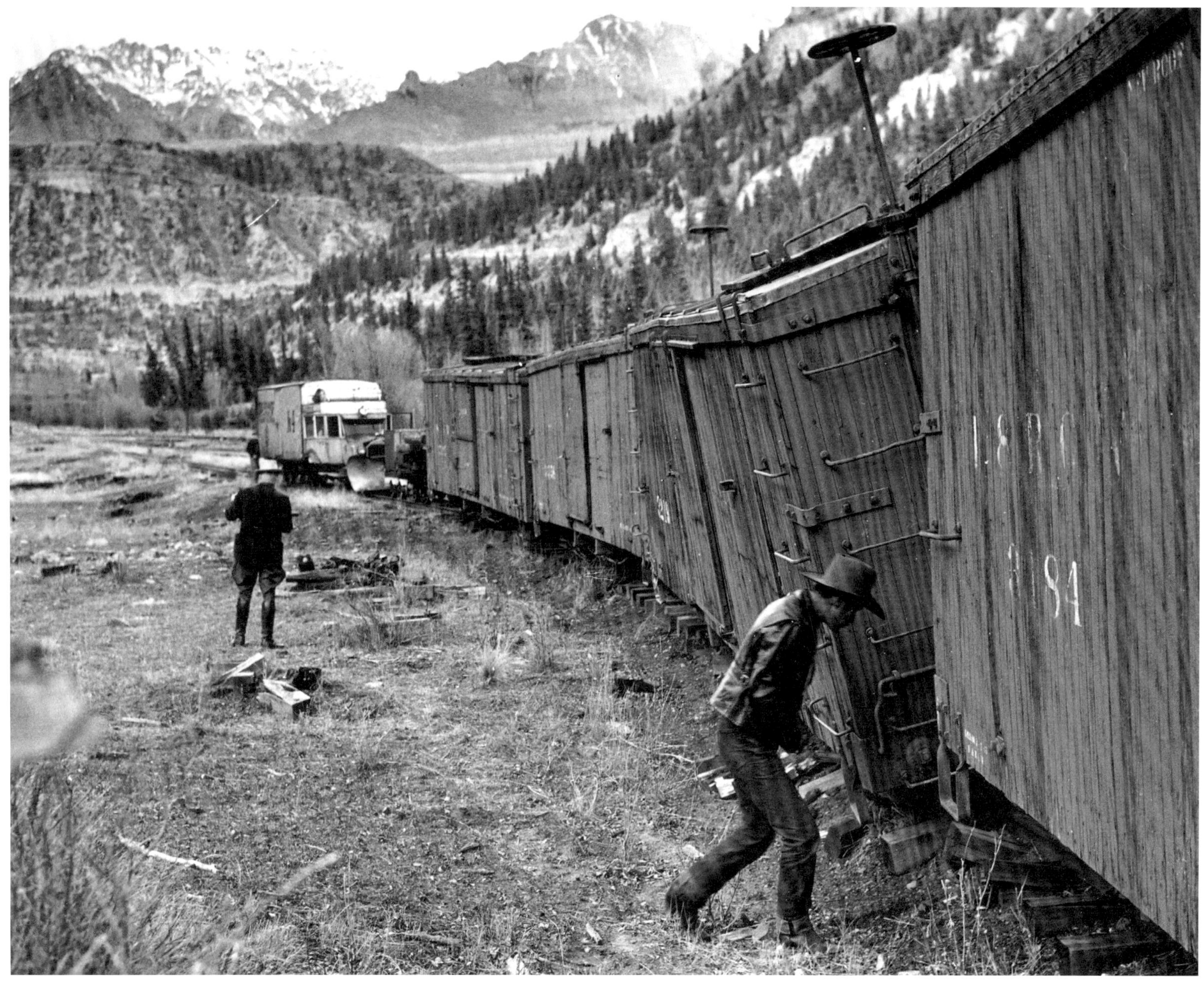

Lucius Beebe (*left, with back to the camera*), stands beside a derailed Rio Grande Southern train, followed in the background by a Rio Grande Southern "Galloping Goose." Charles Clegg. Beebe-Clegg negative 4003.

Courtesy of the California State Railroad Museum.

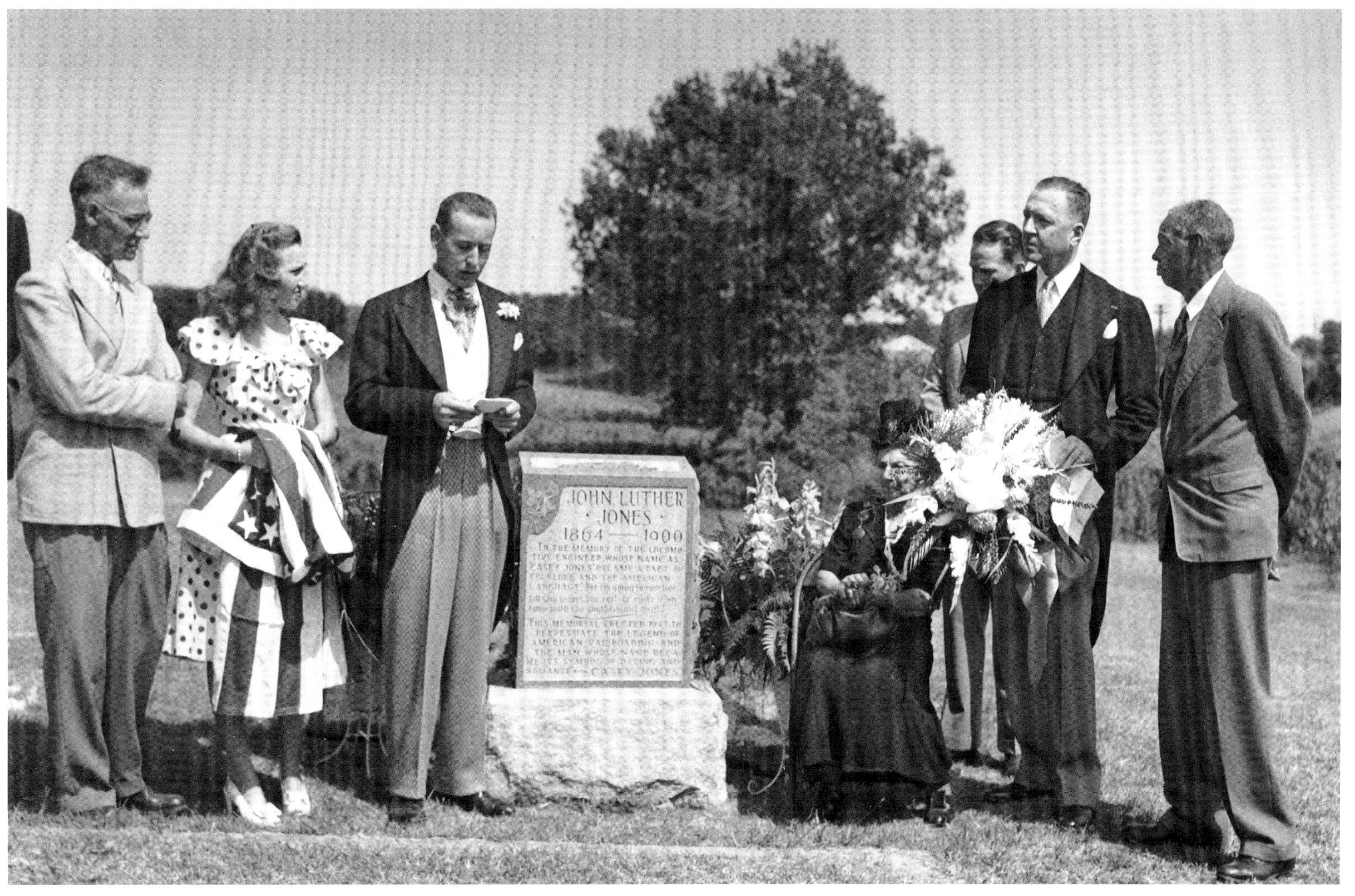

Lucius Beebe and Charles Clegg at the dedication of Casey Jones's grave marker. Jones's wife, Jane Brady Jones, is just to the right of the marker, and his fireman, Sim Webb, is on the far right. Clegg is just to the left of the marker, and Beebe is just to the left of Webb. Photographer unknown. Beebe-Clegg negative 4001.

Courtesy of the California State Railroad Museum.

> *We have always felt that for successful railroad books we must establish what is technically known as "reader identification." This we did with the short lines by chosing* [sic] *only passenger-carrying lines then in actual operation. It was a simple business with the V & T which was and is still receiving enormous assists in publicity and sentiment and, aside from the V & T itself, the Comstock is a tourist natural. It couldn't miss if rightly handled. The same is true of the cable car book if it is done right and priced right with great gobs of San Francisco color material quite incidental to the cars themselves.*

Beebe closed this letter with a manifesto for his and Clegg's publishing program: "Please believe that this lengthy letter represents some extended conversations between Chuck and myself who feel we are getting to the point where we know something of the subject and at least have never, between us, produced anything but a successful railroad job of any sort. We don't plan to, either, and that is why we are going to enquire most shrewdly into the cable car proposition." [61]

Despite their images as bon vivants, Beebe and Clegg would both be termed workaholics today. Beebe took a number of photos in the 1930s, 1940s, and 1950s, but he was primarily a writer. About half of his massive output was devoted to railroading; Beebe, often with Clegg, authored a large oeuvre of railroad books—twenty-one in all.[62] Especially toward the end of his life, the speed and quantity of Beebe's output tended to mar its quality, particularly in terms of factual content. Eight of the Beebe or Beebe-Clegg books appeared during the last five years of Beebe's life; it would be difficult for an author to handle the research for that number of volumes well. Beebe seemed to know that he was running out of time, and he seemed determined to pursue his artistic vision in the years he had left. This sense of urgency and the resulting lack of time devoted to each of these works is apparent in most of them.

Austin Woodward, who worked for Beebe at the *Territorial Enterprise*, said, "In looking back, I'm amazed and impressed with Lucius's prolific output. For each and every weekly issue of the paper, he usually wrote at least one major news article—the headline page one article—and several smaller pieces, plus book reviews, editorials, and major historical features."[63]

Beebe and Clegg began to live part-time in Carson City, Nevada, in 1948. When they were in the area, they resided in their private car, *Gold Coast*, held on trackage in the Virginia & Truckee yards there. In 1950, Beebe resigned from his position at the *New York Herald Tribune*, and he and Clegg then left New York permanently for Virginia City, Nevada. By then, they already owned the then crumbling Piper House, now known as the Piper-Beebe House, which Clegg restored.[64] The move was motivated in part by New York taxes and in part by their tiring of the New York social scene. The decline of the *New York Herald Tribune* after the death of Ogden Reid in 1946 probably played a role in the decision as well.

The very early period of their residence in Nevada, from 1948 to 1950, was devoted to documenting and trying to save the short-line railroad, the famed Virginia & Truckee, which they loved. Beebe also spent time in New York trying to persuade the Mills-Reid family not to dismantle the famed short line.[65] The railroad was abandoned in 1950.[66]

REVIVING THE *TERRITORIAL ENTERPRISE* AND THE PRIVATE RAILROAD CAR

In 1952, Beebe and Clegg purchased the *Virginia City News*, and used its assets to revive the *Territorial Enterprise*, a Virginia City newspaper made famous by Mark Twain in the nineteenth century. Clegg was the editor and Beebe the publisher. As he did in New York, Beebe gathered an impressive circle of friends around the *Territorial Enterprise*, including fiction writer Walter Van Tilburg Clark, historians Bernard DeVoto and Stewart Holbrook, gourmet James Beard, and folklorist Duncan Emrich. For a time, Beebe was also involved in state and civic affairs in Virginia City and Nevada. He was inducted posthumously into the Nevada Writers Hall of Fame in 1992.[67]

Beebe and Clegg did little photography after about 1950. In an interview with Freeman Hubbard, Beebe explained that this was due to the end of the steam era on American railroads. "There are," Beebe said, "no longer any railroad pictures worth taking, with the result that our interest, Clegg's and mine, has been directed of necessity into the legendary past. We are historians of something that was, haunting the roundhouses of yesterday and riding the palace cars of memory."[68]

During this period, Beebe and Clegg were also known for their lavish, private railroad cars. Their first, the *Gold Coast*, originally Georgia Northern/Central of Georgia No. 100, is now at the California State Railroad Museum. Beebe and Clegg purchased it in 1948 and restored it almost immediately. It was of wood construction, and when railroads grew reluctant to operate it they donated it to the Railway and Locomotive Historical Society in 1954.[69] They replaced the *Gold Coast* with the *Virginia City*, which they purchased in 1954; it was originally the Pullman Company's *Crystal Peak*. By 1955, the *Virginia City* was restored and in use by Beebe and Clegg; the car was kept at Sparks, Nevada, as well as at Oakland and Pacific Grove, California. The Charles Clegg Estate sold the car in 1984, and it is currently Amtrak compatible and available for charters.[70] Both cars were redecorated by interior designer Robert Hanley.

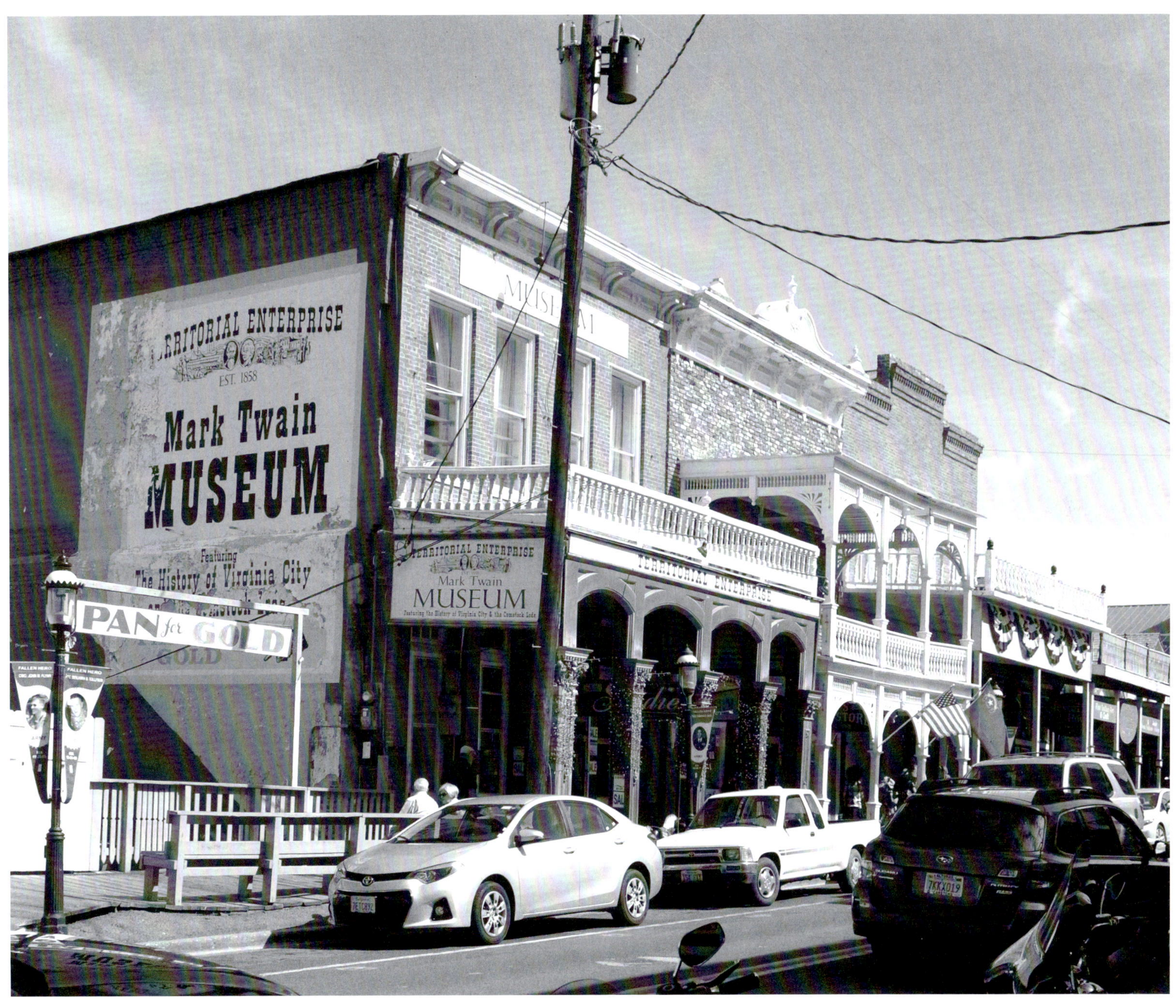

The former offices of the Virginia City, Nevada, newspaper, the *Territorial Enterprise*, which Lucius Beebe and Charles Clegg owned for many years. Photo by author.

Courtesy of the California State Railroad Museum.

In *Mansions on Rails*, Beebe describes a columnist, Herb Caen's, visit to the *Virginia City*. Caen reported, "*The Virginia City* is the only really private railway car in the country. . . . 'It's for pleasure only,' says Mr. Clegg and to prove it mixed Martinis in the drawing room bar and we then walked into the dining room for lunch prepared by Wallace, the chef, and served by Clarence, the steward."[71] With their cars and books such as *Mansions on Rails*, Beebe and Clegg for many years almost single-handedly kept the private car tradition alive in the United States.

ENDINGS

Beebe and Clegg sold the *Territorial Enterprise* in 1960 and from then on lived part of the year in their Virginia City home and part of the year in Hillsborough, California, a wealthy suburb of San Francisco, in a home they purchased in 1957.[72] From 1960 to his death in 1966, Beebe had a column, "This Wild West," in the *San Francisco Chronicle*, and he continued to write for magazines such as *Gourmet*, *Town & Country*, and *Holiday*. In the late 1950s, Beebe began to suffer serious health problems, such as kidney and liver ailments and gout, and he underwent a number of operations. Beebe died of a heart attack in 1966. He is buried in his hometown of Wakefield, Massachusetts.

Clegg spent the first few years after Beebe's death completing Beebe's works. The second volume of *The Trains We Rode* and *The Big Spenders* were published posthumously in 1966 with Clegg's assistance. Clegg also edited, with his friend Duncan Emrich, *The Lucius Beebe Reader*, published in 1967. Clegg, who sold the house in Virginia City in 1978, spent most of his time at the Hillsborough mansion. In his later years, he suffered from an incurable inner-ear disorder, Meniere's disease.[73]

Clegg never seems to have recovered from Beebe's death. He committed suicide through a drug overdose at the Hillsborough villa in 1979—on the day at which he reached the age at which Beebe died. In his suicide note, Clegg blamed his act on a shortage of good servants: "'I am not used to living without full time domestic help—,' he said, 'and I find I cannot do that—'"[74] It was a sad end for a great pioneer of railroad-subject photography.

Clegg's death left his younger sister, Ann Clegg Holloway, as the executor of the Beebe-Clegg estate. She later conveyed most of the Beebe-Clegg papers and photographs—including Beebe's correspondence with fellow railroad authors and photographers Gerald M. Best, Arthur Dubin, and Phil Hastings—to the California State Railroad Museum Library.[75] Other material was donated to the Henry E. Huntington Library, the Nevada Historical Society, the Colorado Railroad Museum, the DeGolyer Collection at Southern Methodist University, the Denver Public Library, the New York Public Library, and the Smithsonian Institution.[76]

The precursor article to this book, published in 2005, noted that "Beebe's life is a sobering lesson in the transience of fame. Although he authored or co-authored almost 40 books, only seven are currently in print, four of them from books-on-demand type publishers."[77] The 2005 article was intended, in part, to help revive Beebe and Clegg's reputation. In 2007, noted photographer, author, and Center for Railroad Photography and Art founder John Gruber authored a retrospective focusing on Beebe and Clegg in the center's periodical, *Railroad Heritage*.[78] Since then, Gruber has worked on a project focused on producing high-quality scans of selected Beebe-Clegg photographs, a portfolio he presented at the center's 2016 conference, and that resulted in a 2018 book, by Gruber with John Ryan and Mel Patrick, entitled *Beebe & Clegg: Their Enduring Photographic Legacy*. These efforts seem to be bearing fruit: publications highlighting, citing, or mentioning Beebe, and to some extent Clegg, have increased dramatically in the past ten years.

BEEBE'S WRITING AND ITS INFLUENCE

This revival of interest is justified for several reasons. The first is Beebe's output as a writer, and, through it, his influence on railroad-subject writing and photography. Beebe was instrumental in founding the railroad picture-book genre and in establishing the railfan hobby in the United States. As the plates will show, both Beebe and Clegg were talented and exceedingly influential railroad-subject photographers.

About half of Beebe's massive written output was devoted to railroading, and almost all of his and Clegg's photography was. With two exceptions, Beebe's and Beebe and Clegg's, railroad books fall into three broad categories: railroad picture albums, illustrated vernacular histories of Western railroads, and books focusing on the luxurious aspects of rail travel.[79]

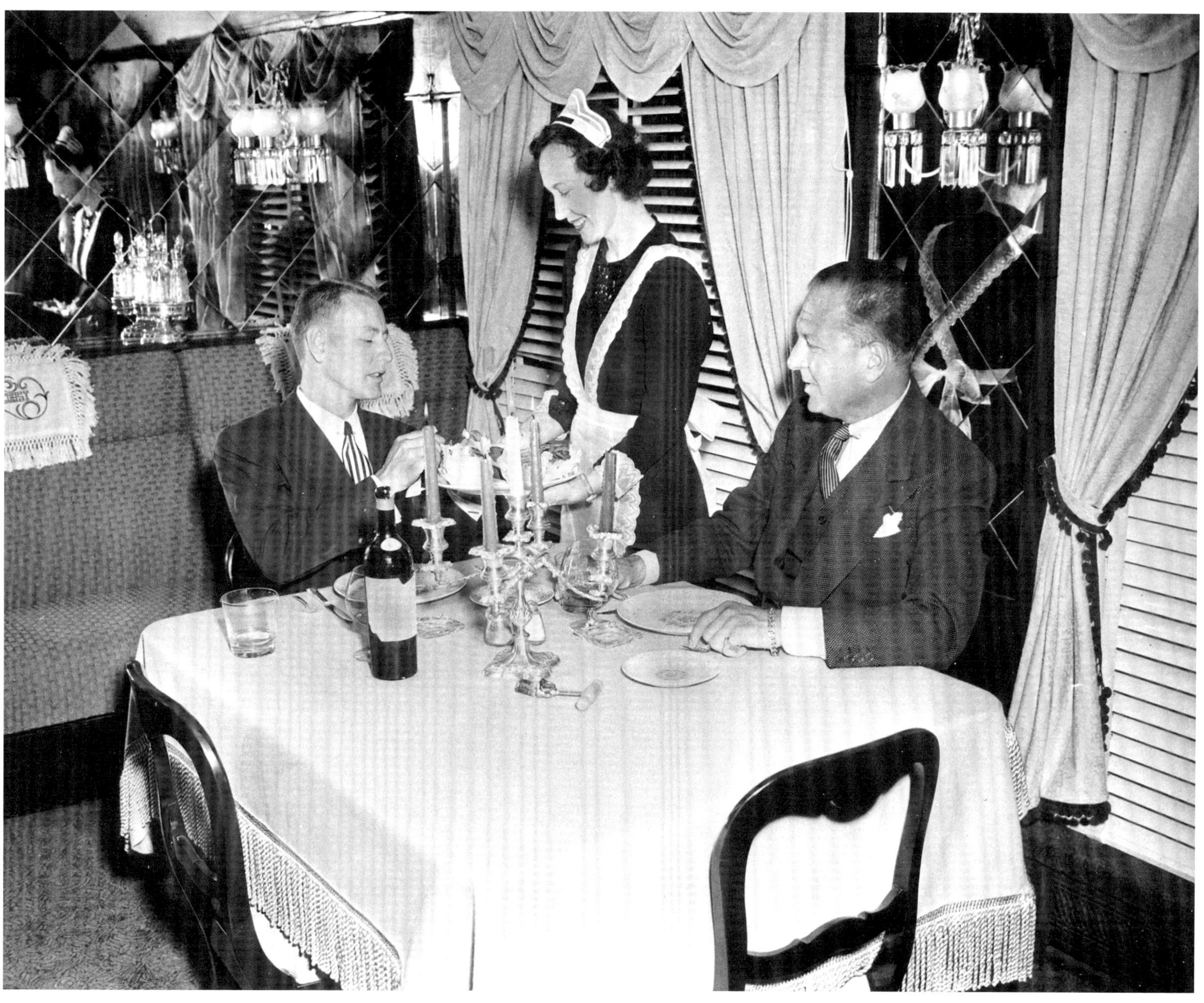

Lucius Beebe (*right*) and Charles Clegg dine on board their private car, the *Gold Coast,* circa 1948–52. Photographer unknown. California State Railroad Museum negative 26564.

Courtesy of the California State Railroad Museum.

The pictorial albums begin with *High Iron* (1938). To this observer, *High Iron, Highball* (1945), *The Age of Steam* (1957), and *Great Railroad Photographs U.S.A.* (1964) stand out in this series. *High Iron* is notable for its innovation, *Highball* as a prelude to the outstanding book *Mixed Train Daily* (1947), and *The Age of Steam* and *Great Railroad Photographs U.S.A* for the excellence of Beebe's illustration choices, which include early or even first photographic book publications of images by Philip R. "Phil" Hastings, H. Reid, Jim Shaughnessy, O. Winston Link, and others.[80]

Another series of Beebe's books focuses on illustrated histories of western American railroads. It begins with *Virginia & Truckee* (1949), which foreshadows Beebe and Clegg's move to the west the following year. Among these books, *The Central Pacific and Southern Pacific Railroads* (1963) stands out as a showcase for more than one hundred photographs by Richard "Dick" Steinheimer.

Beginning with *Mansions on Rails* (1959), Beebe started a new series focusing on the luxury aspects of rail travel. It was a natural subject for this famous writer of articles focusing on wine, gourmet dining, and five-star hotels. In this observer's view, *Mansions on Rails* and *Mr. Pullman's Elegant Palace Car* (1961) stand out as early treatments of subjects—private railroad cars and the Pullman Company—that are still underrepresented in the literature of railroading today. The books are also related to one of Beebe's major archival triumphs—saving many of the Pullman Company's glass plate photographs.[81] Beebe also saved the surviving Fred Jukes collection.

Two books, one of them Beebe and Clegg's acknowledged classic, *Mixed Train Daily,* do not fit into this classification of Beebe and Clegg's railroad-subject work. These books have broader themes. *Mixed Train Daily* is a pictorial, anecdotal, vernacular history of the American short line, and the other, *Hear the Train Blow,* is an idiosyncratic, mostly chronological, illustrated history of the American railroad from its beginnings to the end of the age of steam.

Mixed Train Daily stands as Beebe and Clegg's crowning achievement. In addition to its outstanding photographs, *Mixed Train Daily* may be numbered among the best early books looking at the social history of railroading. What makes it so special? Like the book that inspired it, Archie Robertson's *Slow Train to Yesterday, Mixed Train Daily* is unique in that it captured the societal place and feel of the local train and the short-line railroad and did it in a way that even contemporary readers can appreciate.[82]

Several things set this book apart from Beebe's other work. First, it is the only one of his books for which he did much interviewing of railroaders, and this adds great depth to the volume. Second, Beebe and Clegg took most of the photographs for the book, and it is their work at its best. Third, Beebe and Clegg devoted several years (from about 1945 to 1947) to this book, allowing it to blossom as none of their other railroad subject works do. Finally, in this book, Beebe focuses on a central subject, the theme of short-line railroads in the United States, which avoids the disorganization and spottiness of much of his work.

In reviewing the book for the *New York Times,* Horace Reynolds took Beebe to task for the repetitive nature of his writing. However, Reynolds goes on to say, "But at his best, when he is truly moved, he puts aside his 'columnese' and writes with insight and grace . . . there is precious freight aboard this book." Reynolds also singles out the photography in the book for praise. He writes, "The photographs are many and magnificent. Dynamic and lyrical, they powerfully evoke the sights, sounds and smells of railroading and what these mean to us."[83] It was Beebe's high point as a writer, and Reynolds' review is noteworthy for its insight.

A MIXED LEGACY AS A WRITER

Beebe's books have faults that go beyond the prose style affectations, sketchy research, and fact checking already mentioned. He tended to reuse the same images over and over again; in fact, his oeuvre is riddled with repetition in words, subjects, photographs, and historic images. The majority of his images are unimaginative "smoking wedges." Finally, the design of his books often resembles the worst of Gilded Age illustrated-newspaper layout—a fault that particularly impacts the ambitious survey book *Hear the Train Blow.*

Beebe's treatment of facts goes beyond a lack of attention to, especially in his later works, fabrication. As Arthur Dubin noted in his 2004 interview with this author, Beebe, "with well-intended artistic temperament," sometimes had artists retouch photographs to make them something they were not and then concocted narrative to go with the altered images.[84] Like his prose style, Beebe's veracity as an author deteriorated with age; factual errors appear in the early works, but fabrications proliferate toward the end of Beebe's lifetime. One work that suffers from these outright inventions is *The Trains We Rode*. When unable to locate appropriate photographs, Beebe used photomontage to create images for the book.[85] This practice would be unthinkable in railroad-subject books today.

THE JOINT PHOTOGRAPHIC LEGACY

Beebe and Clegg's influence on railroad subjects goes beyond their written works to their photography. Beginning with *High Iron*, Beebe helped move the genre of railroad-subject photography away from the stultifying roster shot of the 1930s, a style fostered in part by *Railroad Magazine* and the International Engine Picture Club. In its place, particularly through his first four books, Beebe championed a three-quarter front action shot known to railroad subject photographers as the smoking wedge or, in post-steam-era days, the wedge or wedgie shot. This shot, which soon admittedly hardened into another stereotype, saluted pioneers such as Fred Jukes and brought railroad action photography to the general public.

Beebe has often been stereotyped as a photographer of smoking wedges. Jeff Brouws, in his excellent introduction to the work of Richard Steinheimer, quotes passages from *Highliners* and *Great Railroad Photographs, U.S.A.* to present Beebe as an iconoclast of the three-quarter shot.[86] But even a quick flip through *High Iron*, *Mixed Train Daily*, or *The Age of Steam* shows that this is a simplification. Beebe was a habitué and champion of café society New York, and however much he derided modernity in his later years, he was inevitably influenced by Art Deco and modern art and design. The design of *High Iron* and some of the photographs featured there particularly reflect this influence. And although they have not been gathered together in one book until now, Beebe produced excellent portraits focusing on the people of US railroading.

While acknowledging Beebe for his role in the development of the wedge shot and railroad action photography, one should also recognize that, by 1938, the time for this genre of photography—for those with available funds to devote to it—had arrived. Cameras had appeared that could handle action shots; relatively low-cost automobiles allowed the average person to seek out and chase trains without having to ride them; and then the economic boom in the United States following the Great Depression and World War II made it possible for the average person to own a camera and pay for film and processing. For a favored few contributors, the emergence of *Trains* magazine provided an outlet for this type of photography—and soon for the documentary, humanistic approach championed by Phil Hastings, Dick Steinheimer, and Jim Shaughnessy that was to supplant it on the creative cutting edge of this field of work.

In this regard, Charles Clegg, through his own work and his influence on Beebe, deserves more recognition as a talented photographer. Clegg applied the pictorialist principles he learned from J. Ghislain Lootens to produce classic photos depicting American railroading in the context of the built and natural environment surrounding it. By having his work appear in best-selling books with Beebe, he helped pave the way for the holistic view of the railroad through image that we know today. Clegg's influence goes well beyond Hastings, Shaughnessy, Steinheimer, and younger contemporary David Plowden to following generations: to Mel Patrick, Jeff Brouws, and John Gruber, for example. This aesthetic continues to serve as the basis for innovative work by younger photographers of today, such as Scott Lothes and Emily Moser. One arena which Beebe and Clegg did not enter was the realm of night railroad photography; that development awaited the artistry of Phil Hastings, Jim Shaughnessy, Richard Steinheimer, and O. Winston Link.

The period editor of *Trains* magazine, David P. Morgan, is often recognized for his eye for photographic talent. Beebe said of him,

> *The revolt against what he liked to term "miserable wedges of smoke" was spearheaded by David Morgan, powerful and authoritative editor of* Trains *magazine, the devotional reading of True Believers everywhere, and at his editorial fiat head-end action suffered a decline and panned action shots taken from parallel-moving motor cars, personnel portraits, trackside atmosphere and train interiors became the preoccupation of photographers who valued his favor.*[87]

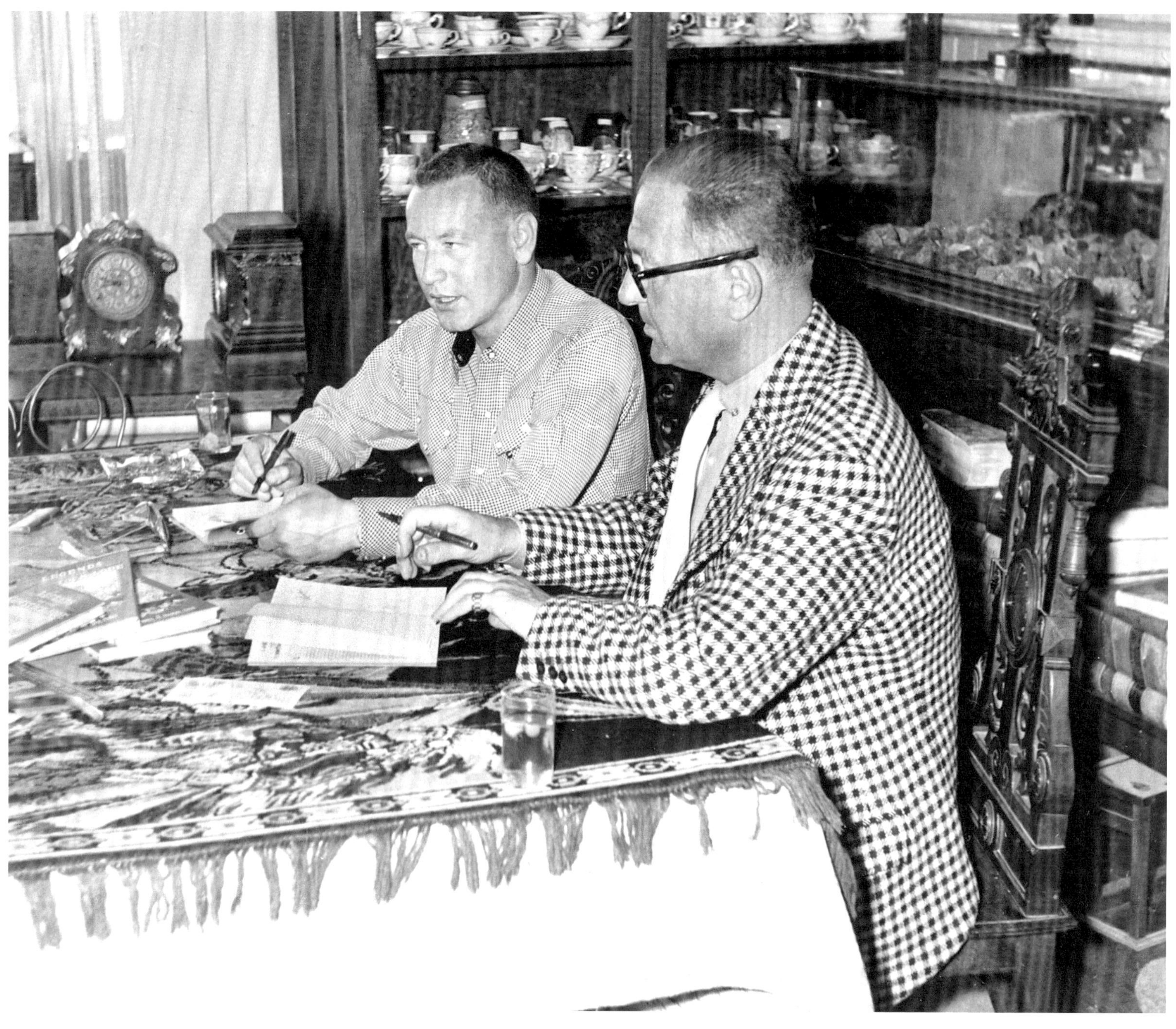

Lucius Beebe (*right*) and Charles Clegg at home. Photographer unknown. California State Railroad Museum negative 33862.

Courtesy of the California State Railroad Museum.

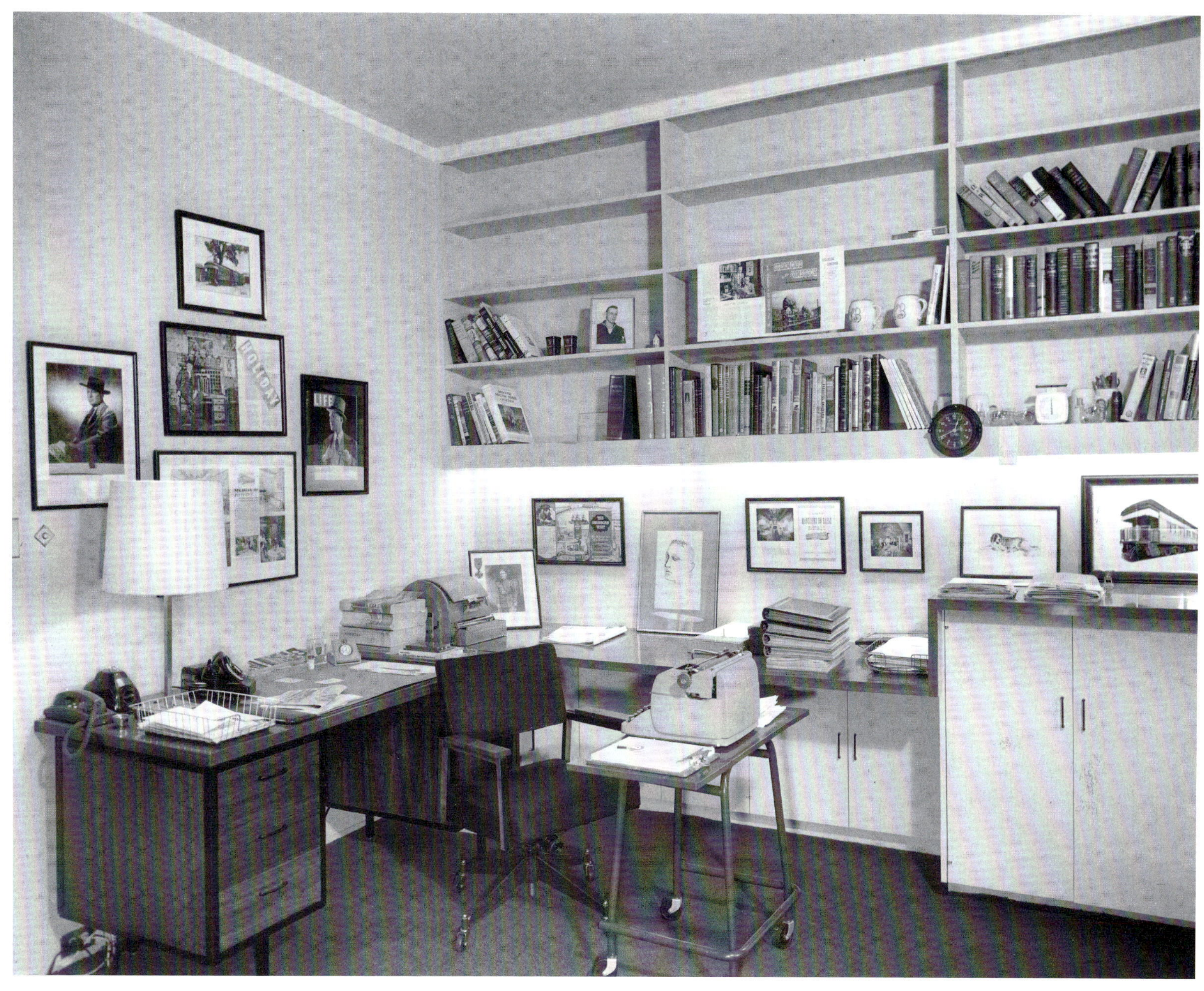

Lucius Beebe's study at his and Charles Clegg's home in Hillsborough, California. Photo by the Parton Studio, San Mateo, California. Beebe-Clegg negative 4010.

Courtesy of the California State Railroad Museum.

Beebe and Clegg, who had an important role in the production and design of their joint works, had an uncanny eye for talent equal to that of Morgan's. Their role in fostering many photographic careers, including those of Richard Steinheimer, Jim Shaughnessy, O. Winston Link, and many others, deserves more attention.

Beebe and Clegg's appreciation for railroad-subject photography went well beyond images resembling their own work. Most notably, they were the first to publish O. Winston Link's famed railroad-subject photos in a book. Some of these images were wedge shots, but some were Link's world-famous posed nighttime tableaux—images as different from Beebe and Clegg's work as can be imagined. Link is perhaps as much an ancestor of contemporary work by art-photography figures like Jeff Wall and Gregory Crewdson as he is of today's railroad-subject work. The early recognition given Link by Beebe and Clegg is notable. Also notable is Beebe's great championing of the work of an early, groundbreaking railroad-subject photographer, Fred Jukes.[88]

GREATER SOCIETAL INFLUENCES

Beebe wrote about many topics. His other books include books of poetry and poetry criticism; monographs, mostly written for hire, highlighting great hotels and restaurants; a book about Boston, *Boston and the Boston Legend*; a series of autobiographical sketches of café society, *Snoot if You Must*; *The Stork Club Bar Book*; and a series of illustrated, vernacular histories of the American West.[89]

Beebe's significance goes beyond his work as a writer and photographer. Another aspect of his work and life that deserves consideration is his role in depicting and glamorizing New York's café society of the Prohibition, Great Depression, and World War II years. Although he denied it, Beebe is often credited with coining the term "café society." Currently, interest in café society has increased dramatically, including a focus on period cocktails and motion pictures. To this observer, the similarities between the Great Depression and our recent Great Recession are the main drivers of this development. In any event, Beebe's role in café society has great significance for those interested in the period, be they devotees of a revival of the cocktail hour or students of the history of New York City.

A related reason for increased interest in Beebe's work is his groundbreaking role as an American food critic. The United States of his day was not renowned for its gastronomic achievements; at the time our country stood in the shadow of France, Italy, and even Great Britain in that regard. Beebe was one of the first noted food critics from the United States, and as such, he played a role in improving appreciation for fine dining, for wine, and for spirits and mixed drinks. The leadership shown by Beebe and other pioneers of his day, such as Julia Child and James Beard, resulted in the present-day food culture that prevails in much of the United States.[90] It was Lucius Beebe who wrote in 1938 that "no other city in the world offers such a variety of restaurants as New York, or such a wide range of quality."[91]

As mentioned earlier, Lucius Beebe's public and noted relationships with Jerome Zerbe and Charles Clegg also deserve attention. An interesting opportunity for future research on Beebe is work delineating his influence on acceptance of LGBTQ relationships in the United States.

Until recently, Beebe's star has been on the wane, and Clegg's reputation has always stood in the shadow of his partner's oversized image. Given Beebe's contributions to railroad history and his and Clegg's contributions to railroad-subject photography, the time has come for a Beebe and Clegg retrospective—perhaps even a revival. Whatever the future, as Lucius Beebe—originator of the railroad photo book, proponent of railroad action photography, publisher of O. Winston Link photography in book form, author of *Mixed Train Daily*—said, "May the grass grow green where once the light iron ran."[92]

1 THE THREE-QUARTERS SHOT

Lucius Beebe is generally considered a master of—and perhaps the major proponent of—a railroad-subject image style known as the "three-quarters" view. Also known as a wedge or wedgie, the three-quarters shot seems to be one of the most natural ways of depicting a train. Plate 1 is an excellent and early Beebe example of this type of image. To take a three-quarters view, the photographer stands at the edge of the tracks, faces the train, and aims her or his camera at a slight diagonal towards the train. Three-quarters shots of trains have been taken as long as railroading and photography have coexisted, but images of trains in motion from this viewpoint had to await the development of high-speed shutters. Action, rather than static, images of this nature were pioneered by photographers such as Albert F. Bishop. J. Foster Adams, and Fred Jukes during the 1890s and the first decade of the twentieth century.[1]

During the years just preceding the release of *High Iron*, the three-quarters shot was eclipsed in popularity by the roster shot: a documentary portrait of a locomotive or, less commonly, another type of rolling stock. Roster shots were often traded through the "International Engine Picture Club" feature in *Railroad Man's Magazine*, later *Railroad Stories* and then *Railroad Magazine*.[2] The roster shot, especially if it was intended to be traded, had to follow strict guidelines: a side view taken at a ninety-degree angle from the locomotive; no distracting background; enough light to illuminate all of the running gear (locomotive wheels, rods, and cylinders); and a motionless engine, posed with its rods down.

Because of its association with the blue-collar, working-class *Railroad Magazine*, with a readership drawn heavily from the ranks of railroad employees, the roster shot hobby was seen as even more déclassé than the railfan hobby in general.[3] It is likely that this aspect of roster shots, combined with the lack of creative innovation that the genre commanded, led Beebe to champion the three-quarters view of a moving steam locomotive followed by a train.

Champion it he did, with increasing fervor—and a somewhat binding lack of creativity—as he aged. In 1938's *High Iron* and the three following books, Beebe made a strong and vibrant case for the three-quarters shot. *High Iron* presented one or two photos to a page, a dramatic step forward in design that is still emulated by the best railroad-subject photography books.[4] The book includes more than fifty such images taken by Beebe himself, many of them landmark photographs of the genre.

Beebe's most extensive early photographic manifesto is found not in *High Iron* but in his next book, 1940's *Highliners*. In it, Beebe states,

> *The perfect railroad action photograph—with its rural background, its clarity of definition of all moving parts, its indication of speed through smoke and steam exhaust, its full-length view of the entire train, and its absence of any object or matter to distract the attention from the locomotive and consist themselves—is not easy to come by. . . .*
>
> *Railroad photography in its most satisfactory form is conditioned by a technique that is neither known nor understood by photographers honored and successful in other specialized fields of endeavor. . . .*
>
> *Not all photographs in this collection abide by the most rigid classic requirements. Some have been taken from other than the three-quarter head-on angle required by exacting collectors of action shots. Many show the left side of the locomotive and consequently do not include the power reverse gear. Still others, faute de mieux, include no steam exhaust or index of speed or motion whatsoever.*[5]

Already, Beebe was describing the three-quarters shot in a way just as limiting as the conventions of the roster shot that it was superseding in popularity.

This portfolio presents the three-quarters shot as Beebe and, later, Charles Clegg saw it, and it shows how this type of action shot could and did broaden out into a more inclusive view of railroading. Plates 1 to 6 are classic three-quarters images, with a steam engine in motion, showing smoke, and leading a train—usually a passenger train—that trails off in the distance. Plate 7, a noted image by Charles Clegg, shows one way a photographer can move away from the standard three-quarters shot. The Baltimore & Ohio train in the image is at a wedge angle to Clegg's camera, but Clegg is shooting from overhead rather than trackside, adding complexity and depth to the image. Plate 29, a Midland Terminal Railroad image by Clegg, demonstrates a similar approach.

In plates 8 to 10, harbingers of Clegg's later environmental pictorialist approach, Beebe's camera is far enough from the tracks that the speeding locomotive is framed by a characteristic background: the Deep South, the California coast, and the Sierras.

Plate 11 is a classic wedge shot by Beebe that, uncharacteristically for him, depicts a diesel locomotive. Plates 12 and 13 depict two of the massive steam locomotives that ruled the rails of the western United States towards the end of the age of steam, and both also demonstrate the effects a photographer can achieve when a steam engine produces large amounts of smoke and steam, especially in the winter (plate 13). In plates 14, 15, and 16, Beebe and Clegg achieve a pastoral within the confines of the wedge shot and demonstrate another much-used technique by framing the locomotive with trees.

Plates 17 to 27 show how a wedge shot can proclaim its environment; in this case, the American South and border-state regions, such as West Virginia and southern Indiana. Plate 17, one of Clegg's best-known images, could easily be called an environmental portrait rather than a three-quarters image. To achieve a different effect, Clegg shot the train on an unusual Y bridge, positioned his camera farther back than for a standard wedge shot, shot from a curved segment of the bridge, and got a view slightly angled rather than dead center. Plate 22 is a more conventional Beebe image taken on a bridge. In plate 18, Beebe framed the entire short-line mixed train of the Wadley Southern, creating an archetypical view of the trains that he, Clegg, and Archie Robertson described for posterity.[6] Plates 20 and 23 show motorcars, and plate 24 is an unusual three-quarters view, because the locomotive is pulling the train running backwards, with its tender in the front.

In plates 28 to 34, we see three-quarters shots depicting one of the regions most beloved by Beebe and Clegg: the mountains of Colorado, including the narrow-gauge lines of the Denver & Rio Grande Western and the narrow-gauge Rio Grande Southern. Plates 28 and 31 emphasize the high grandeur of the Colorado Rockies through vertical framing, in which the train fills a bit more than the bottom third of the image, with the mountains in the background rising to the top, or almost to the top, of the frame. Plate 35, an image of the Amador Central in California by Beebe, shows the same device, but in this case the top two-thirds of the image is filled by the pillar of smoke being produced by a small engine, No. 7.

Portfolio 1 ends with four three-quarter shot images of another of Beebe and Clegg's favorite regions: the area near Virginia City, Carson City, and Reno, Nevada. Plates 36 and 37 depict their beloved Virginia & Truckee Railroad. Plate 38 shows the nearby Tonopah & Goldfield Railroad, and plate 39, another overhead view by Clegg, shows the narrow-gauge Southern Pacific Owens Valley branch, a survivor of the Virginia & Truckee–affiliated Carson & Colorado.

These photos span the years from the mid-1930s to about 1950, also the years when Beebe and Clegg were active as photographers. By about 1950, the three-quarters shot was being eclipsed as a cutting-edge mode of railroad-subject photography by work showing the entire environment of American railroading. These new "environmental" images were produced by Phil Hastings, Jim Shaughnessy, Dick Steinheimer, and their colleagues—a group of photographers championed by *Trains* editor David P. Morgan.

There are at least two ironies inherent in this development. The first is that all of these photographers were inspired at least in part by *Mixed Train Daily* and especially by Clegg's broader photographic approach to American railroading. Clegg was not only one of the greatest influences on American railroad-subject photography beginning in the late 1940s; he was also a major artistic influence on Beebe. As portfolio 4 will show, both of these men closed their photographic careers with broad-based images of American railroading that rival the best taken by Hastings, who is often considered the early master of this genre.

Second, although Beebe often jousted in print with those advocating a broader approach to railroad-subject photography, he had an eye for talent that rivaled Morgan's legendary prowess in that regard. Beebe was an early advocate for photographers such as Hastings, Shaughnessy, and H. Reid; he worked extensively with Dick Steinheimer; and in *Great Railroad Photographs, U.S.A.* and *The Trains We Rode: Volume II*, he was the first to give book publication to railroad-subject photographs by O. Winston Link.[7] Beebe's judgment in all of these cases was exceptional. Beebe's early recognition of Link is especially notable; Link's reputation is still rising, and he is often cited as the greatest railroad-subject photographer of the twentieth century.

With its placement of one or two three-quarters shots per page, *High Iron* remains the prototype for all of the railroad picture books that have followed, including Link's masterwork, *Steam, Steel & Stars.*

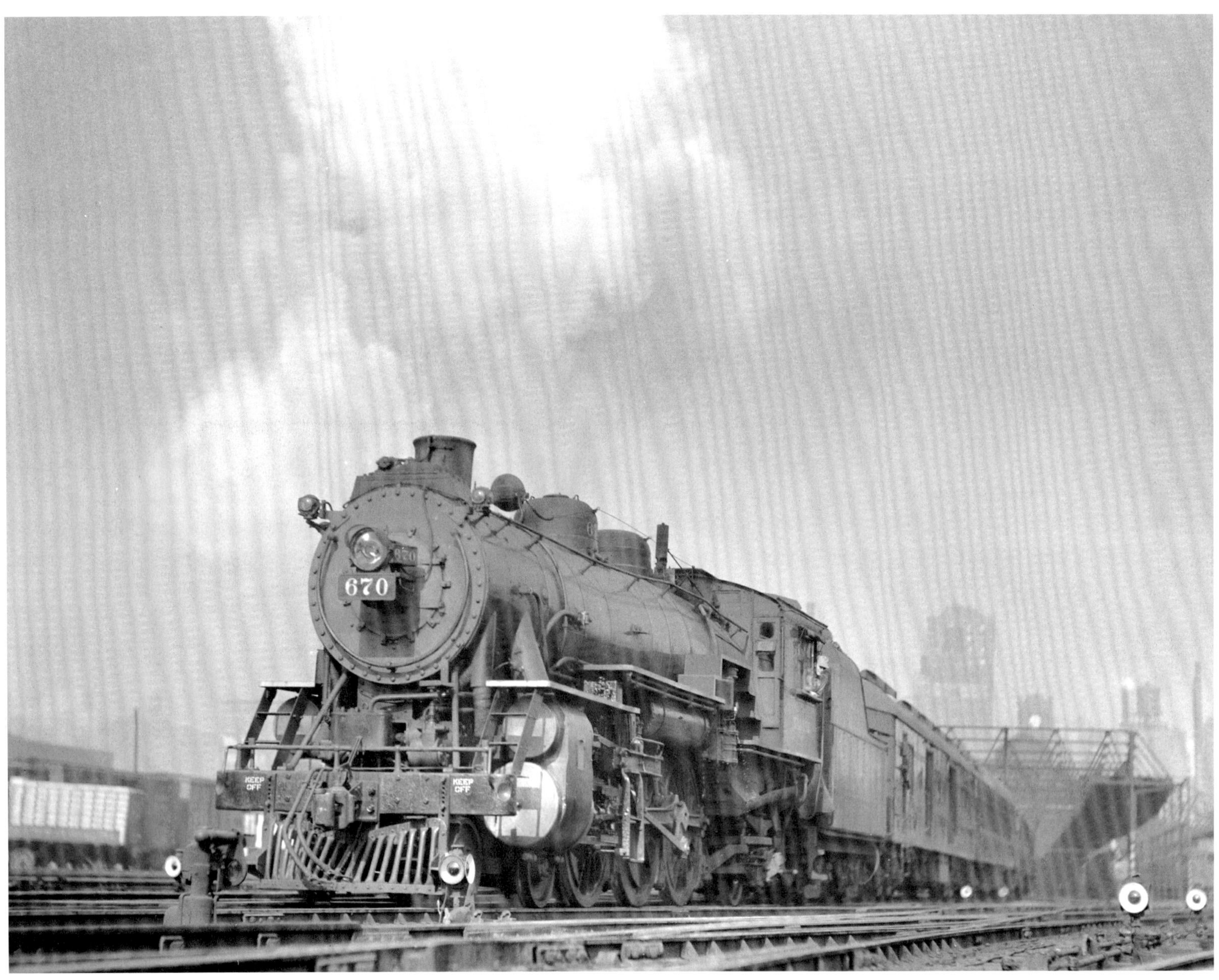

Plate 1. The *Banner Blue* on the Wabash Railroad. Taken at Dearborn Station, Chicago, Illinois, 1935. Lucius Beebe. Beebe-Clegg negative 670.

Courtesy of the California State Railroad Museum.

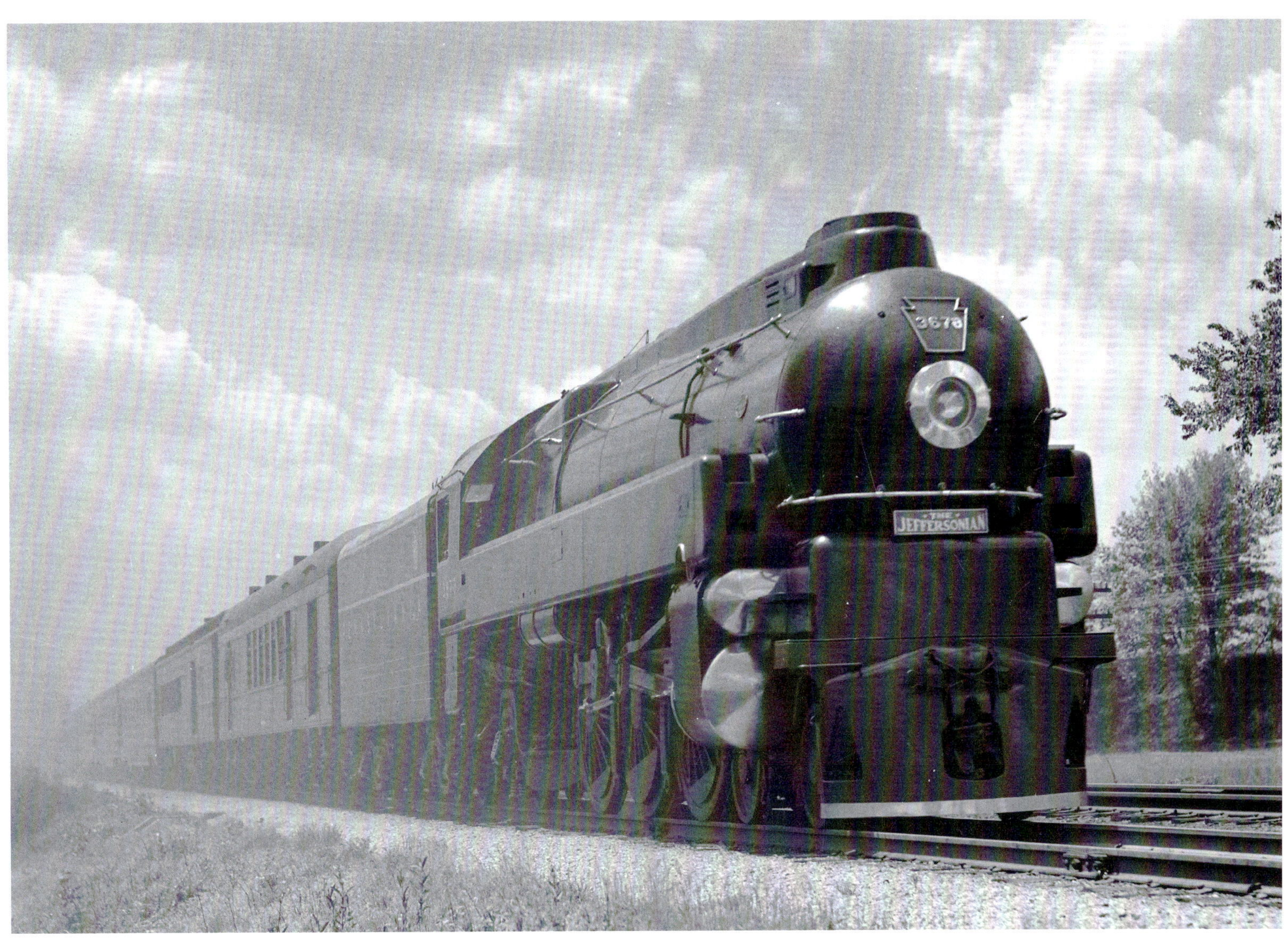

Plate 2. The *Jeffersonian* on the Pennsylvania Railroad, crossing Illinois during the 1930s. Note that, as published in books such as *Highball,* this photo was a composite; the impressive pall of smoke was added to this image. Lucius Beebe. Beebe-Clegg negative 873.

Courtesy of the California State Railroad Museum.

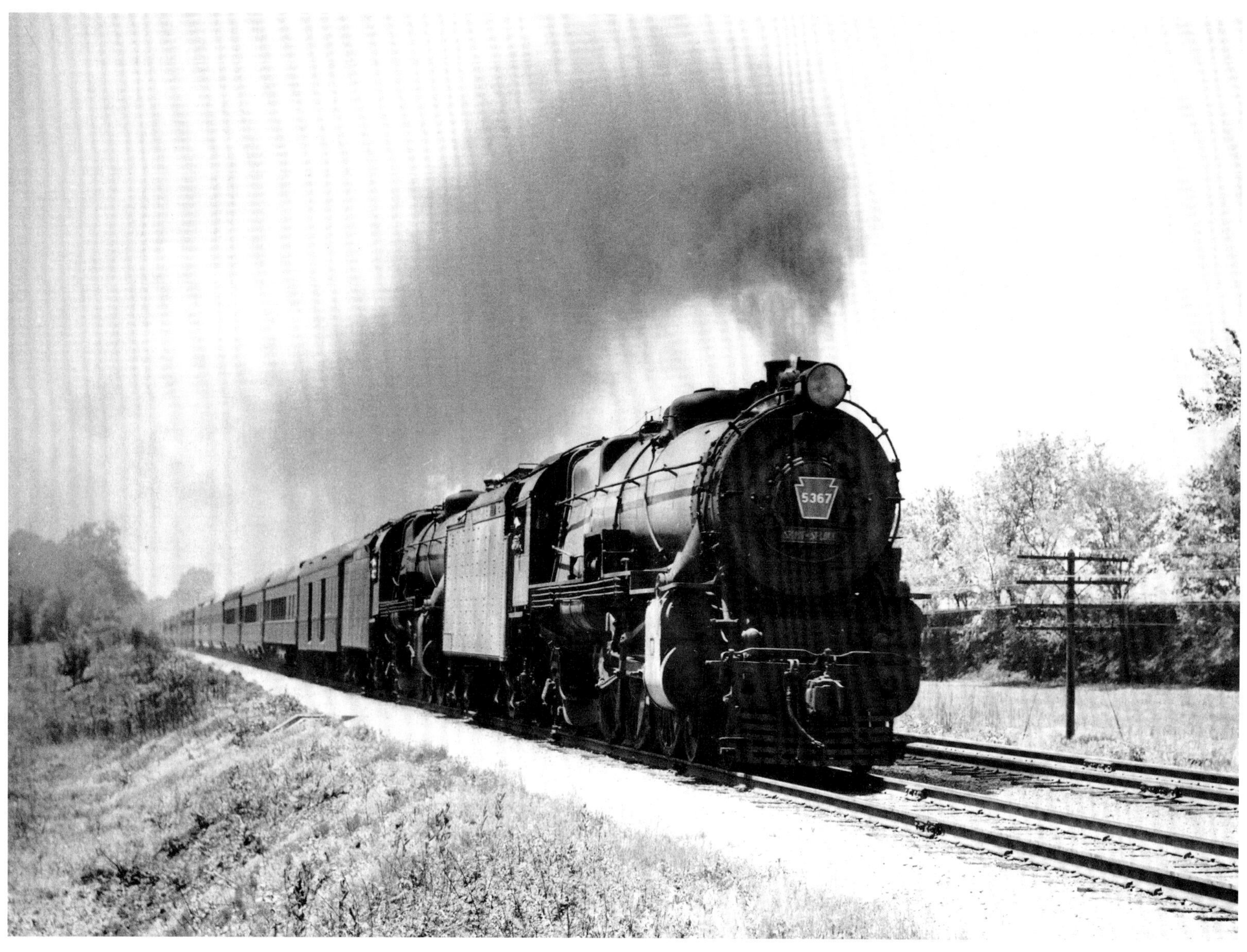

Plate 3. The Pennsylvania Railroad's *Spirit of St. Louis* at speed during the 1930s. Lucius Beebe. Beebe-Clegg negative 4005.

Courtesy of the California State Railroad Museum.

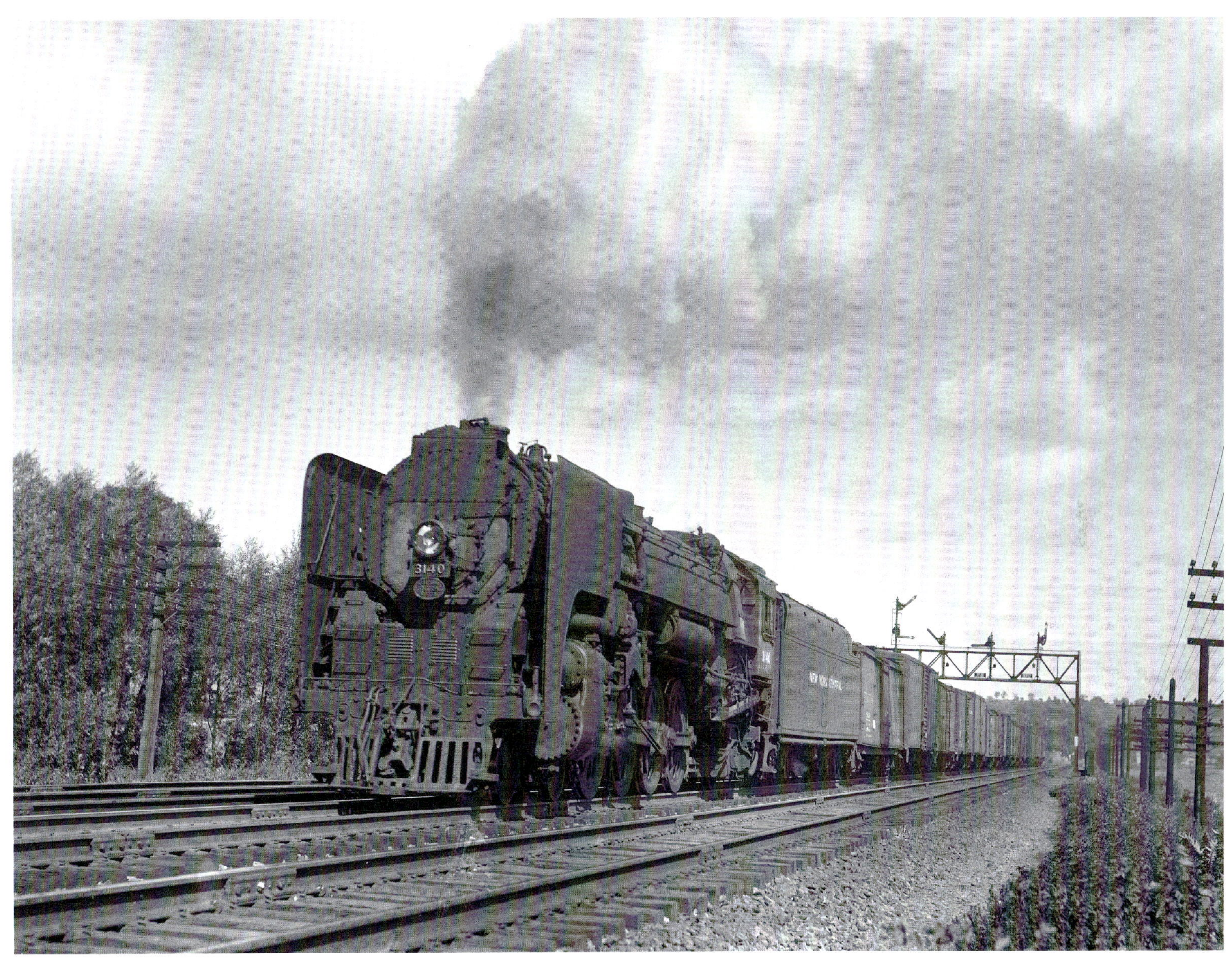

Plate 4. New York Central engine 3140 with train. Lucius Beebe or Charles Clegg. Beebe-Clegg negative 2649.

Courtesy of the California State Railroad Museum.

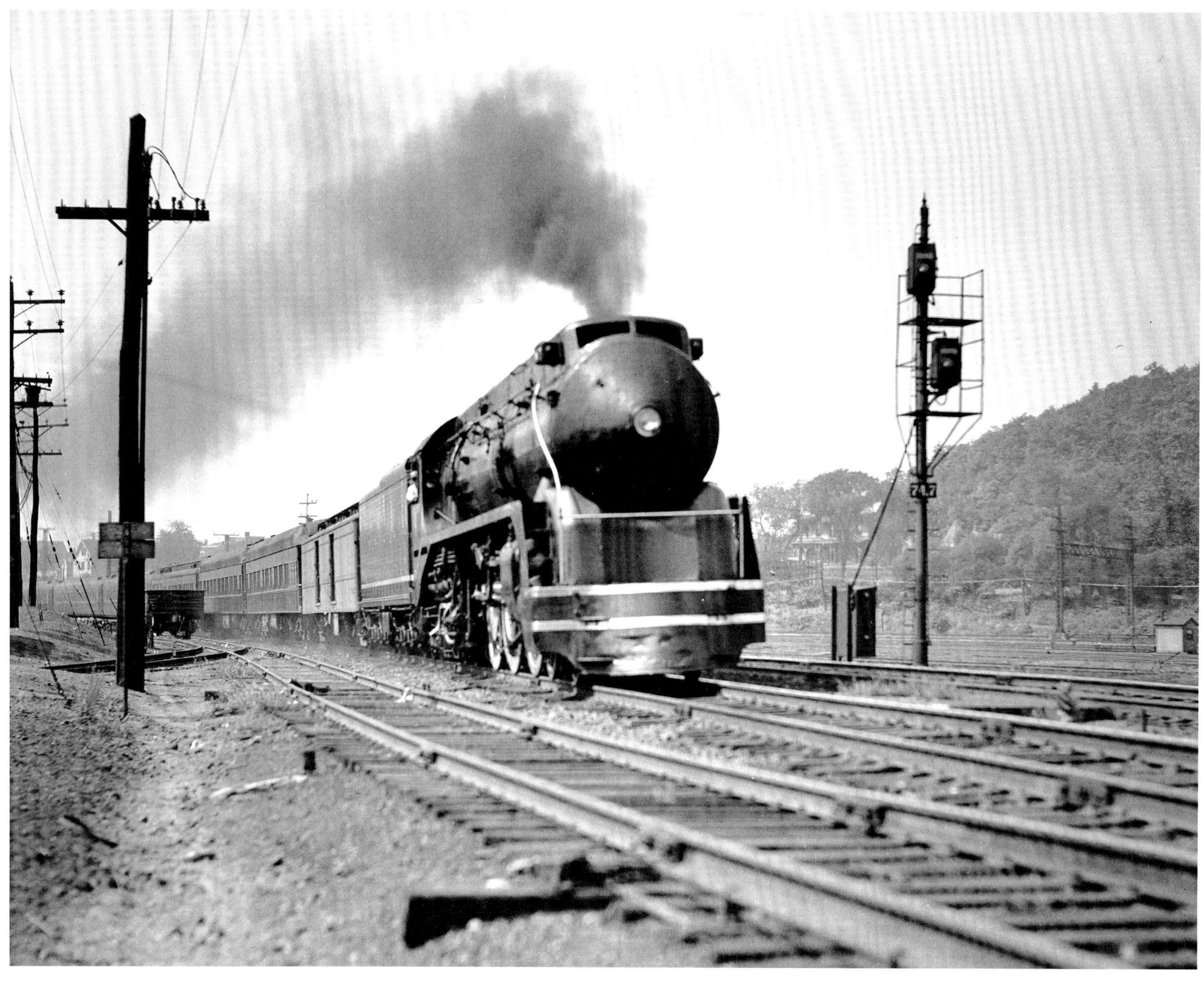

Plate 5. New Haven (New York, New Haven & Hartford Railroad) "Shoreliner Class" locomotive with train. Attributed to Lucius Beebe. Beebe-Clegg negative 2635.

Courtesy of the California State Railroad Museum.

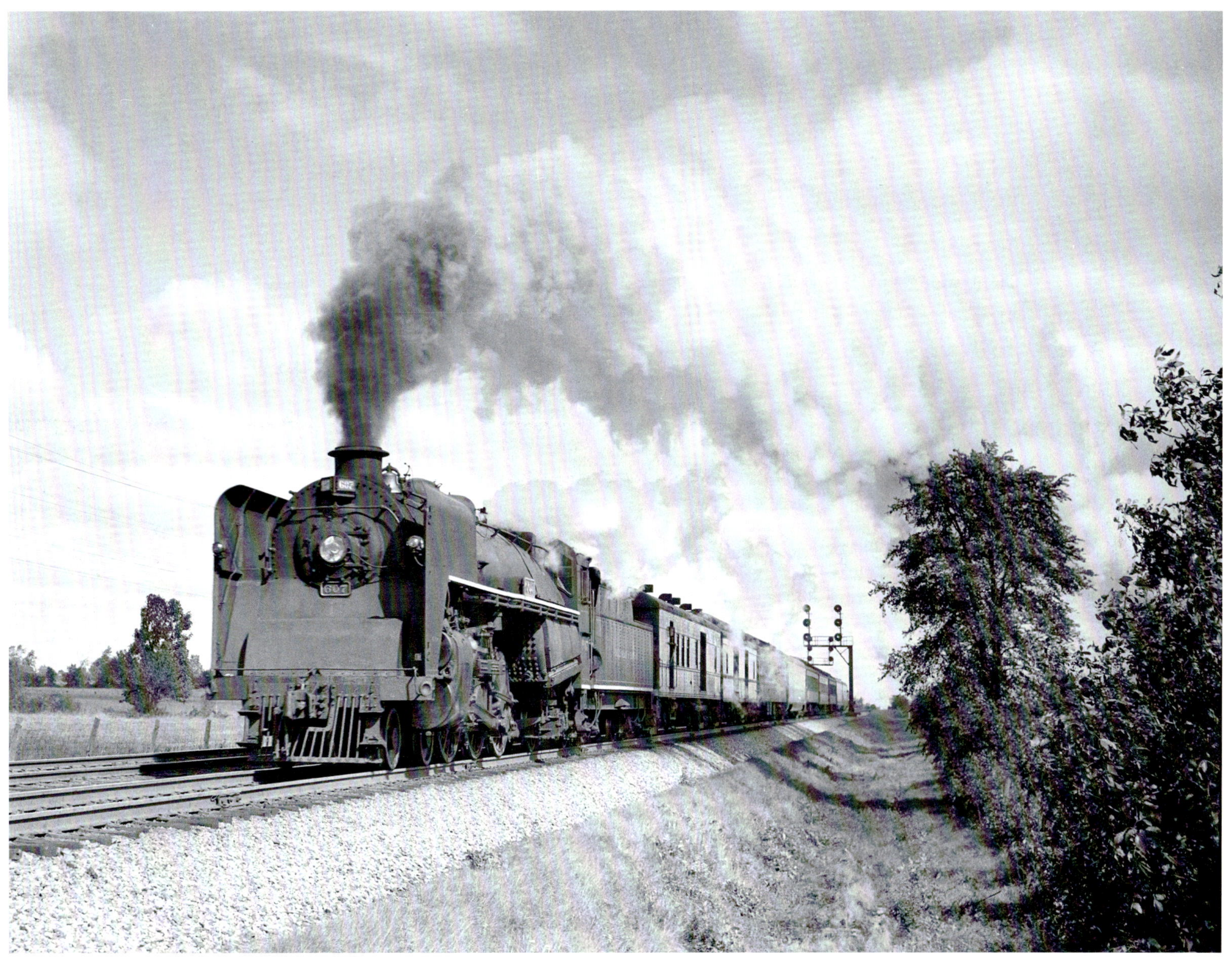

Plate 6. The Delaware & Hudson Railway's *Laurentian*. Charles Clegg. Beebe-Clegg negative 391.

Courtesy of the California State Railroad Museum.

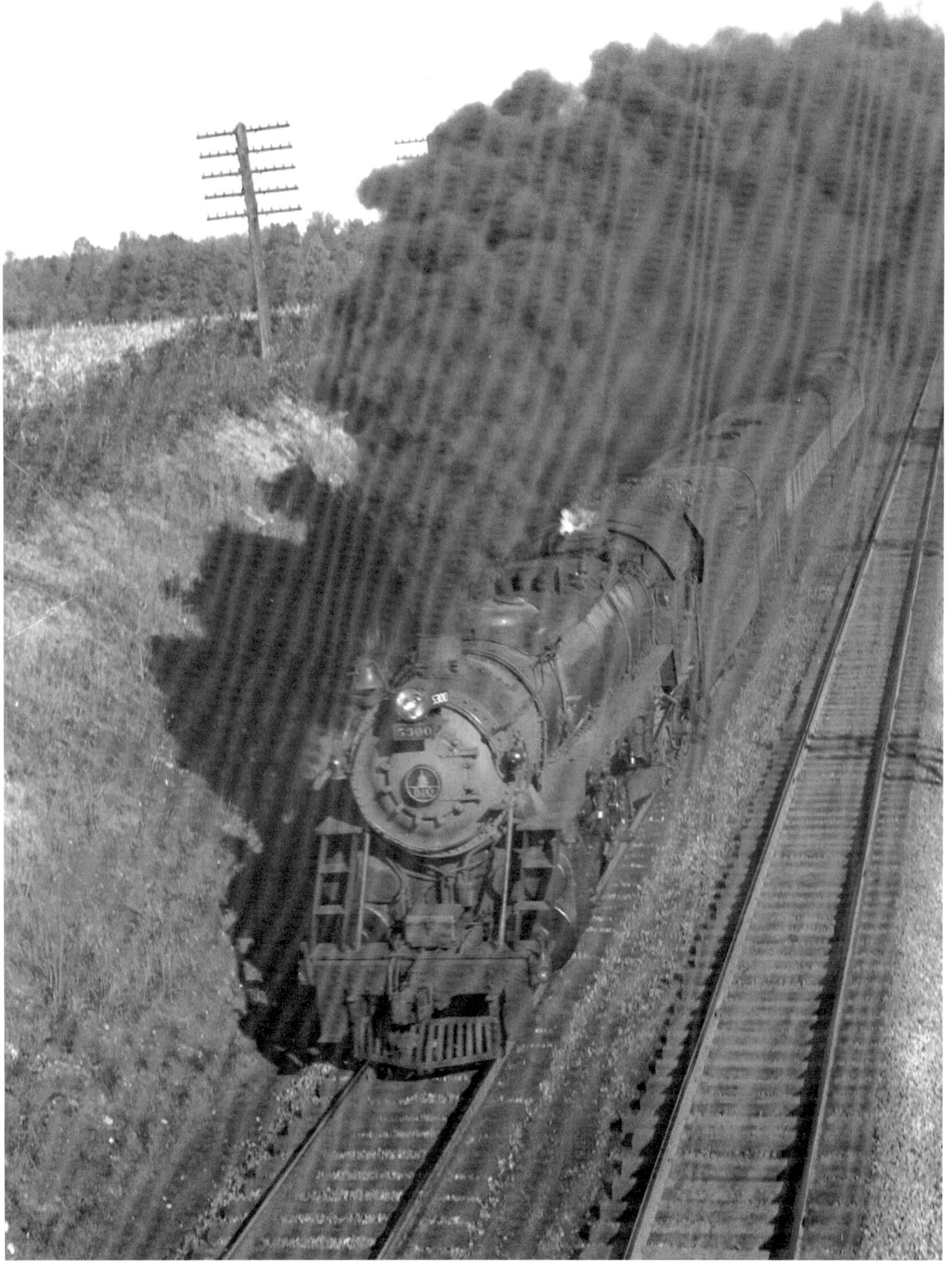

Plate 7. The Baltimore & Ohio Railroad's *National Limited* in Maryland. Charles Clegg. Beebe-Clegg negative 87.

Courtesy of the California State Railroad Museum.

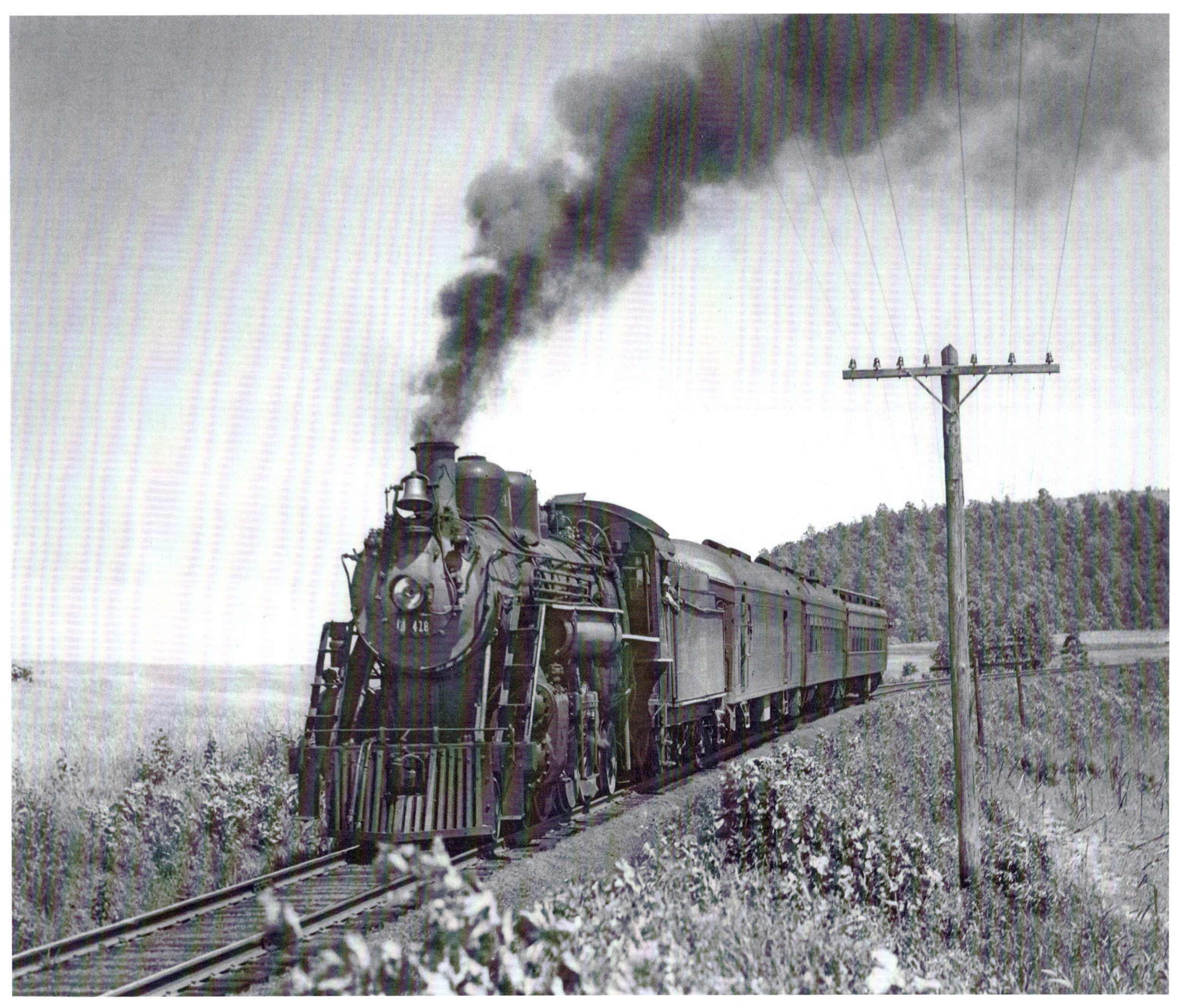

Plate 8. A Central of Georgia Railway local passenger train near Albany, Georgia, 1944. Lucius Beebe. Beebe-Clegg negative 4004.

Courtesy of the California State Railroad Museum.

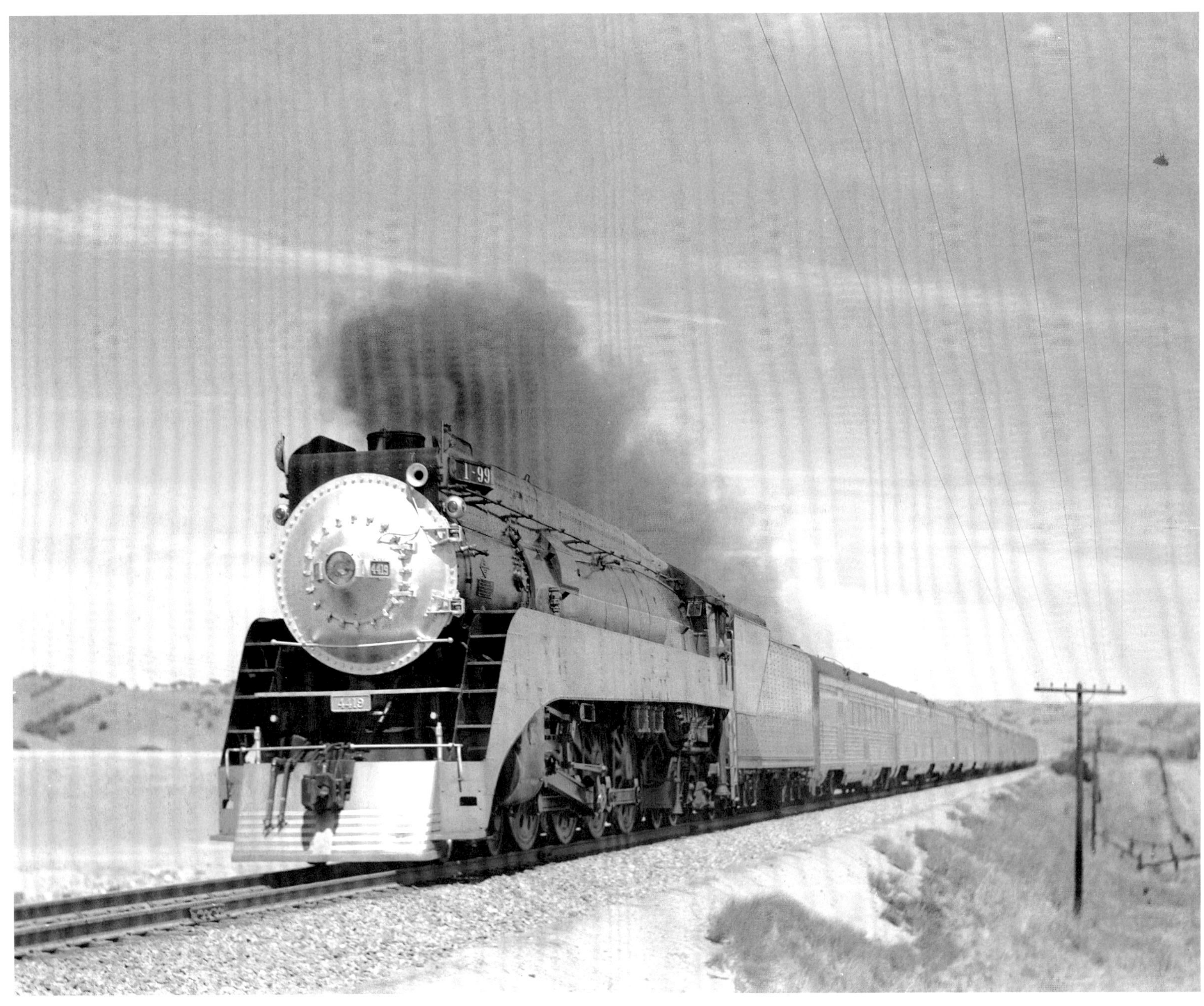

Plate 9. The first section of the Southern Pacific's *Daylight*, at Surf, California, in 1938. Lucius Beebe. Beebe-Clegg negative 1823.

Courtesy of the California State Railroad Museum.

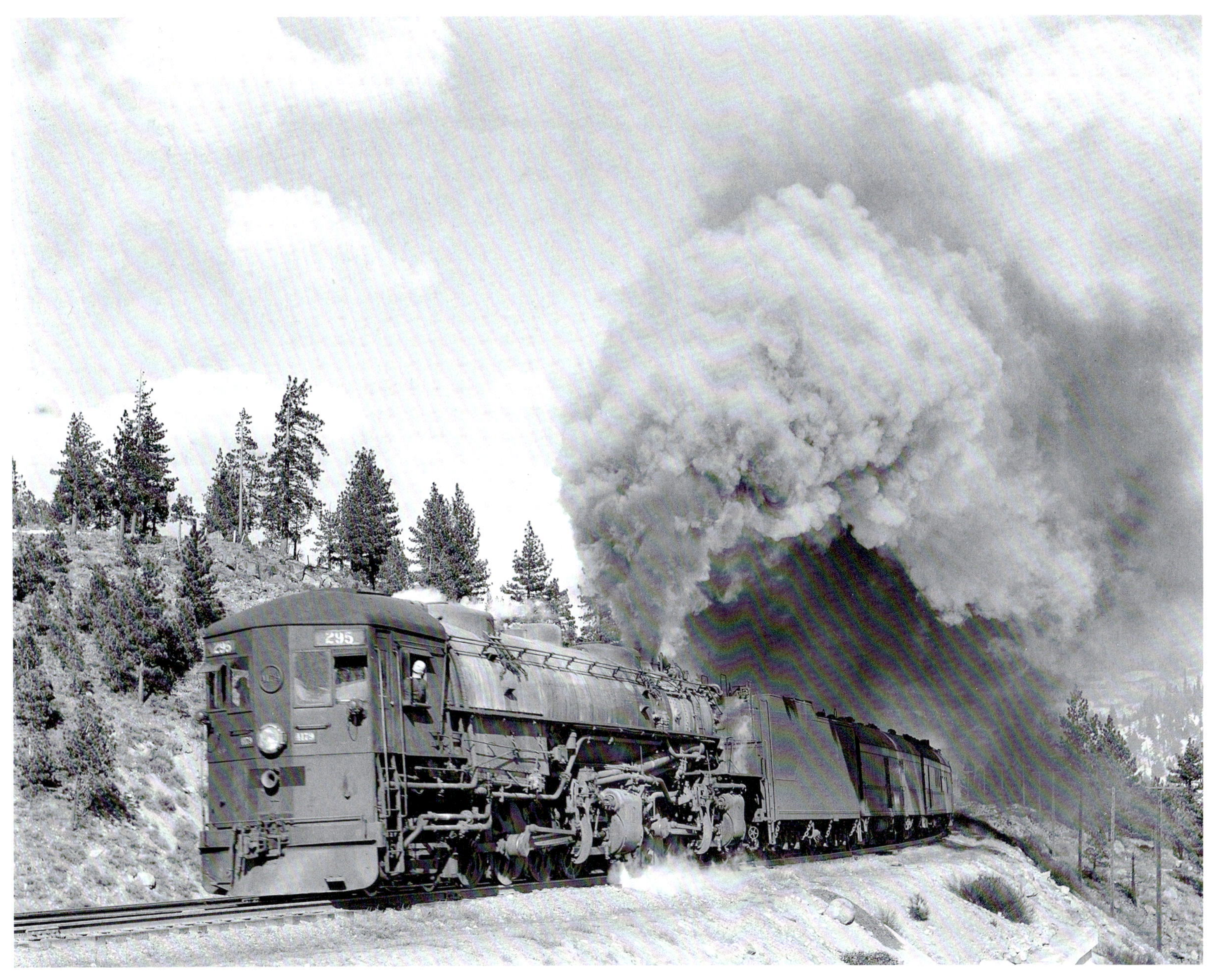

Plate 10. "Almost to Timberline." Southern Pacific local No. 295, near Truckee, California. The train is headed by a famed Southern Pacific "cab-forward" steam locomotive. The worker looking back from the cab is the fireman, who is checking his fire by watching the smoke from the cab-forward's stack behind him. Lucius Beebe. Beebe-Clegg negative 1777.

Courtesy of the California State Railroad Museum.

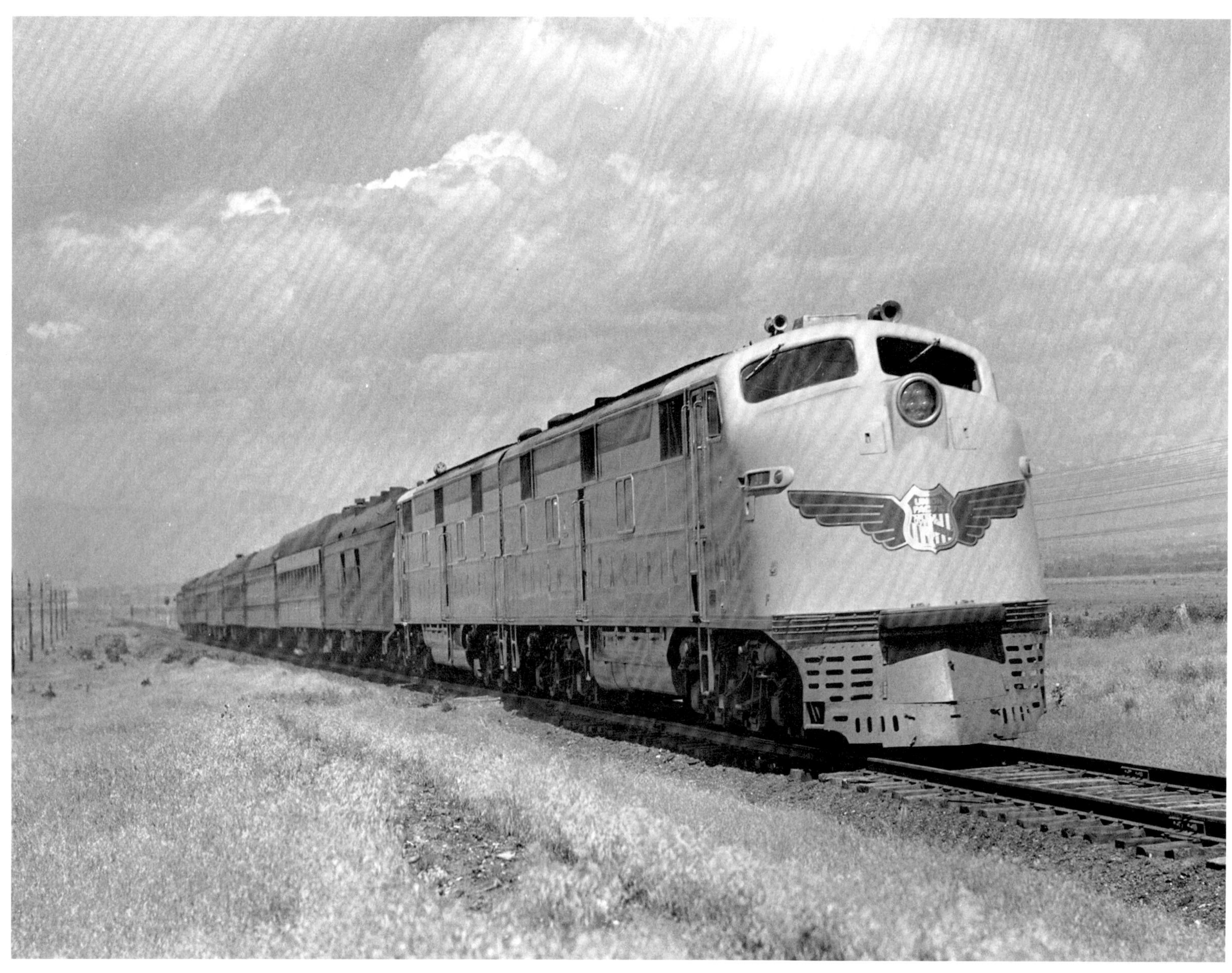

Plate 11. A diesel-hauled Union Pacific passenger train. This photo, from 1941's *Trains in Transition,* depicts an early usage of the diesel locomotive in the United States. It is also one of a limited number of diesel locomotive images taken by Lucius Beebe. Lucius Beebe. Beebe-Clegg negative 804.

Courtesy of the California State Railroad Museum.

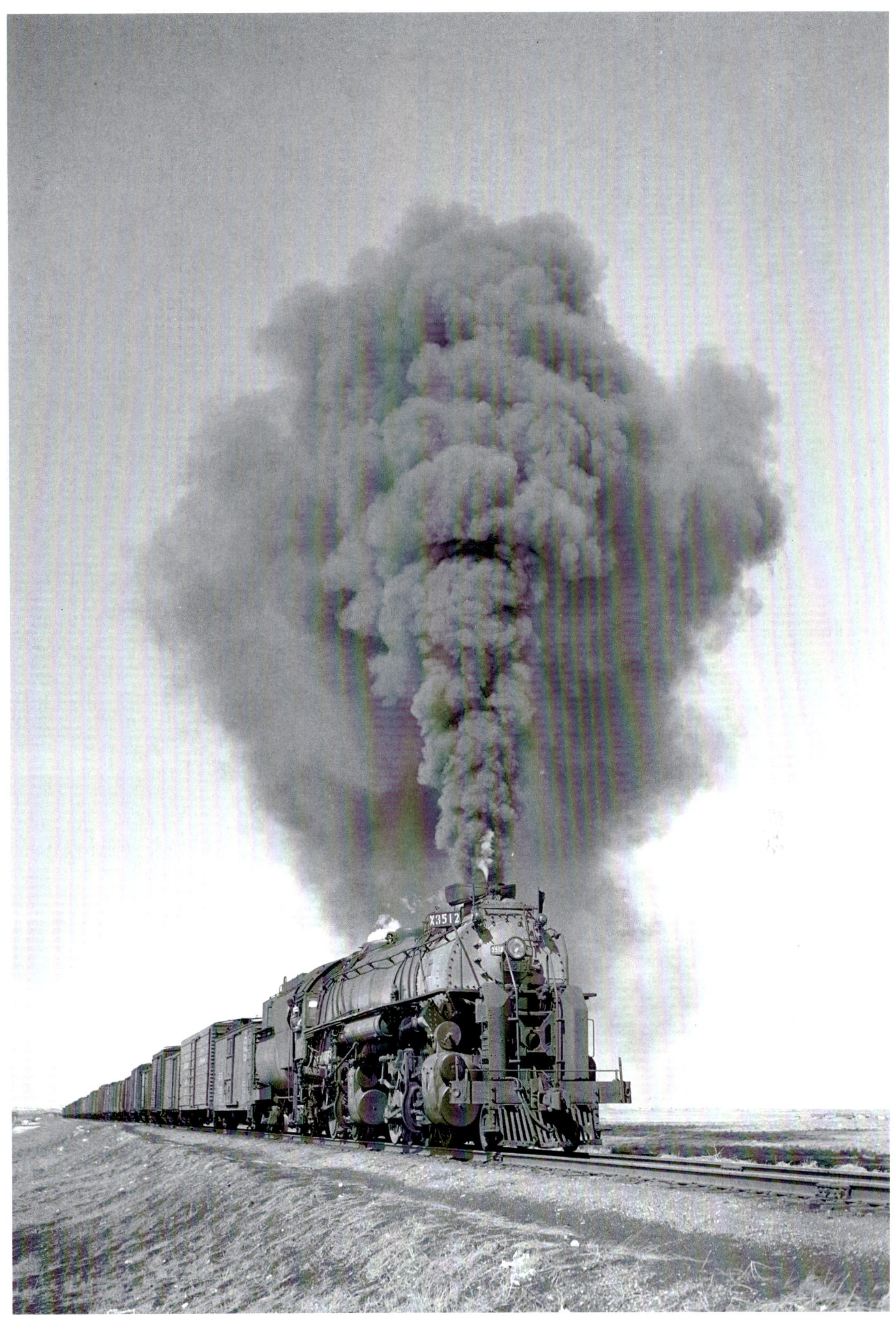

Plate 12. Union Pacific freight, led by engine 3512. Charles Clegg. Beebe-Clegg negative 845.

Courtesy of the California State Railroad Museum.

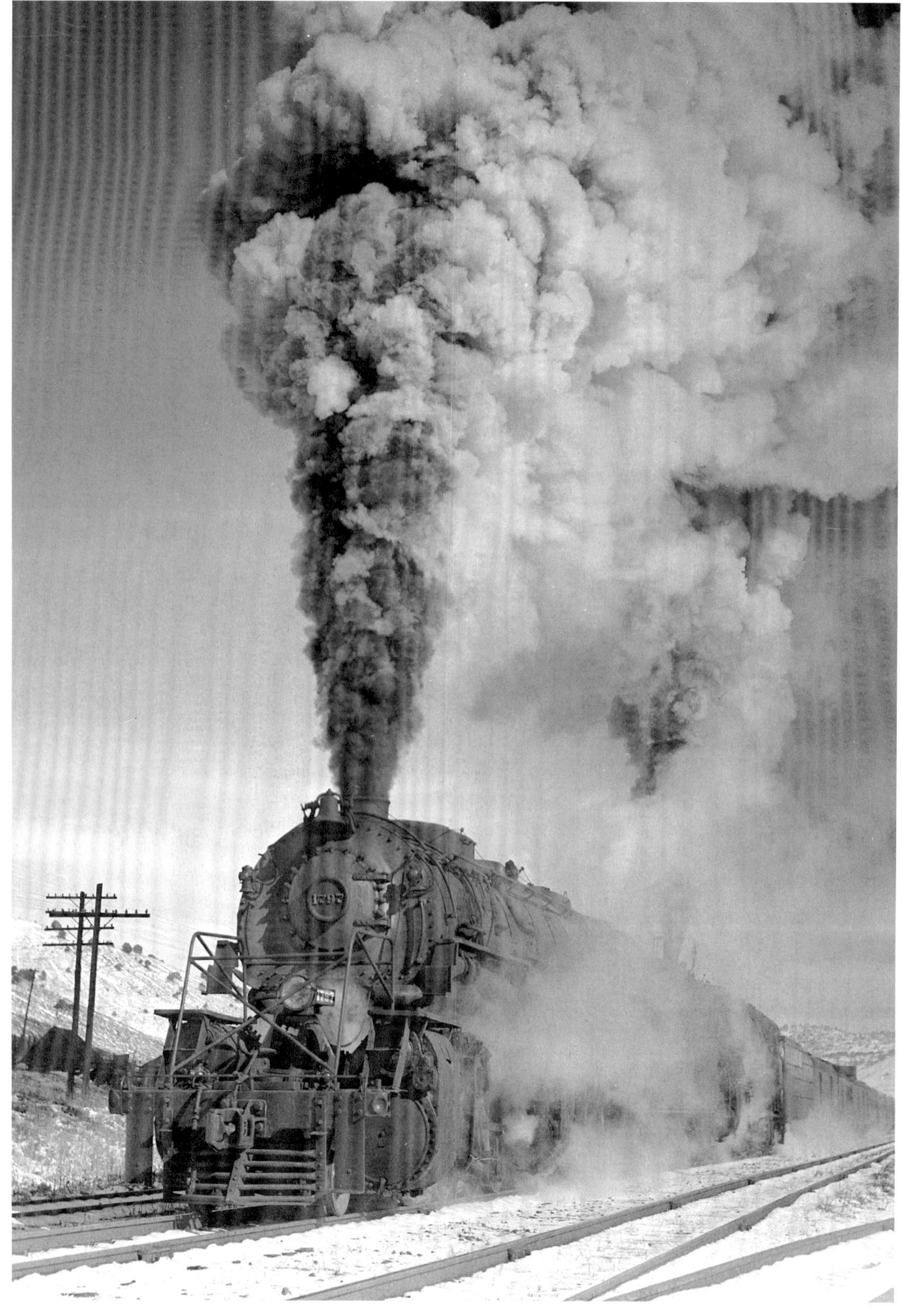

Plate 13. Santa Fe engine 1797, with a passenger train. Lucius Beebe. Beebe-Clegg negative 1601.

Courtesy of the California State Railroad Museum.

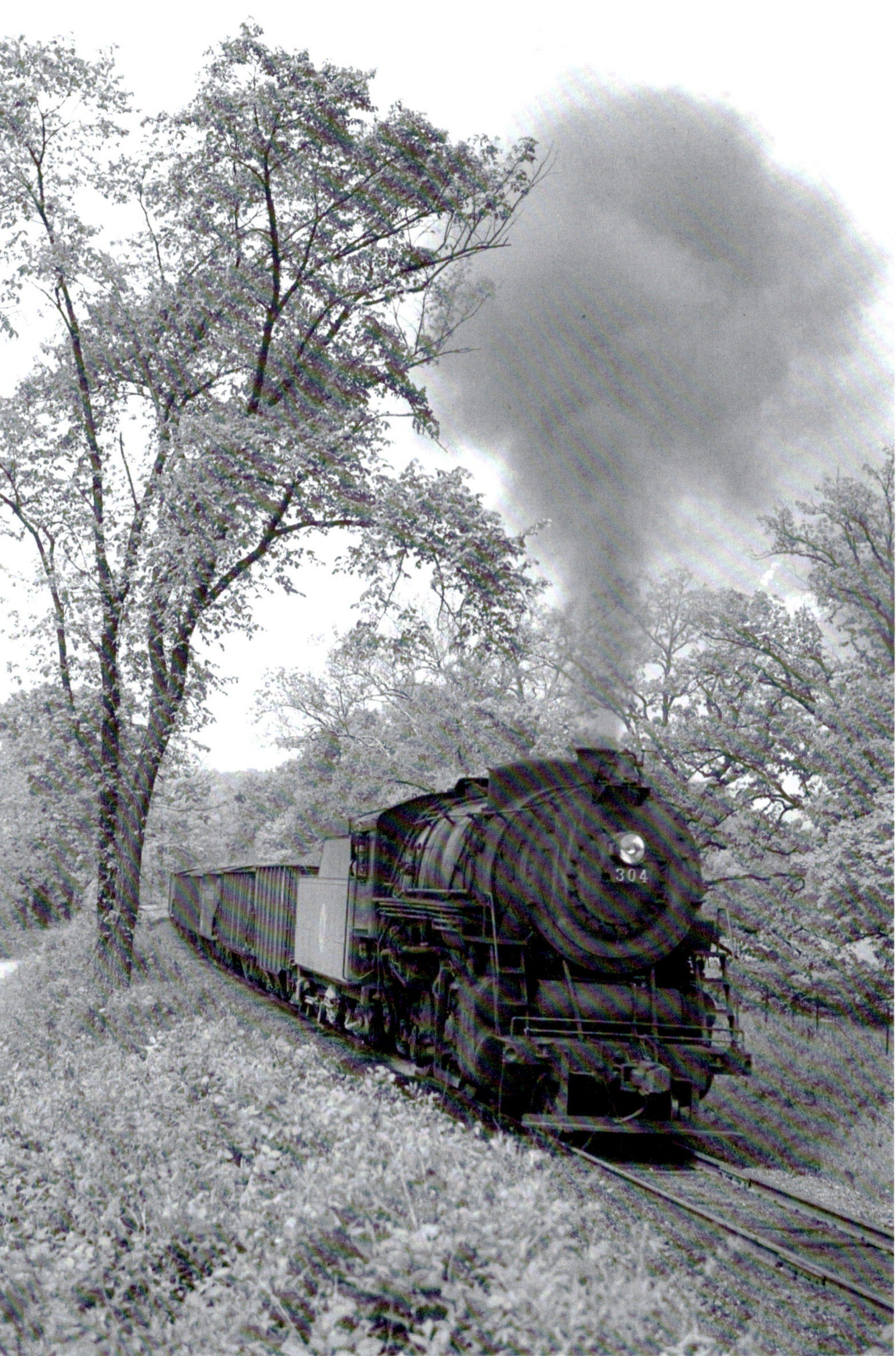

Plate 14. A Lehigh & New England Railroad coal train led by "Consolidation" 304 at Gainesburgh Junction, New Jersey. Charles Clegg. Beebe-Clegg negative 1173.

Courtesy of the California State Railroad Museum.

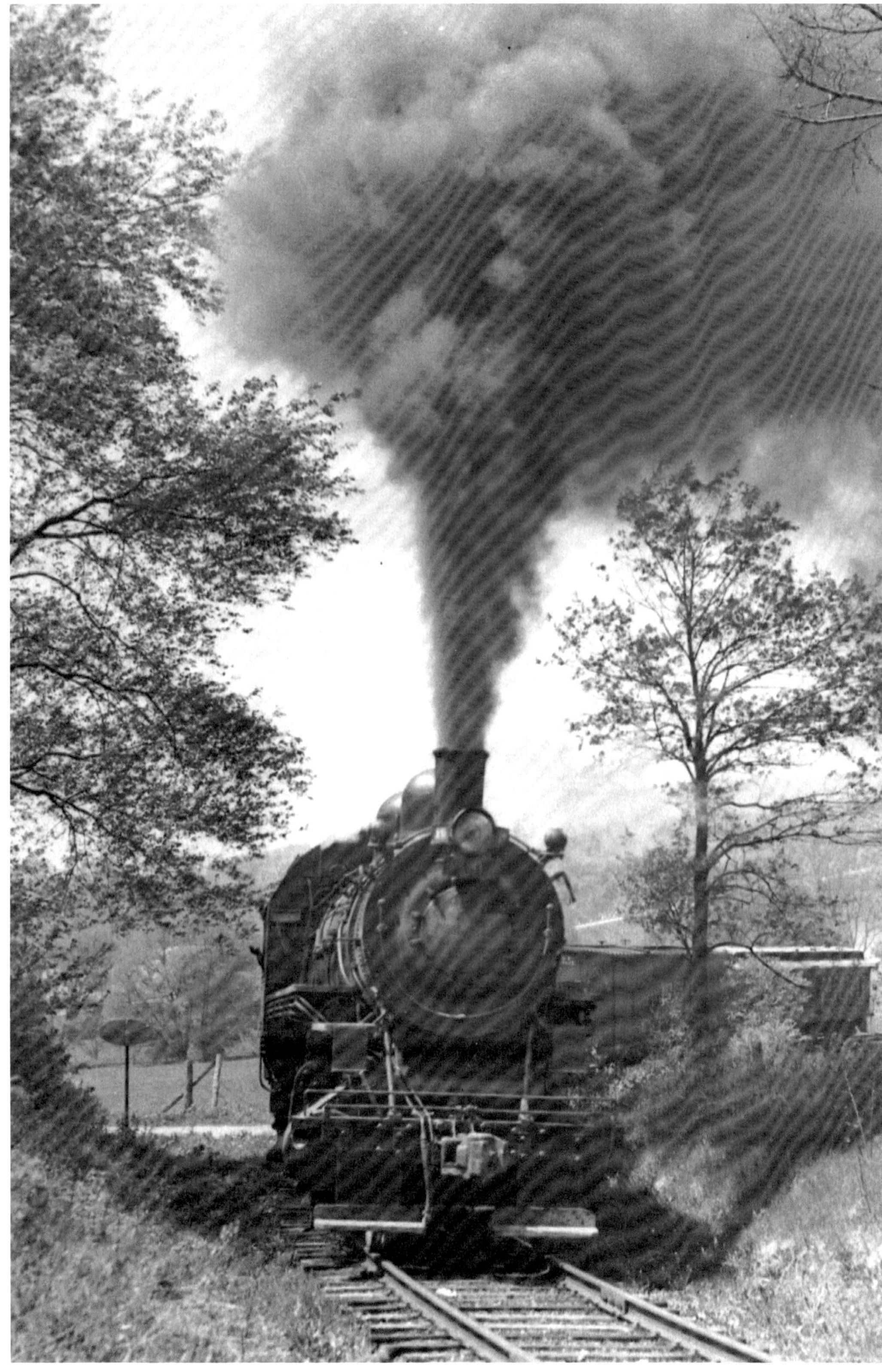

Plate 15. The daily mixed train of the Bellefonte Central Railroad, running westbound from Bellefonte to State College, Pennsylvania, at a location called Horseshoe Curve. Lucius Beebe. Beebe-Clegg negative 1168.

Courtesy of the California State Railroad Museum.

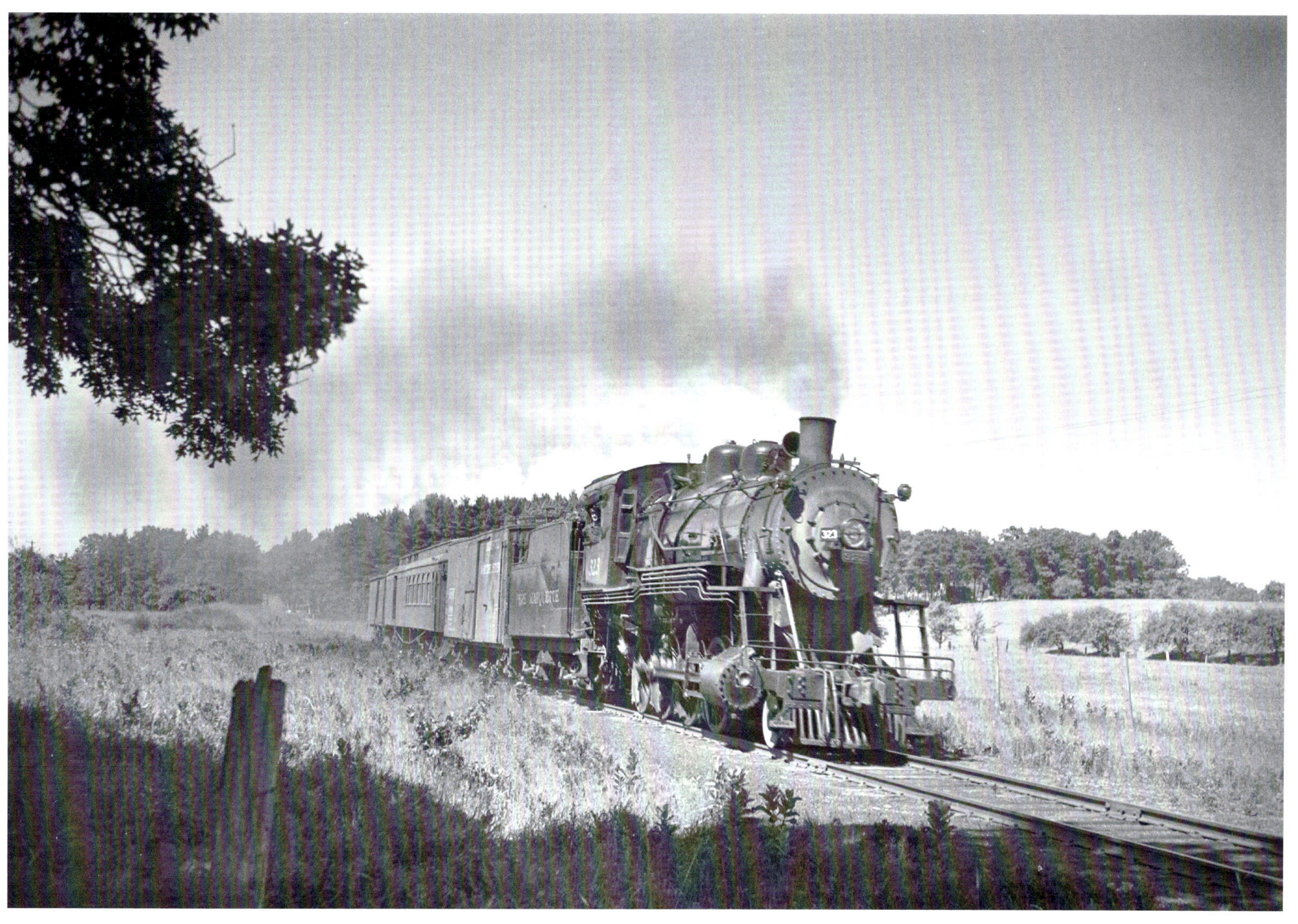

Plate 16. Pere Marquette 323 leads a short train on the Manistee & North-Eastern, controlled by the larger Pere Marquette Railway at the time. Charles Clegg. Beebe-Clegg negative 3000.

Courtesy of the California State Railroad Museum.

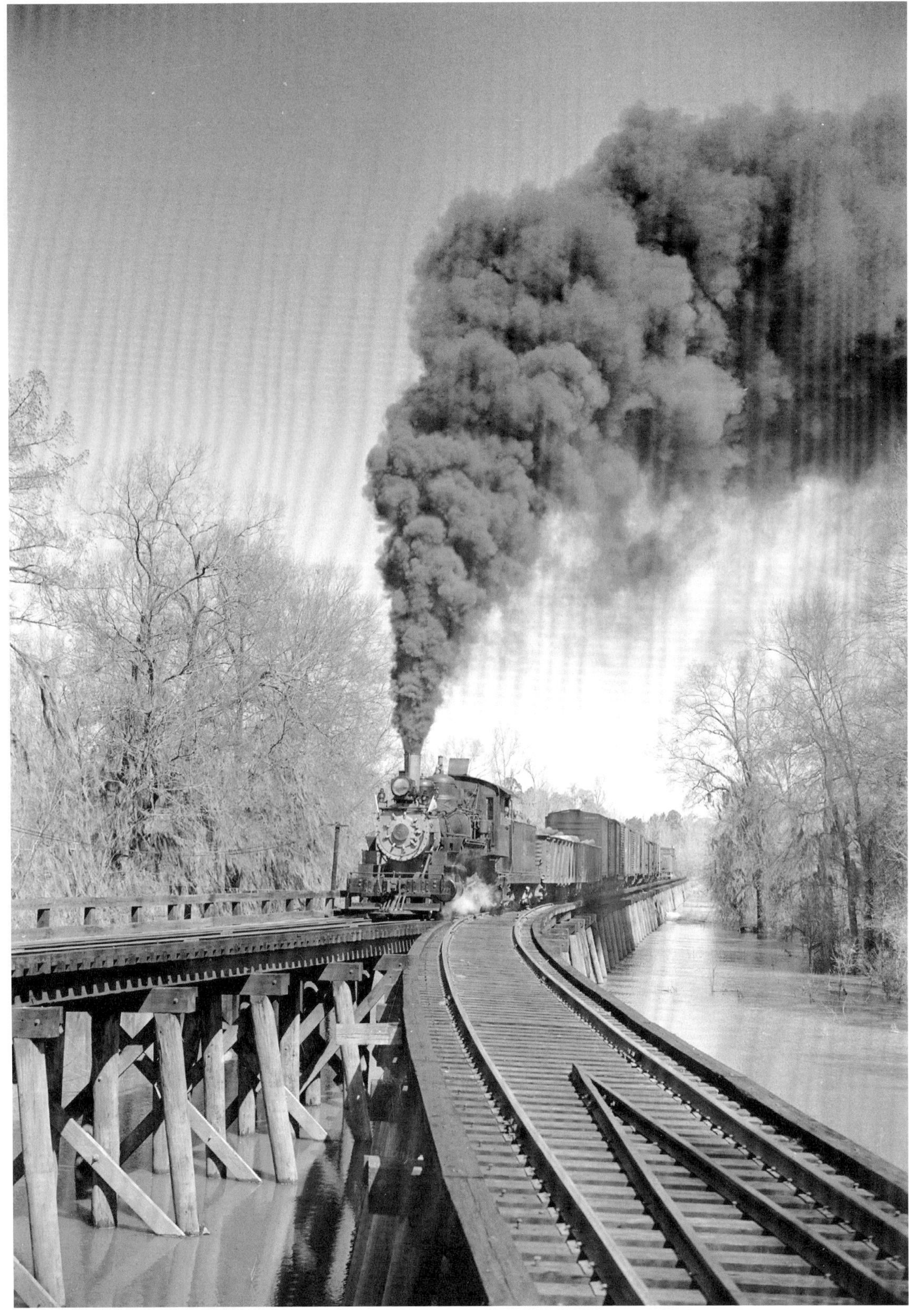

Plate 17. The morning eastbound mixed train of the Tremont & Gulf Railroad crosses a trestle east of Rochelle, Louisiana. The Tremont & Gulf, which connected with the Missouri Pacific Railroad in Rochelle, carried passengers on its mixed trains in a caboose. Charles Clegg. Beebe-Clegg negative 612.

Courtesy of the California State Railroad Museum.

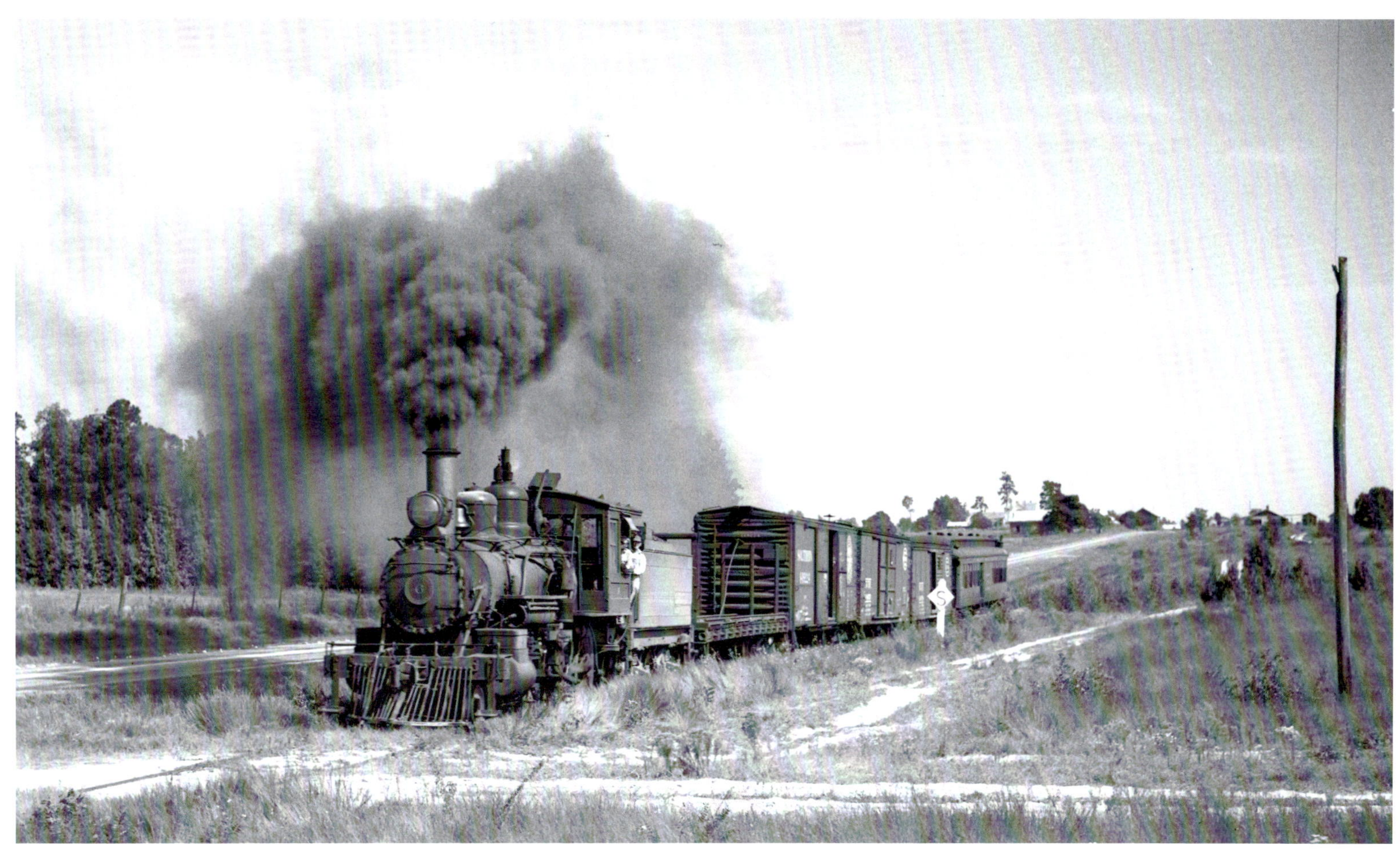

Plate 18. Wadley Southern Railway train arriving at Swainsboro, Georgia, its southern terminus. Lucius Beebe. Beebe-Clegg negative 882.

Courtesy of the California State Railroad Museum.

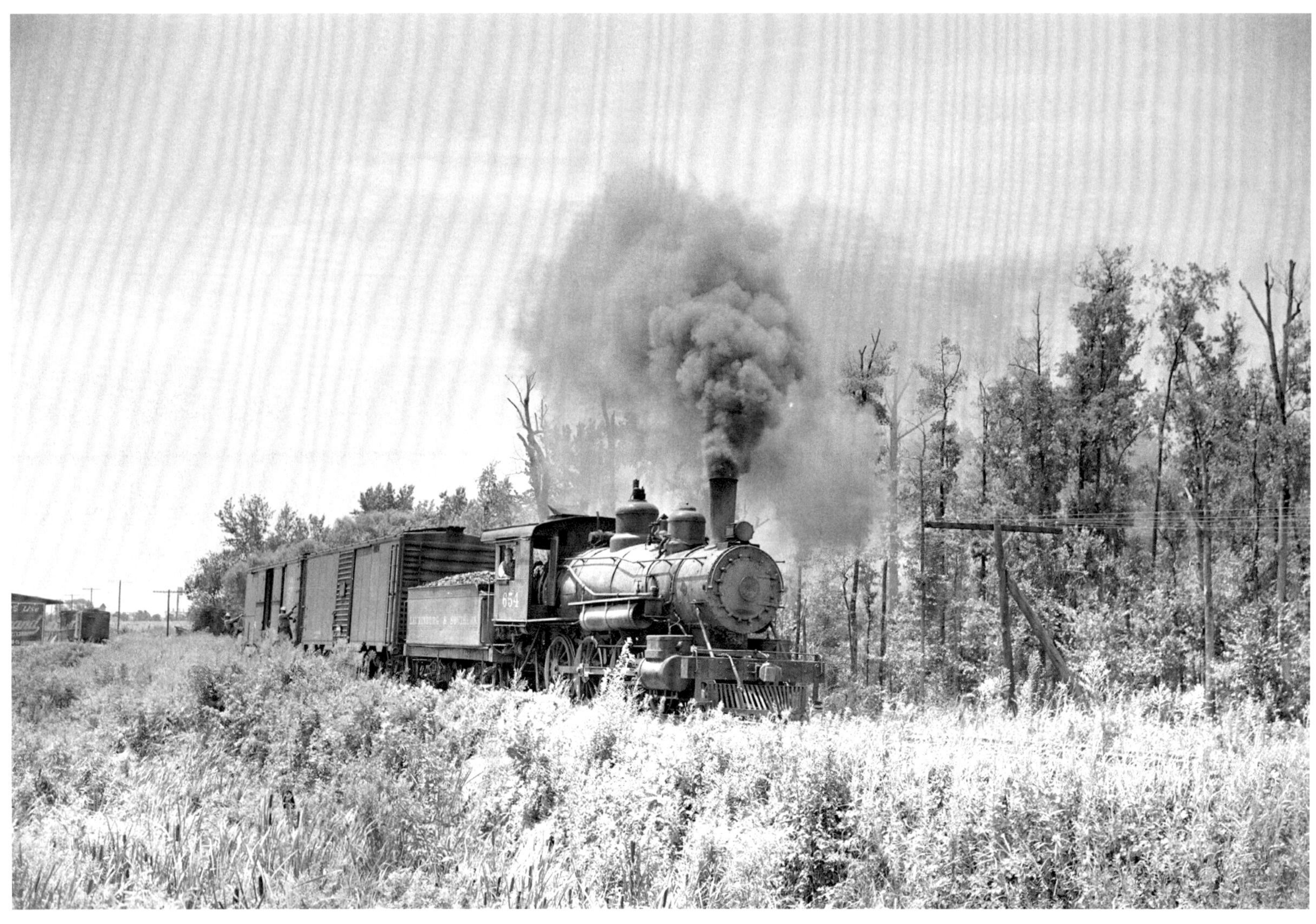

Plate 19. Laurinburg & Southern 654 with a short train. Charles Clegg. Beebe-Clegg negative 2439.

Courtesy of the California State Railroad Museum.

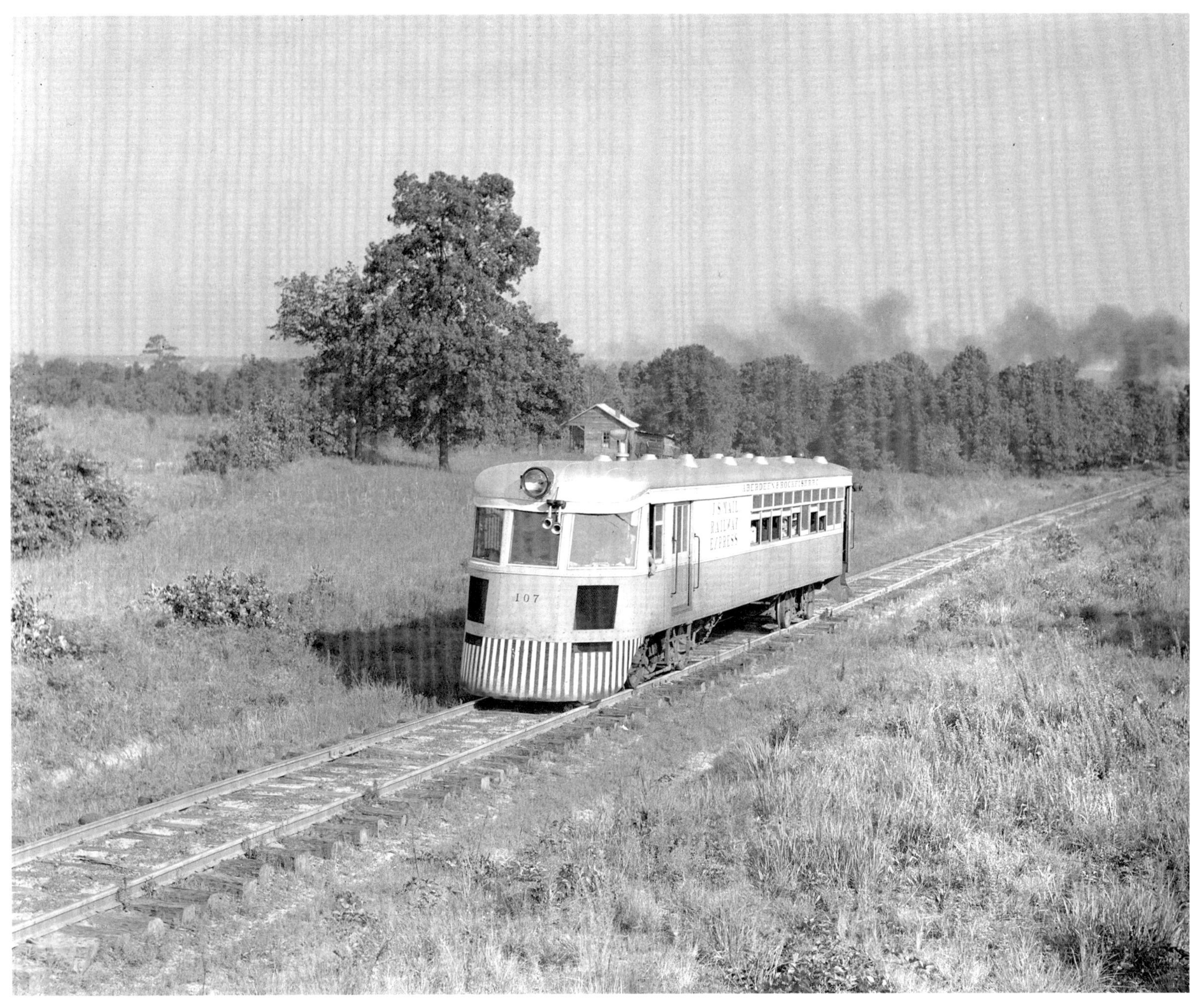

Plate 20. Aberdeen & Rockfish motorcar 107. This motorcar was rebuilt from a wrecked J. G. Brill Company motorcar, Aberdeen & Rockfish 103, in 1941. It was sold to a Cuban purchaser in about 1948. Lucius Beebe. Beebe-Clegg negative 15.

Courtesy of the California State Railroad Museum.

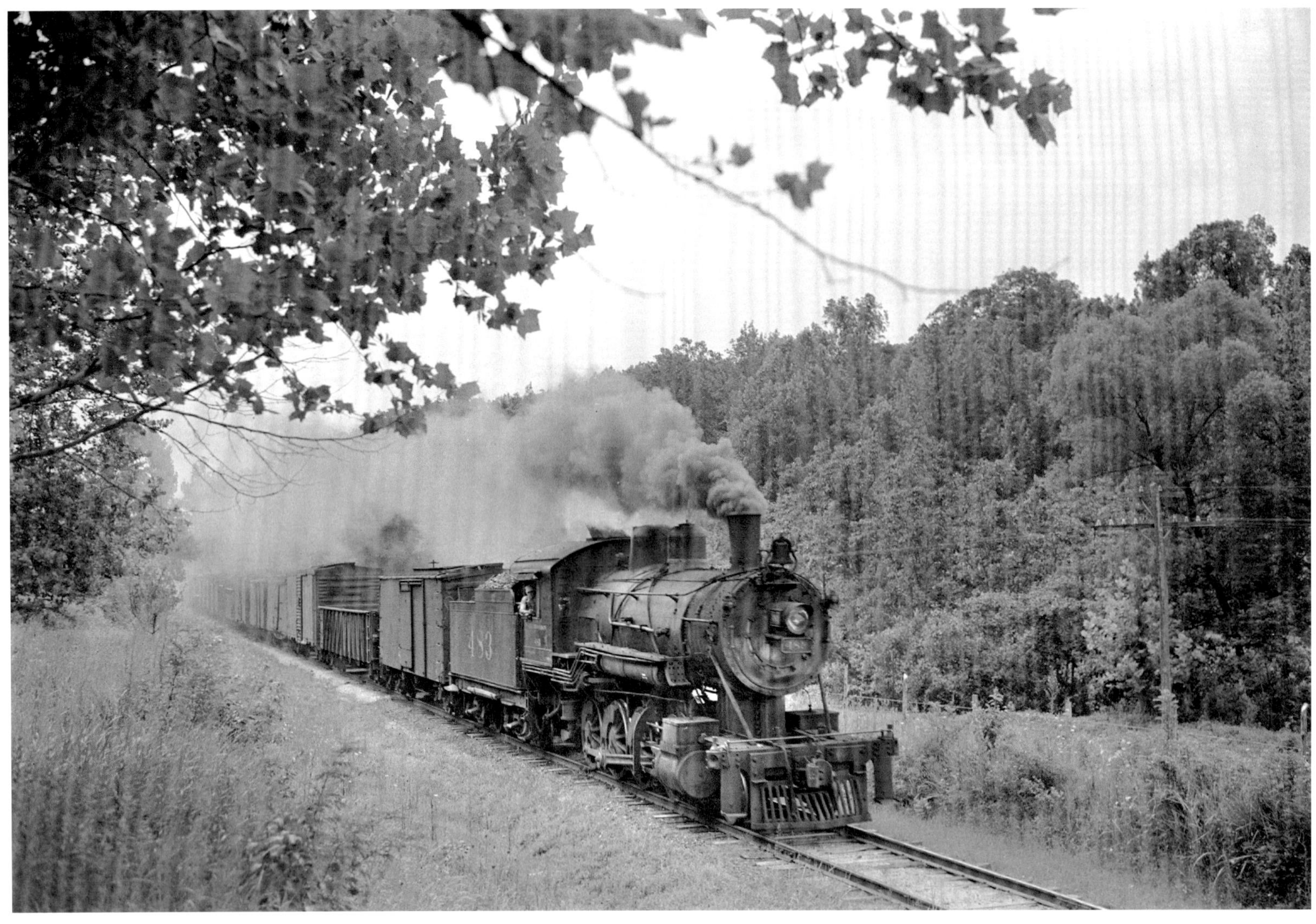

Plate 21. Atlantic & Yadkin locomotive 483 with train. Lucius Beebe. Beebe-Clegg negative 1467.

Courtesy of the California State Railroad Museum.

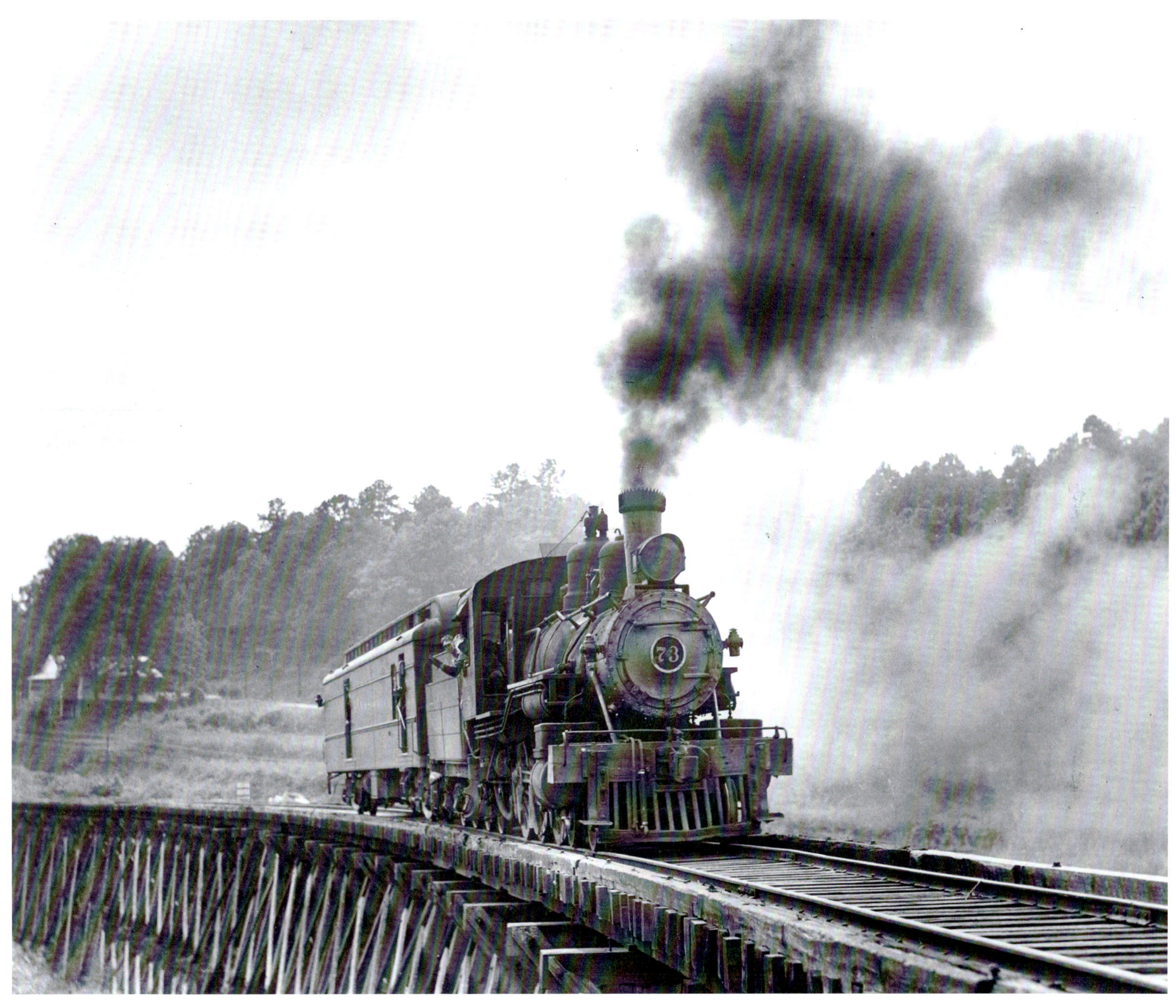

Plate 22. The Tallulah Falls Railroad's No. 73 pulls a single mail and express car across a trestle between Cornelia, Georgia, and Franklin, North Carolina. Lucius Beebe. Beebe-Clegg negative 4006.

Courtesy of the California State Railroad Museum.

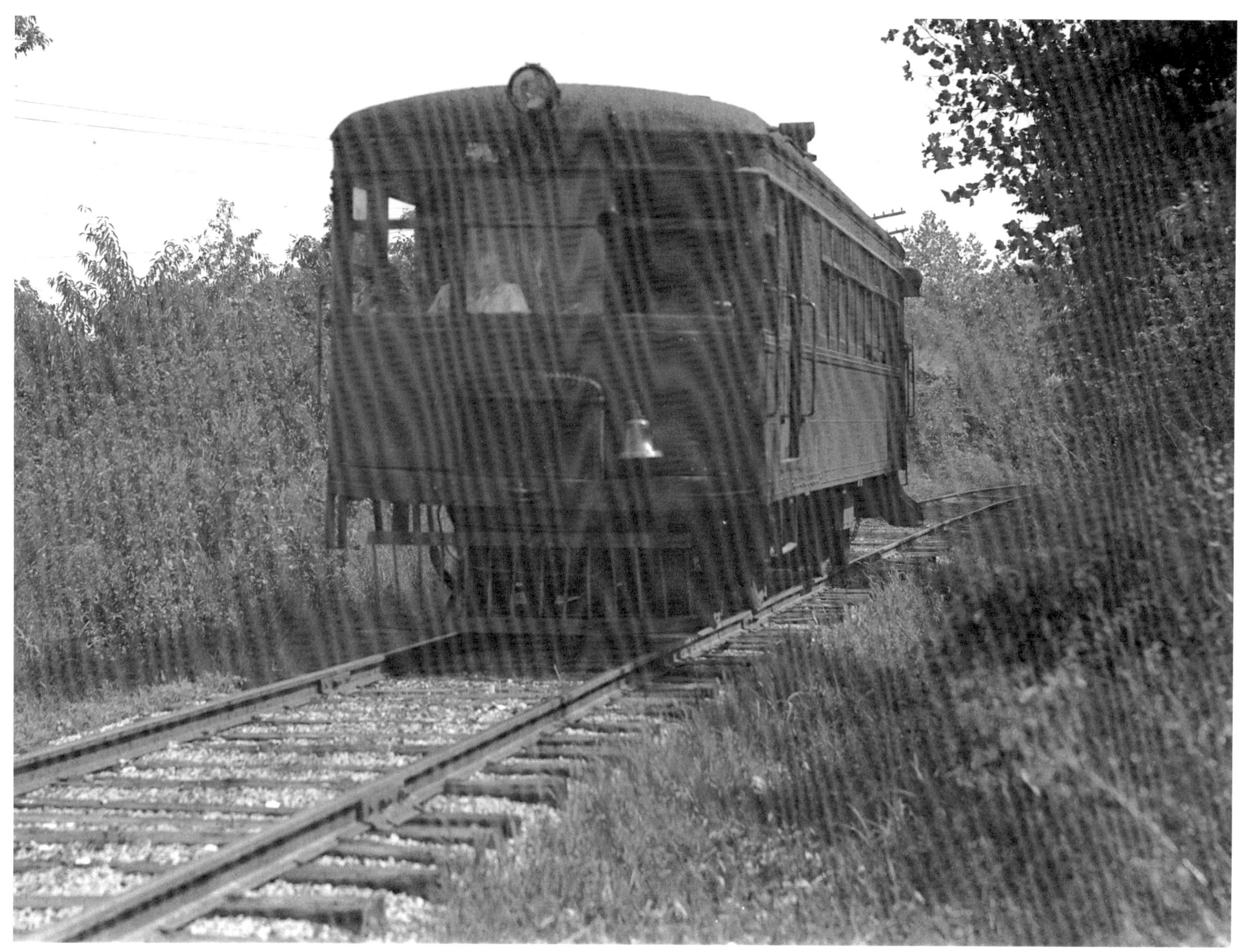

Plate 23. Frankfort & Cincinnati motorcar M55-1, a Brill Railcar. Photo by Lucius Beebe or Charles Clegg. Beebe-Clegg negative 2171.

Courtesy of the California State Railroad Museum.

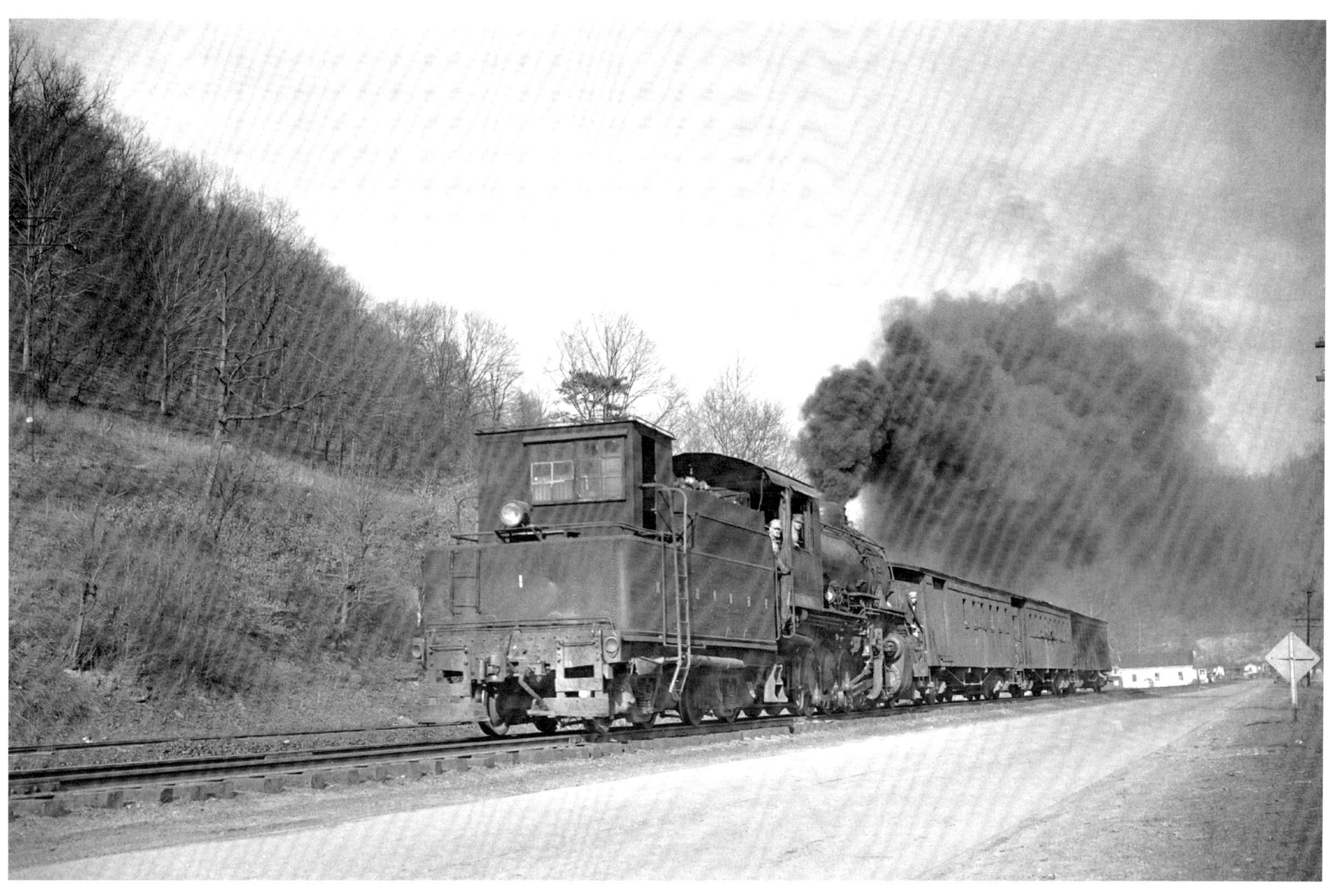

Plate 24. Kelley's Creek & Northwestern Railroad No. 1 with a passenger train. The train was run for miners. Photo by Lucius Beebe or Charles Clegg, probably Charles Clegg. Beebe-Clegg negative 2473.

Courtesy of the California State Railroad Museum.

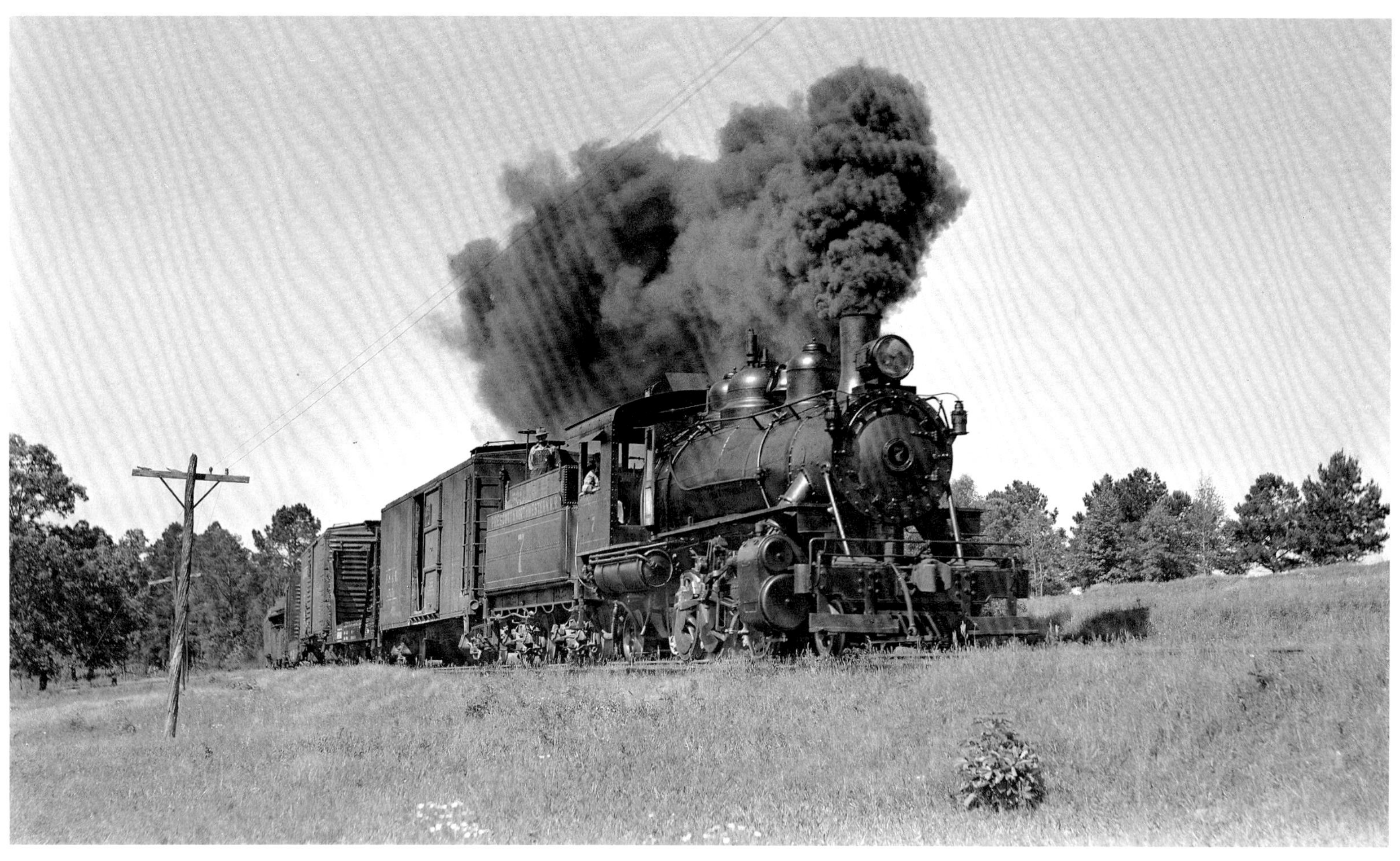

Plate 25. Prescott & Northwestern Railroad No. 7 with a mixed train. Lucius Beebe. Beebe-Clegg negative 3380.

Courtesy of the California State Railroad Museum.

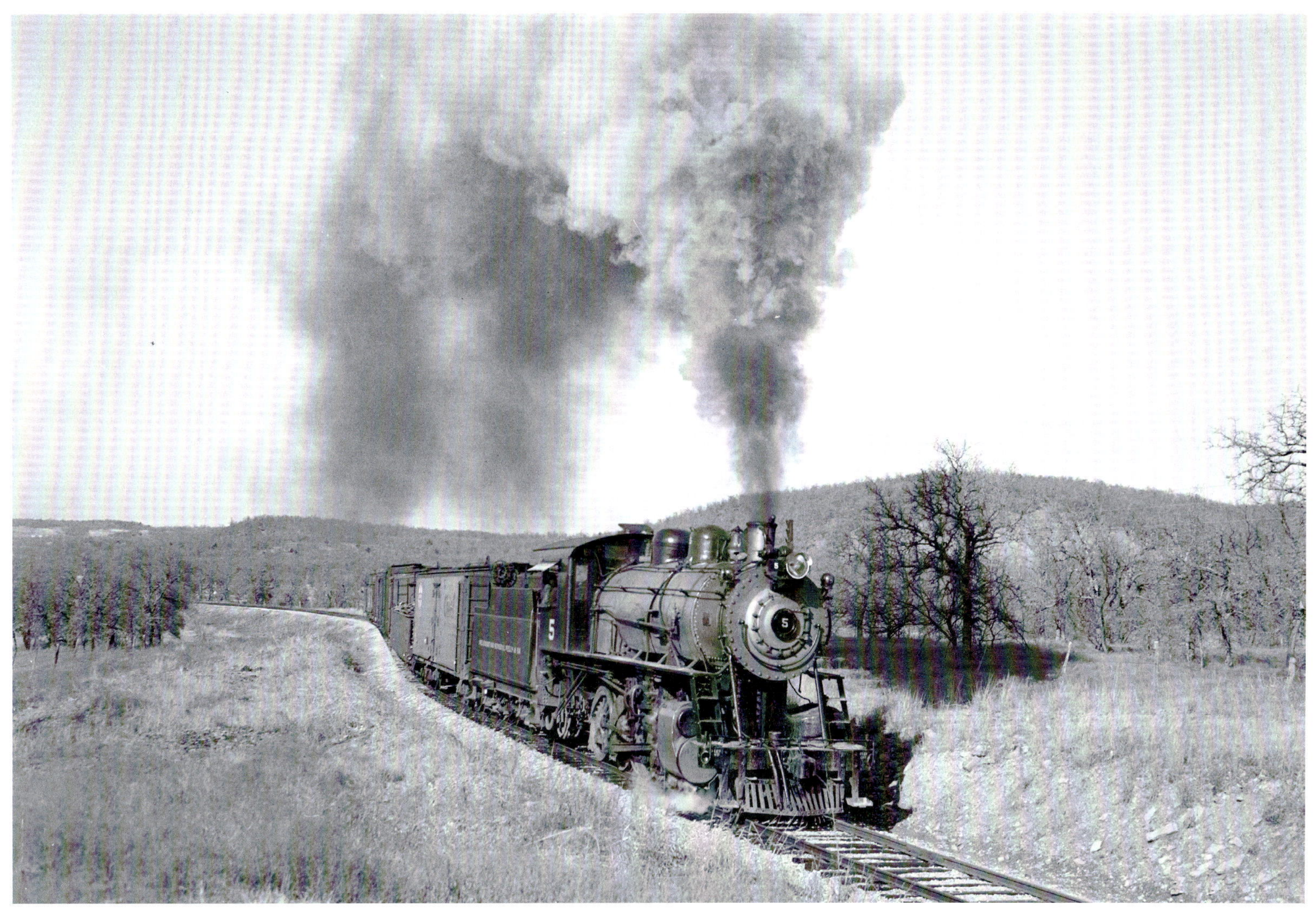

Plate 26. Weatherford, Mineral Wells & Northwestern Railway No. 5 with a train. Charles Clegg. Beebe-Clegg negative 3522.

Courtesy of the California State Railroad Museum.

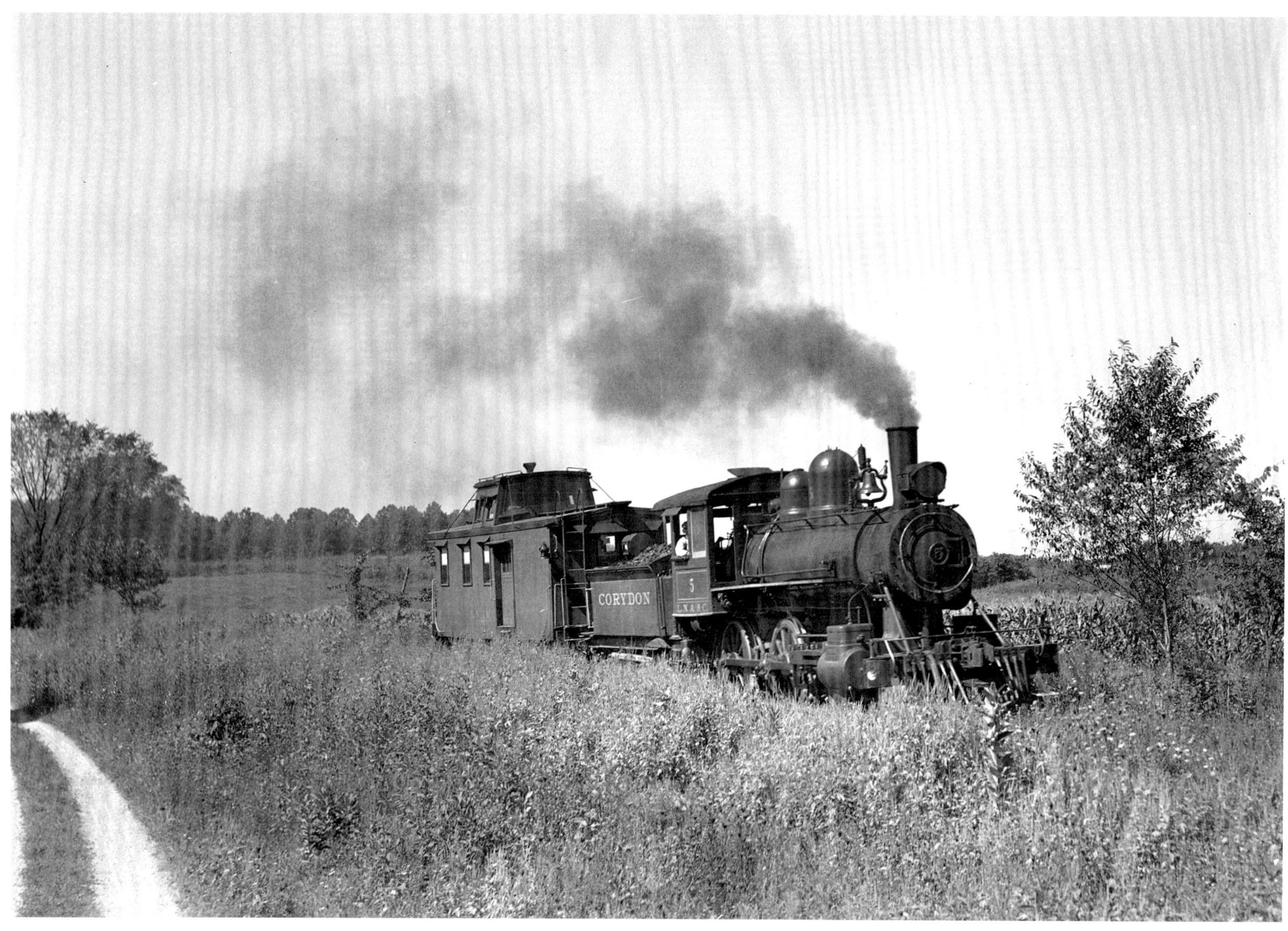

Plate 27. Louisville, New Albany & Corydon Railroad No. 5 with a "caboose hop." Lucius Beebe. Beebe-Clegg negative 1164.

Courtesy of the California State Railroad Museum.

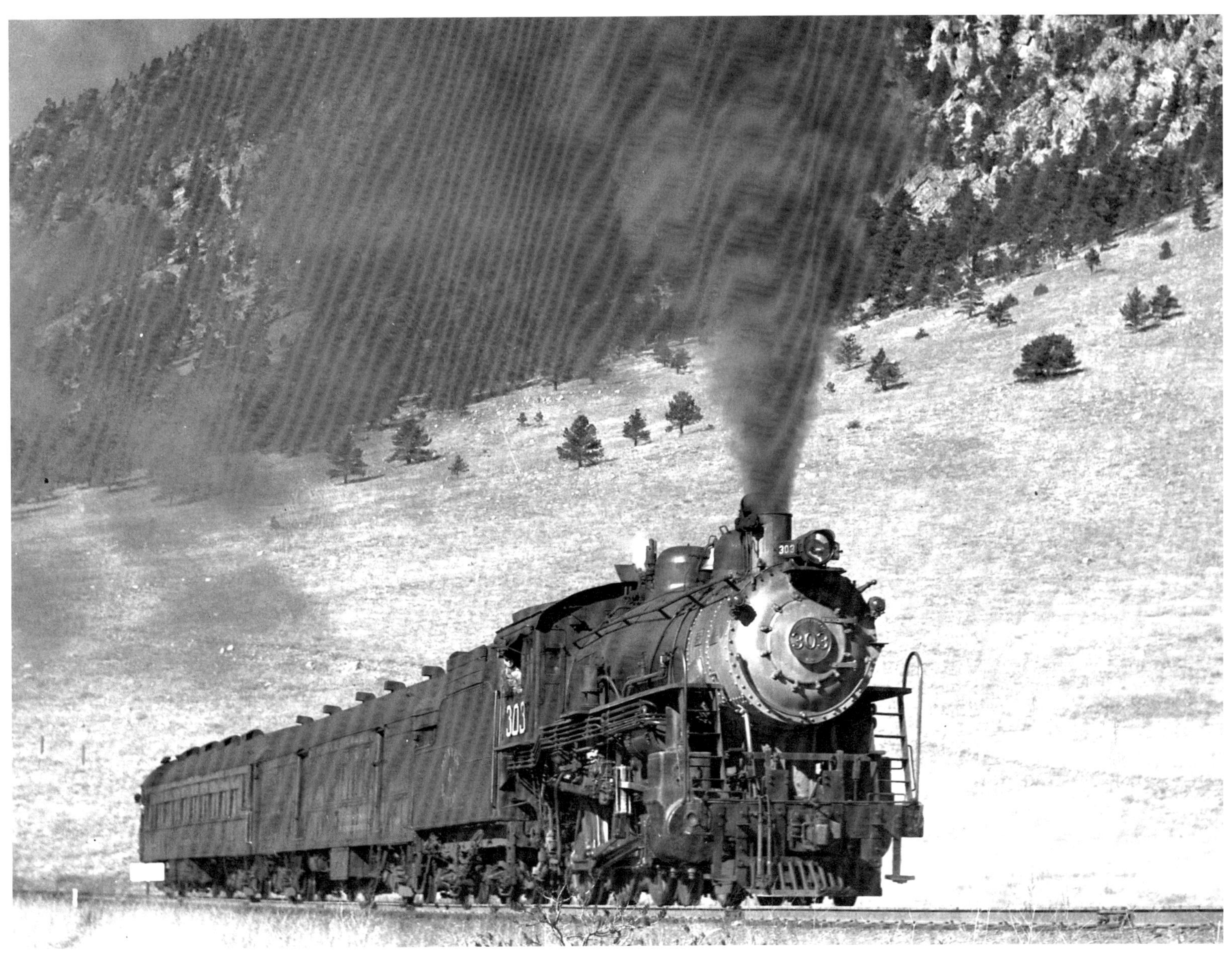

Plate 28. The Denver & Salt Lake Railway's train No. 1 on a grade between Coal Creek, Colorado, and the portal of the railroad's tunnel No. 1. Photo by Lucius Beebe or Charles Clegg (credited to Beebe in *Mixed Train Daily* and to Clegg in *Rio Grande: Mainline of the Rockies*). Beebe-Clegg negative 2208.

Courtesy of the California State Railroad Museum.

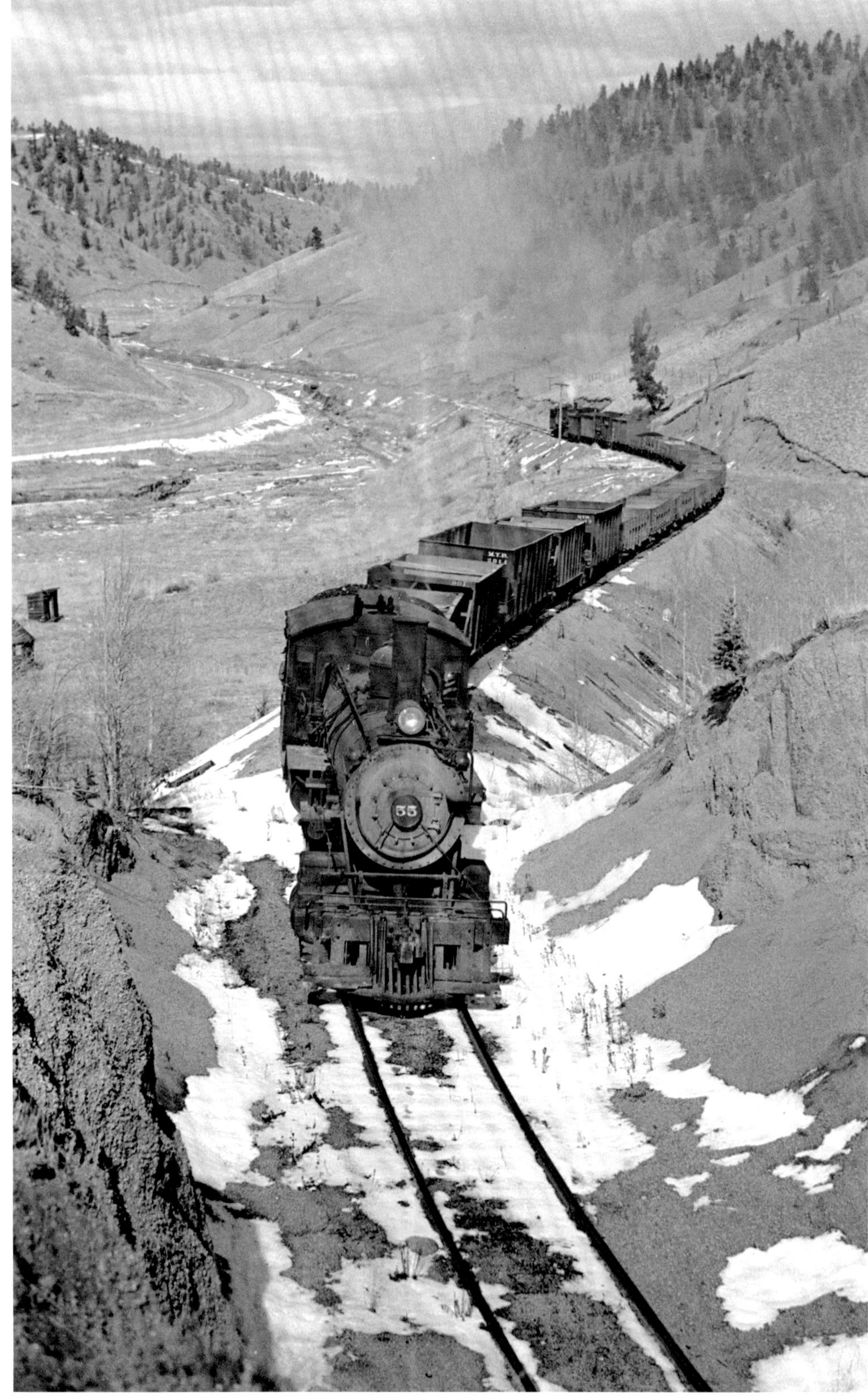

Plate 29. "The Hounds of Spring." Two Consolidations on Colorado's Midland Terminal Railway haul a train of ore empties upgrade at Midland, Colorado. Charles Clegg. Beebe-Clegg negative 2374.

Courtesy of the California State Railroad Museum.

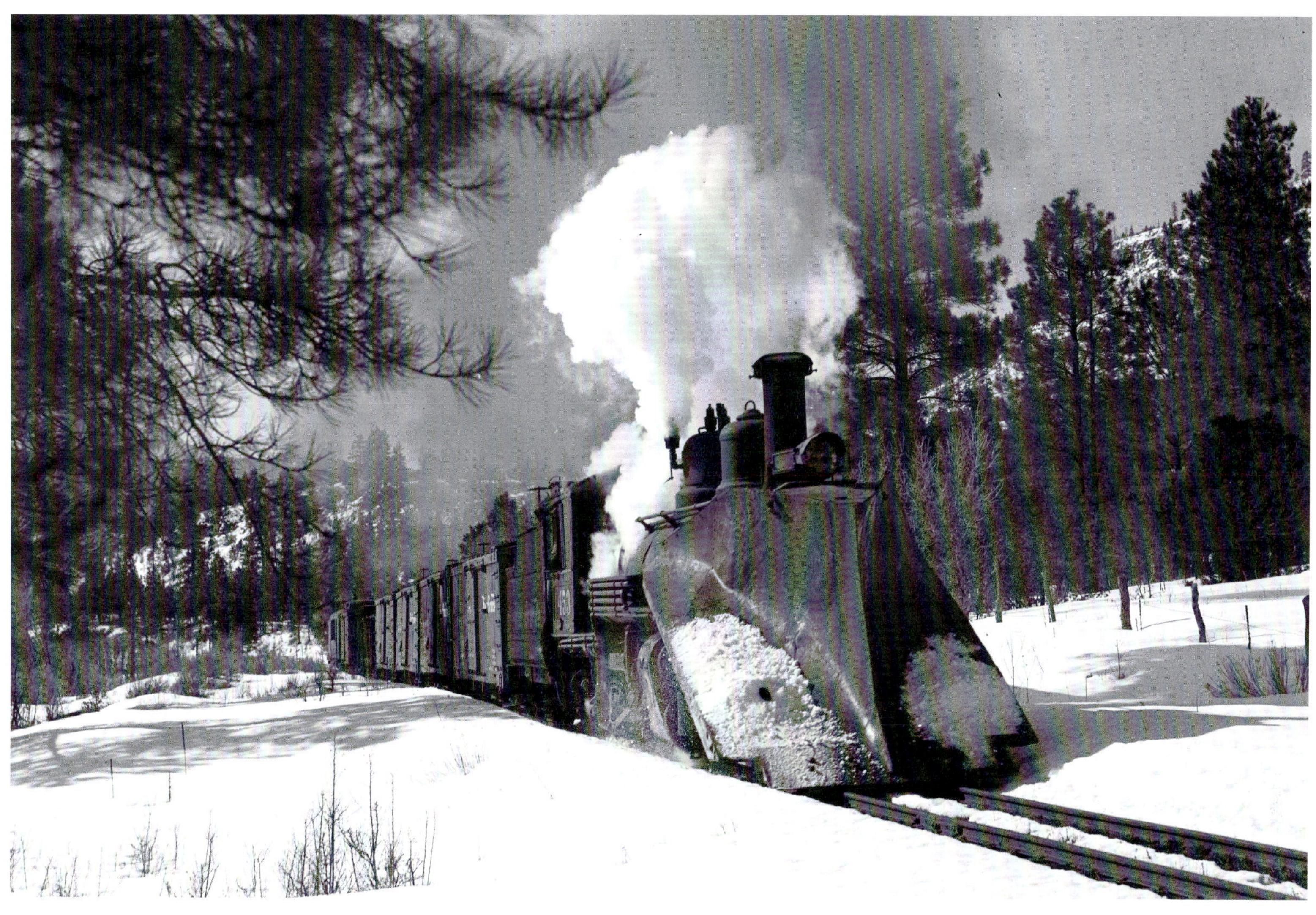

Plate 30. "The Deep Snows Near Timberline." The Denver & Rio Grande Western's Silverton train, running from Durango to Silverton, Colorado, uses a wedge plow to clear the snow brought to the area by the blizzard of March 1945. The train, shown here almost at the timberline in Animas Canyon, is a mixed train, with both a coach and a caboose at the end. Lucius Beebe. Beebe-Clegg negative 1124.

Courtesy of the California State Railroad Museum.

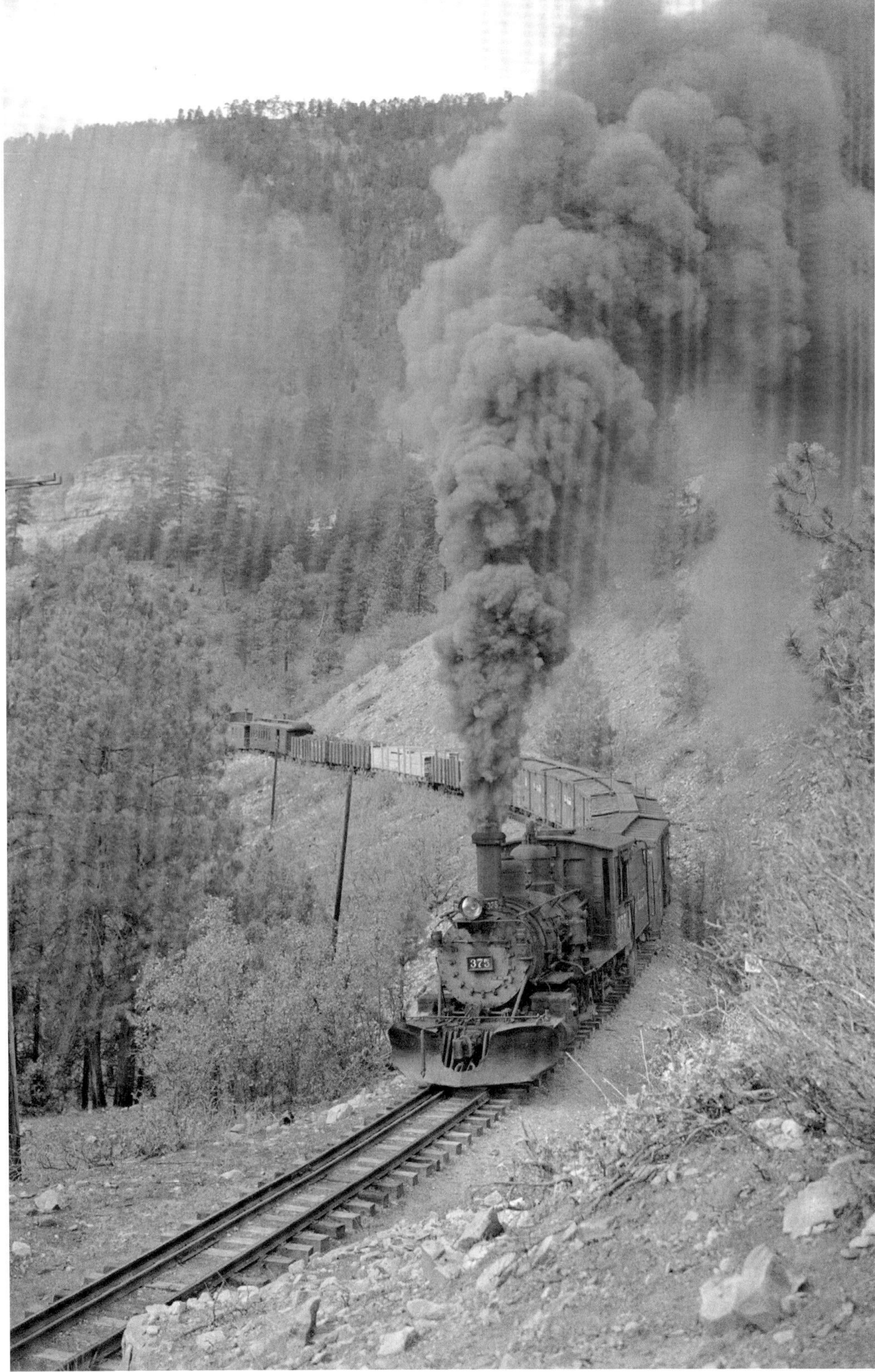

Plate 31. "Above the Canyon of Lost Souls." The Denver & Rio Grande Western's twice-a-week mixed train from Durango to Silverton, Colorado, climbs in Animas Canyon at Rockwood, Colorado. Charles Clegg. Beebe-Clegg negative 3240.

Courtesy of the California State Railroad Museum.

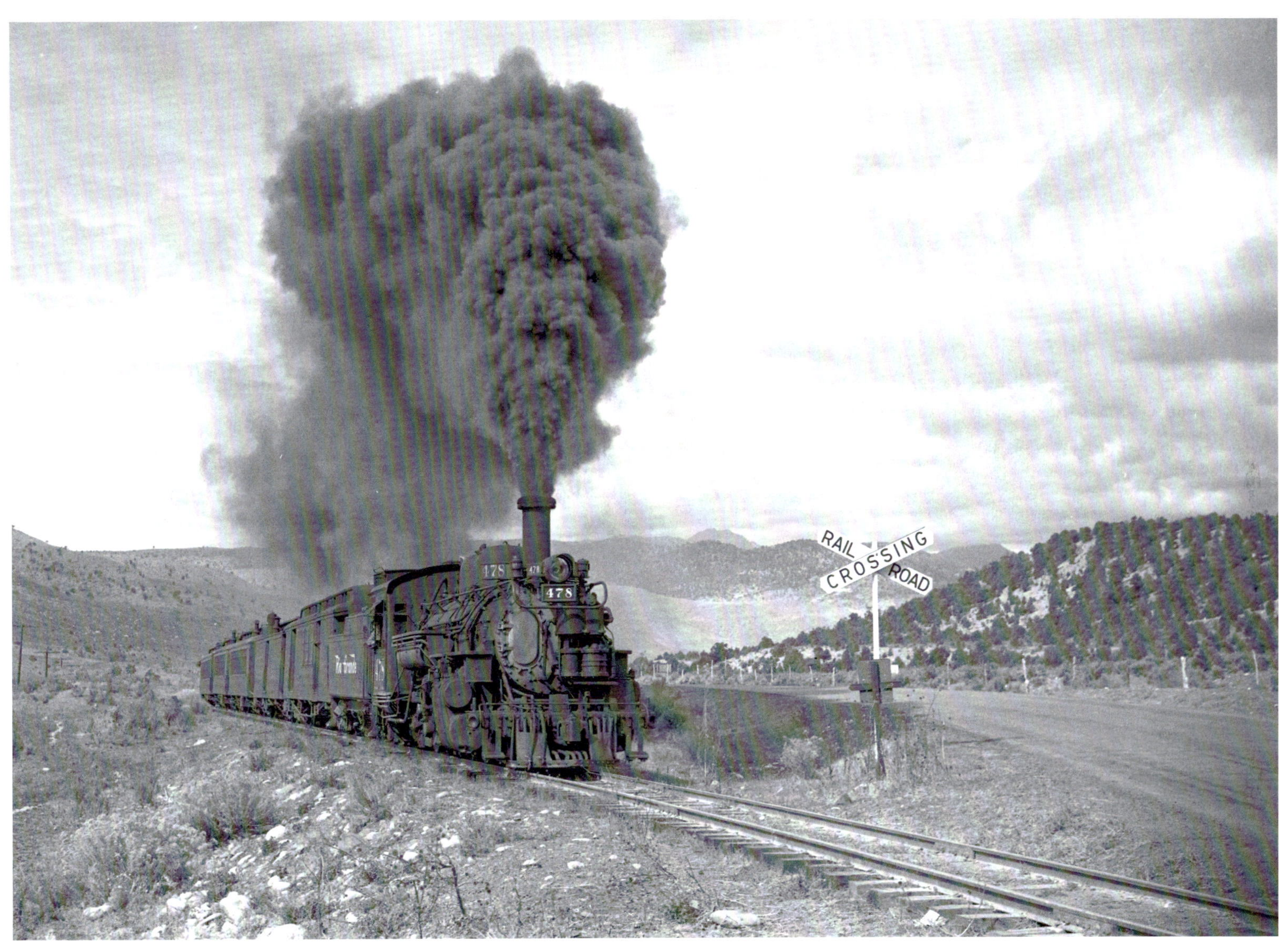

Plate 32. "The *San Juan*." Famed Denver & Rio Grande Western narrow-gauge passenger train, the *San Juan*, climbs out of Durango, Colorado in 1945. Charles Clegg. Beebe-Clegg negative 1541.

Courtesy of the California State Railroad Museum.

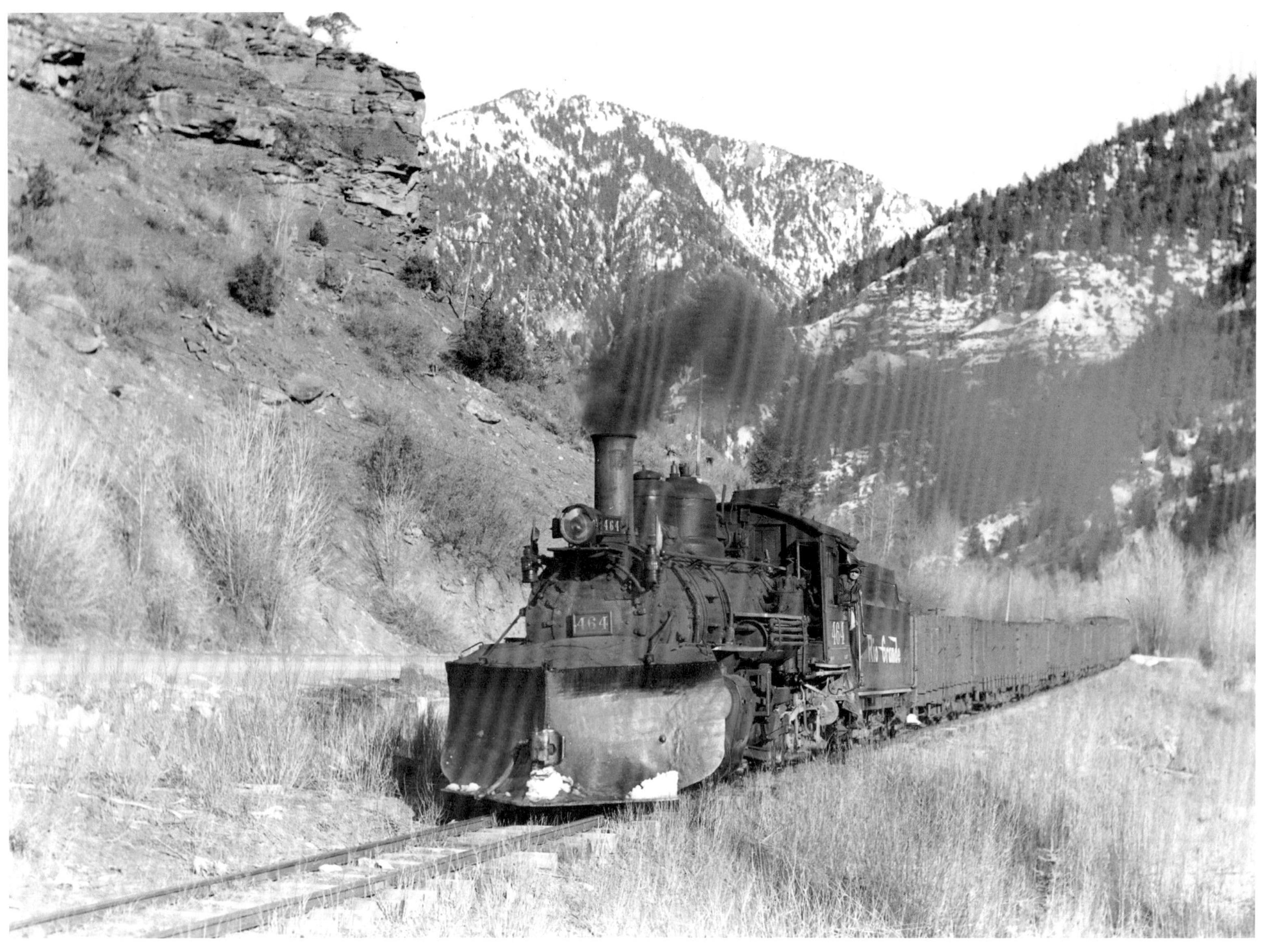

Plate 33. "Destiny in Humble Guise on the Narrow Gage." A Rio Grande Southern Railroad freight, led by a borrowed Denver & Rio Grande Western narrow-gauge locomotive, No. 464, near Vanadium, Colorado. Although Lucius Beebe didn't know it at the time (March 1945), the cars trailing No. 464 are filled with radioactive ores bound for secret facilities racing to produce the first atomic bombs during World War II. Lucius Beebe. Beebe-Clegg negative 4007.

Courtesy of the California State Railroad Museum.

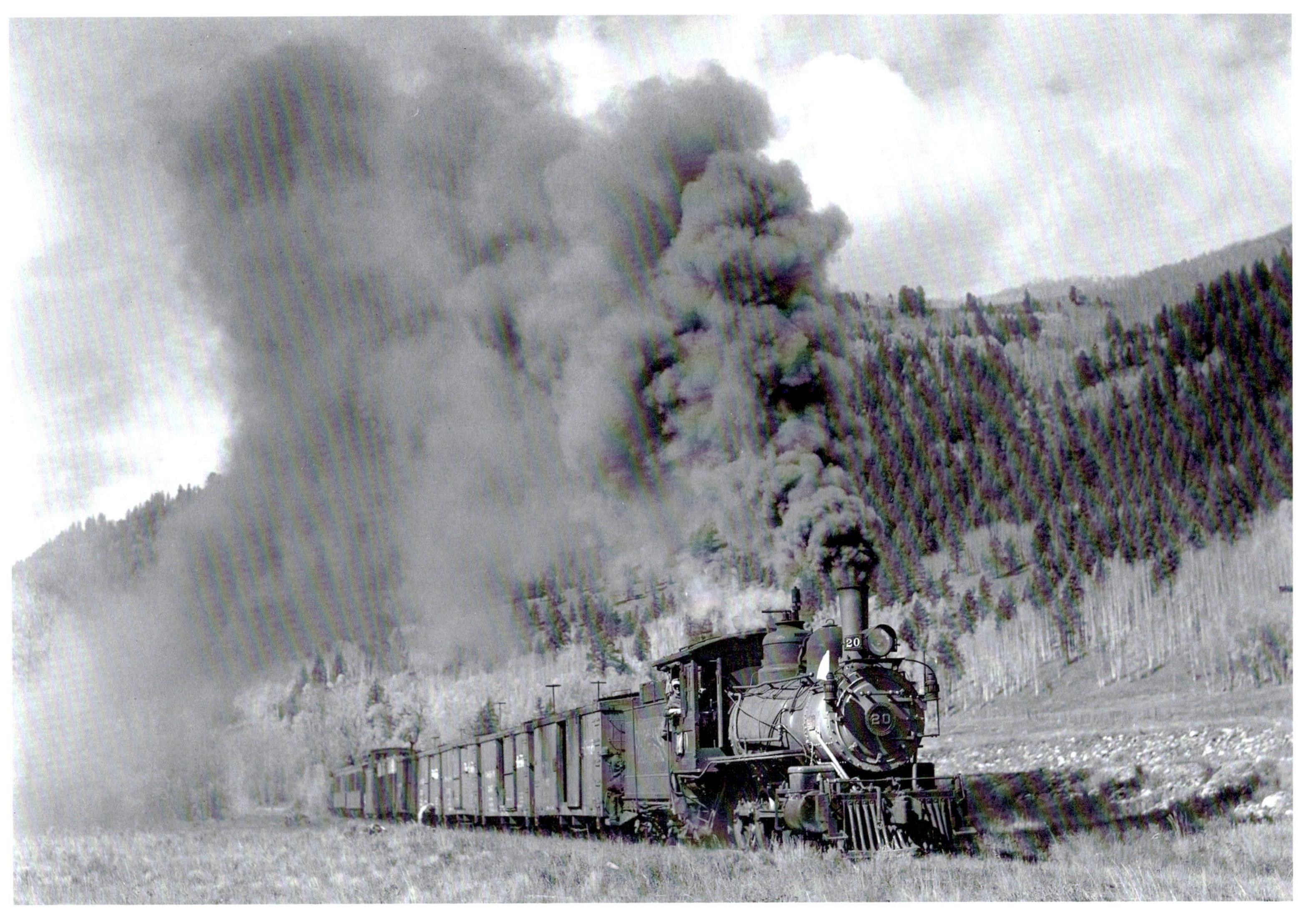

Plate 34. Rio Grande Southern No. 20 with train. Lucius Beebe. Beebe-Clegg negative 3067.

Courtesy of the California State Railroad Museum.

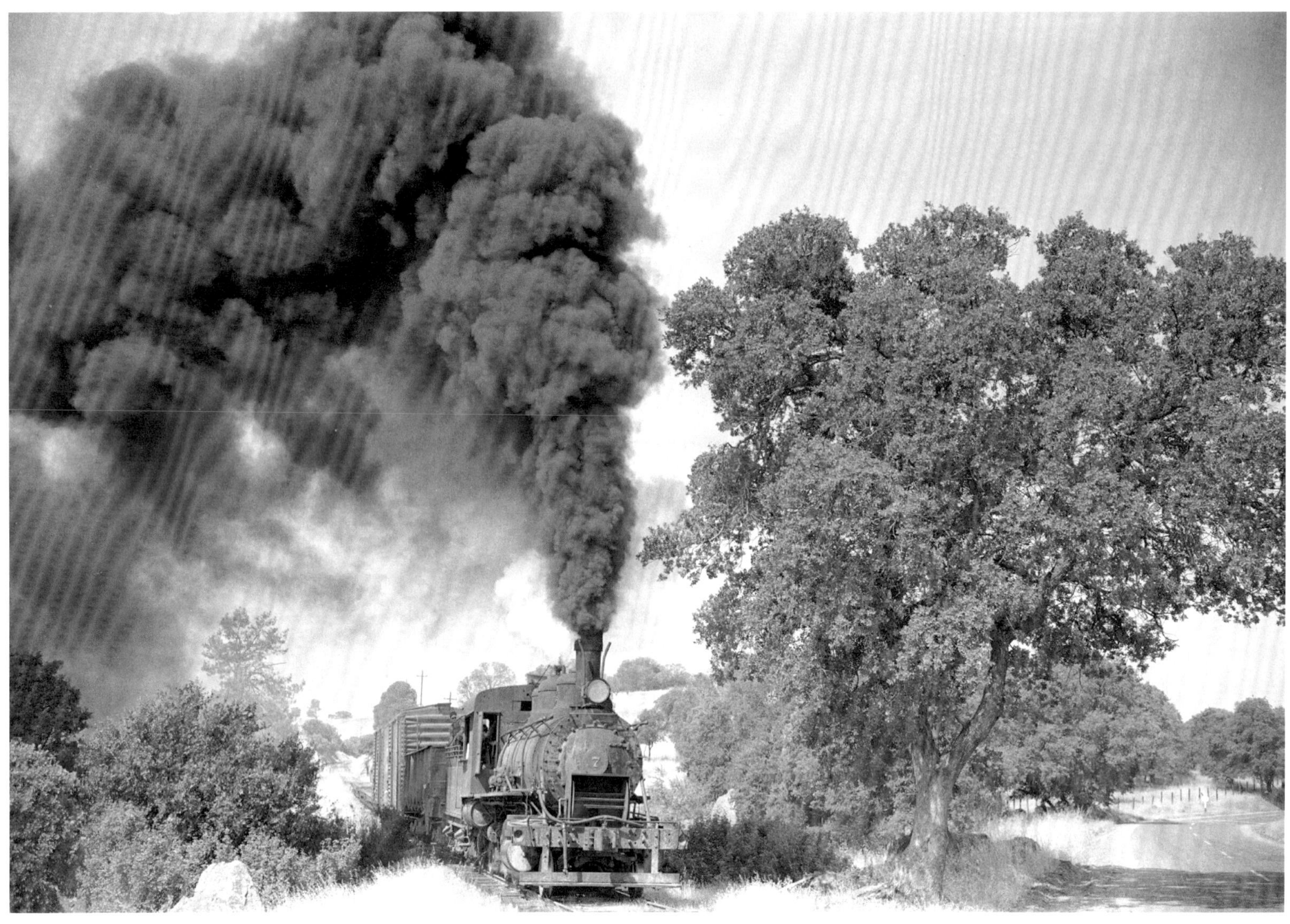

Plate 35. "Working Steam in the Bret Harte Hills." Amador Central No. 7 with train. Lucius Beebe. Beebe-Clegg negative 1460.

Courtesy of the California State Railroad Museum.

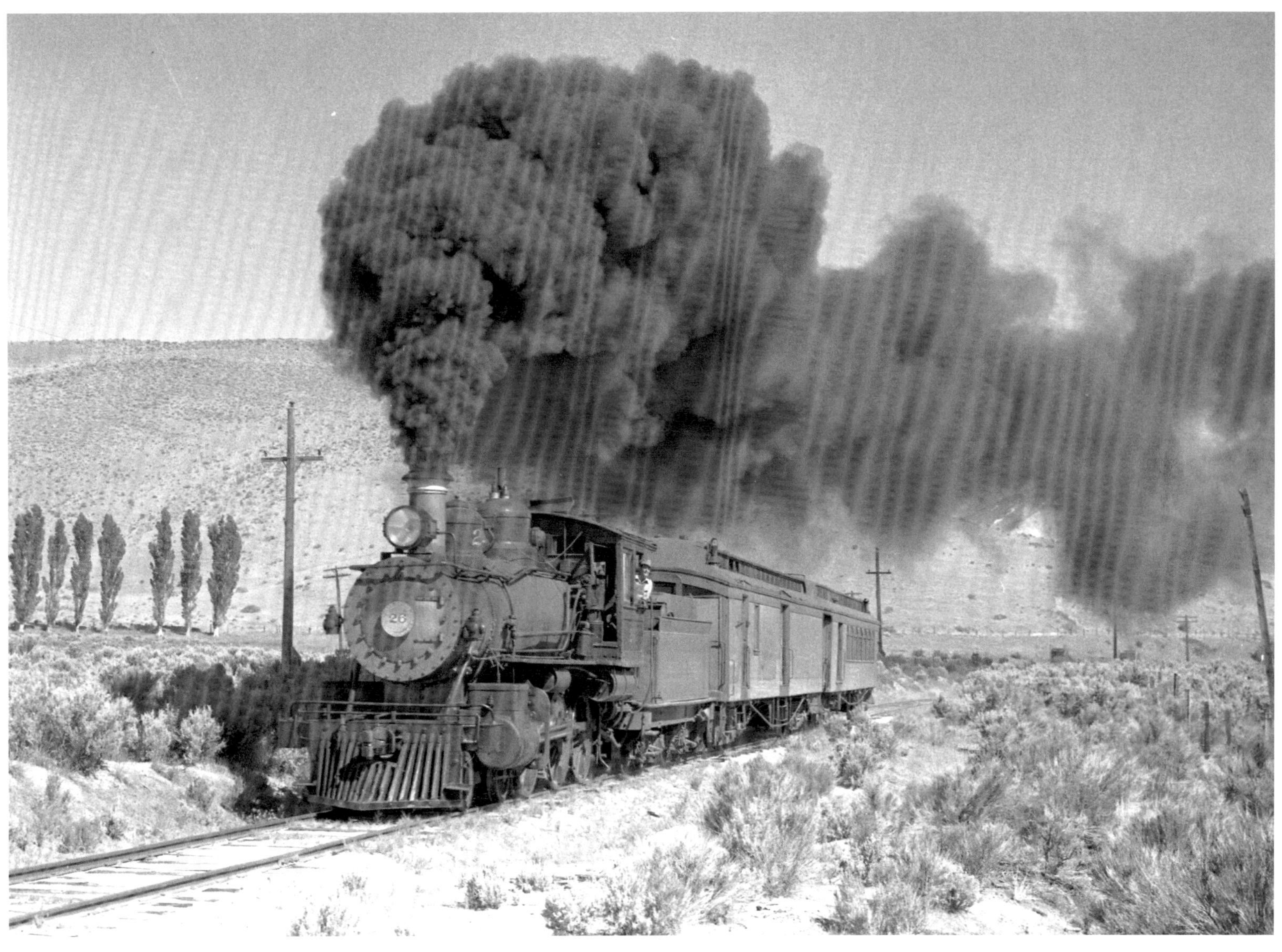

Plate 36. "Ghost Train to Yesterday." A passenger train, led by No. 26, on Nevada's famed Virginia & Truckee Railroad. The V&T ran from Reno through Carson City to Minden, Nevada, at the time. Charles Clegg. Beebe-Clegg negative 1160.

Courtesy of the California State Railroad Museum.

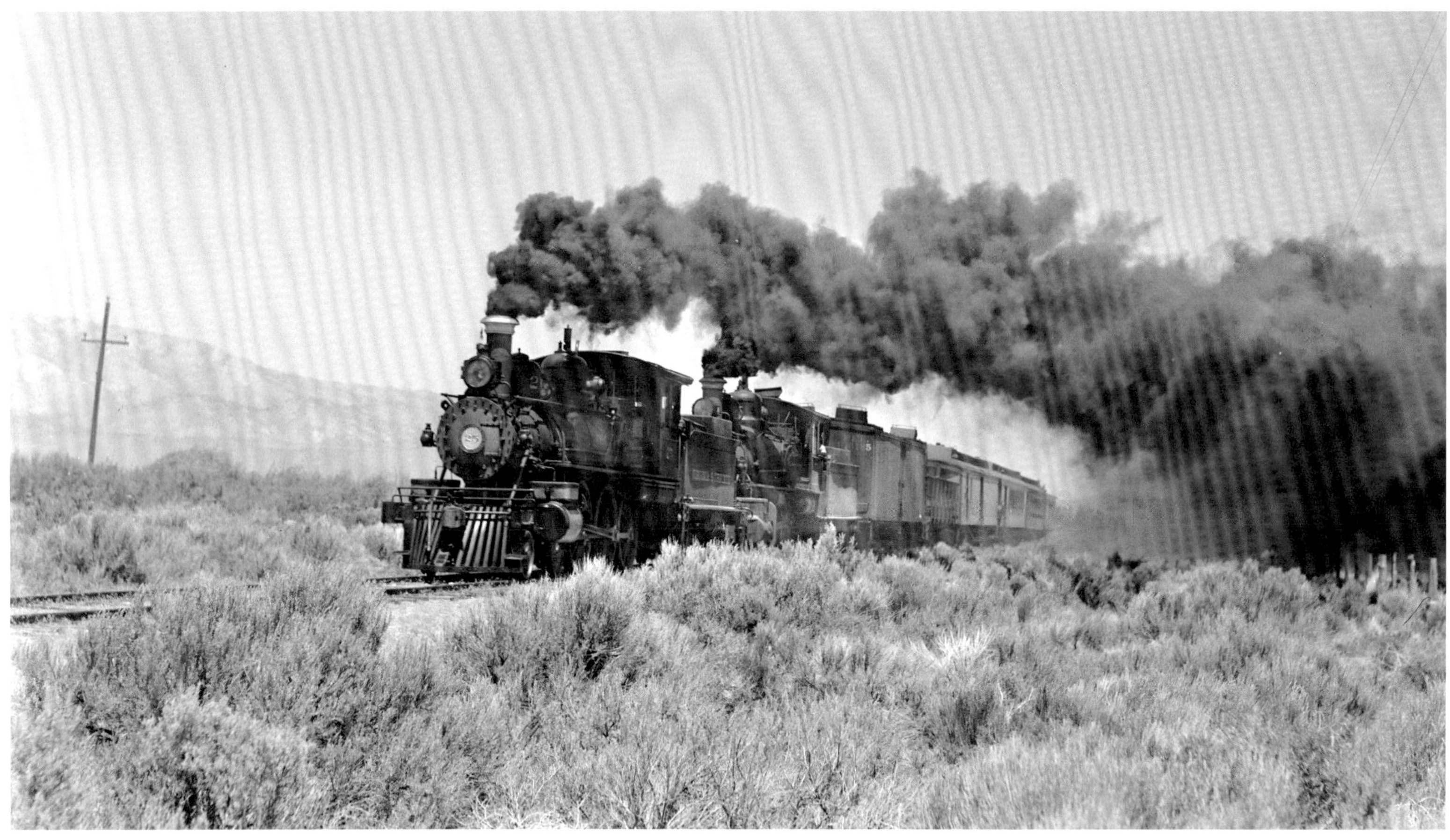

Plate 37. "Smoke and Glory in the Grand Manner." A double-header on the Virginia & Truckee Railroad, with engines No. 25 and 26. This train, shown passing through the Minden meadows in Nevada, was a special, including the club car *Julia Bulette*, run for Lucius Beebe and Charles Clegg. Lucius Beebe. Beebe-Clegg negative 1299.

Courtesy of the California State Railroad Museum.

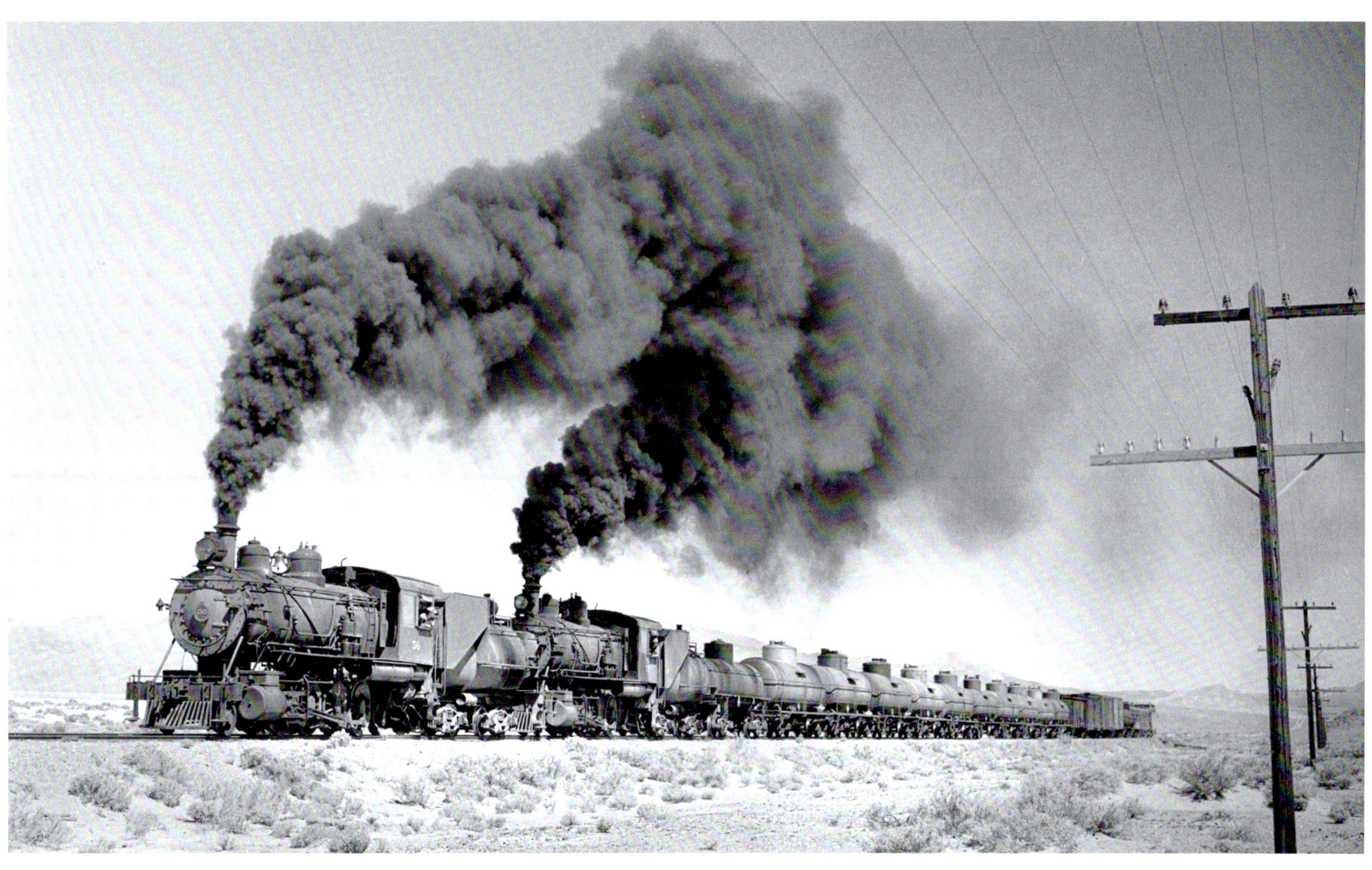

Plate 38. A double-headed train on Nevada's Tonopah & Goldfield Railroad bringing fuel to the aviation field at Tonopah. Charles Clegg. Beebe-Clegg negative 577.

Courtesy of the California State Railroad Museum.

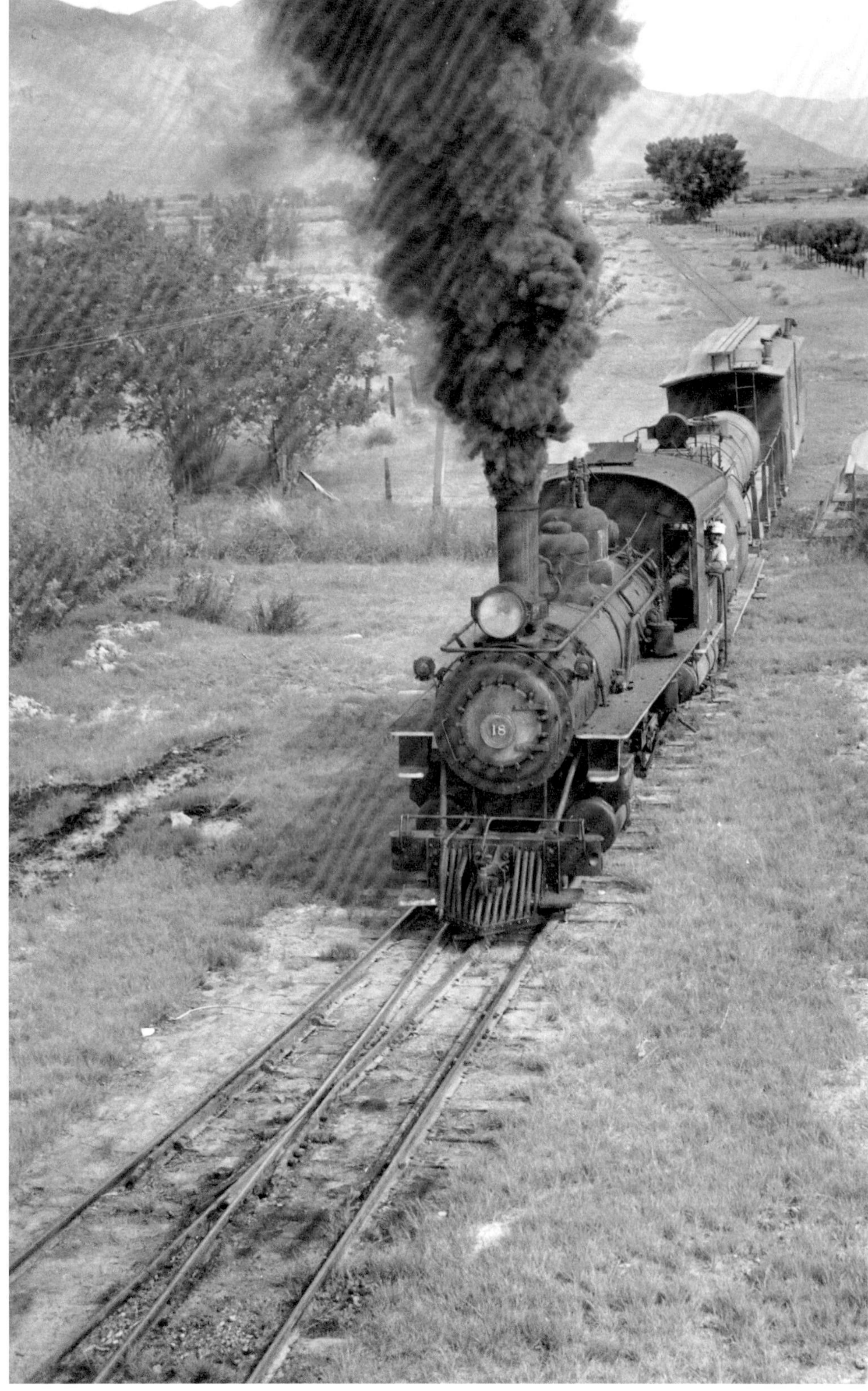

Plate 39. "From the Water Tower at Laws." Southern Pacific narrow-gauge locomotive No. 18 blasts upgrade into the yard at Laws, California, at the northern end of the SP's famed Owens Valley branch. The short trains often featured in Beebe-Clegg photographs provide mute testimony as to why these railroads did not survive into our times. Charles Clegg. Beebe-Clegg negative 4011.

Courtesy of the California State Railroad Museum.

2 A MODERNIST VIEW OF THE AMERICAN RAILROAD

Today, we often think of Lucius Beebe at least in part as the ultraconservative writer who led the *Territorial Enterprise* during the 1950s and then published the far-right column "This Wild West" for the *San Francisco Chronicle*.

But we must remember that before he met Charles Clegg and then moved to Nevada and California, Beebe was a habitué of Prohibition- and Great Depression–era New York. During much of the 1930s, Jerome Zerbe, arguably the first of the paparazzi, was Beebe's partner. Judging from the photographs included in *High Iron* and the 1936 *Town & Country* article "Keeping up with the Casey Joneses," Beebe also knew color photography pioneer Ivan Dmitri (Levon West).[1]

The 1930s in New York were a time and place of creative ferment. Walker Evans held his first major exhibit, "American Photographs," at the Museum of Modern Art (MoMA) in New York in 1938, the same year Beebe's *High Iron* was released. "American Photographs" was the first one-person photography exhibit at MoMA. At about that time, O. Winston Link started his career as a staff photographer with Carl Byoir & Associates in New York.[2] Earlier in the decade, *Fortune* was established and *Life* was purchased and transformed by Henry Luce; the latter publication was to revolutionize American photojournalism. The early 1930s also saw the landmark Edward Hopper exhibit at MoMA (1933); Hopper's oeuvre includes many paintings with railroad subject matter.[3]

As the partner of Jerome Zerbe, Beebe was inevitably exposed to the Art Deco style and to modernism in the visual arts and literature. His interest in railroads also led Beebe to Henry Dreyfuss, who redesigned the *Twentieth Century Limited*, and to Leslie Ragan, who created promotional posters for that great train.[4]

Conventional wisdom typecasts Lucius Beebe as a wedge-shot railroad photographer, while Charles Clegg, whose reputation has been under his partner's shadow, is seen as an early proponent of a wider, environmental approach to railroad subjects. Perhaps the link between their work and modernism has been cloaked by the exaggeratedly Victorian nature of both Beebe's writing style and Beebe and Clegg's Gilded Age lifestyle. Beebe and Clegg's work shows a clear impact of modernism, however, particularly Beebe's early photographs, perhaps the result of Jerome Zerbe and Ivan Dmitri's influence. Another possible influence is the range of railroad and cruise line posters produced in a high modernist style during the 1930s; as a frequent passenger on trains and ocean liners, Beebe would have seen many such images. This portfolio seeks to make the modernist aspects of Beebe and Clegg's work clear.

Especially in his early work, Beebe often shot exaggeratedly tight, closely cropped images both of locomotives and of passenger cars. Beebe often stepped beyond his usual emphasis on steam locomotives to depict early diesels as well. Since most early diesel locomotives were designed in an Art Deco style clearly influenced by period automotive design, these icons of the 1930s were subjects that demanded a modernist approach.

Plates 40 to 43 are views of this type. The three by Beebe—plates 40, 41, and 43—were all featured in his early books. Plate 41 shows a New York Central streamlined "Hudson" locomotive, an Art Deco classic, a design by Henry Dreyfuss. Plate 42 is by Clegg, and, as the caption notes, shows the influence Beebe had on his partner's photography.

Plates 44 to 46 are similar modernist photos taken by Beebe early in his photographic career, depicting early, diesel-powered passenger trains: the Denver & Rio Grande Western's *Prospector* and the Burlington-Rock Island's *Sam Houston Zephyr.* As modernist views of innovative if ultimately unsuccessful trains with notable Art Deco styling, these images are an excellent example of style appropriately reflecting subject.

Plates 47 to 49, all by Beebe and all featured in his early books, are tightly cropped views of steam locomotive running gear. Plates 47 and 49, although taken at an angle, show the influence of artist and photographer Charles Sheeler, who lived close to New York City and was very active there from the 1920s on. As a Manhattan habitué, Beebe would undoubtedly have been aware of Sheeler's work, which included a retrospective exhibit at MOMA in 1939 and the film (with Paul Strand) *Manhatta* from 1921.[5] An angular view shooting towards a steam engine's cylinders that depicts an engineer's nightmare tangle of rods, bolts, and pipes, plate 48 is a stunning and unique image.

Both Beebe and Clegg delighted in observing and recording the vernacular trappings, which may now be seen as outsider art, often found on short-line steam locomotive front ends and smokestacks, particularly in the southern United States. Plates 50 to 54 are images of this kind, all of them tightly and cleanly framed, modernist in outlook despite their subjects. The folk-art Indian shooting an arrow above an American eagle depicted in plate 51 is an excellent example of outsider art. In plate 54, Beebe conveys the personality of the short line Ferdinand Railroad in one shot.

Charles Clegg found great interest in tightly framed images of railroad rolling stock details, such as archaic trucks and link and pin couplers. Plates 55 to 56 are images of this type. Plate 57 shows Beebe following Clegg's lead in photographic treatment of a subject.

Clegg's gifted eye was also drawn to tightly formatted images of wayside signs and locomotive-service equipment. Plates 58 to 64 are images of this type. Modernist in tone and likely all taken during the 1940s, these images stand out as ahead of their time. By the 1980s and 1990s, with the publication of John Stilgoe's *Metropolitan Corridor* and Michael Flanagan's *Stations: An Imagined Journey,* such images were integral components of some of the most significant works focusing on American railroads.[6] Probably due to the popularity of *Mixed Train Daily,* Clegg's influence on these and other observers of the American railroad is palpable.

Plate 65, a tightly cropped view of the Apache Railway's logo, is similar to now-noted work by Walker Evans and Jack Delano.[7] Evans's 1957 portfolio of images of railroad heralds for *Fortune* certainly could have been informed by this photograph, which appeared in *Mixed Train Daily.*[8]

Plate 66, a well-known image by Beebe that first appeared in *Trains in Transition,* shows his eye for modernist views, his sense of humor, and his interest in railroad folklore. The image depicts "Bozo Texino," an example of another long-standing, railroad-related area of American outsider art: the hobo moniker. Hobo monikers are, in many ways, the precursor of the now-ubiquitous graffiti found on American railroad freight cars; anathema to the industry, most railfans, and legal authorities, they are a respected area of outsider art in the view of most art critics and cultural observers.[9] Our survey of Beebe and Clegg's modernist work concludes with plate 67, Beebe's tightly cropped portrait of a steam locomotive whistle, originally published in *Highball.*

A clean modernist approach is arguably absent from most of today's railroad-subject photography. Given the dramatic simplification that has overtaken American railroading as long distance passenger services have dwindled to one provider, Amtrak, and major railroads have consolidated into seven large systems, two of them largely Canadian, a contemporary, modernist approach seems suited to many present-day, standardized and simplified railroad subjects. Given their modernist work, Beebe and Clegg can show the way for railroad photographers today.

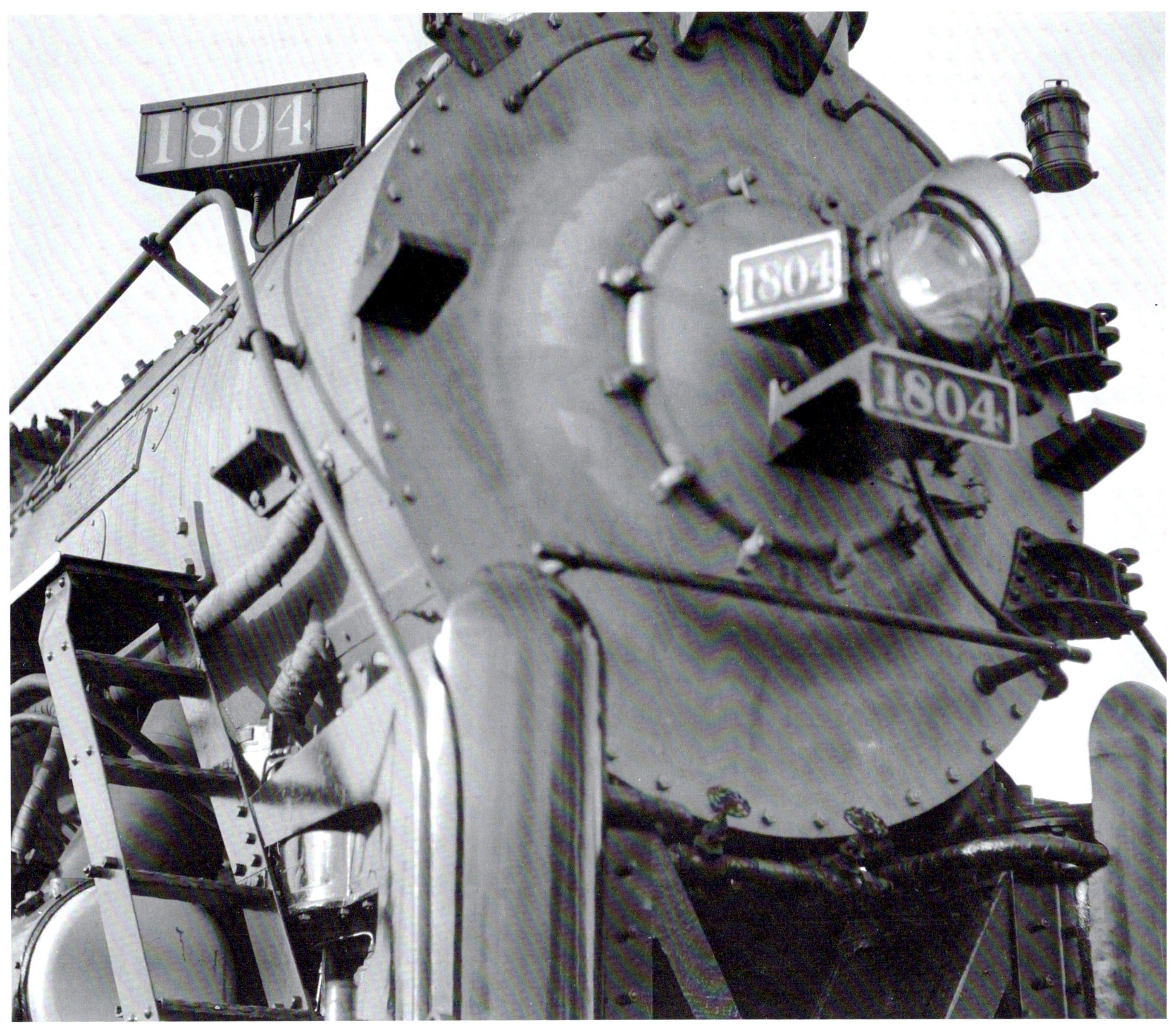

Plate 40. Engine 1804, the first image in the introduction of Lucius Beebe's first book, *High Iron*, published in 1938. Note the tight, almost disorienting cropping of the photo, a characteristic of Beebe's modernist work. Lucius Beebe. Beebe-Clegg negative 1126.

Courtesy of the California State Railroad Museum.

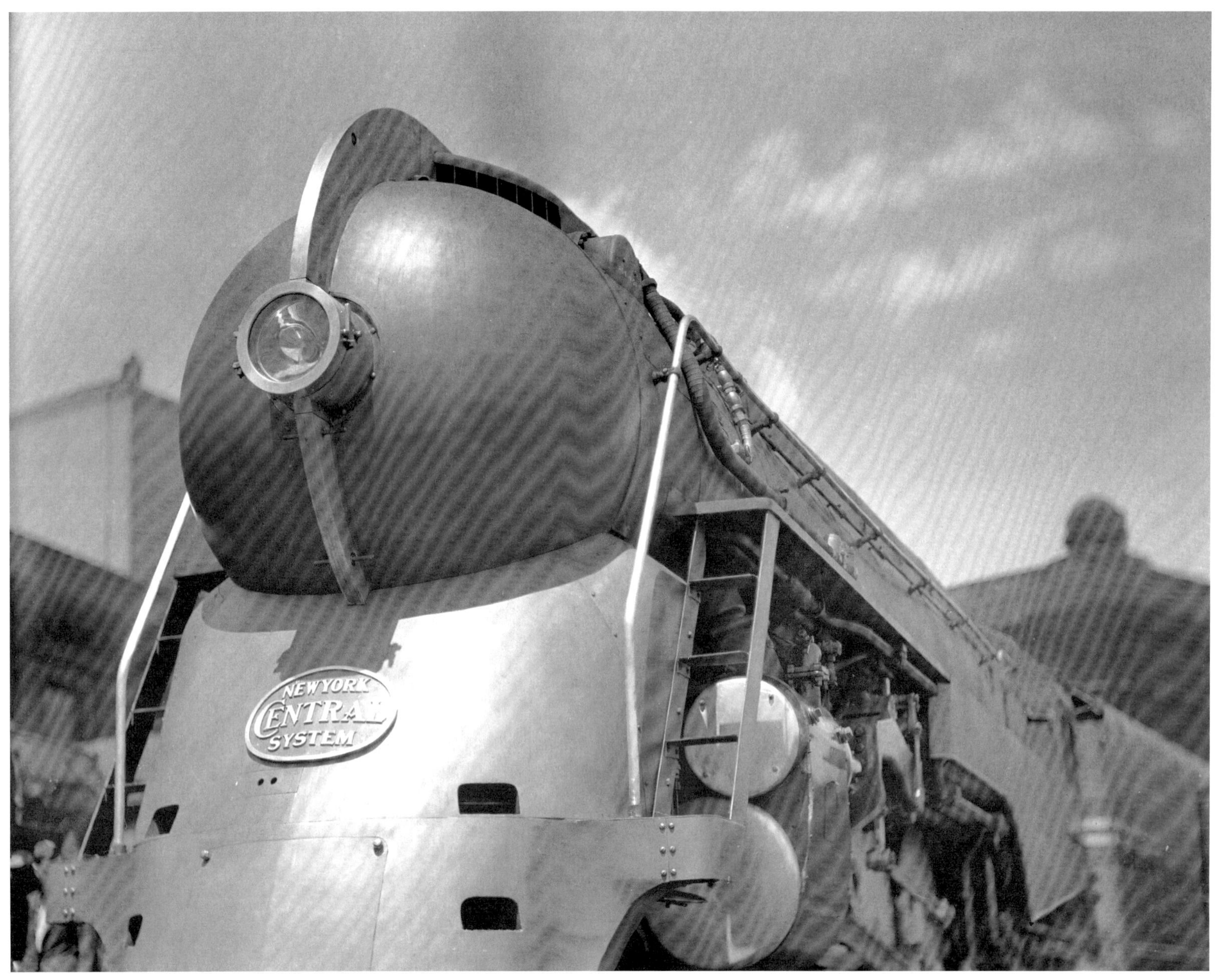

Plate 41. Streamlined New York Central steam locomotive, also from *High Iron*. This is a four-six-four "Hudson" streamlined with a design by Henry Dreyfuss. Note the very tight framing. Lucius Beebe. Beebe-Clegg negative 3742.

Courtesy of the California State Railroad Museum.

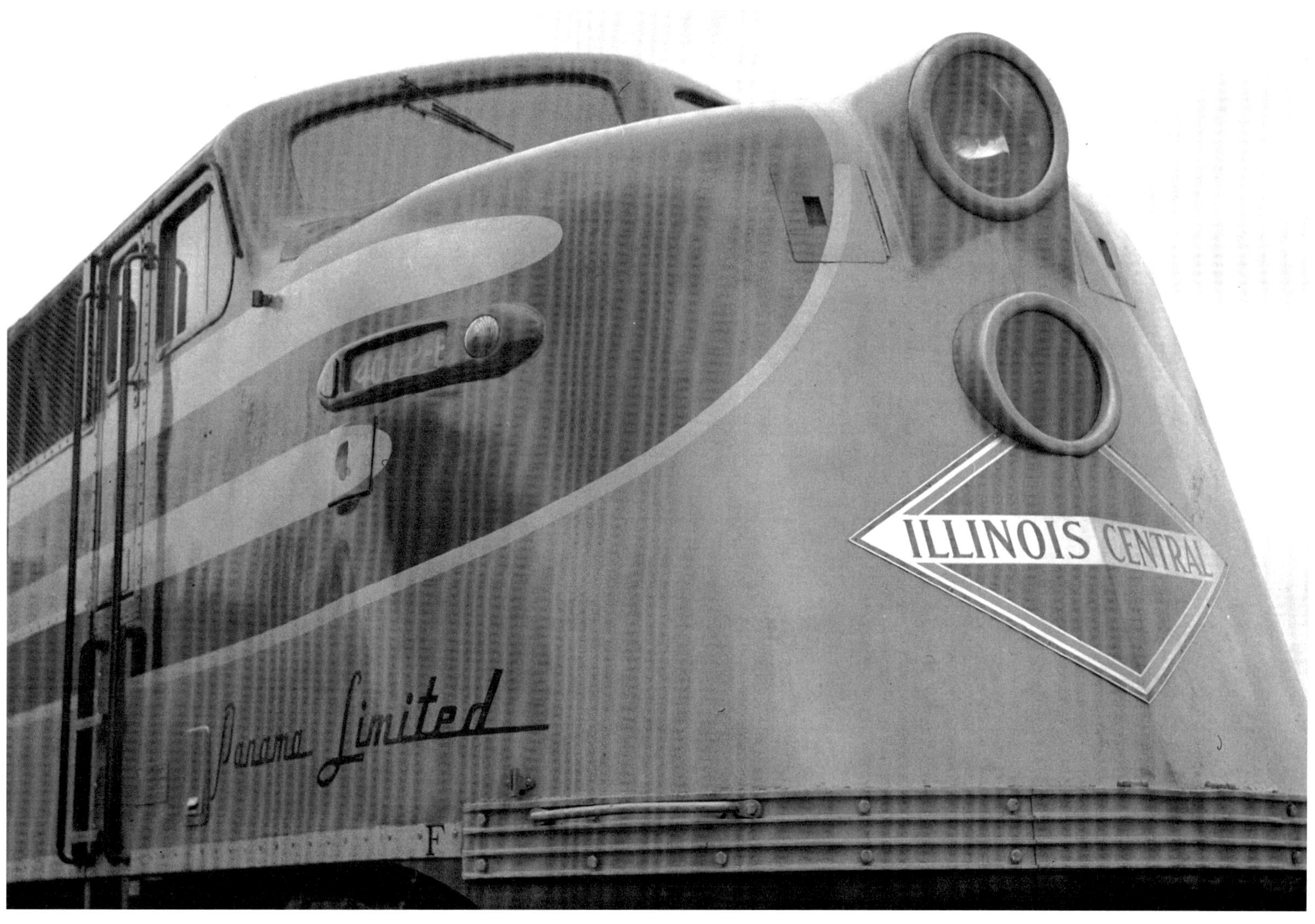

Plate 42. An Illinois Central diesel, the first image in the "Portrait Gallery" chapter of *Highball: A Pageant of Trains* (1945). This photo is by Charles Clegg, but the framing here closely mimics that of Beebe's modernist work. As in much of Beebe's modernist work, the subject is a streamlined locomotive or passenger car, often clearly influenced by the Art Deco movement. Charles Clegg. Beebe-Clegg negative 1135.

Courtesy of the California State Railroad Museum.

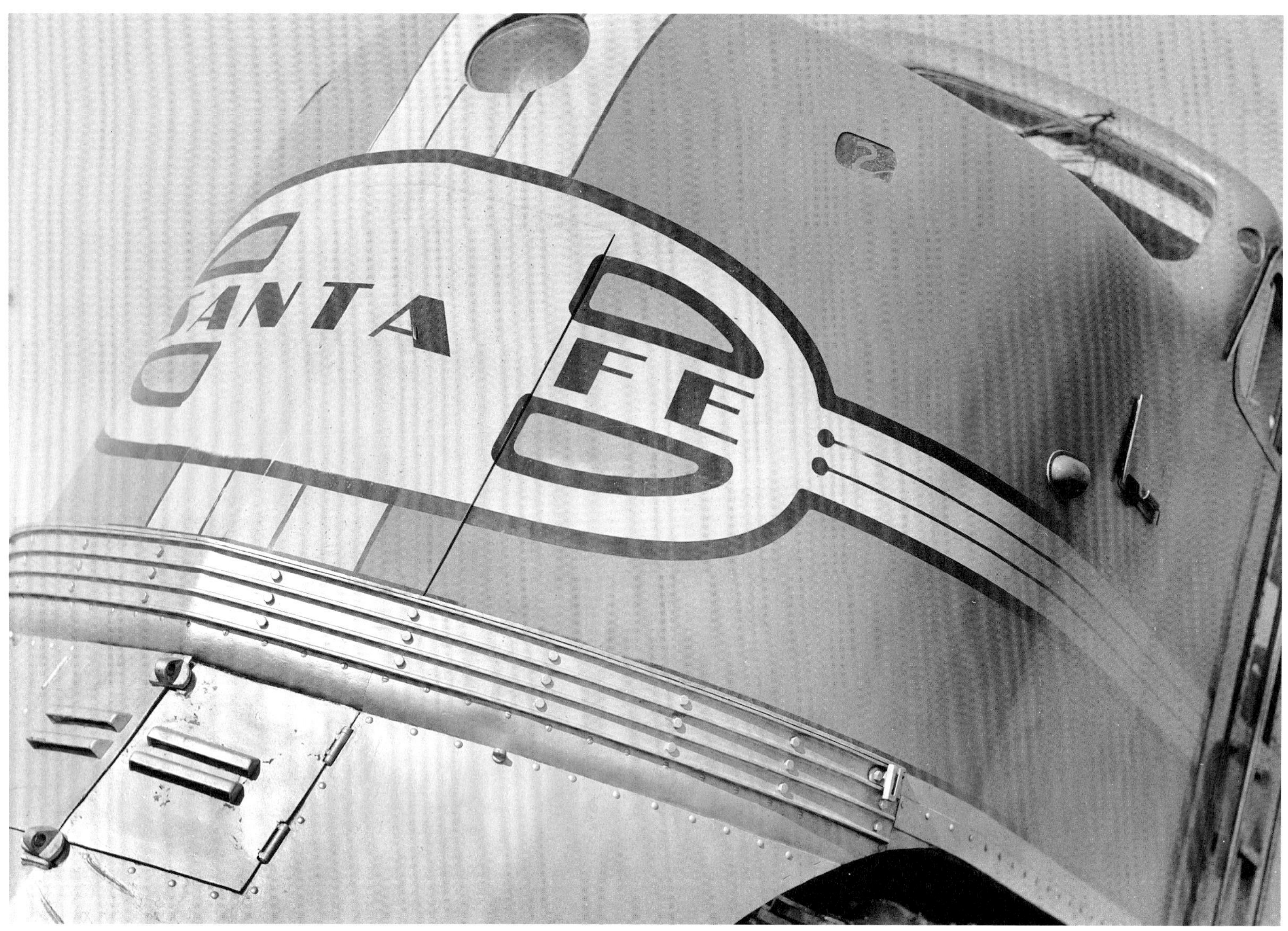

Plate 43. "*Super Chief* Symbol." A very closely cropped, streamlined Santa Fe diesel, from the book *Highliners* (1940), showing the *Super Chief* at La Junta, Colorado. Beebe's modernist views often featured diesel locomotives; he rarely photographed diesels otherwise. Lucius Beebe. Beebe-Clegg negative 1010.

Courtesy of the California State Railroad Museum.

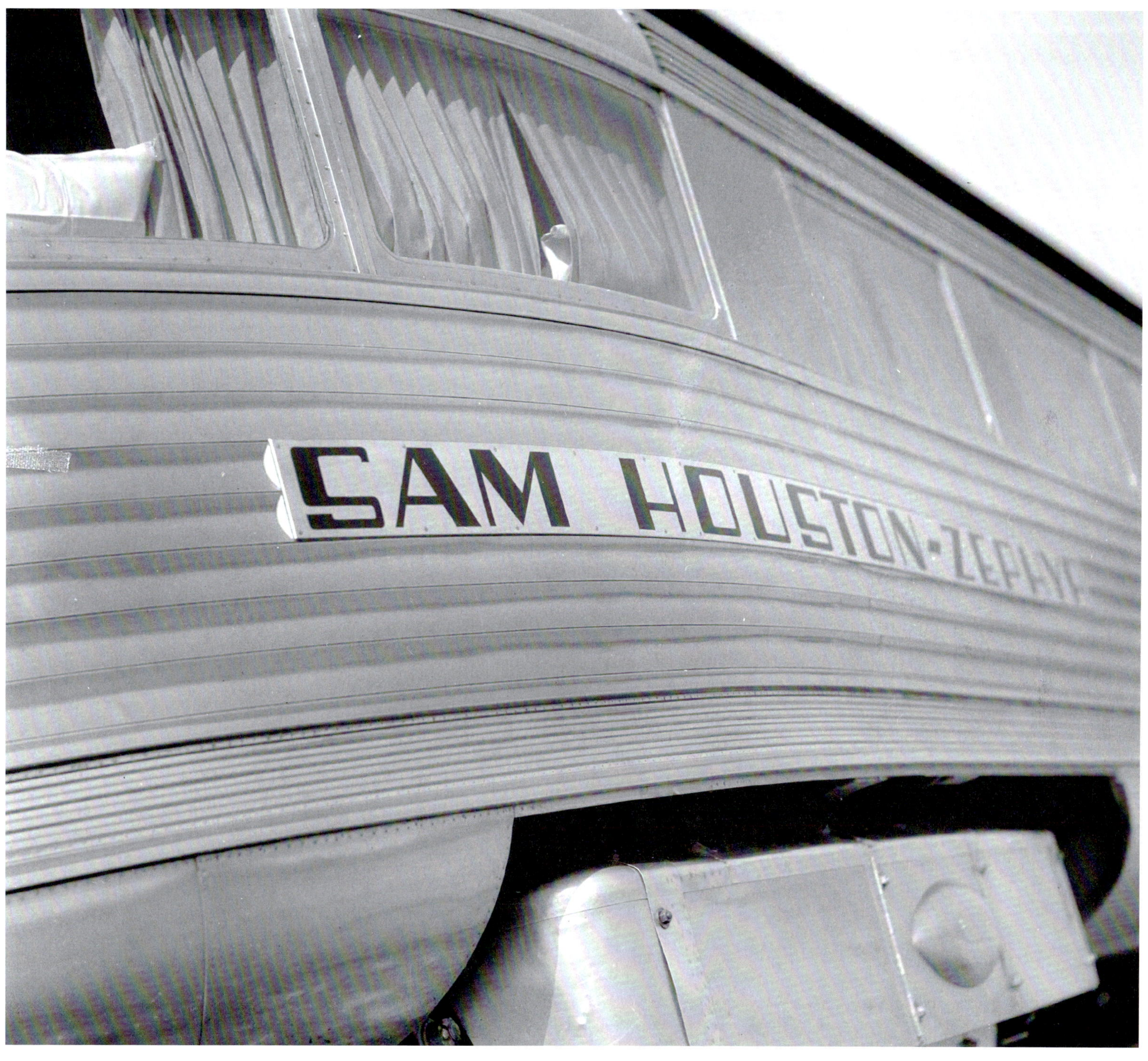

Plate 44. A tightly framed image of the *Sam Houston Zephyr*, focusing on its streamlining and nameplate, from *High Iron*. Lucius Beebe. Beebe-Clegg negative 3681.

Courtesy of the California State Railroad Museum.

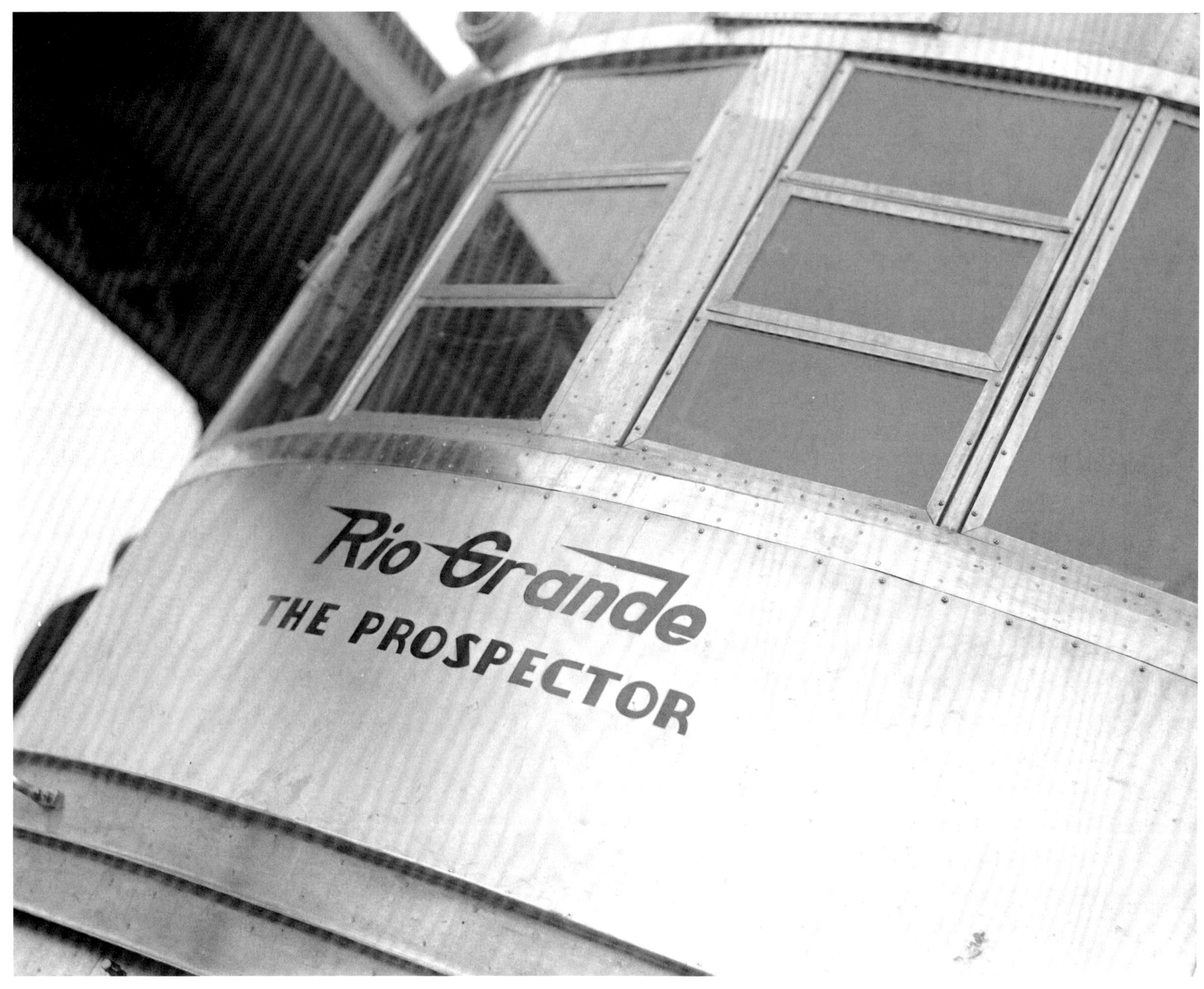

Plate 45. A tightly framed shot of the Denver & Rio Grande Western's streamlined *Prospector*. The photo was not taken on the D & RGW; Beebe captured the *Prospector* on its first run as it left the Budd Company plant in Philadelphia, Pennsylvania. Lucius Beebe. Beebe-Clegg negative 3794.

Courtesy of the California State Railroad Museum.

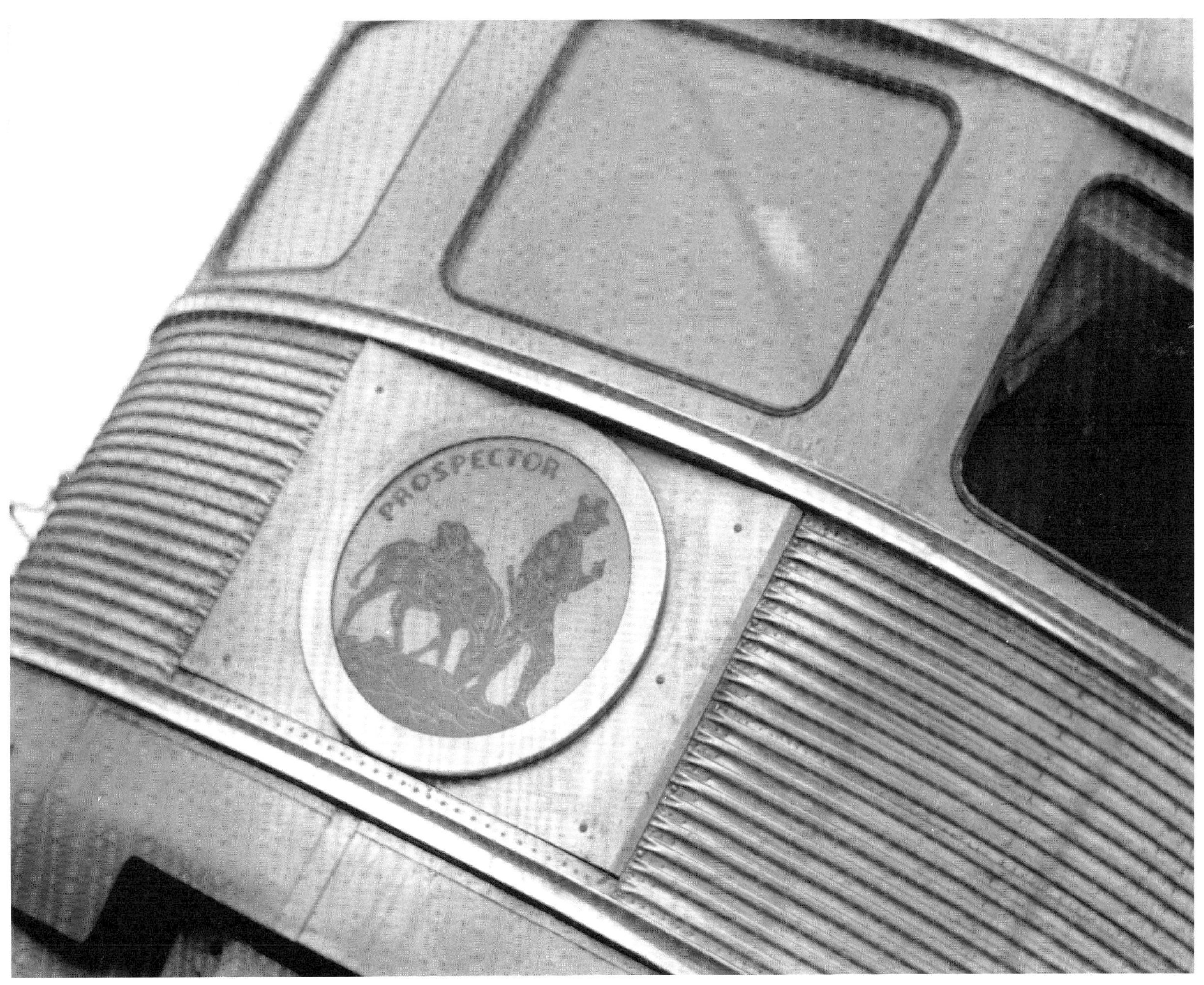

Plate 46. The drumhead of the Denver & Rio Grande Western's *Prospector,* from *Trains in Transition* (1940). Lucius Beebe. Beebe-Clegg negative 1103.

Courtesy of the California State Railroad Museum.

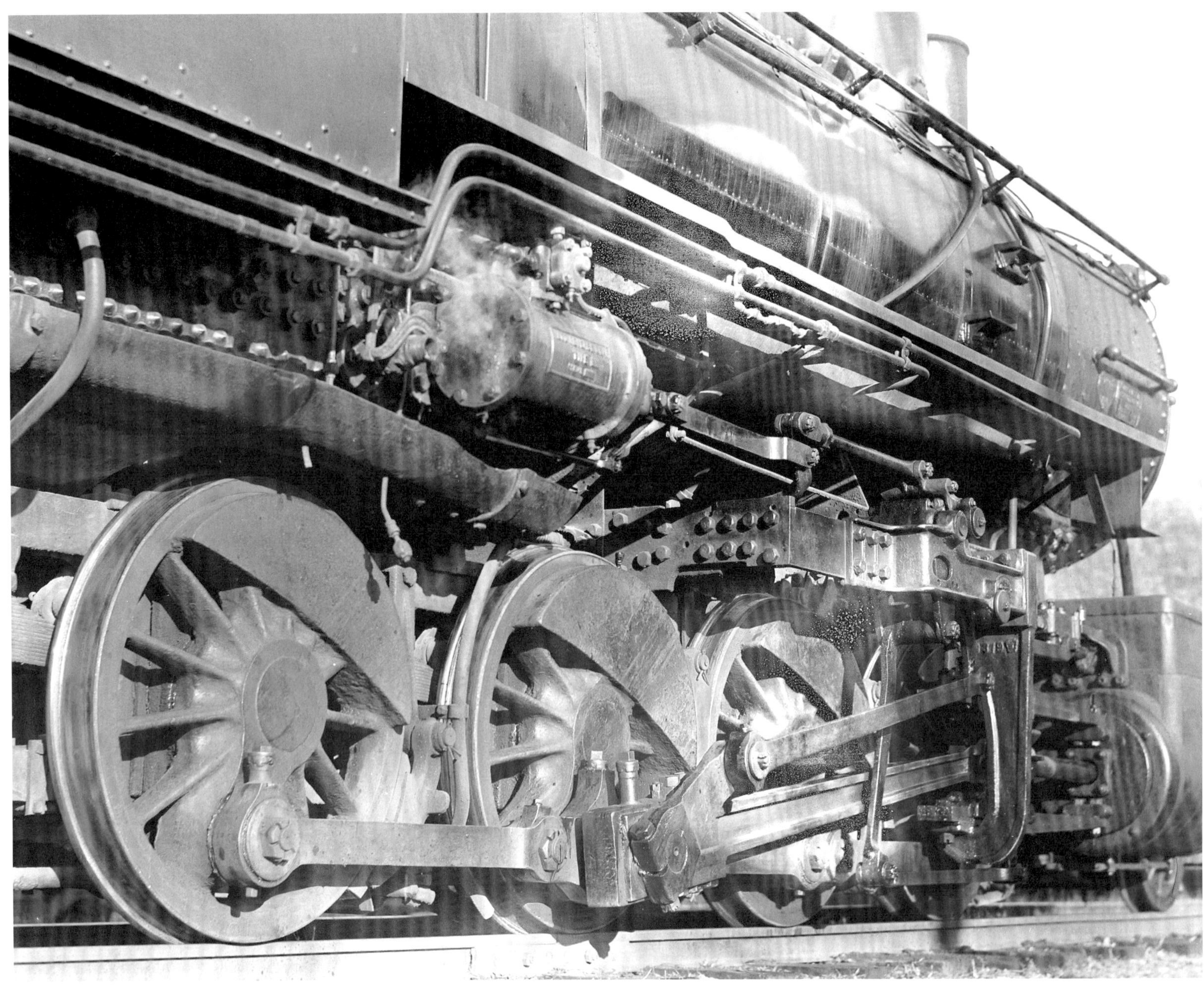

Plate 47. A Lucius Beebe steam engine close-up, the image above the table of contents in *Highball: A Pageant of Trains* (1945). Note the possible influence of Charles Sheeler in this image. Lucius Beebe. Beebe-Clegg negative 1149.

Courtesy of the California State Railroad Museum.

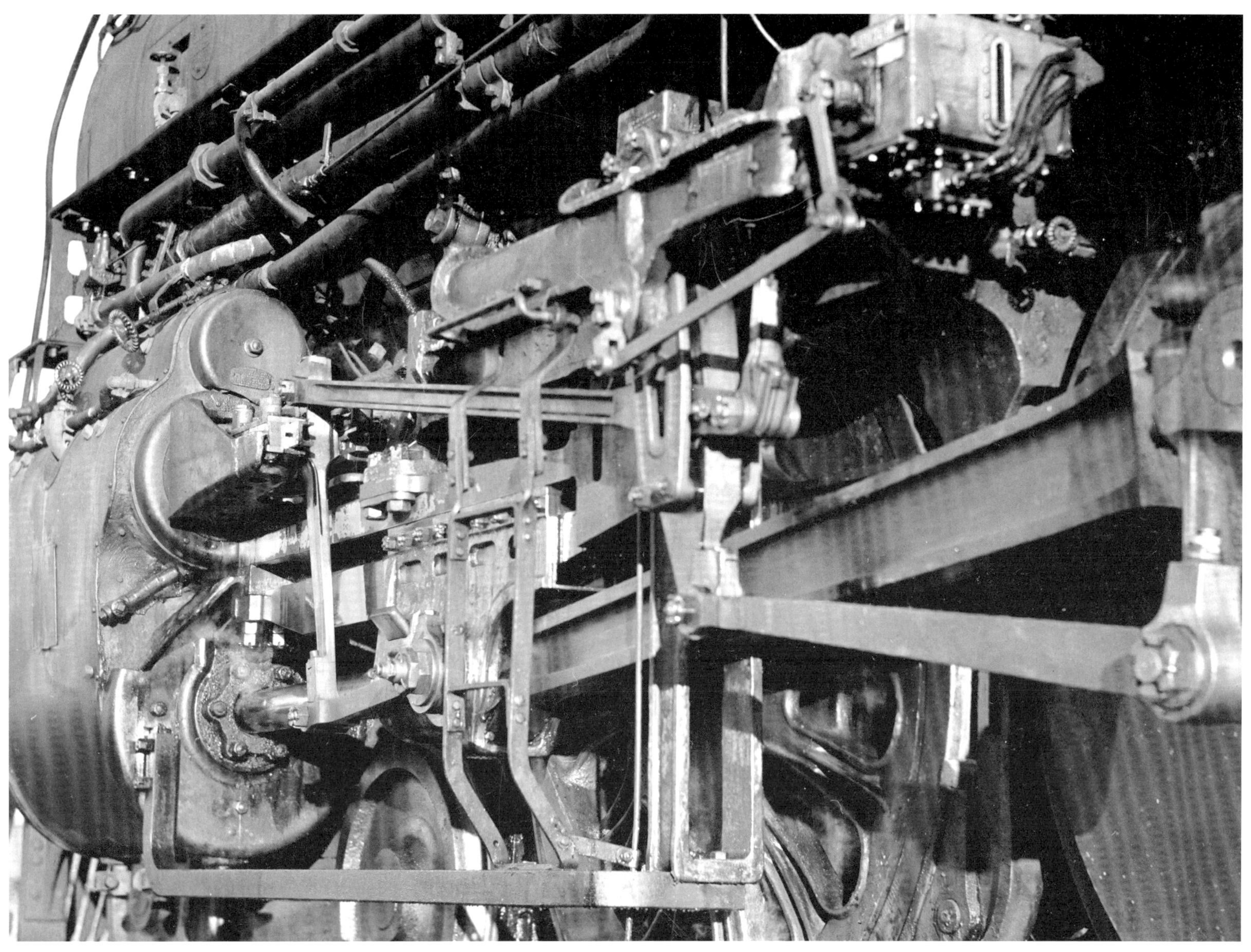

Plate 48. "Symbols of Integrated Power." The valve gear and part of the rod assembly of an Atchison, Topeka & Santa Fe Railway four-eight-four "Northern" passenger locomotive. Another steam engine close-up, this one a stunning assemblage of cylinders, rods, and wheels, where the Sheeler influence develops into a unique vision of Beebe's own. Lucius Beebe. Beebe-Clegg negative 1019.

Courtesy of the California State Railroad Museum.

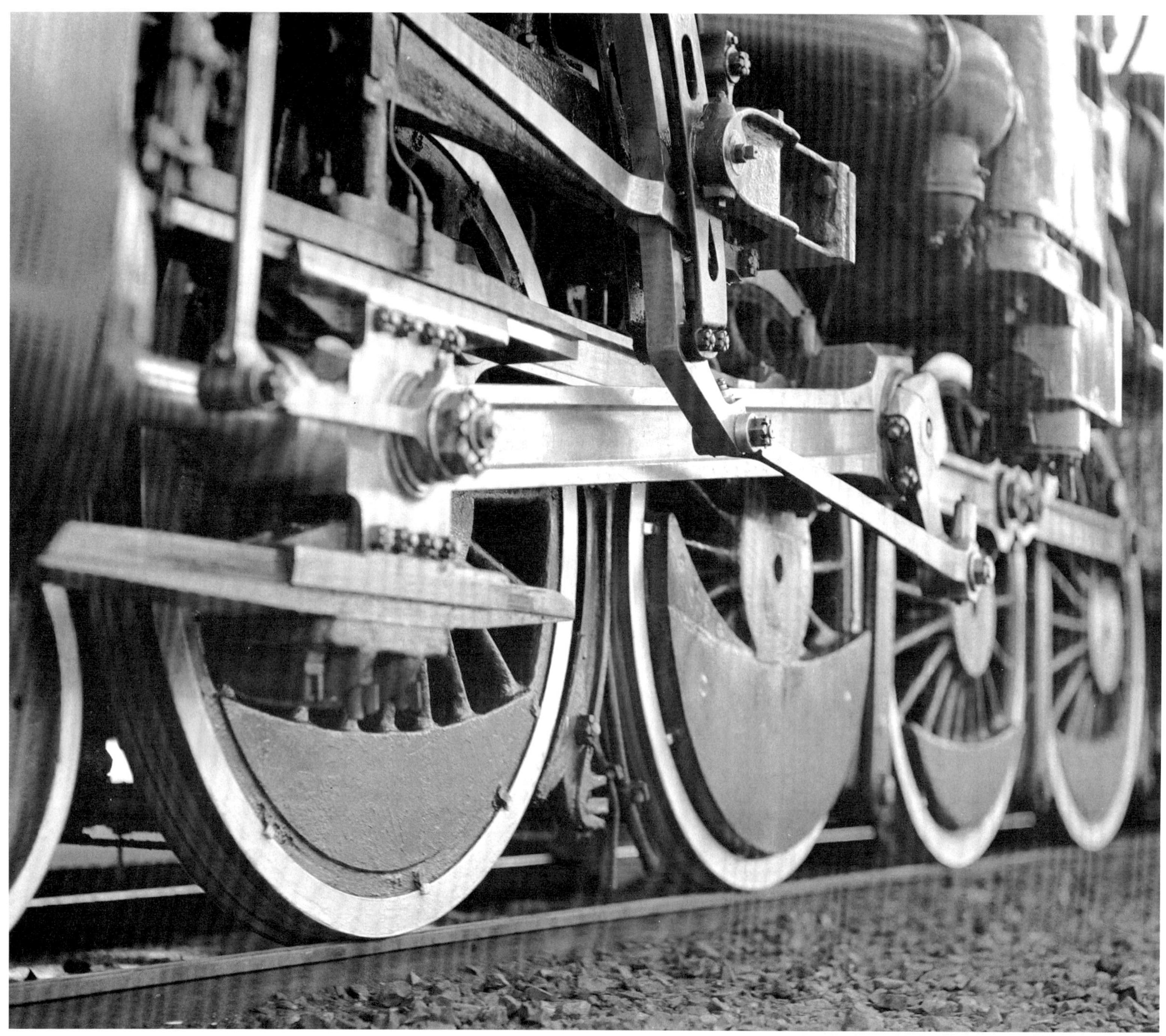

Plate 49. A steam engine close-up emphasizing the locomotive's driving wheels. This image introduces the "Power" chapter in *High Iron* (1938). Beebe often used his tightly formatted, modernist images to introduce books or sections of books. Lucius Beebe. Beebe-Clegg negative 1724.

Courtesy of the California State Railroad Museum.

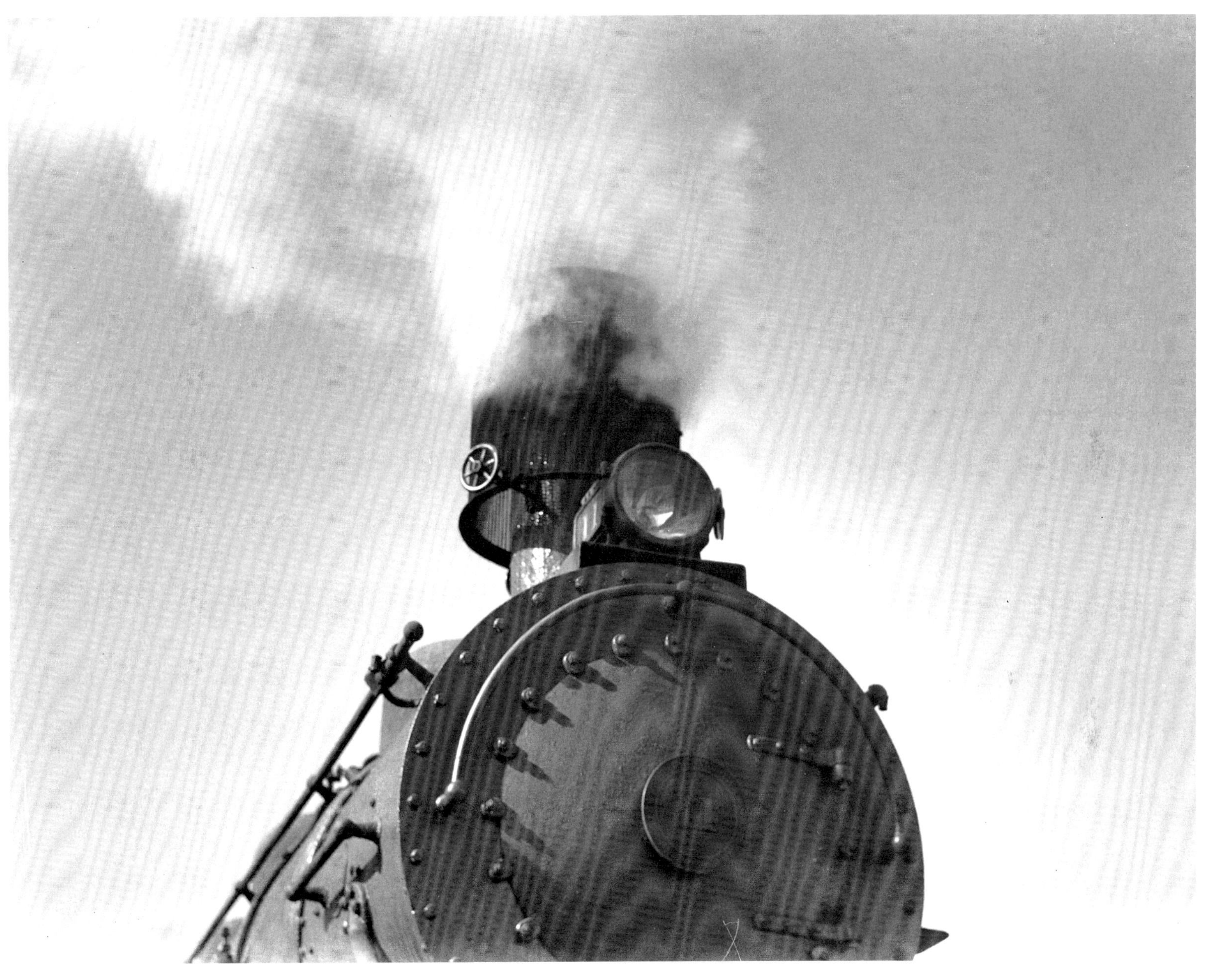

Plate 50. A tight close-up of Raritan River No. 11, emphasizing its unusual spark arrestor. Lucius Beebe. Beebe-Clegg negative 1153.

Courtesy of the California State Railroad Museum.

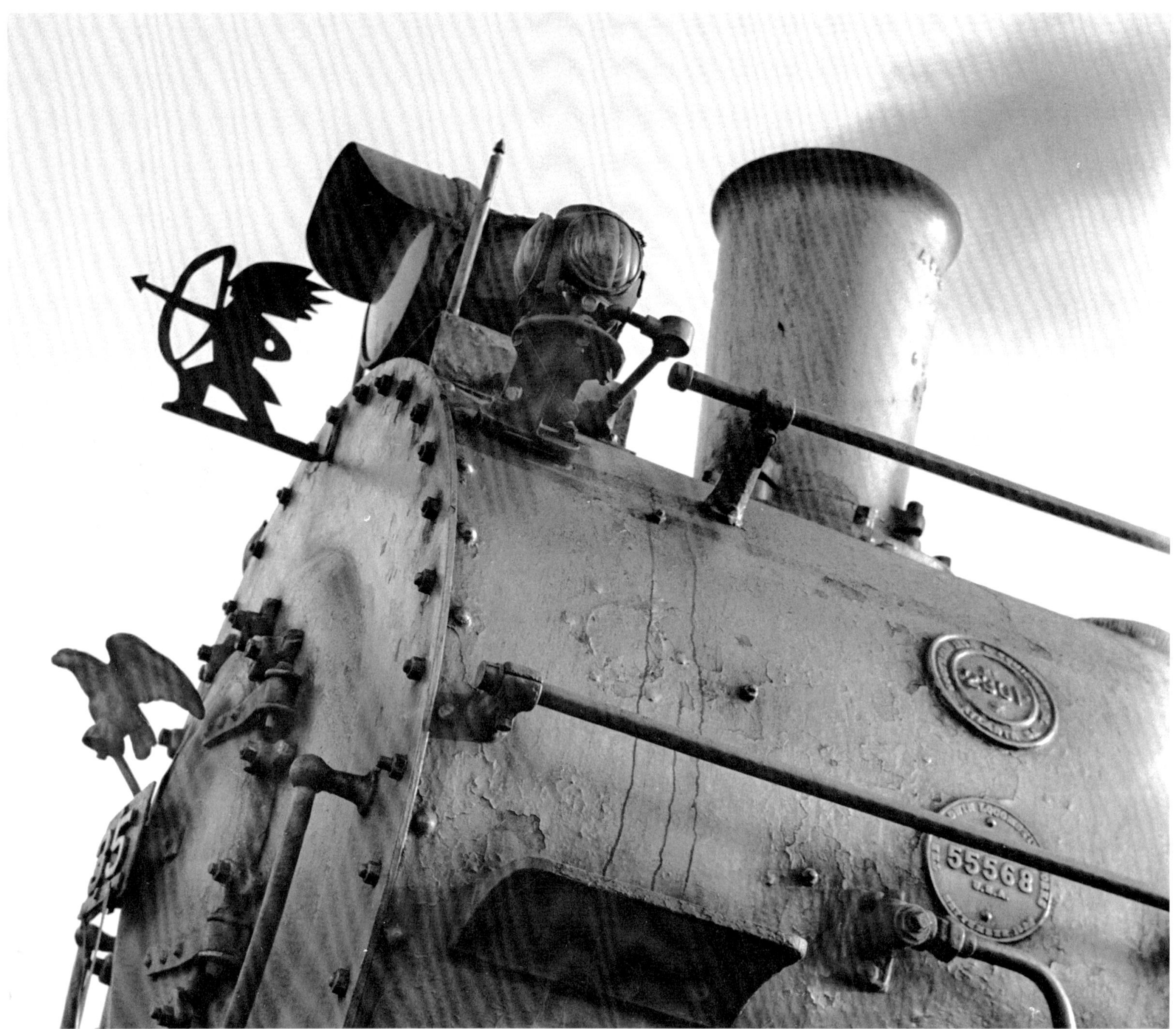

Plate 51. A Charles Clegg close-up of Aberdeen & Rockfish Railroad No. 35, emphasizing its cut-out, folk-art Indian with bow and arrow, and the American eagle added just above its number plate. Charles Clegg. Beebe-Clegg negative 2812.

Courtesy of the California State Railroad Museum.

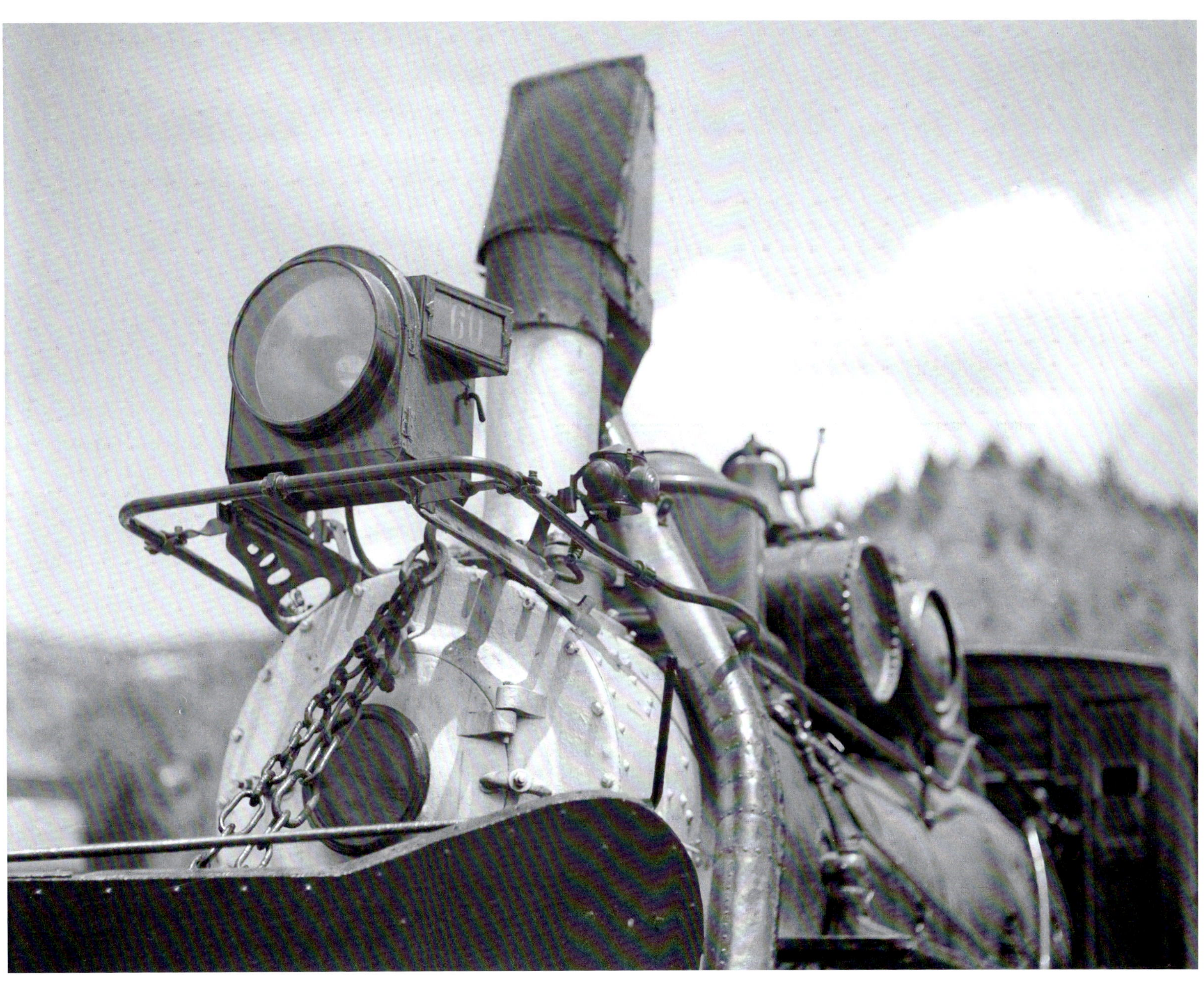

Plate 52. "Never Again to Georgetown, to Silver Plume." Colorado & Southern Railway narrow-gauge steam locomotive No. 60 on display at Idaho Springs, Colorado. Another Lucius Beebe close-up of the front of a steam engine, emphasizing its spark arrestor. Lucius Beebe. Beebe-Clegg negative 289.

Courtesy of the California State Railroad Museum.

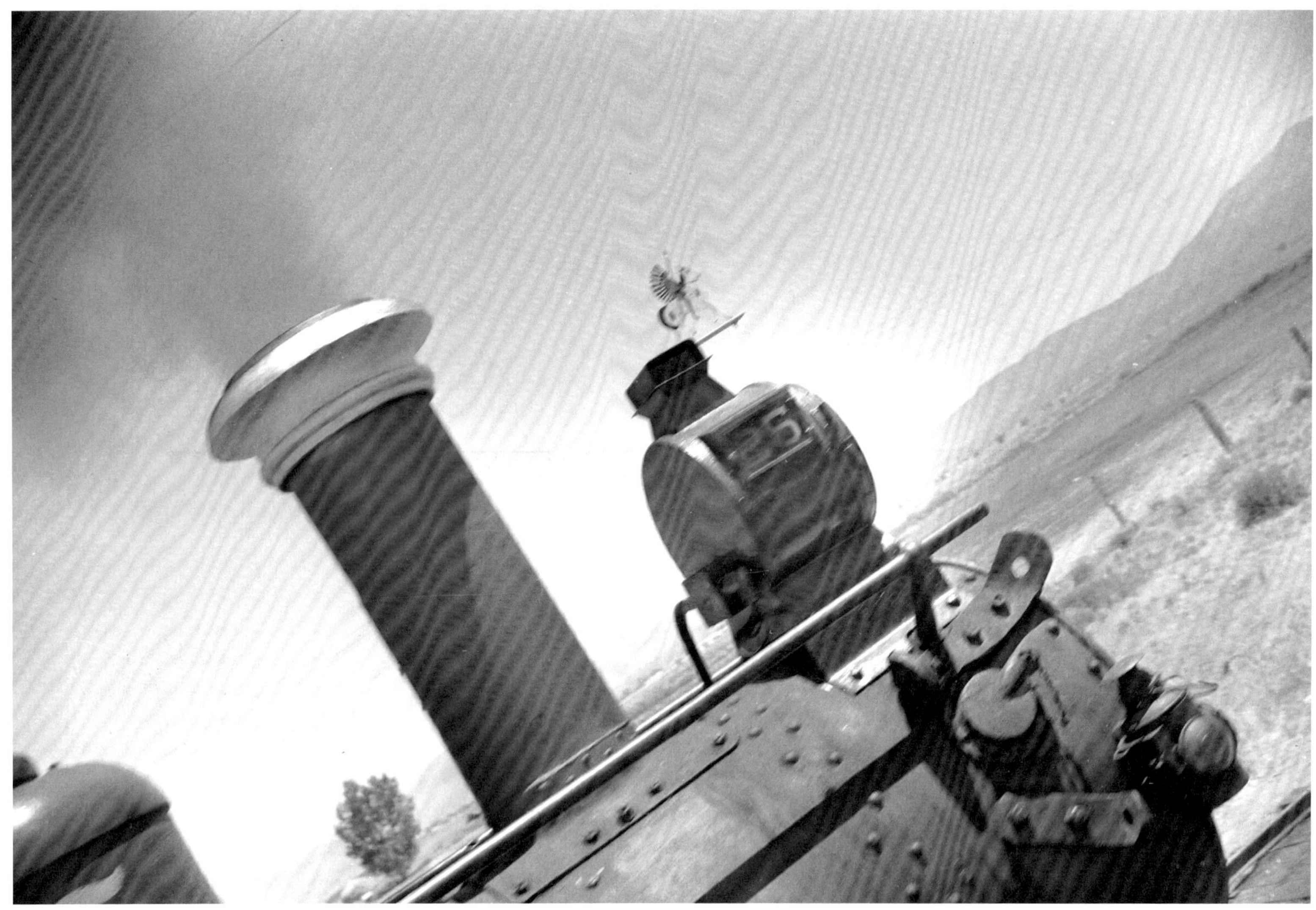

Plate 53. Virginia & Truckee No. 25, taken in June 1946. Another close-up of a steam engine front end, this one from the side and behind, rather than from the front. Lucius Beebe or Charles Clegg. Beebe-Clegg negative 1416.

Courtesy of the California State Railroad Museum.

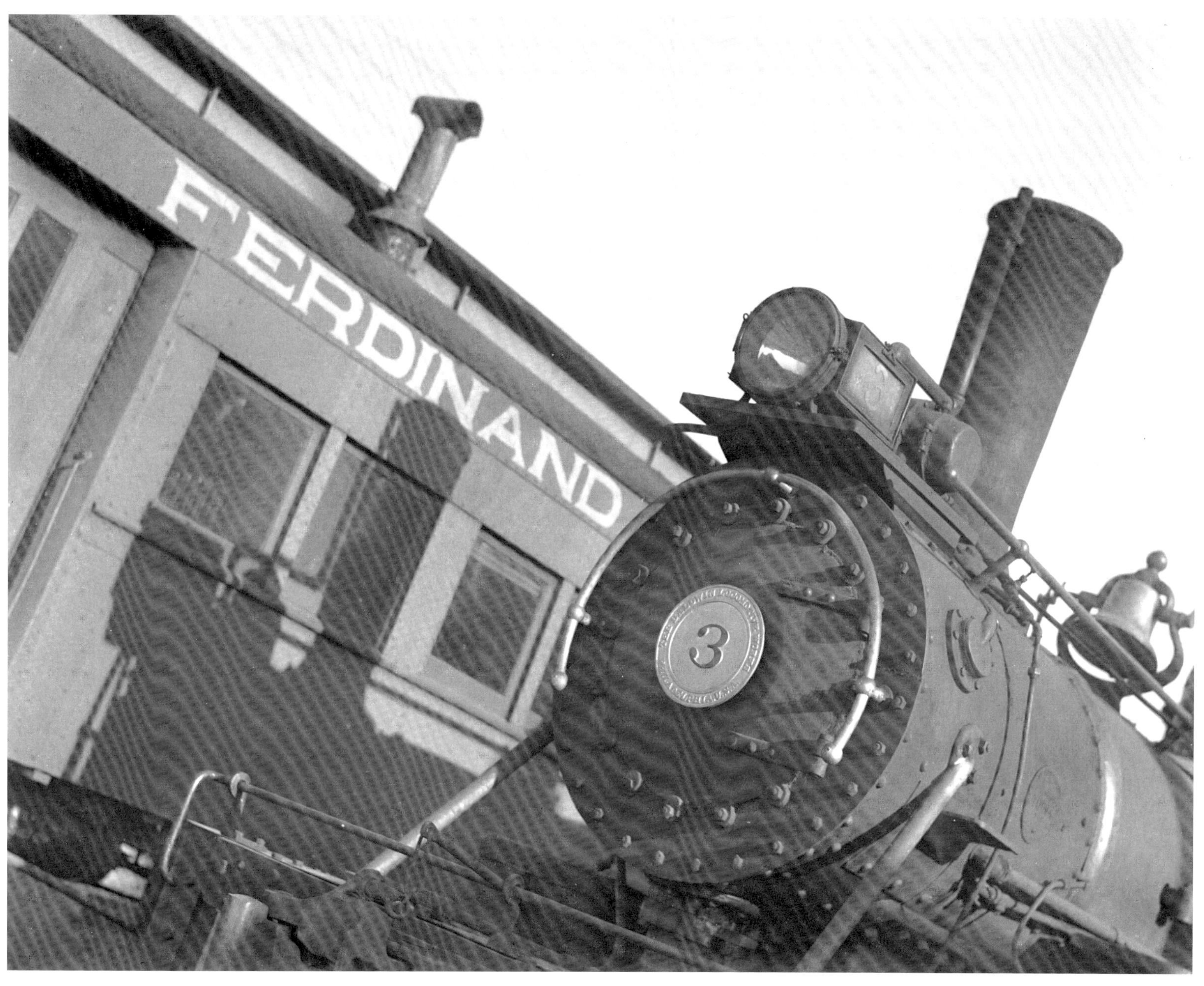

Plate 54. "This is the Whole of the Ferdinand Railroad." This photo captures the spirit of an American short line in one concise image. The Ferdinand Railroad ran in southern Indiana. Lucius Beebe. Beebe-Clegg negative 442.

Courtesy of the California State Railroad Museum.

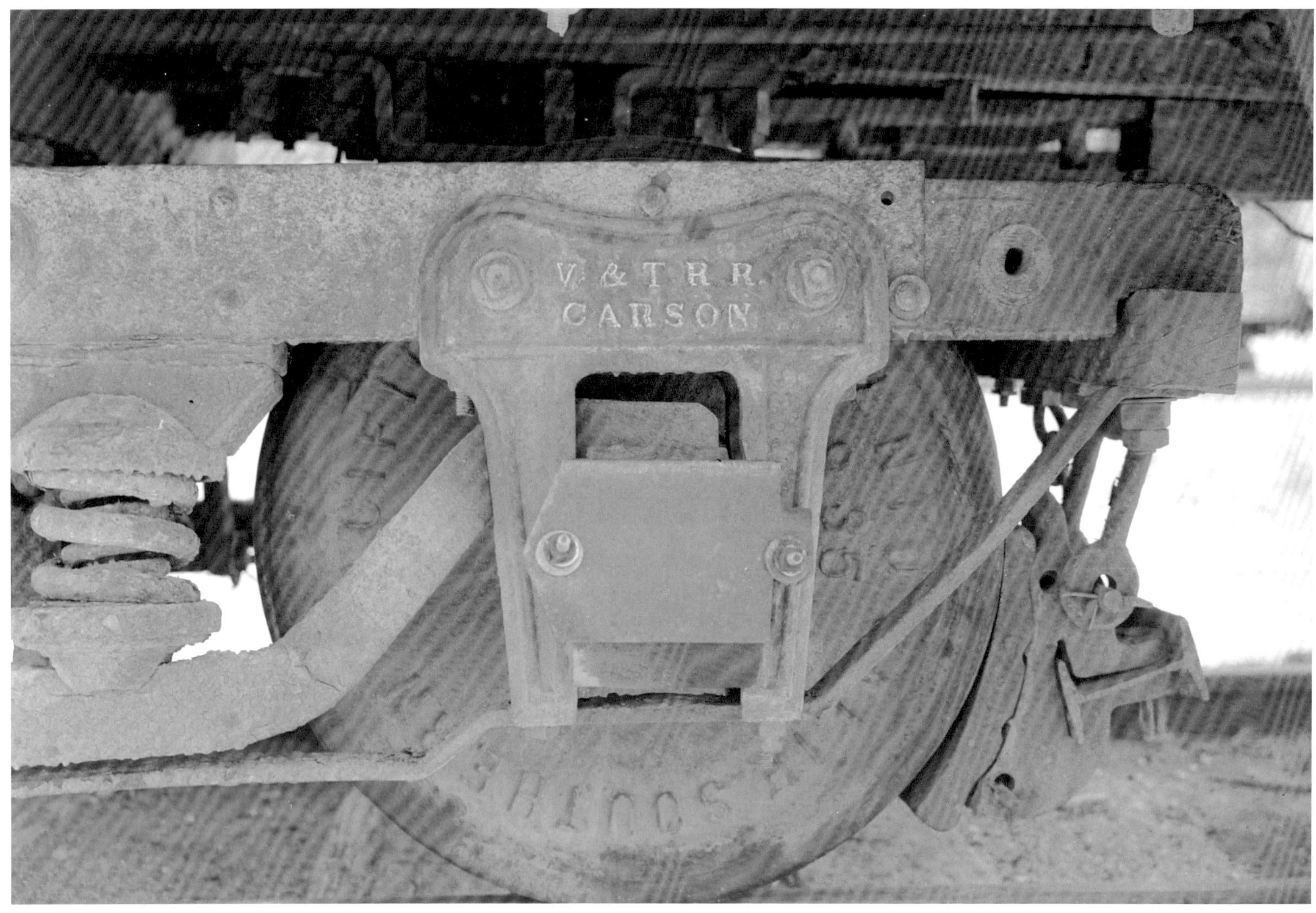

Plate 55. A Clegg detail photo, of part of a truck of the narrow-gauge combine then located in Owenyo, California, on the Southern Pacific's narrow-gauge Owens Valley branch. As the photo shows, part of the assembly was cast in the Virginia & Truckee's Carson City shops many years before. Railroads do not tend to change quickly. Charles Clegg. Beebe-Clegg negative 1235.

Courtesy of the California State Railroad Museum.

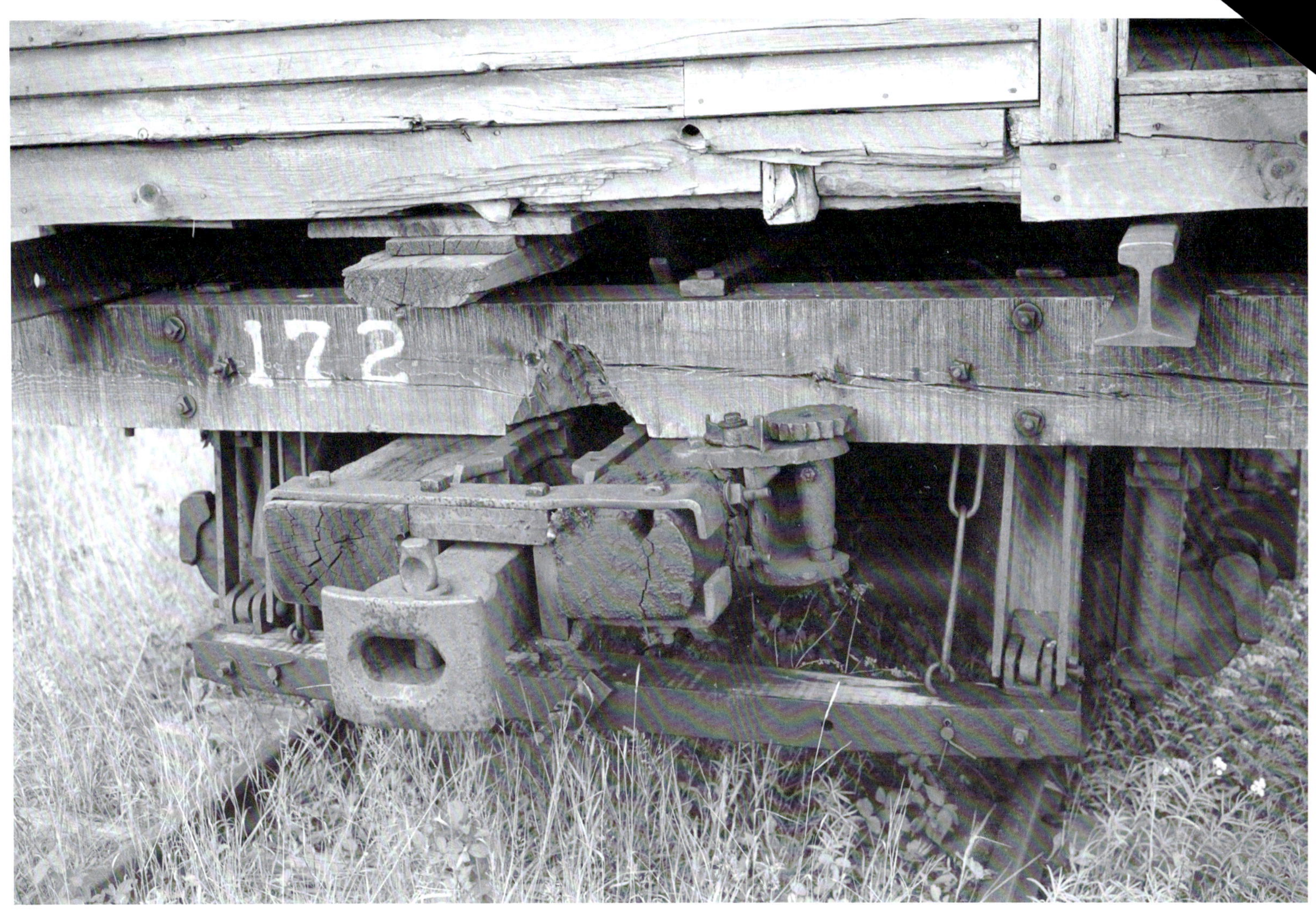

Plate 56. A wonderful Charles Clegg close-up, of a link and pin coupler and draft gear on a homebuilt passenger car of the Grasse River Railroad, at Childwold, New York, in 1945. The Grasse River was owned by a logging company. Charles Clegg. Beebe-Clegg negative 2232.

Courtesy of the California State Railroad Museum.

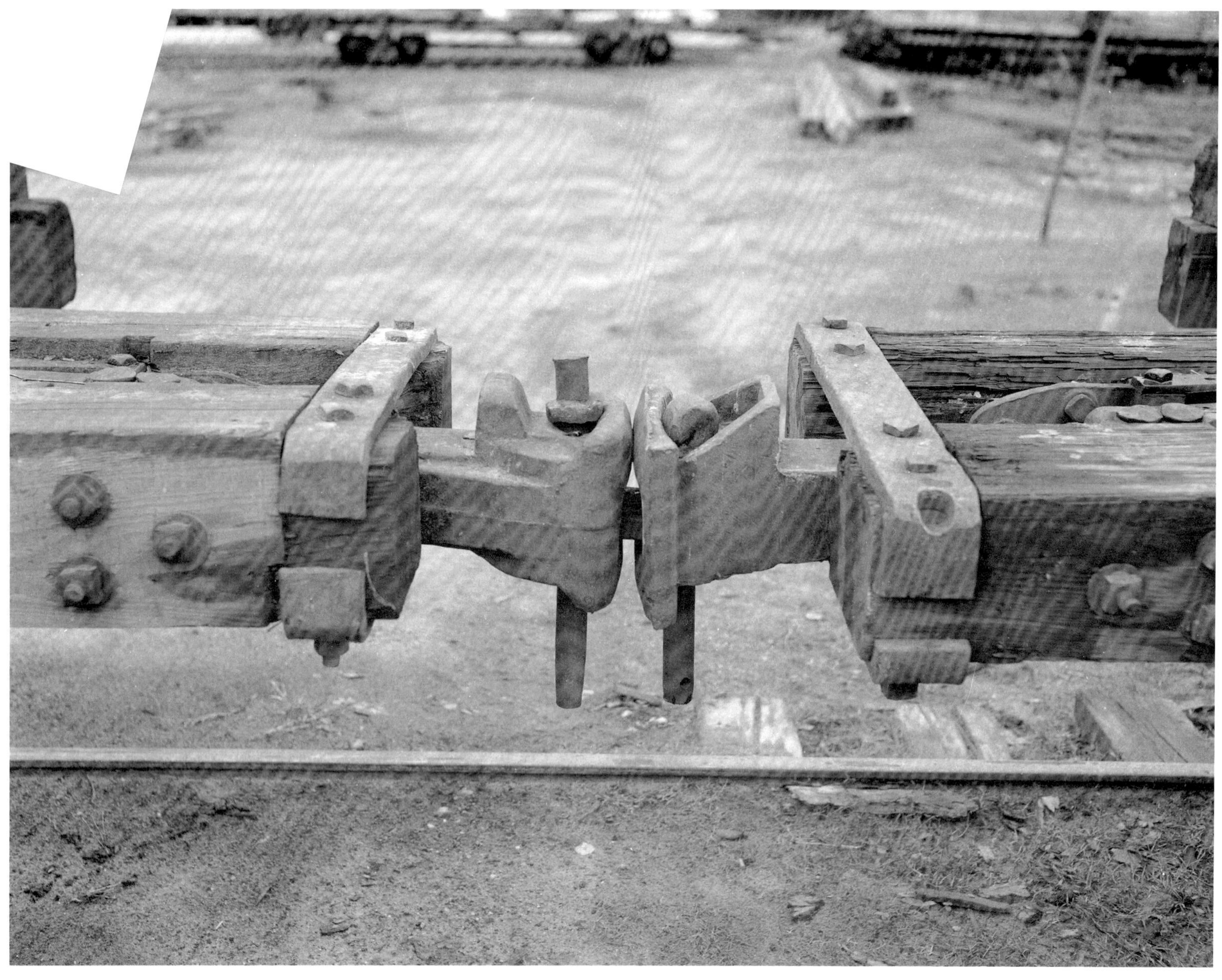

Plate 57. Link and pin couplers on the Moscow, Camden & San Augustine Railroad. Lucius Beebe. Beebe-Clegg negative 2836.

Courtesy of the California State Railroad Museum.

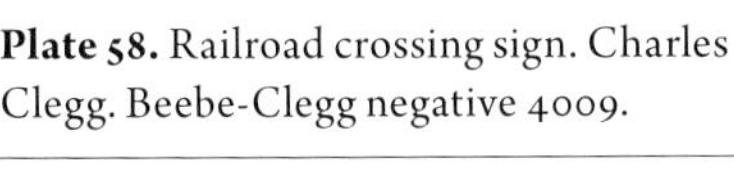

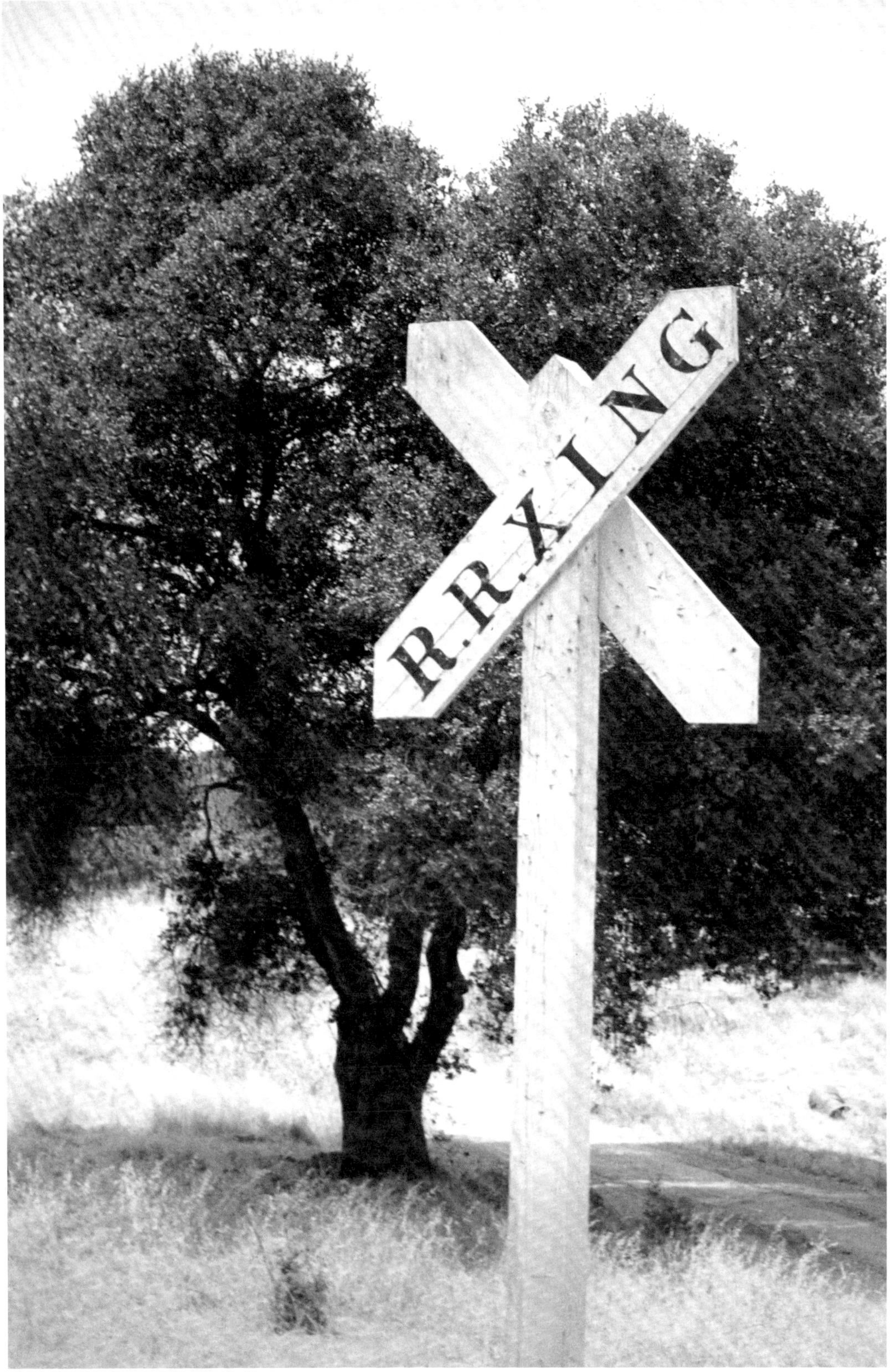

Plate 58. Railroad crossing sign. Charles Clegg. Beebe-Clegg negative 4009.

Courtesy of the California State Railroad Museum.

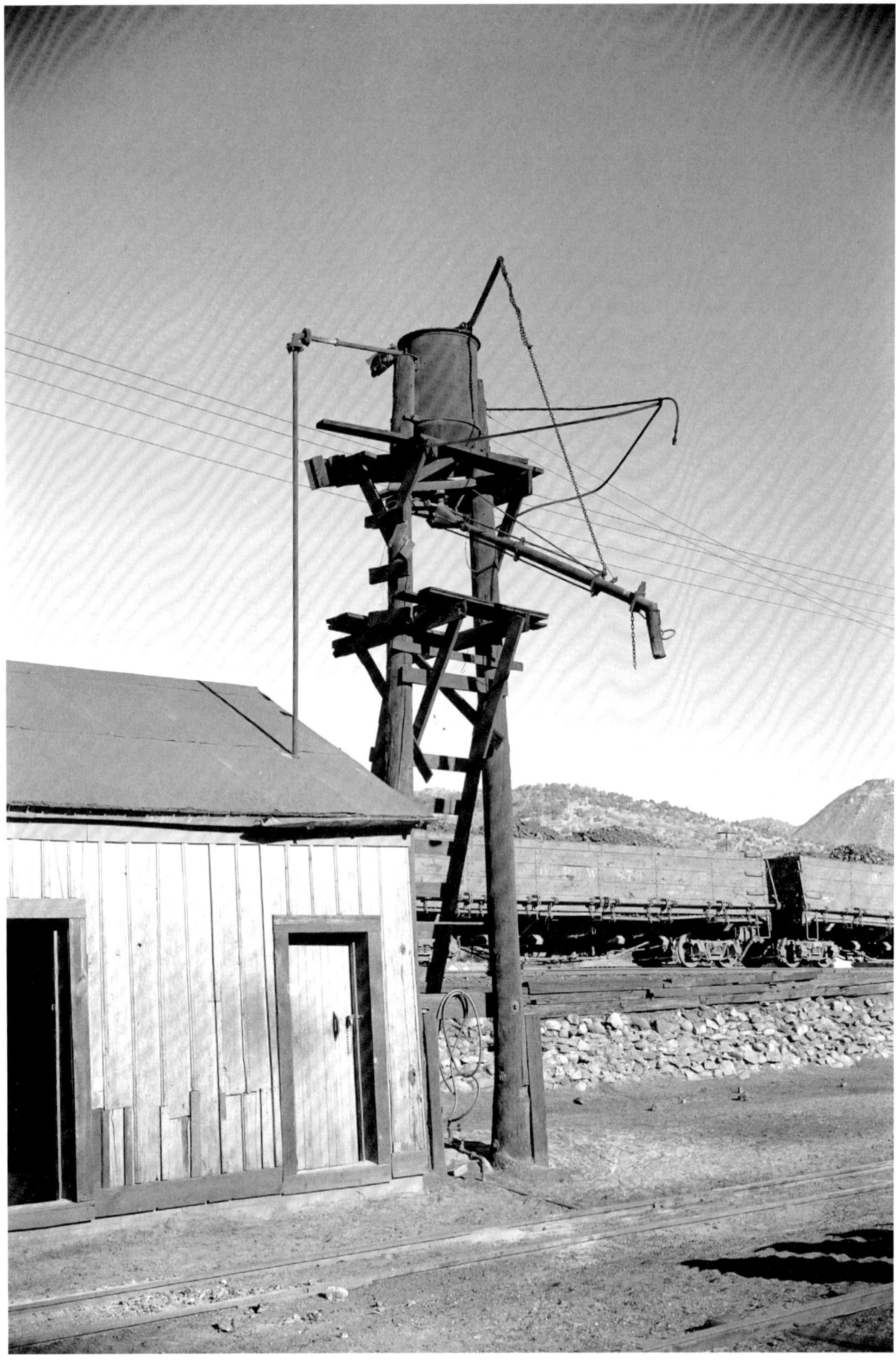

Plate 59. Sand house on Denver & Rio Grande Western narrow gauge, Durango, Colorado. Lucius Beebe or Charles Clegg. Beebe-Clegg negative 3201.

Courtesy of the California State Railroad Museum.

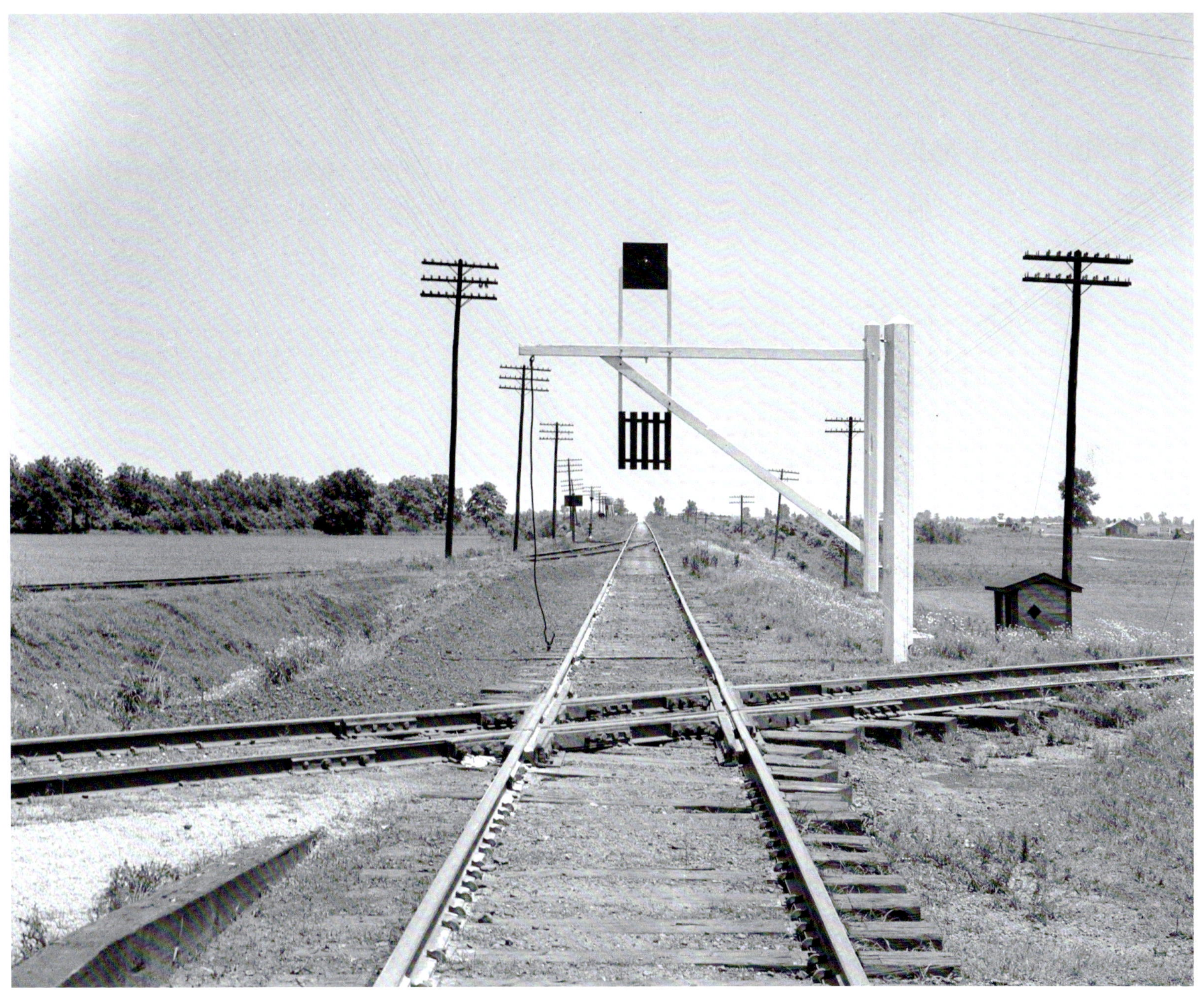

Plate 60. Two railroads crossing at grade, with a crossing gate and sign. On the Columbus & Greenville Railway. Charles Clegg. Beebe-Clegg negative 329.

Courtesy of the California State Railroad Museum.

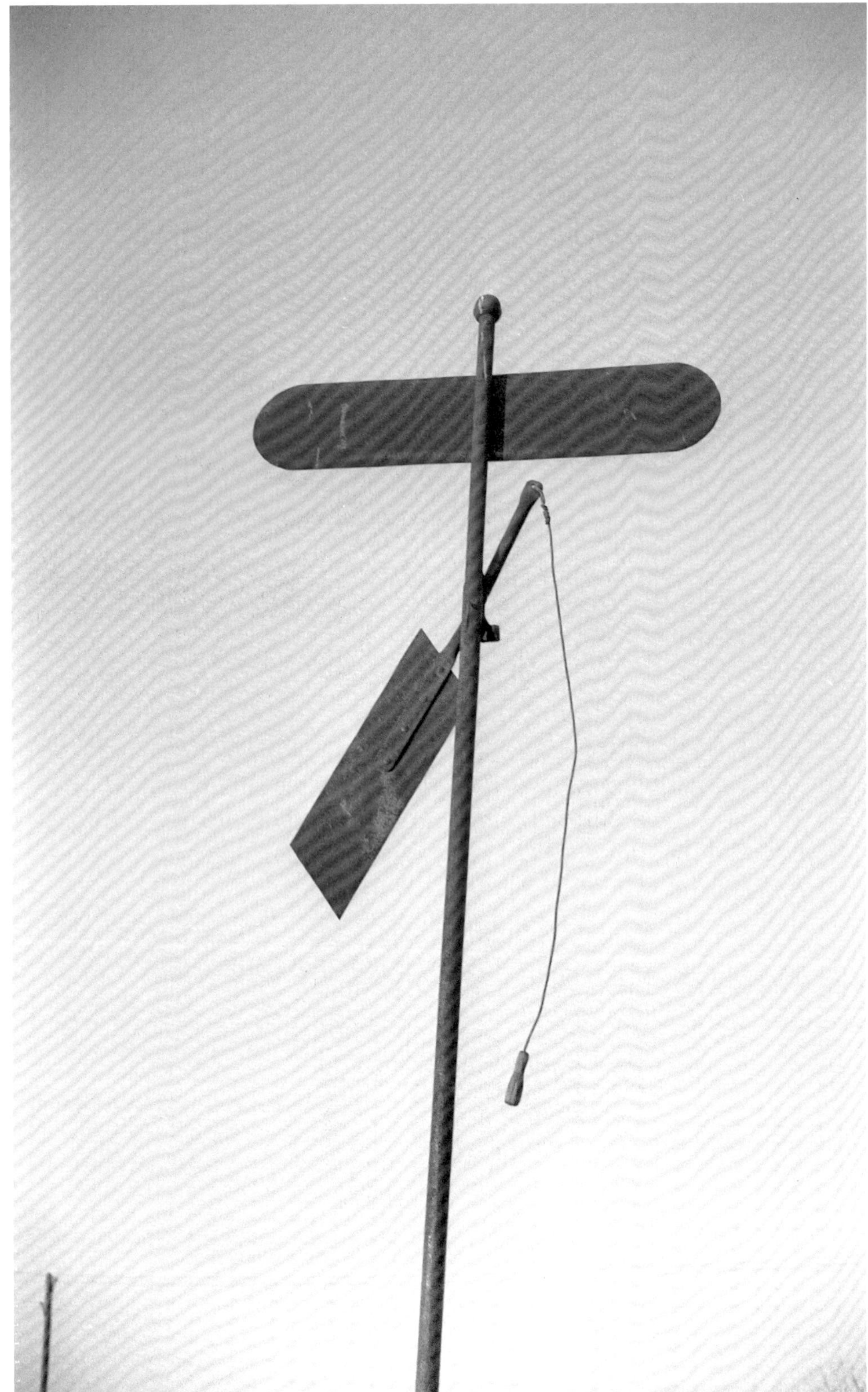

Plate 61. On the Carolina & Northwestern Railway. Charles Clegg. Beebe-Clegg negative 1588.

Courtesy of the California State Railroad Museum.

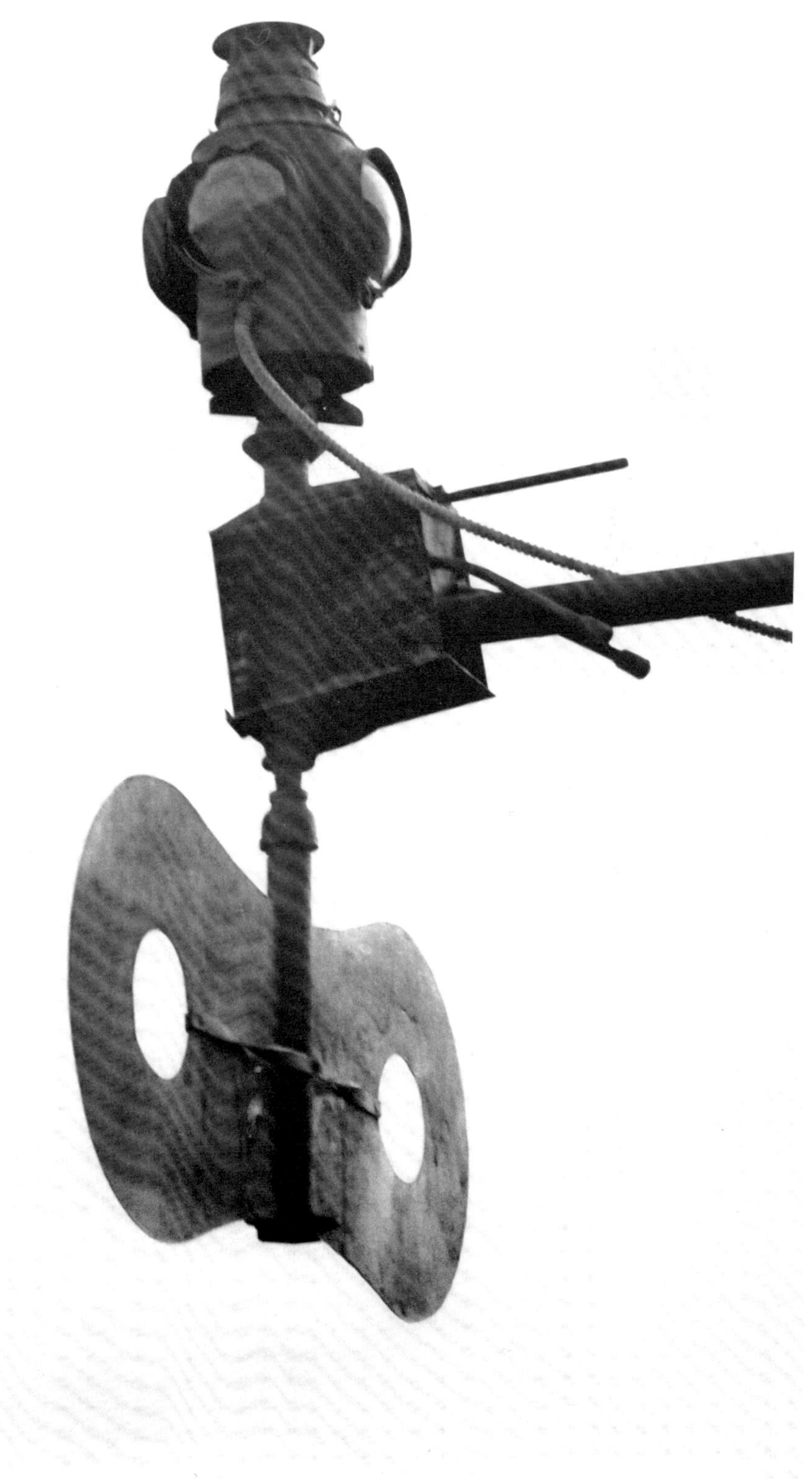

Plate 62. The order board at Blanca, Colorado, on the San Luis Valley Southern Railway, also known as the Southern San Luis Valley Railroad. Charles Clegg. Beebe-Clegg negative 4012.

Courtesy of the California State Railroad Museum.

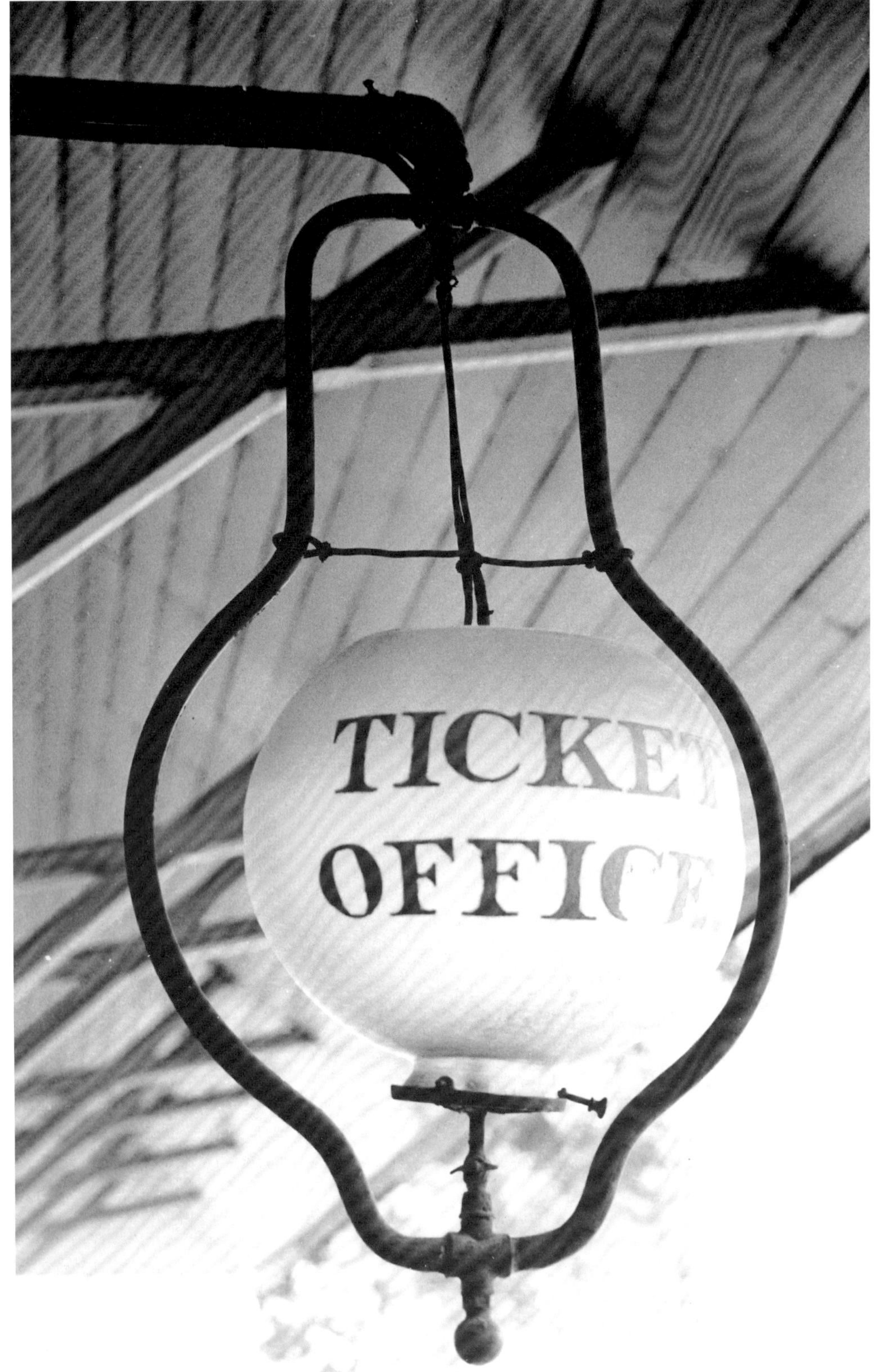

Plate 63. The "Ticket Office" globe sign outside the waiting room at the Virginia & Truckee's station in Carson City, Nevada. Charles Clegg. Beebe-Clegg negative 4013.

Courtesy of the California State Railroad Museum.

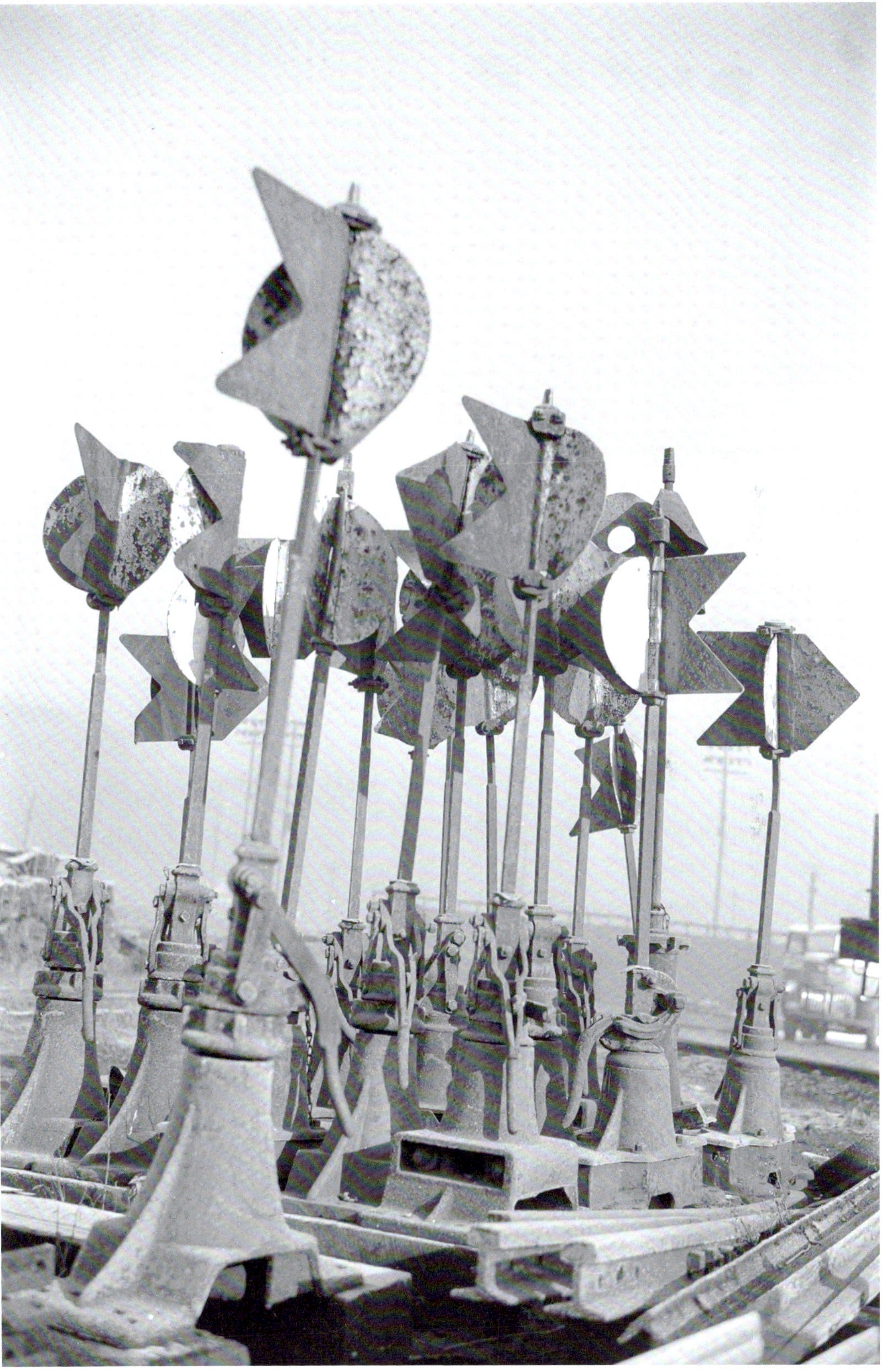

Plate 64. The disused switch stands of the Cranberry to Pineola and Boone, North Carolina, section of the Tweetsie (East Tennessee & Western North Carolina Railroad), abandoned in 1940, await scrapping in Johnson City, Tennessee. Charles Clegg. Beebe-Clegg negative 2751.

Courtesy of the California State Railroad Museum.

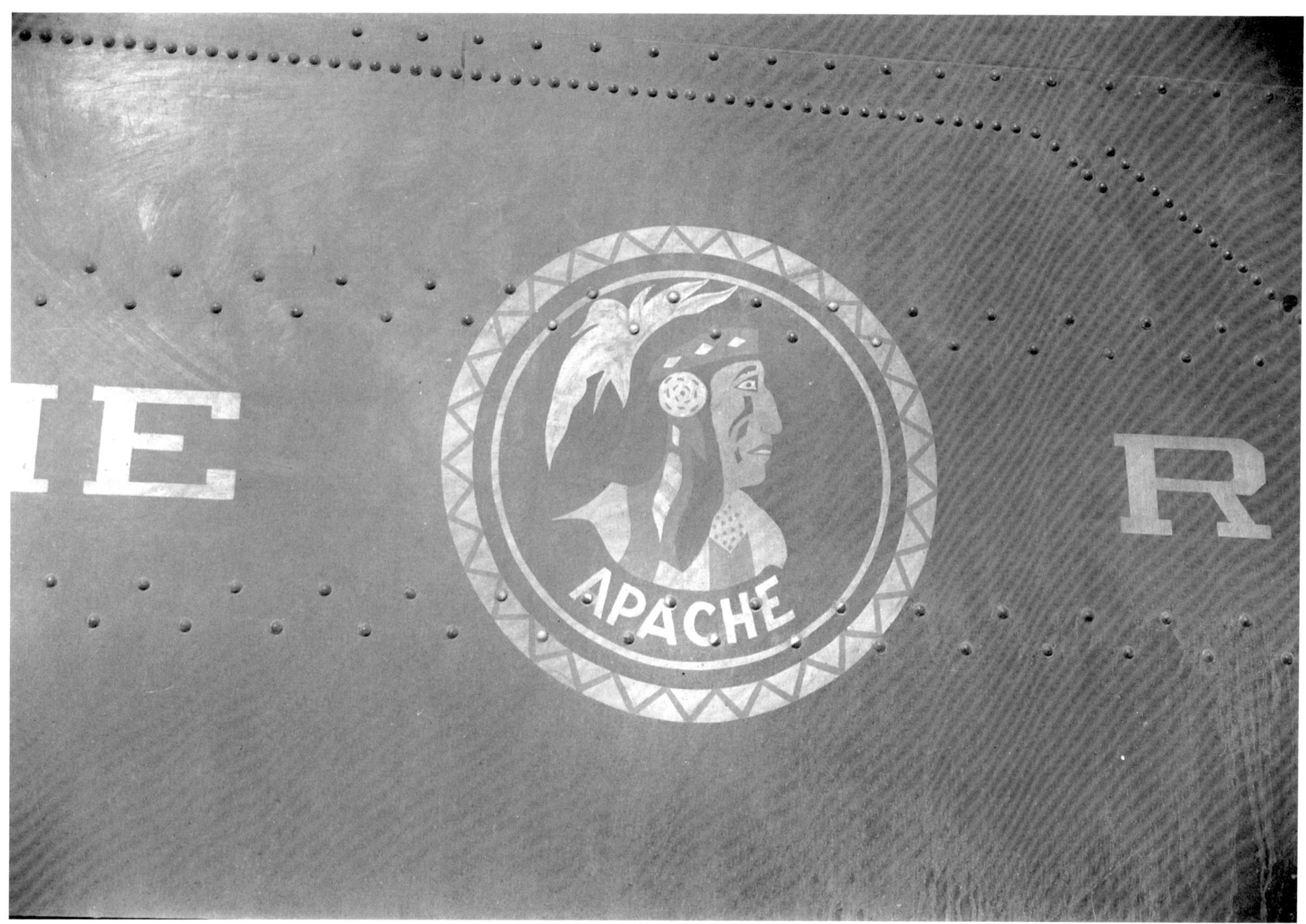

Plate 65. Railroad logo on a steam locomotive tender, Apache Railway. Charles Clegg. Beebe-Clegg negative 1083.

Courtesy of the California State Railroad Museum.

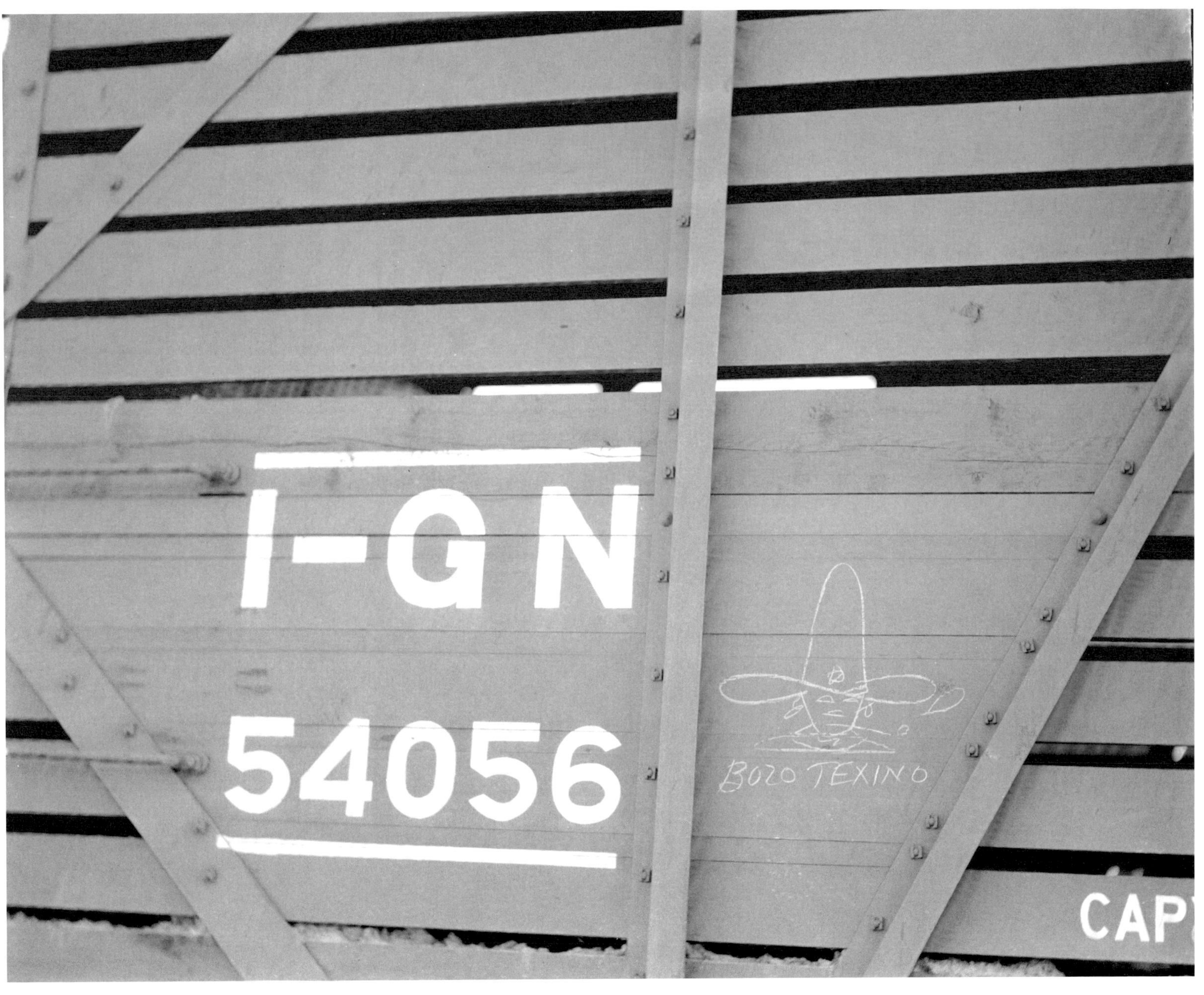

Plate 66. "The Whistler of the Boxcars." Lucius Beebe's photographic document of the famed "Bozo Texino" moniker, created by J. H. McKinley, a Missouri Pacific engineman from San Antonio, Texas. Beebe took this view of an International Great Northern freight car in the Santa Fe yards at San Bernardino, California. Lucius Beebe. Beebe-Clegg negative 3363.

Courtesy of the California State Railroad Museum.

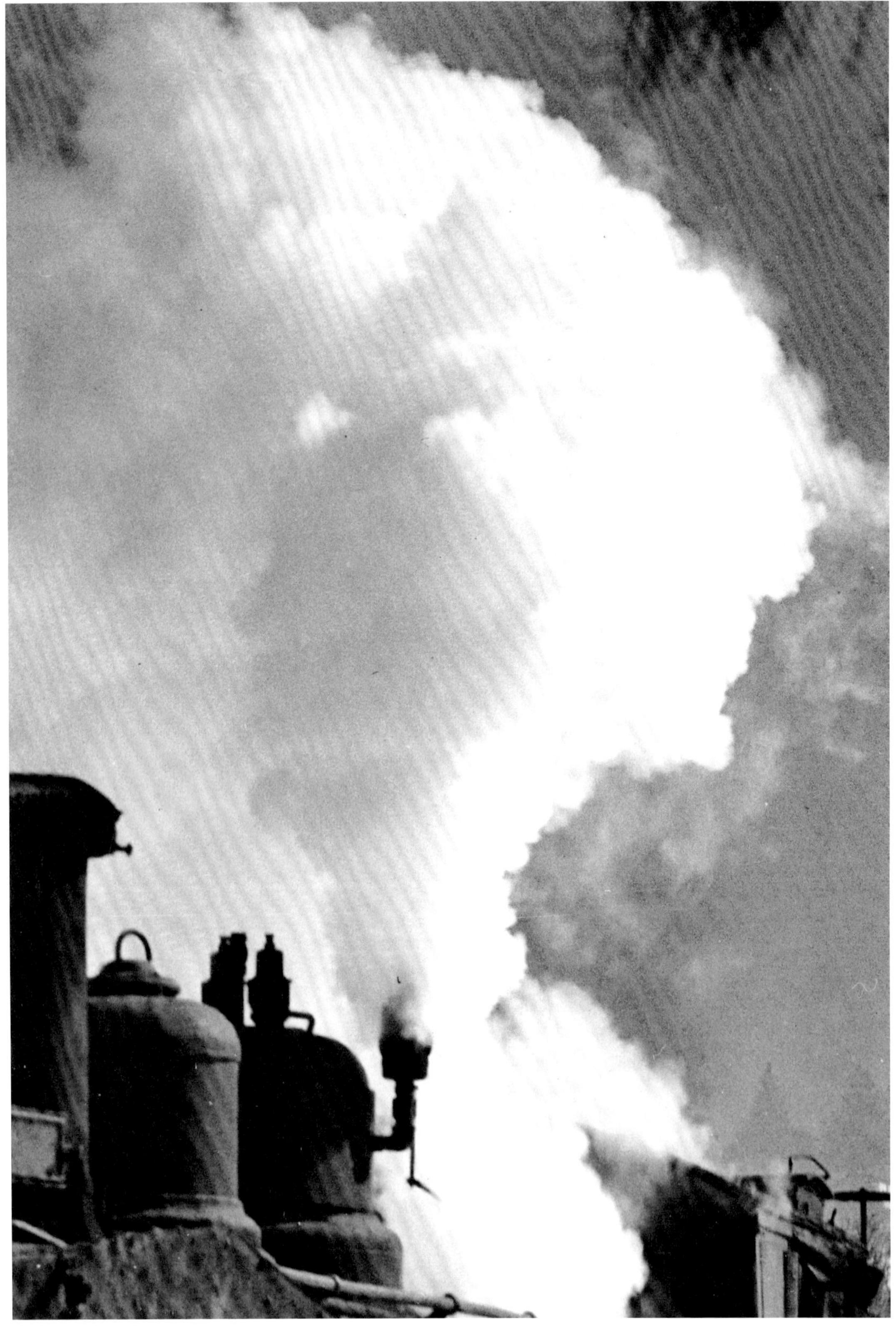

Plate 67. Engine whistling, used at the top of the "Whistle Code" section of *Highball*. Lucius Beebe. Beebe-Clegg negative 4021.

Courtesy of the California State Railroad Museum.

3 RAILROADERS

Railroading is an interesting line of work. Largely male, highly paid, dangerous and exacting, not generally requiring a college education, working class but, at least in the past, composed of workers highly respected in their communities, it is one of the few remaining professions in the United States that can provide a well-paying job to workers without a college degree. The major "Class One" railroads employ one of most unionized workforces left in the United States today.

Lucius Beebe was a well-known spokesperson of the opposite side of American society—of wealth, of laissez-faire, of luxury travel, of gourmet dining. He is not often mentioned as a notable creator of portraits of American railroad workers, and in this observer's view at least, this omission seems to be less a reflection of Beebe's photographic work than of our perception of his attitudes.

Another reason for the neglect of Beebe and Charles Clegg's portraiture is that their published portraits are scattered throughout their vast and disparate output of railroad photography books. Portfolio 3 brings a selection of their most notable portraits together for the first time. Viewed as a collection of work, Beebe and Clegg's portraits stand, like Jack Delano's, as a notable depiction of American railroaders just as the industry was about to transform. Unlike Delano's contemporary images, which did not become well-known until the 1970s, Beebe and Clegg's portraits were pored over by all of the American railroad-subject photographers who followed them. The influence of their work on Phil Hastings is obvious, and an unacknowledged influence on O. Winston Link seems likely.

This is not to say that Beebe and Clegg concentrated on portraits; compared to later, noted railroad-subject photographers, their oeuvre is relatively deficient in images of railroad workers. According to many contemporary accounts, Beebe had a patrician manner that may have affected the empathy a photographer needs to take great portraits. His background may also have lessened his interest in blue-collar railroad workers. These assumptions about Beebe have some validity, but they have often been overdrawn. If his work is to be taken as a guide, Beebe's empathy for railroad workers increased with time, reflecting the influence of Charles Clegg, who had an abiding interest in depicting the people of railroading in the context of their surroundings.

Portraits of railroaders were common before Beebe and Clegg, but most were posed images of proud men with the trains under their care or of engineers either in cab windows or "oiling around" with the long-spout oil can, an archetype of steam railroading. One of the first photographers to go beyond this stilted treatment was Lewis Hine, especially in his work for *Fortune*, *Survey Graphic*, and *U.S. Camera*, and in his book, *Men at Work*.[1] Hine was closely associated with New York City, and Beebe would likely have been familiar with Hine and his photography.[2]

Beebe's *High Iron*, which includes a number of fine portraits, was published in 1938, just six years after *Men at Work*. Like their modernist work, this is another area where Beebe's photos influenced Charles Clegg, whose portraits of railroaders in the 1940s closely resemble Beebe's earlier images.

Plates 68 to 70 show railroaders lubricating the iron horse, but these are not staged or stereotypical photographs. In plate 68, one of Beebe's best-known portraits, a worker, with his helper, is using a grease gun to lubricate a Union Pacific steam engine. It is an unusual view later emulated by O. Winston Link. Plates 69 and 70 show workplaces very different from the Union Pacific's locomotive-servicing location in Laramie, Wyoming. In plate 69, Beebe shows a railroader using a comically small oil can to lubricate one of the Sumpter Valley Railway's unusual narrow-gauge "Mallet" steam locomotives. In plate 70, Clegg depicts a worker oiling a Camino, Placerville & Lake Tahoe Railroad "Shay" geared locomotive, an engine normally used on industrial railroads serving the lumber industry.

One of Beebe's favorite portraits was that of a fireman silhouetted against the tender of a steam locomotive and filling the tank with water. He was a master of this type of image. Plates 71 to 74 are other examples of this type of photograph. Plates 71 and 72 are early images, originally from *High Iron* and *Trains in Transition*. Plate 73 is a little-known image, taken on the Morristown & Erie Railway and showing, at the left, the brick base of this cold-climate water tank. Plate 74 shows a short line, the Amador Central's, less sophisticated method of taking on water. Plate 75, a closely related image, shows another short line, the Gainesville Midland Railroad's, bucket-brigade method for filling a steam locomotive's sand dome.

Plates 76 and 77, one Beebe's and the other attributed to Beebe, show a fireman and an engineer working on camelback locomotives.[3] Plate 76 is much published, but its renown is justified; it is one of Beebe's greatest portraits.

Beebe and Clegg had a special affection for eccentric short lines of the southern and western United States. In plate 78, we see a Tweetsie (East Tennessee & Western North Carolina) engine crew with their possum. In plate 79, Beebe depicts with stark realism the elderly engine crew working on a short line in rural Texas, the Wichita Falls & Southern Railroad. The photo seems to say that the end is near for these men, their locomotive, and the railroad itself—as proved to be the case.

In plates 80 to 84, we see railroad operating employees, such as conductors, brakemen, and flagmen, and a type of employee rarely depicted in railroad-subject photographs: supervisors and managers. Plate 80 shows an inspection car on the "Katy" (Missouri-Kansas-Texas Railroad) and the railroaders using it; given their dress clothes and fedoras, they are clearly managerial. In plate 81, Clegg shows an intricate set piece on a southern short line, the Georgia & Florida. At a whistle-stop shelter with a tie pile and a lonely dirt road in the background, a trainman watches from a Jim Crow coach at the end of a mixed train. As he looks on, a bystander watches as a passenger boards the coach.

In plate 82, a trainman, probably a conductor, waits on the steps of a Copper Range Railroad coach. The ramshackle coach provides an interesting contrast to the trainman's natty full uniform. Plate 83, which shows the influence of Archie Robertson, is another full scene, showing a trainman, probably a conductor, in freight-railroading garb, helping a group of women and girls in immaculate, light-colored dresses detrain. The image was taken on the Louisville, New Albany & Corydon Railroad, which carried passengers in its caboose.[4] Finally, plate 84, by Clegg, shows a group of Native Americans boarding a "Galloping Goose" railcar.

Plates 85 to 91 show freight railroaders at work. In plate 85, by Clegg, a trainman, probably a head-end brakeman, stands on a steam-engine tender in a view reminiscent of Beebe's views of firemen watering steam engines.

Plate 86 is an excellent example of the power of cropping an image. As originally taken, this image is marred by pedestrian framing; John Gruber calls it "amateurish."[5] When Beebe published this image, probably with Clegg's assistance, it was cropped tightly in order to focus on the Rio Grande Southern head-end brakeman ("head shack," in Beebe's words).[6] As the caption notes, in this image, Beebe was able to include every imaginable icon representing steam-era freight railroad brakemen. As cropped, it is a stunning and historic portrait. When taken with plate 86, plates 87 and 88 form a series showing this brakeman and his crewmates in action and "decorating" (working on, riding) the car tops, a practice outlawed long ago.

Plate 89 takes us to rural North Carolina, where a trainman stands on the platform of his caboose and watches the photographer, Clegg. In plate 90, another iconic portrait of steam-era freight railroading, Clegg depicts Southern Pacific freight conductor J. A. Brennan in his caboose. Finally, in plate 91, Clegg shows a Mississippi & Alabama trainman, probably a head brakeman, riding on the switch-engine-type pilot of his train's locomotive.

Plates 92 to 94 show a less commonly photographed facet of American railroading before the decline of passenger service: the ubiquitous mail, express, and baggage service provided by US railroads at a time when payment for mail carriage helped keep passenger trains running. Plate 92, by Clegg, shows a crew member on the Stewartstown Railroad in Pennsylvania handling sacks of mail. The dolly loaded with mail sacks seems comically large compared to the tiny diesel locomotive in the background.[7] Plates 93 and 94 take us to the Deep South. Plate 93, by Clegg, shows Central of Georgia trainmen, probably a conductor and a baggageman, and a consignee looking on as three other workers manhandle a heavily loaded baggage cart over the rails of a siding. Plate 94 shows the importance of mail carriage to the passenger train industry at the time, as a baggage cart is loaded with mail sacks from a Louisiana & North West Railroad railcar.

The work of the railroad employees who helped maintain American railroads is relatively poorly depicted in period photographs. Clegg sometimes took images of this nature. Plate 95 shows a Manchester & Oneida section gang working on a riotously weed-grown right-of-way, and plate 96, a rare image, shows a worker, probably a signalman, who has ridden his speeder out on the line to light signal lamps, such as this switch lamp. The worker, switch stand, track, and speeder are cleverly framed by the archaic highball signal towering over the scene. Note that the highball signal also has two kerosene lamps, which are reached by a narrow ladder running up the signal mast.

As Beebe noted in a number of his writings, disabled or elderly railroad employees were often given crossing-tender jobs, in many cases as a form of relief in the days before social security, health insurance, and retirement plans. The final image in this portfolio, plate 97, by Clegg, shows a crossing tender at his shack on the Norwood & St. Lawrence Railroad in the far reaches of upstate New York.

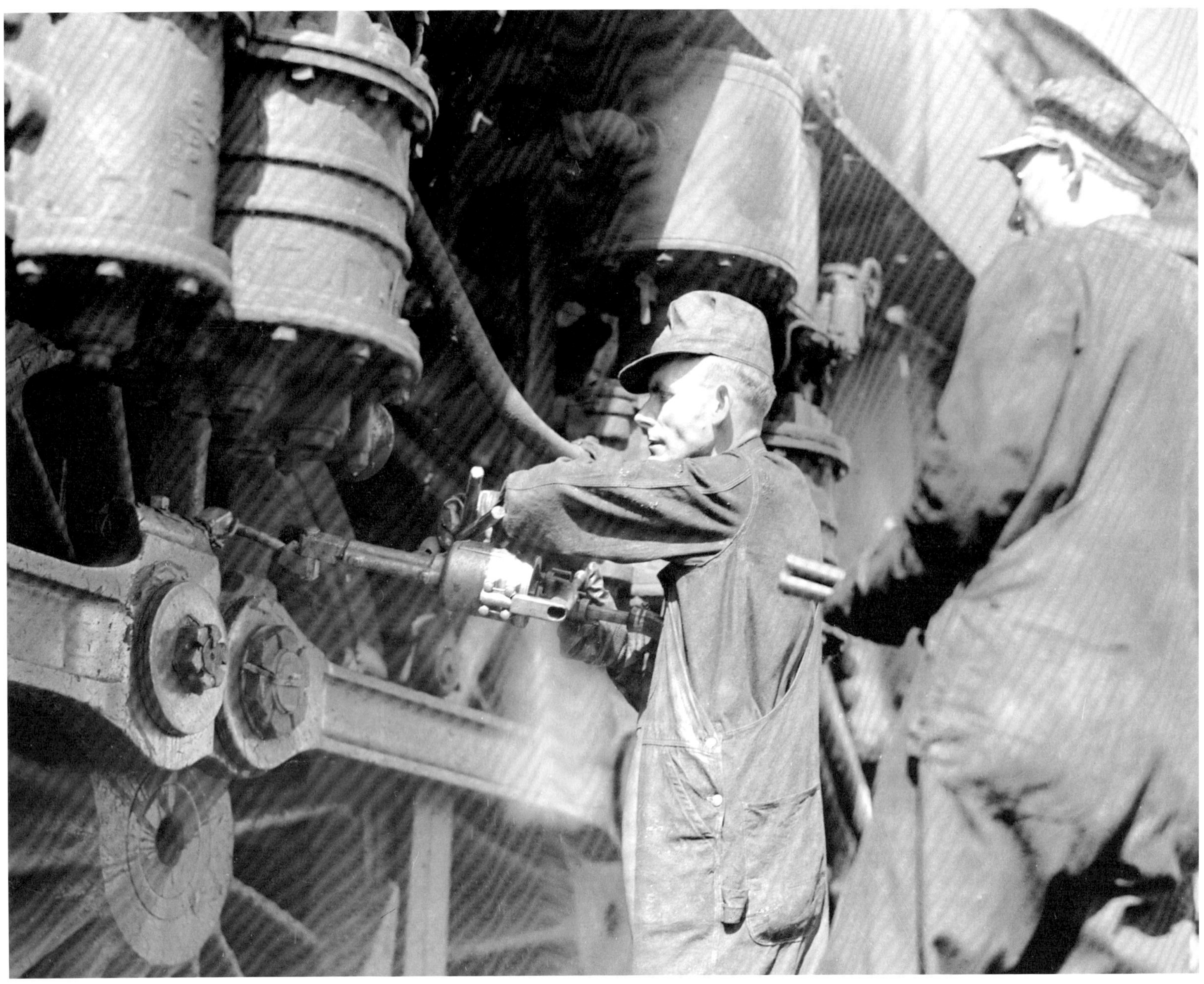

Plate 68. "Service for Side Rods." A Union Pacific service crew lubricating a four-eight-two locomotive leading the *Overland Limited* at Laramie, Wyoming. Beebe later identified this photo as having been taken on the Southern Pacific at Lordsburg, New Mexico. Lucius Beebe. Beebe-Clegg negative 805.

Courtesy of the California State Railroad Museum.

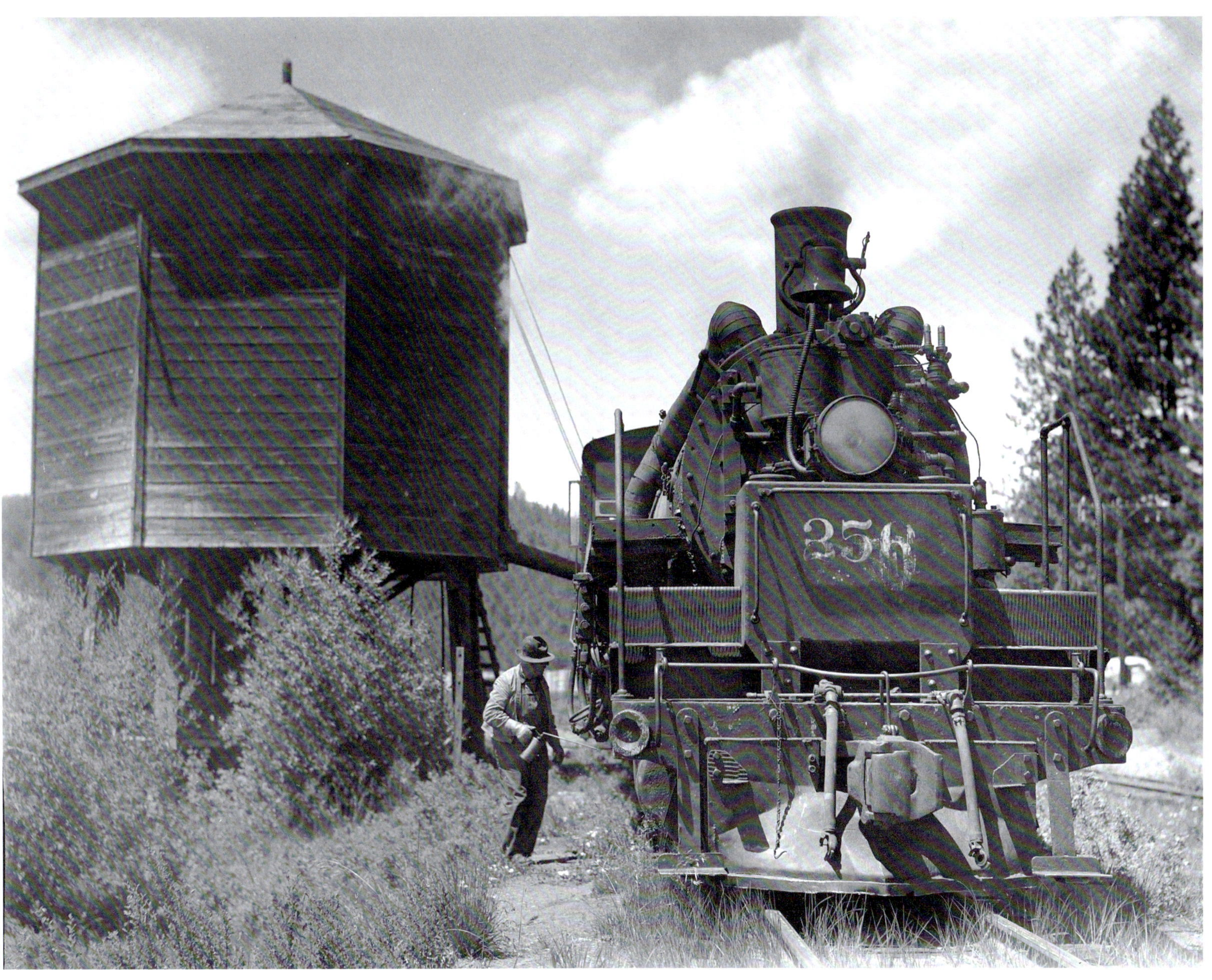

Plate 69. Crew member servicing a locomotive at a water stop on the Sumpter Valley Railway. Lucius Beebe. Beebe-Clegg negative 2052.

Courtesy of the California State Railroad Museum.

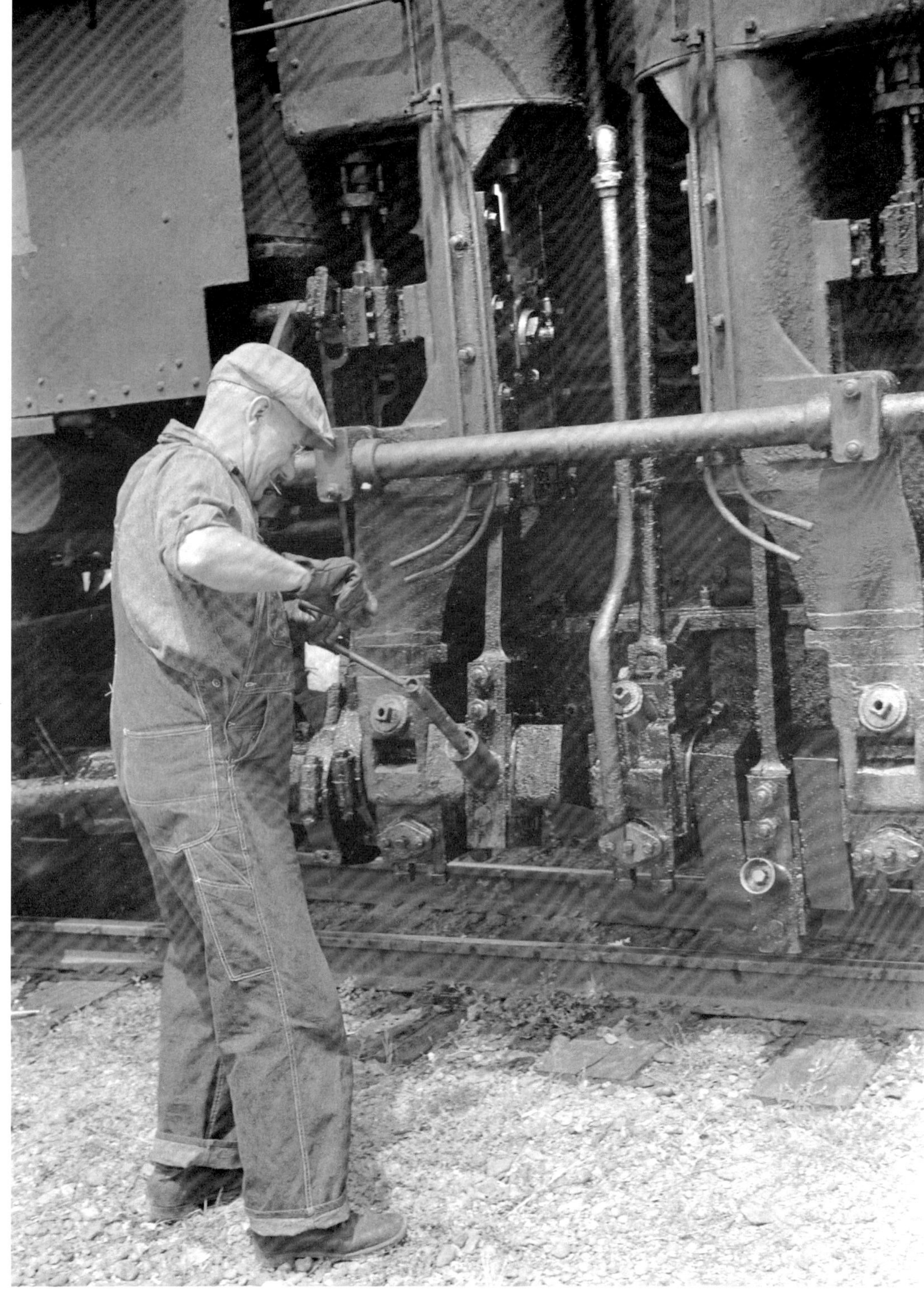

Plate 70. Crew member oiling a Camino, Placerville & Lake Tahoe Railroad "Shay" geared steam locomotive. Charles Clegg. Beebe-Clegg negative 1331.

Courtesy of the California State Railroad Museum.

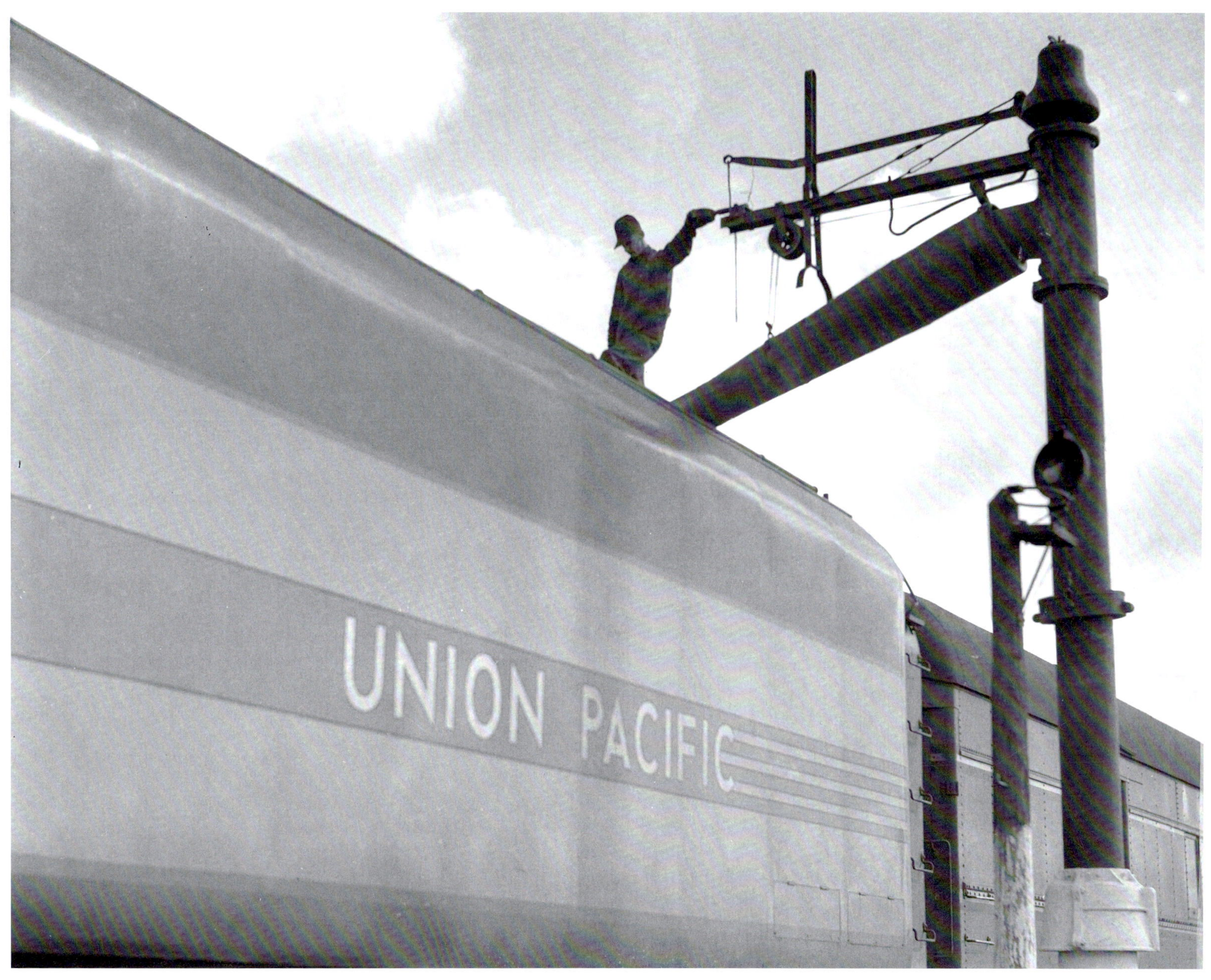

Plate 71. A Union Pacific fireman taking on water. Lucius Beebe was a master of this classic view of the steam era; he repeated this type of image a number of times, usually with excellent results. He used this photograph in several of his books. Lucius Beebe. Beebe-Clegg negative 809.

Courtesy of the California State Railroad Museum.

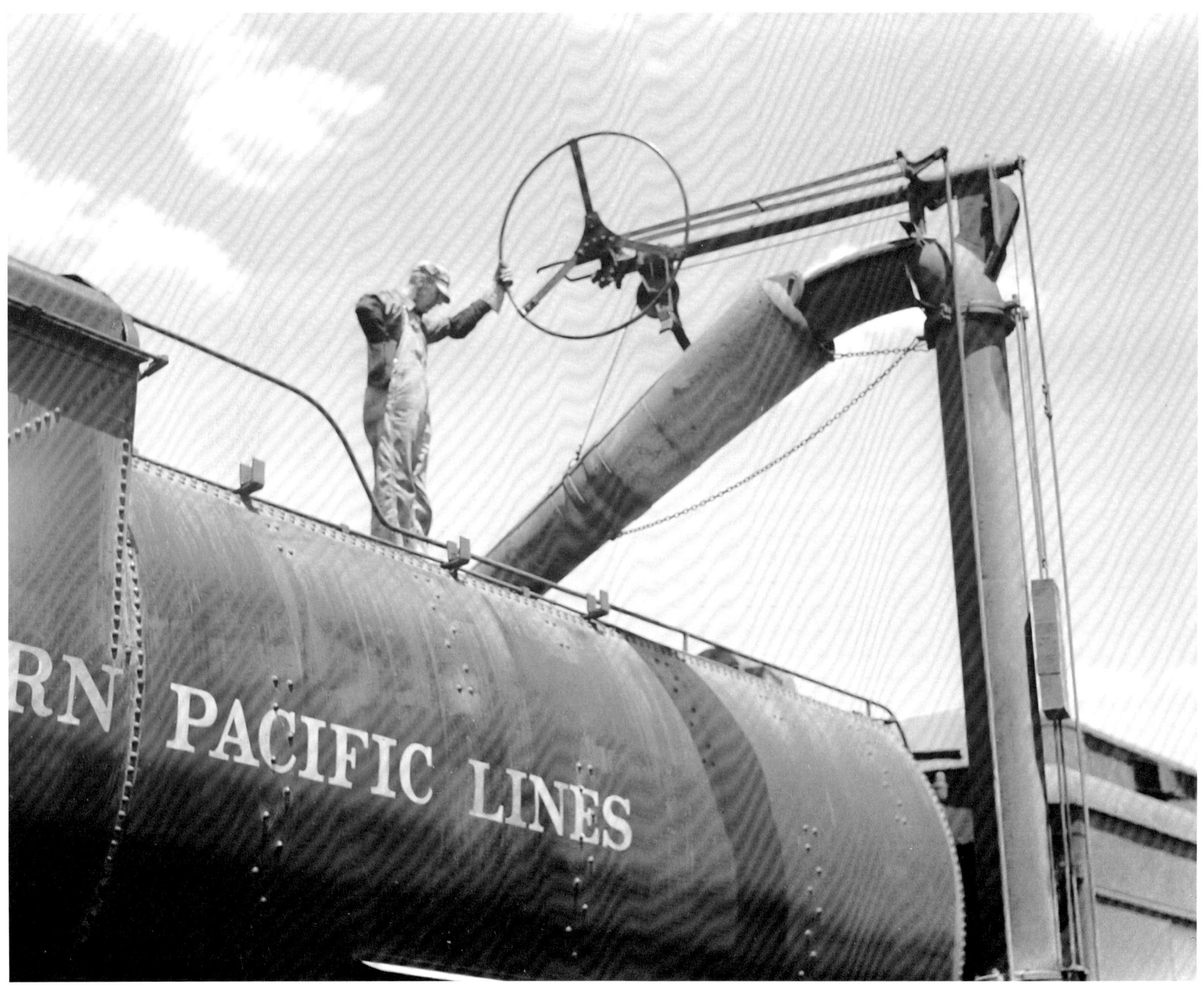

Plate 72. A Southern Pacific fireman. This photograph opened the introduction to *Trains in Transition*. Lucius Beebe. Beebe-Clegg negative 3792.

Courtesy of the California State Railroad Museum.

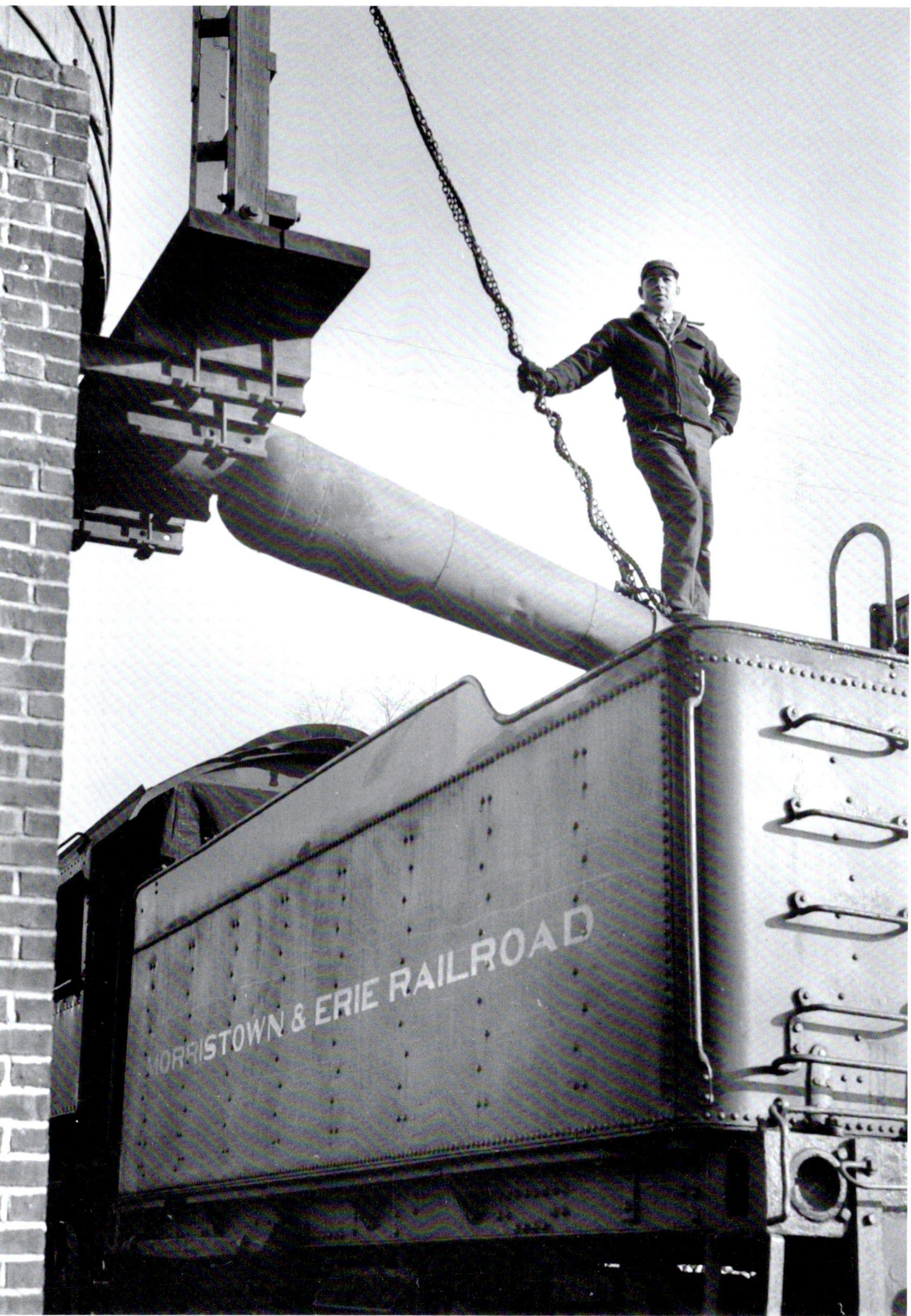

Plate 73. Watering up a steam locomotive on the Morristown & Erie Railway, Whippany, New Jersey. This water tank still stands today. Lucius Beebe or Charles Clegg. Beebe-Clegg negative 2849.

Courtesy of the California State Railroad Museum.

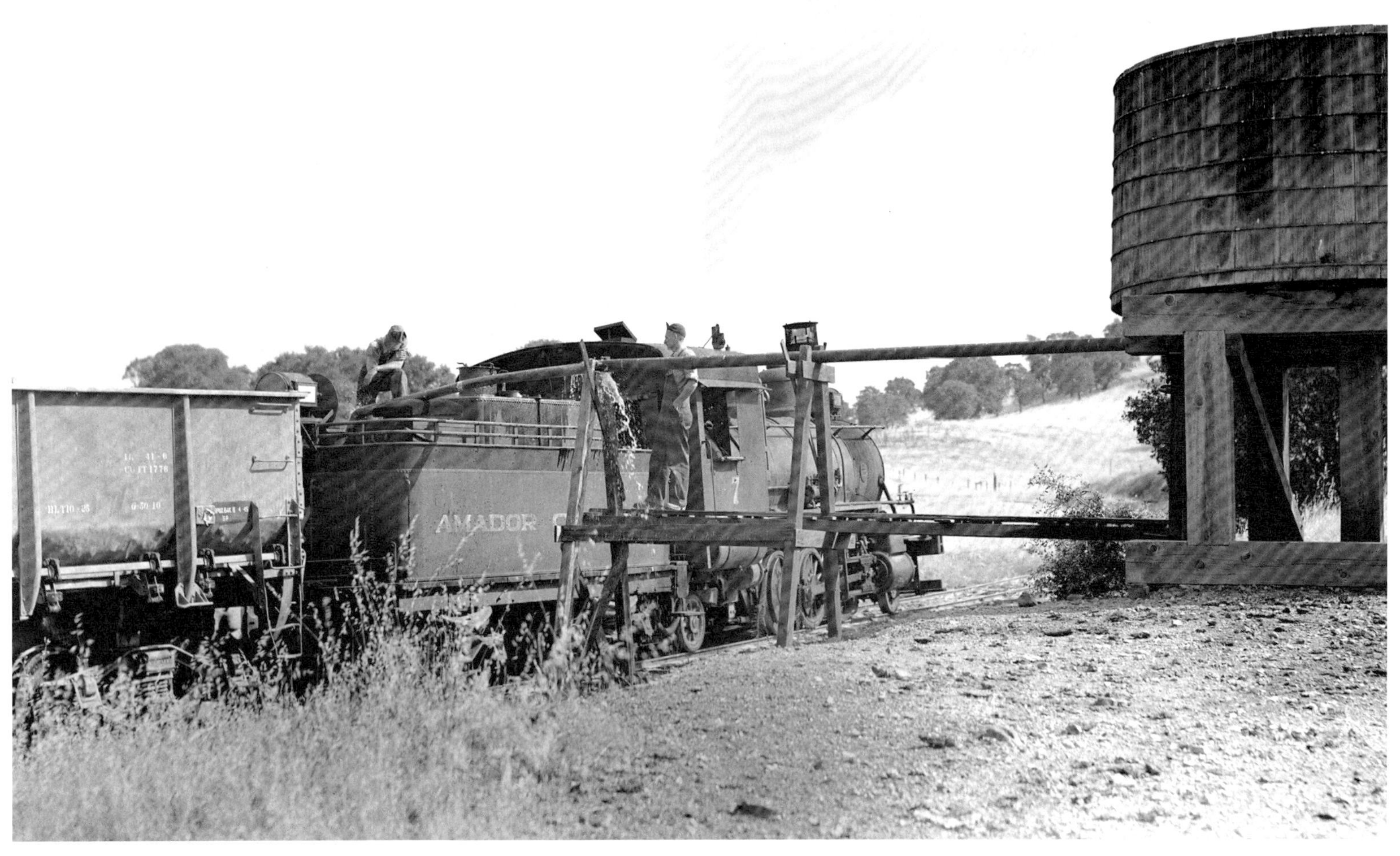

Plate 74. Watering up on the Amador Central. Lucius Beebe or Charles Clegg, probably Charles Clegg, as a similar photo by Clegg appears in *Mixed Train Daily*. Beebe-Clegg negative 2813.

Courtesy of the California State Railroad Museum.

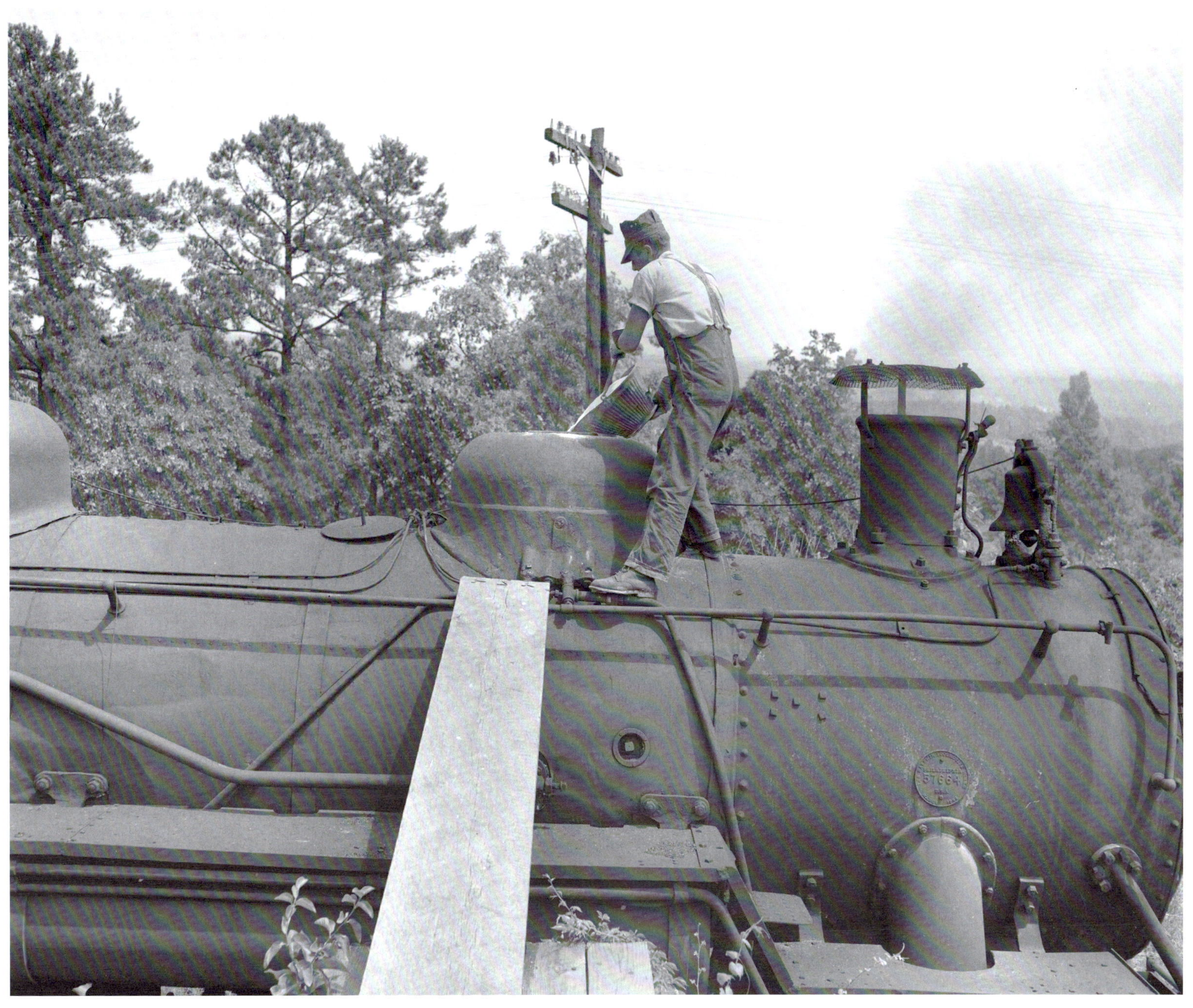

Plate 75. Filling a sand dome by hand on the Gainesville Midland Railroad, locomotive No. 207. Lucius Beebe. Beebe-Clegg negative 3562.

Courtesy of the California State Railroad Museum.

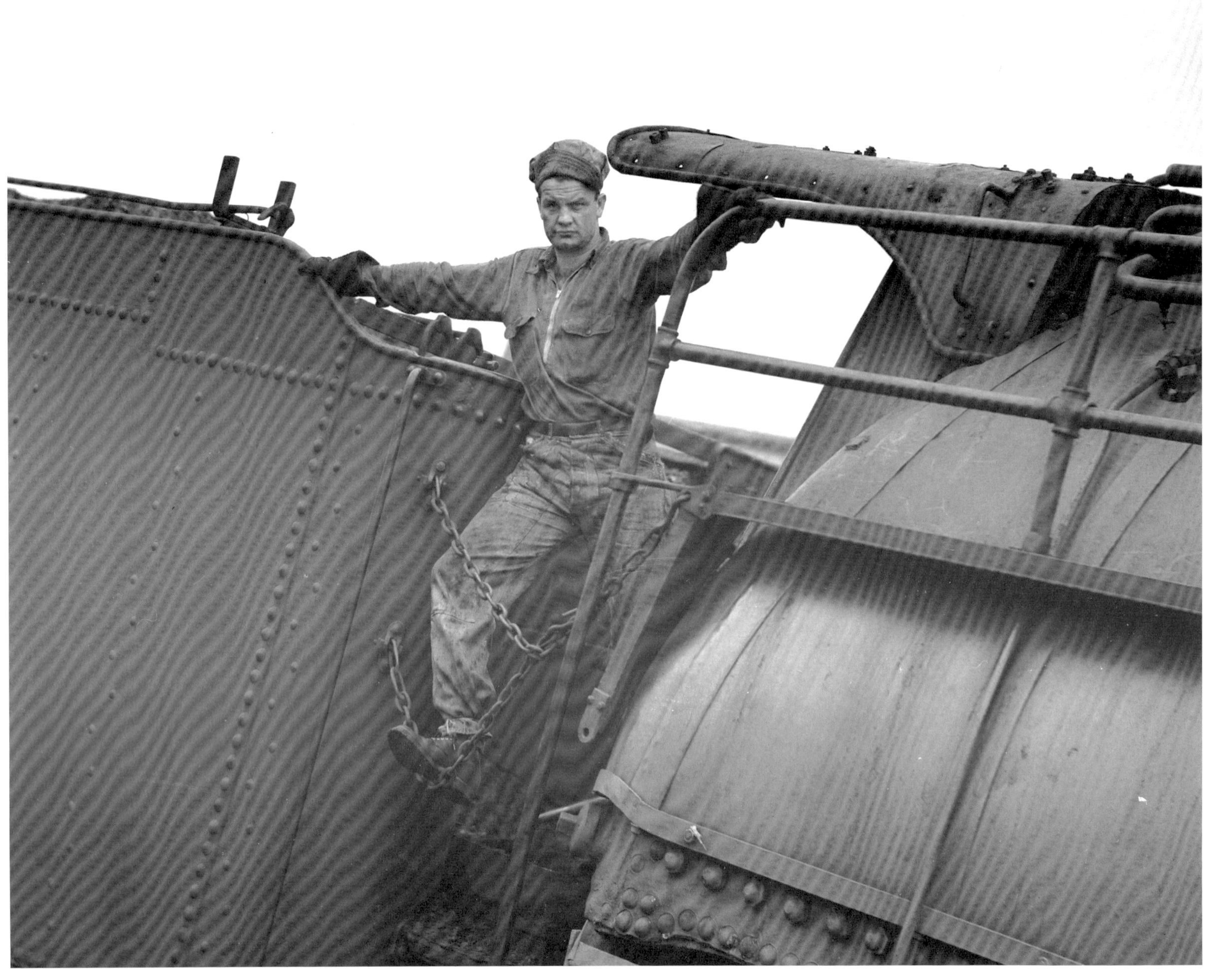

Plate 76. Another classic Beebe railroader image, a fireman in the rear cab of a Central Railroad of New Jersey camelback locomotive. Lucius Beebe. Beebe-Clegg negative 2536.

Courtesy of the California State Railroad Museum.

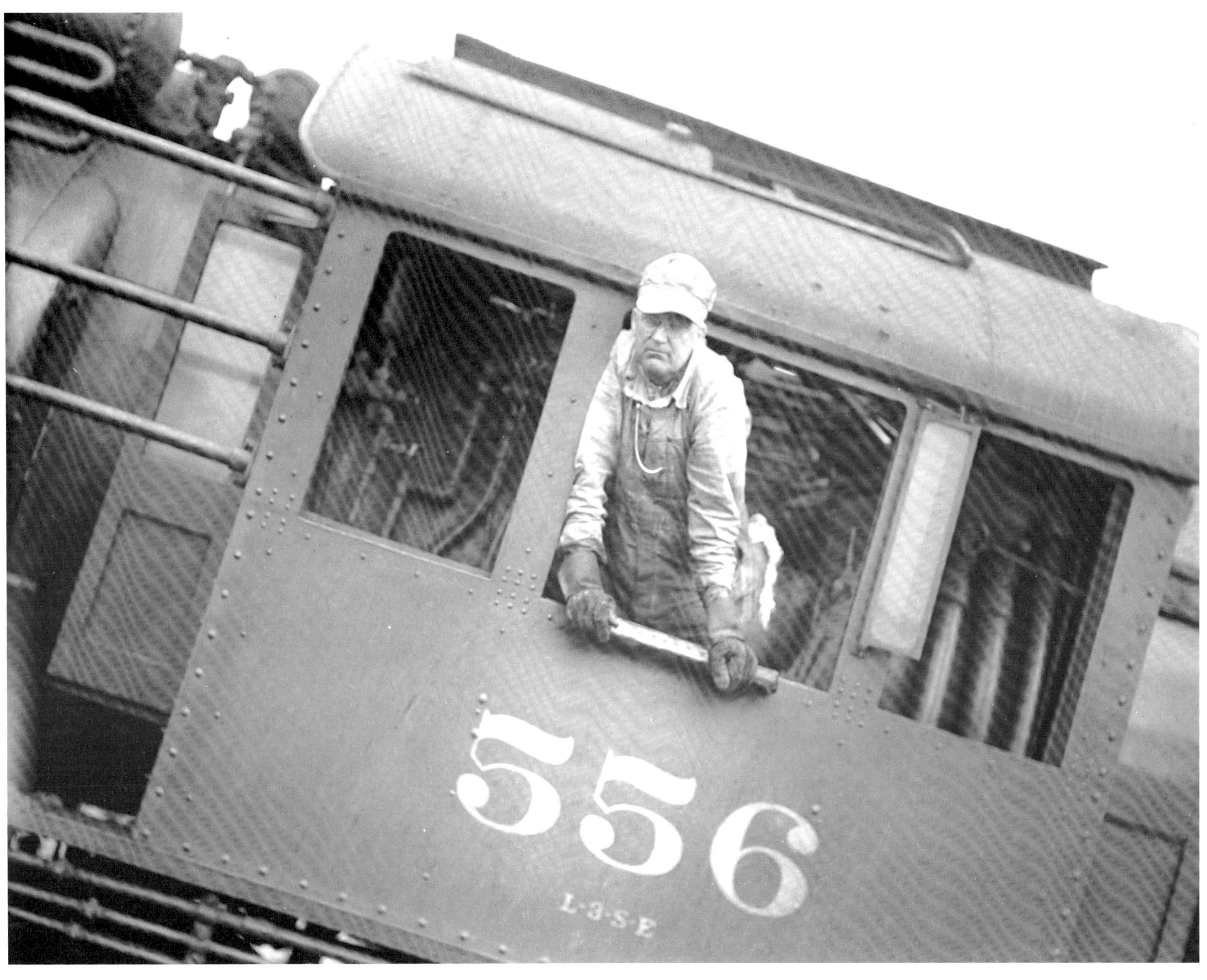

Plate 77. The engineer of Reading steam locomotive No. 556, a camelback, watches the photographer. Lucius Beebe or Charles Clegg, probably Lucius Beebe. Beebe-Clegg negative 2584.

Courtesy of the California State Railroad Museum.

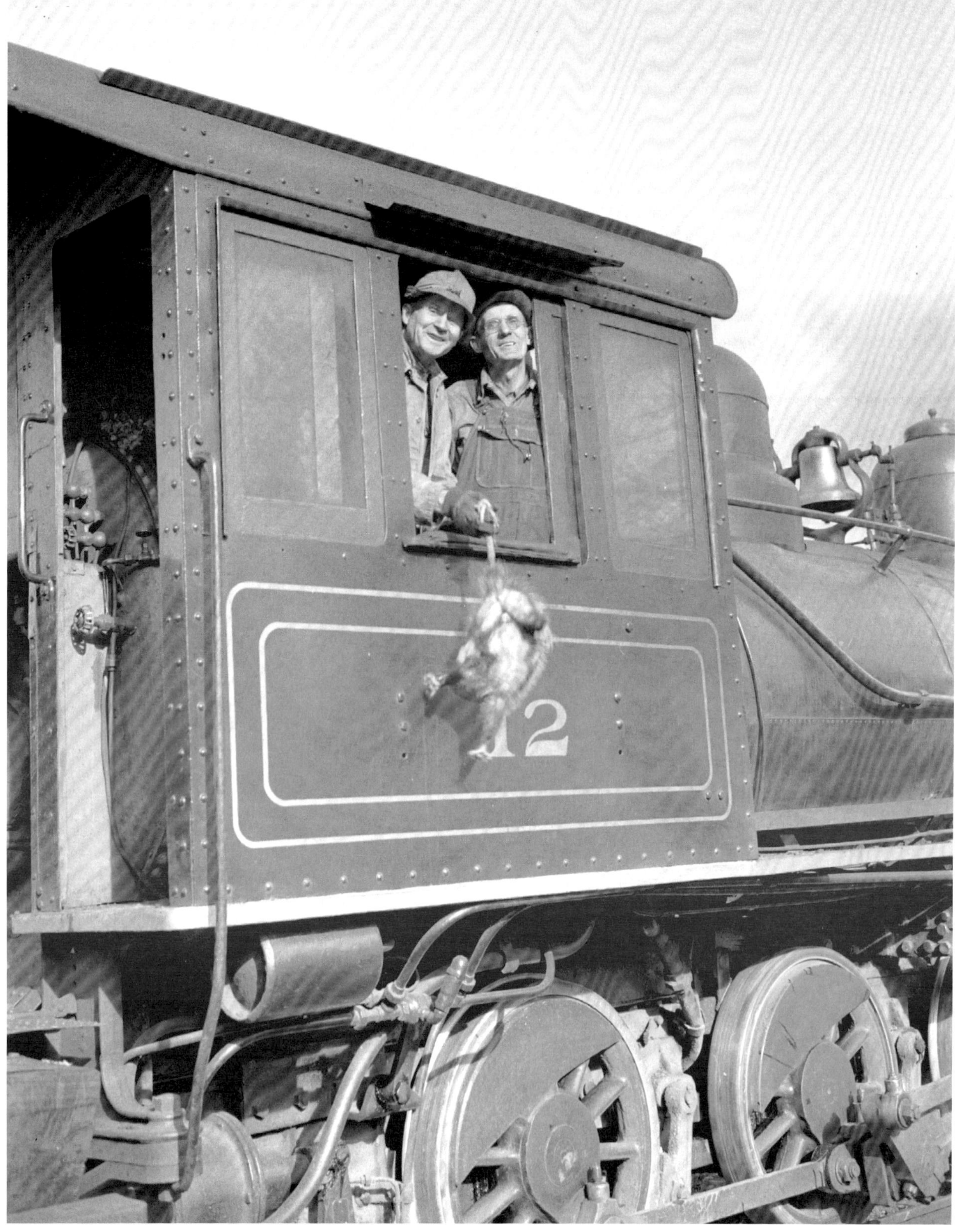

Plate 78. The engine crew of East Tennessee & Western North Carolina No. 12, a locomotive now at Tweetsie Railroad in Blowing Rock, North Carolina, shows off the possum they caught. Lucius Beebe or Charles Clegg; this photo is probably by Charles Clegg, as a similar photo by Clegg appears in *Mixed Train Daily*. Beebe-Clegg negative 2748.

Courtesy of the California State Railroad Museum.

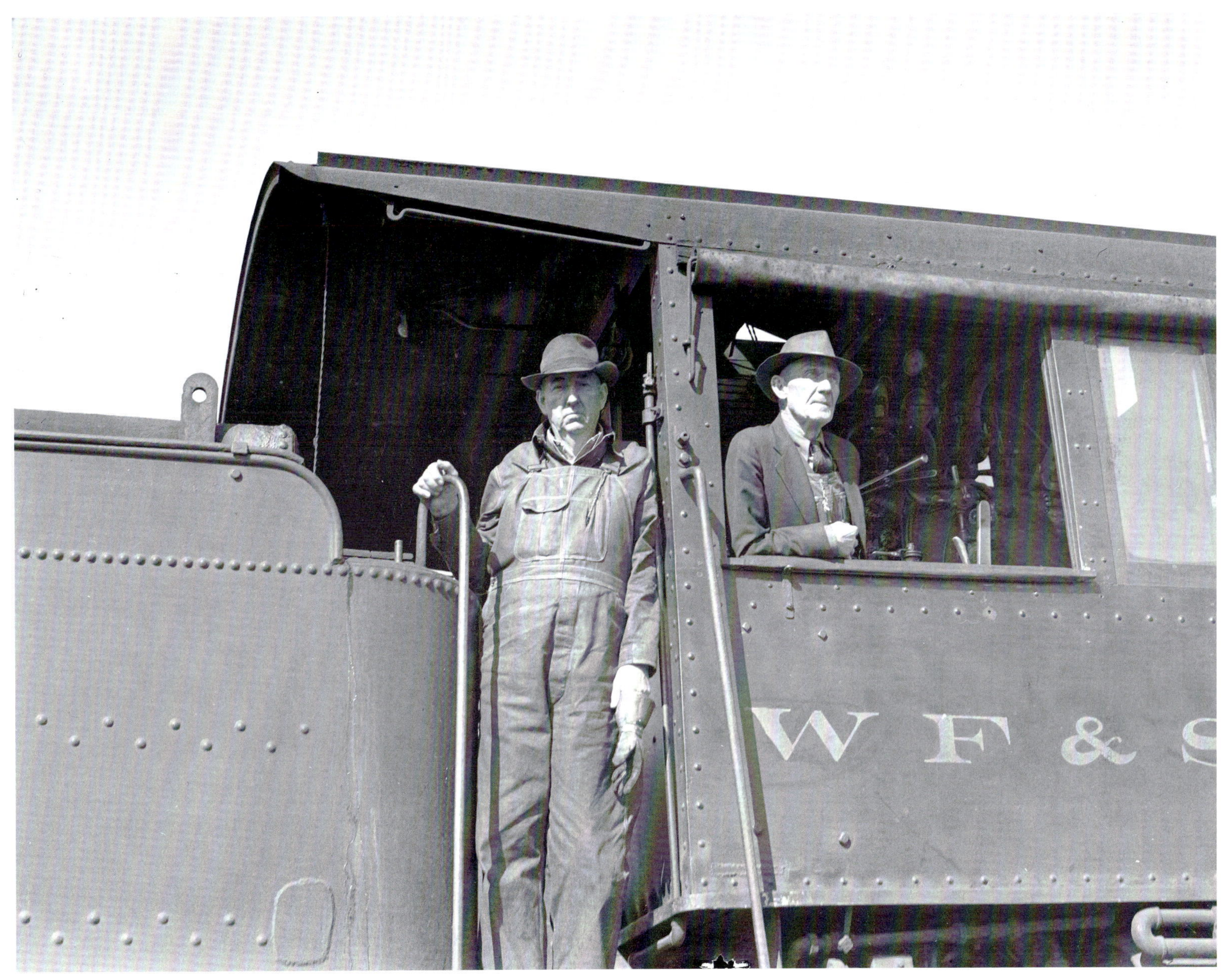

Plate 79. The dour, elderly crew of a Wichita Falls & Southern Railroad locomotive taken in 1944 or 1945. Lucius Beebe. Beebe-Clegg negative 797.

Courtesy of the California State Railroad Museum.

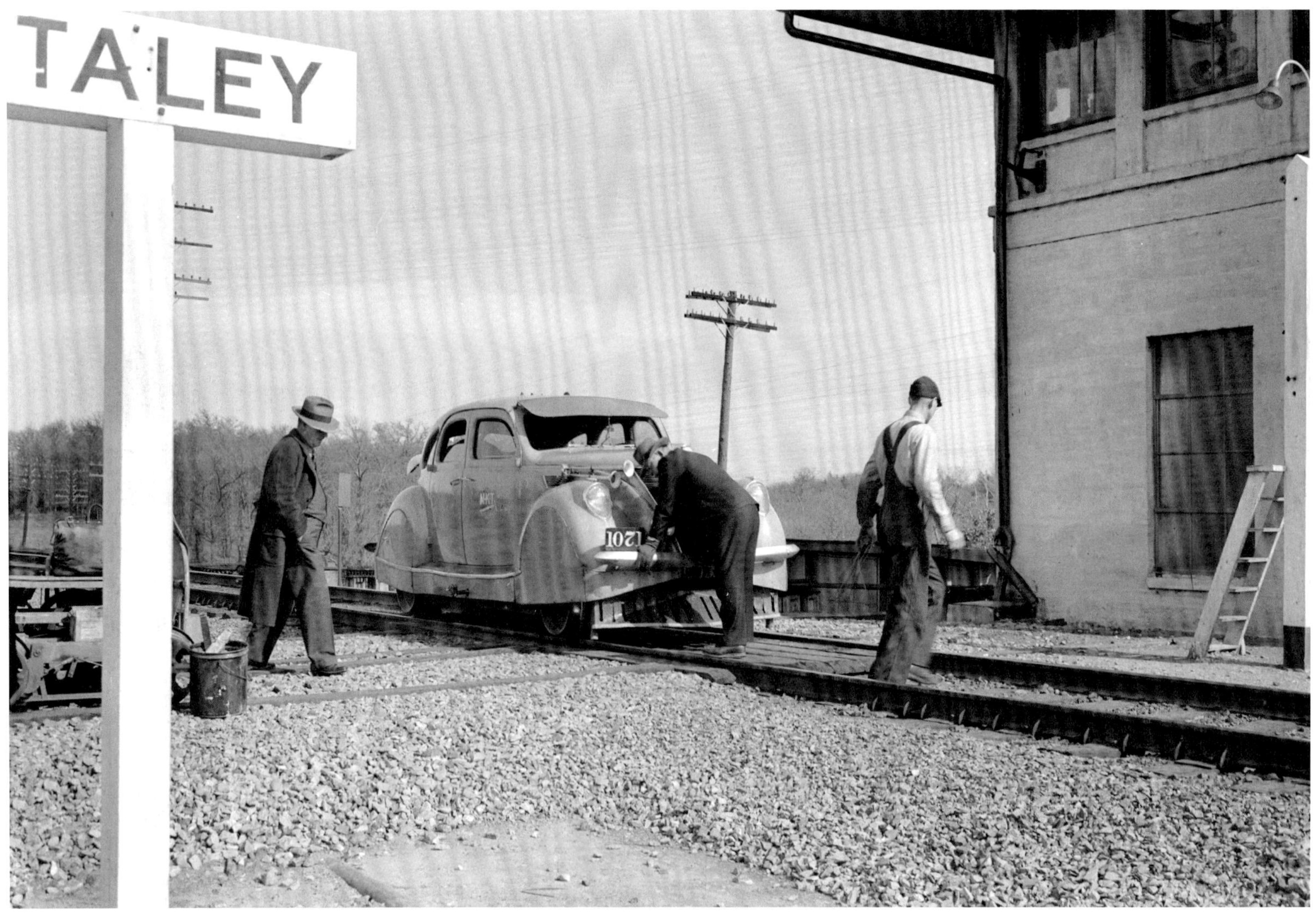

Plate 80. A "Katy" (M-K-T, or Missouri-Kansas-Texas Railroad) inspection car, at Staley Tower in Oklahoma, near Denison, Texas. Lucius Beebe or Charles Clegg. Beebe-Clegg negative 2885.

Courtesy of the California State Railroad Museum.

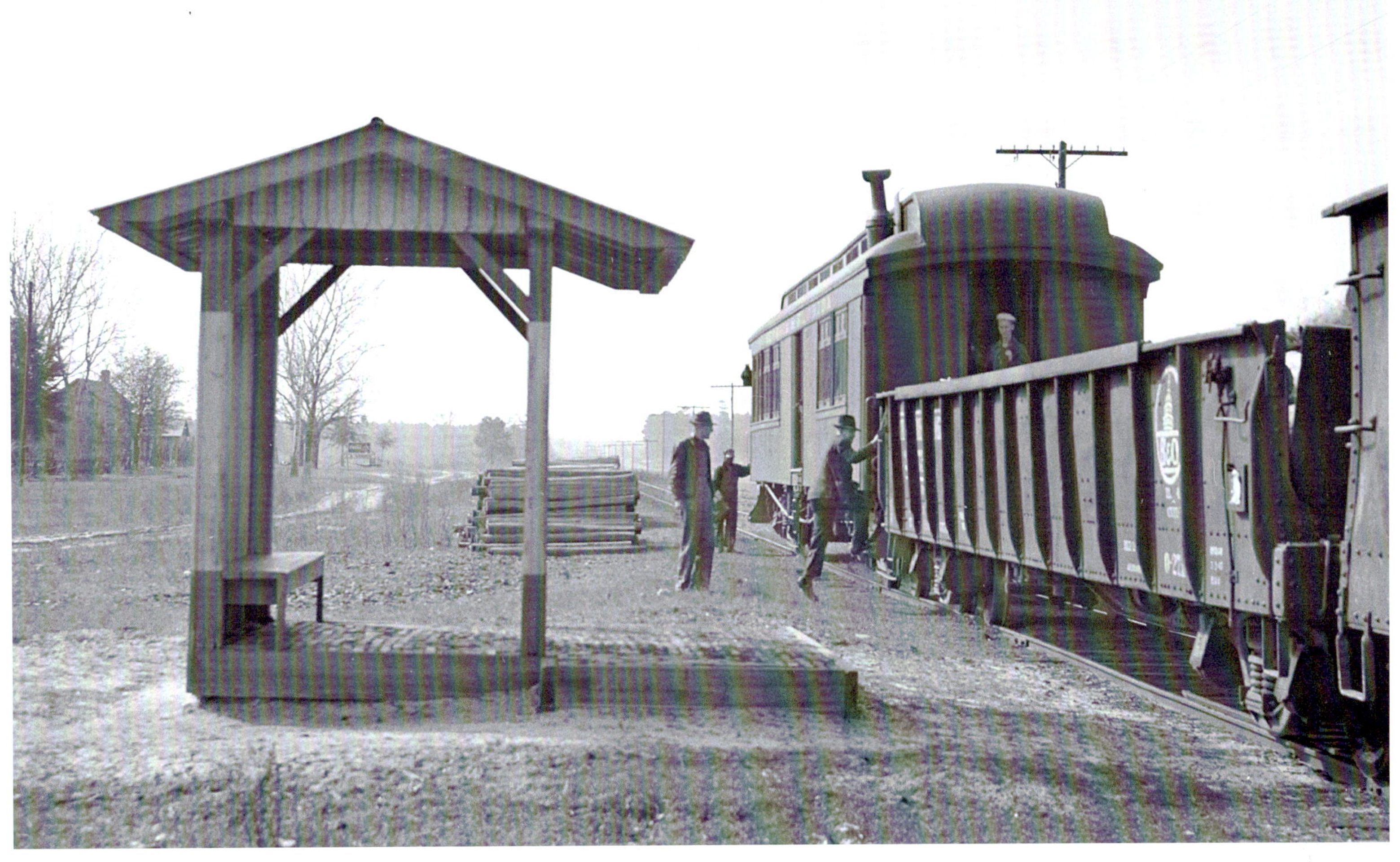

Plate 81. Folks board a Georgia & Florida mixed train as a crew member looks on from the rear. Note the Jim Crow coach, the unusual passenger shelter, and the person standing in the open coach door above the gondola car. Charles Clegg. Beebe-Clegg negative 2177.

Courtesy of the California State Railroad Museum.

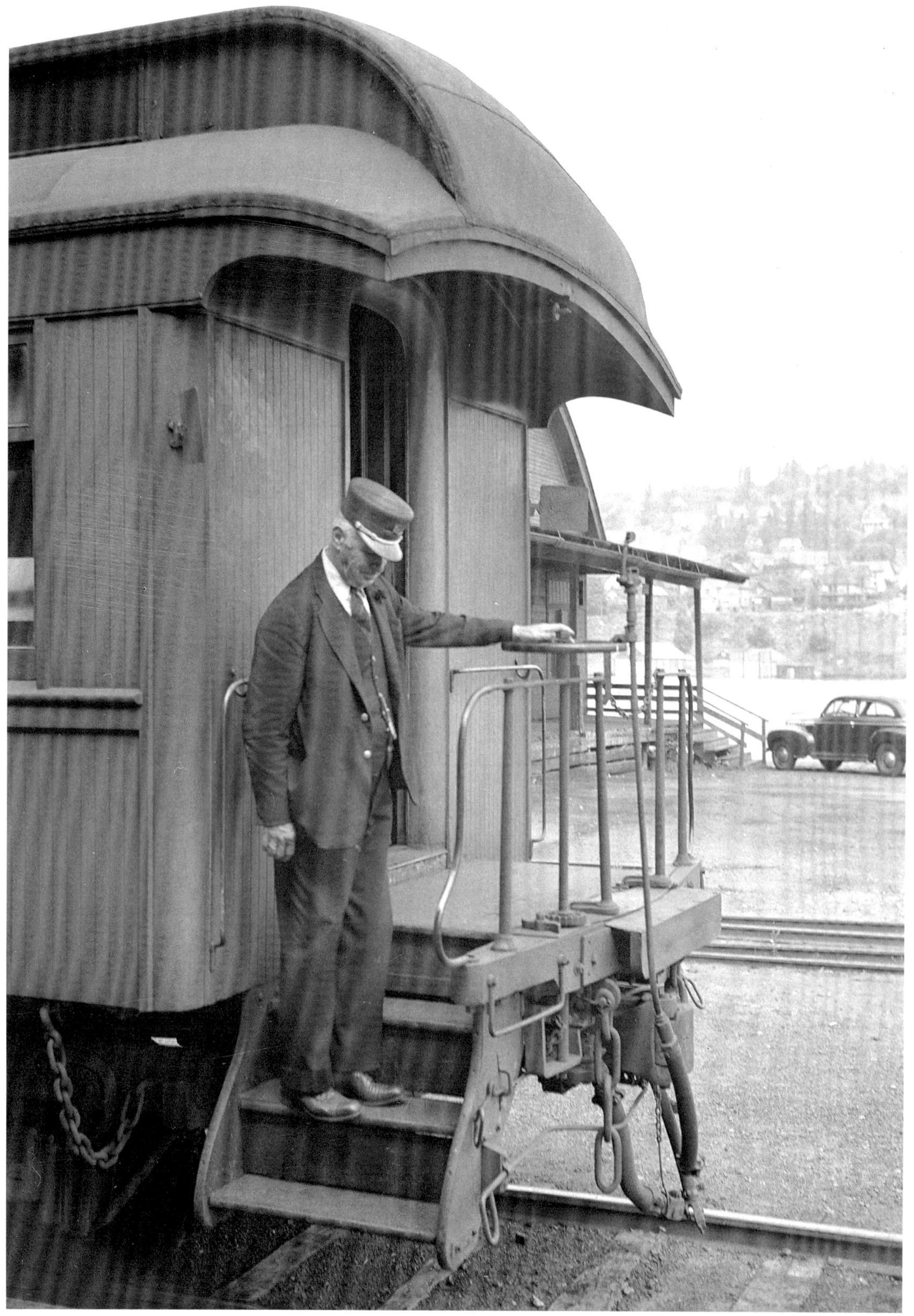

Plate 82. A uniformed Copper Range Railroad train crew member, probably the conductor, stands on the steps at the end of his train, his hand on the brake wheel, July 1946. Lucius Beebe or Charles Clegg. Beebe-Clegg negative 265.

Courtesy of the California State Railroad Museum.

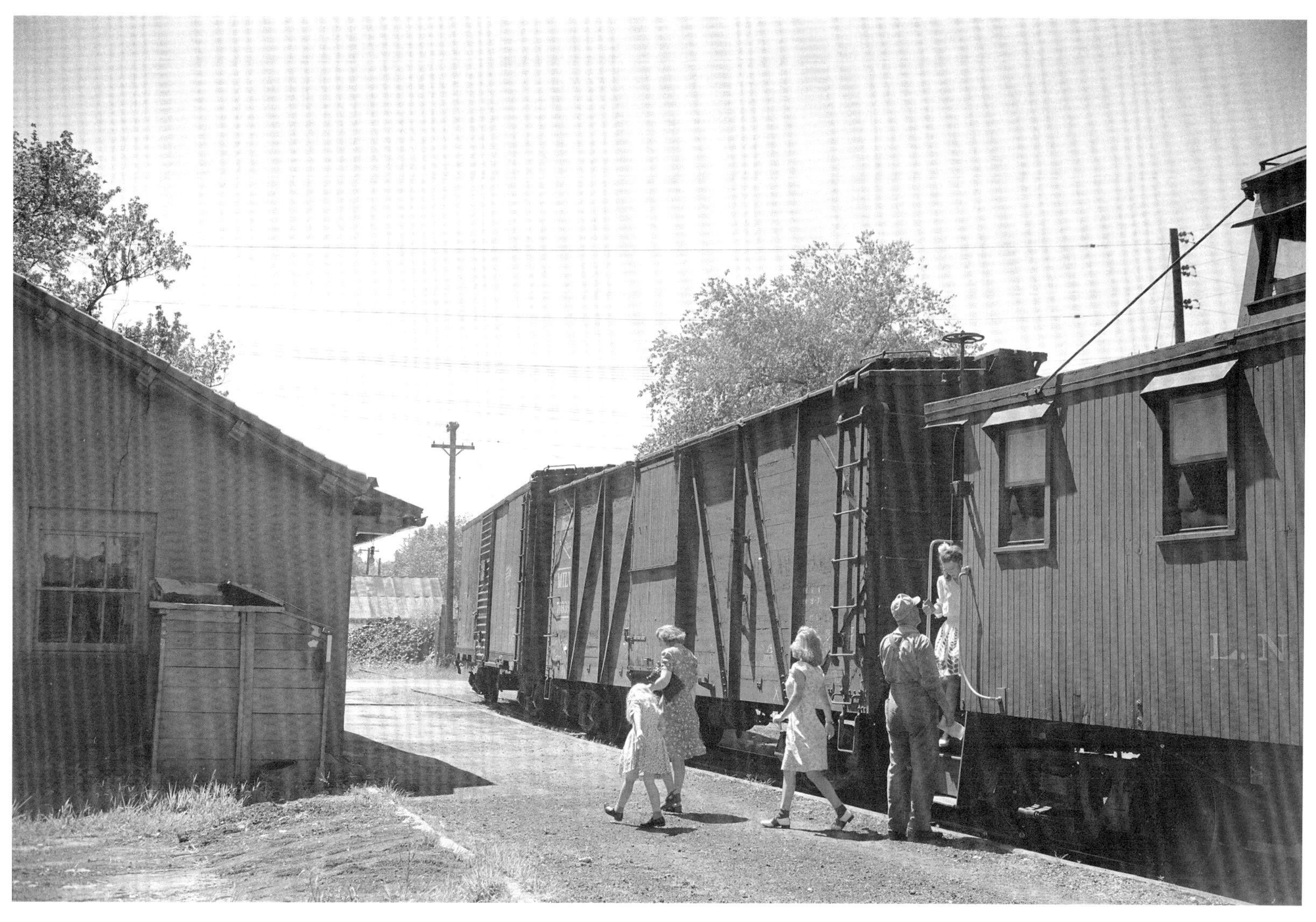

Plate 83. A crew member, probably the conductor, assists as passengers leave the caboose, which served as passenger accommodations on the Louisville, New Albany & Corydon Railroad, The location is Corydon, Indiana. Charles Clegg. Beebe-Clegg negative 2797.

Courtesy of the California State Railroad Museum.

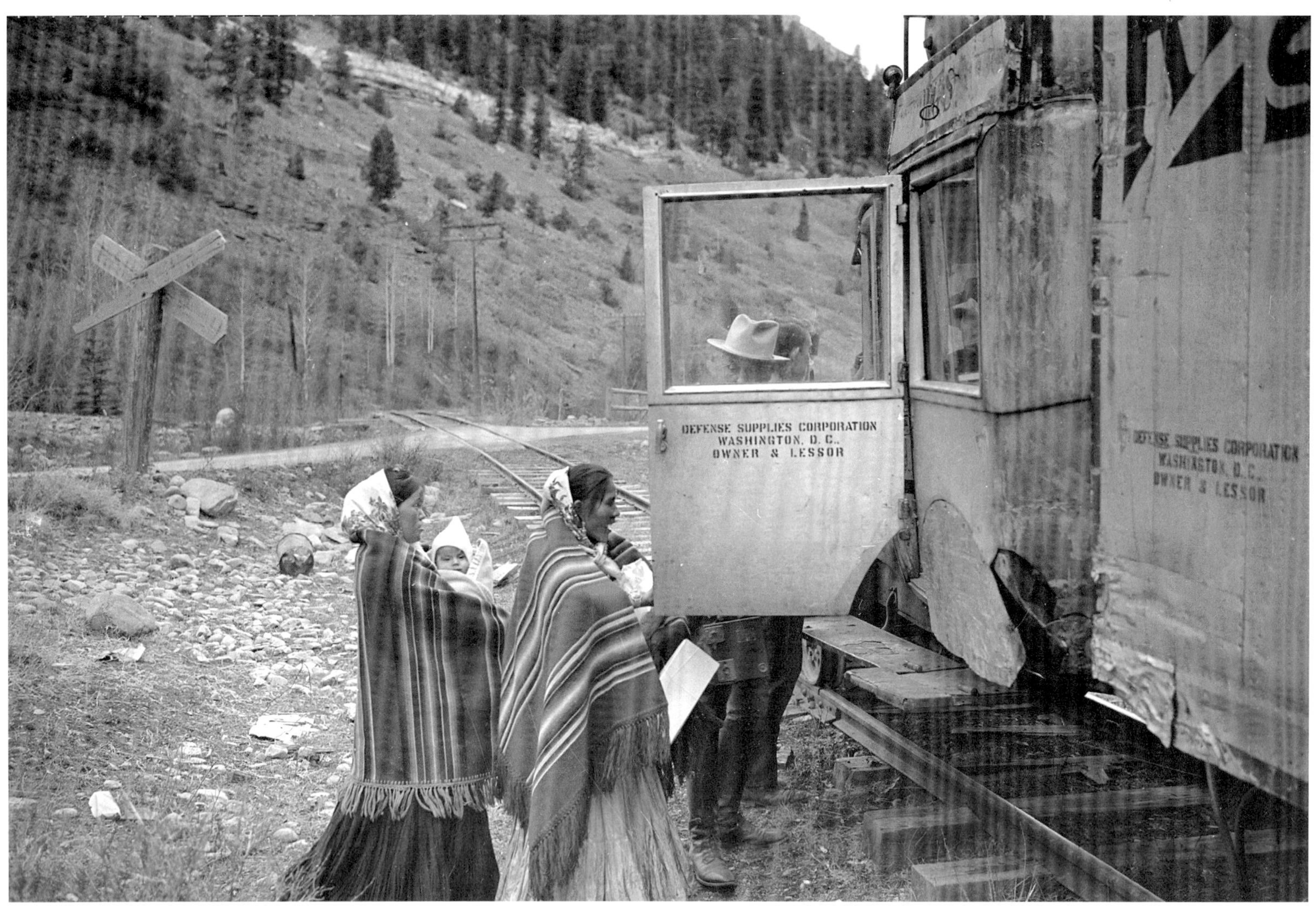

Plate 84. "Three and a Half Fares for the Goose," Rico, Colorado. Charles Clegg. Beebe-Clegg negative 3322.

Courtesy of the California State Railroad Museum.

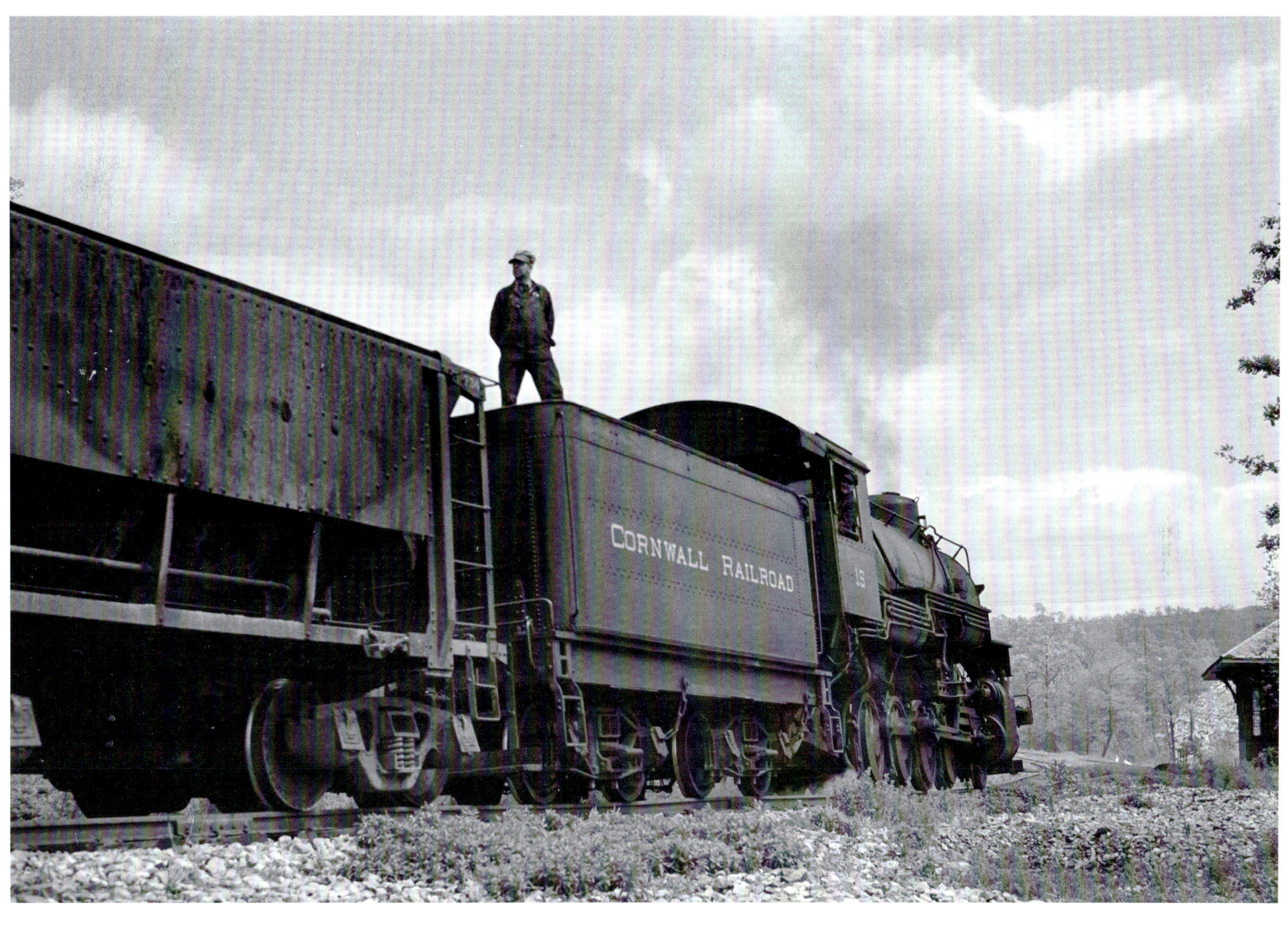

Plate 85. A crew member, probably a head-end brakeman, rides the tender on the Cornwall Railroad. Charles Clegg. Beebe-Clegg negative 3782.

Courtesy of the California State Railroad Museum.

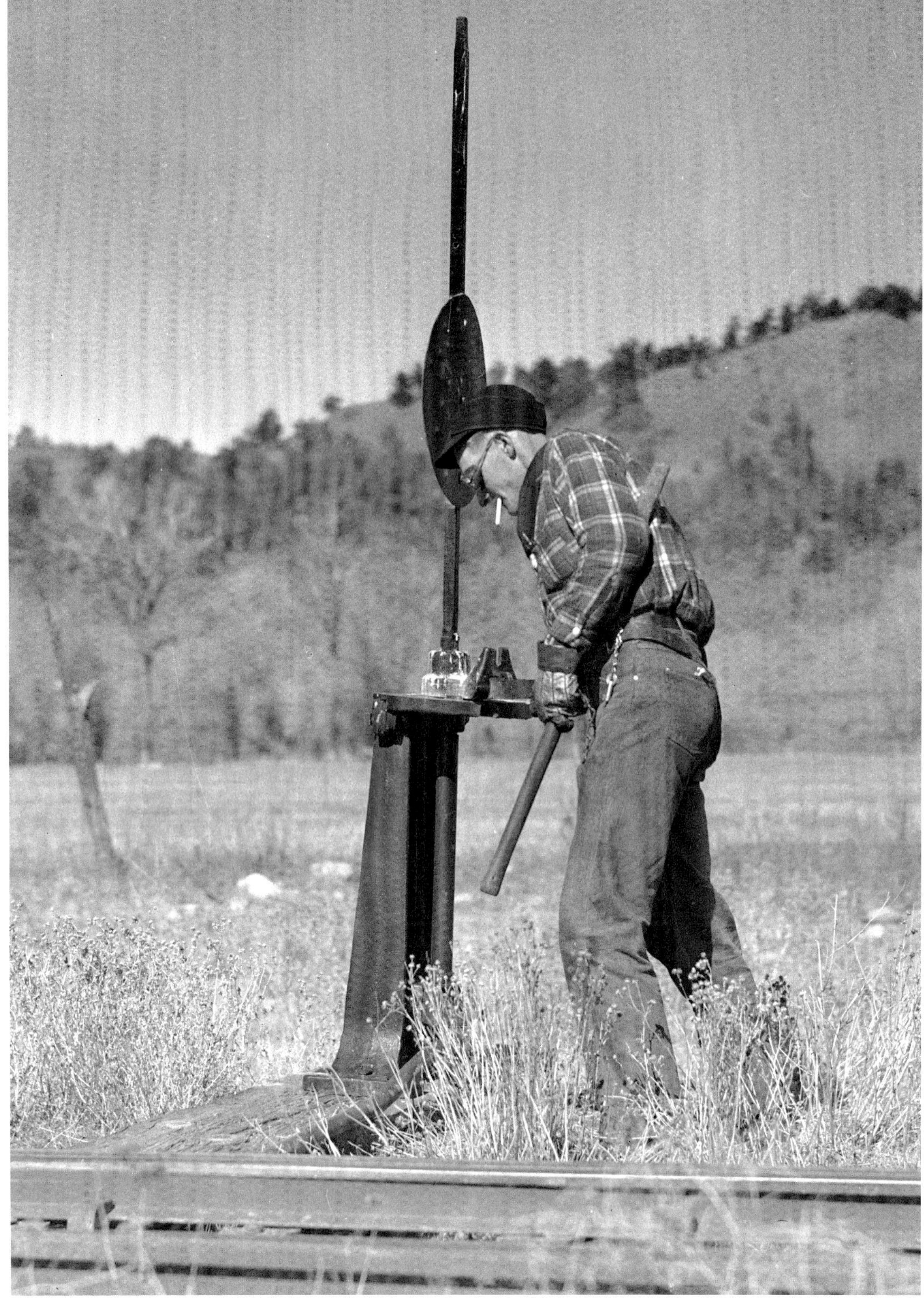

Plate 86. A Rio Grande Southern head-end freight brakeman at Mancos, Colorado. Note the goggles, brake club, gloves, switch key hanging from a heavy belt, "thousand-mile shirt," jeans, and hat. Beebe captured, even created, the visual archetype of a steam-era American brakeman. Lucius Beebe. Beebe-Clegg negative 3207.

Courtesy of the California State Railroad Museum.

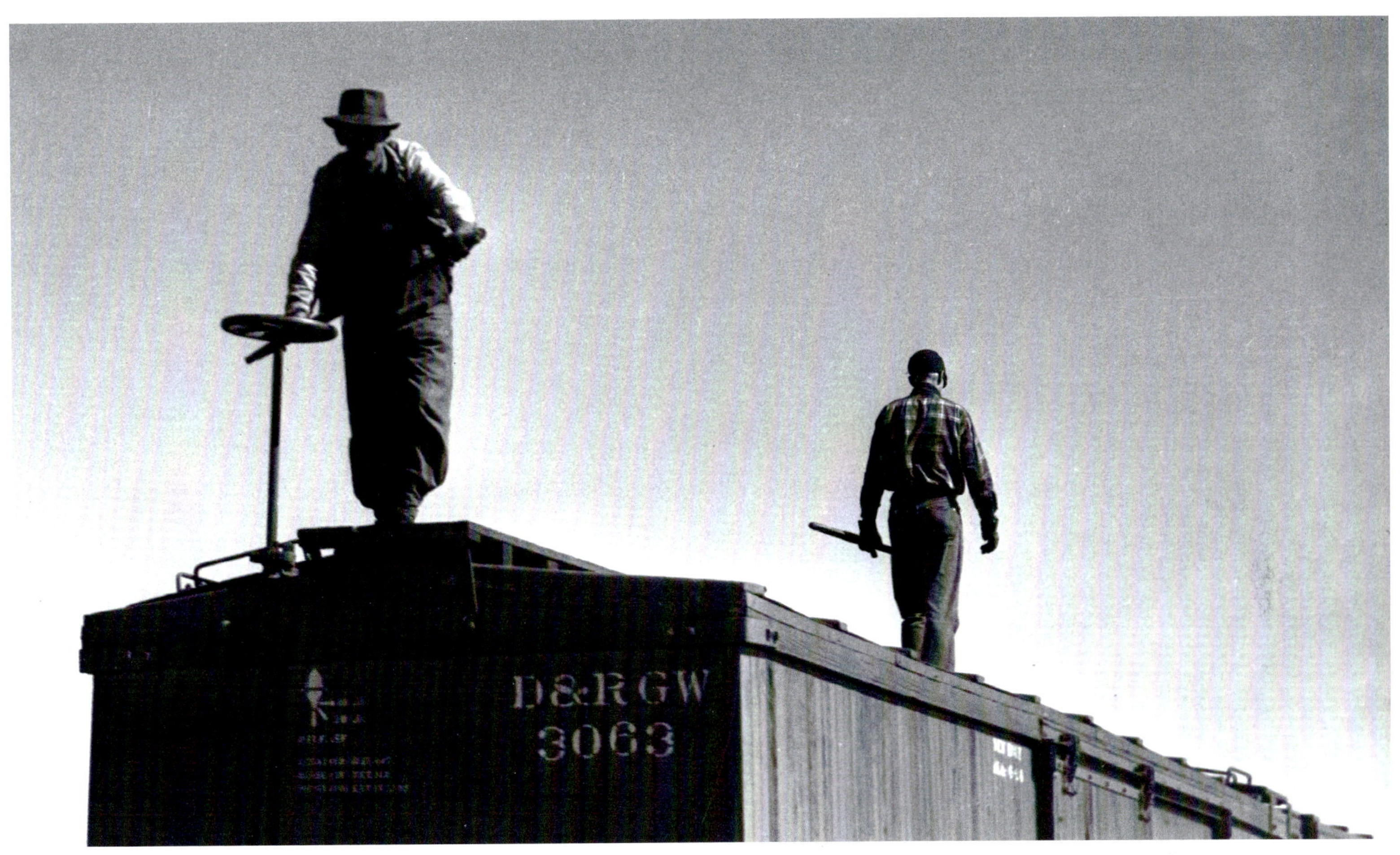

Plate 87. Two crew members decorate the car tops of a Rio Grande Southern freight. The freight car is a Denver & Rio Grande Western narrow-gauge boxcar; note the high brake wheel. The man farthest from the photographer appears to be the same brakeman featured in plate 86. Lucius Beebe or Charles Clegg, Beebe-Clegg negative 3264.

Courtesy of the California State Railroad Museum.

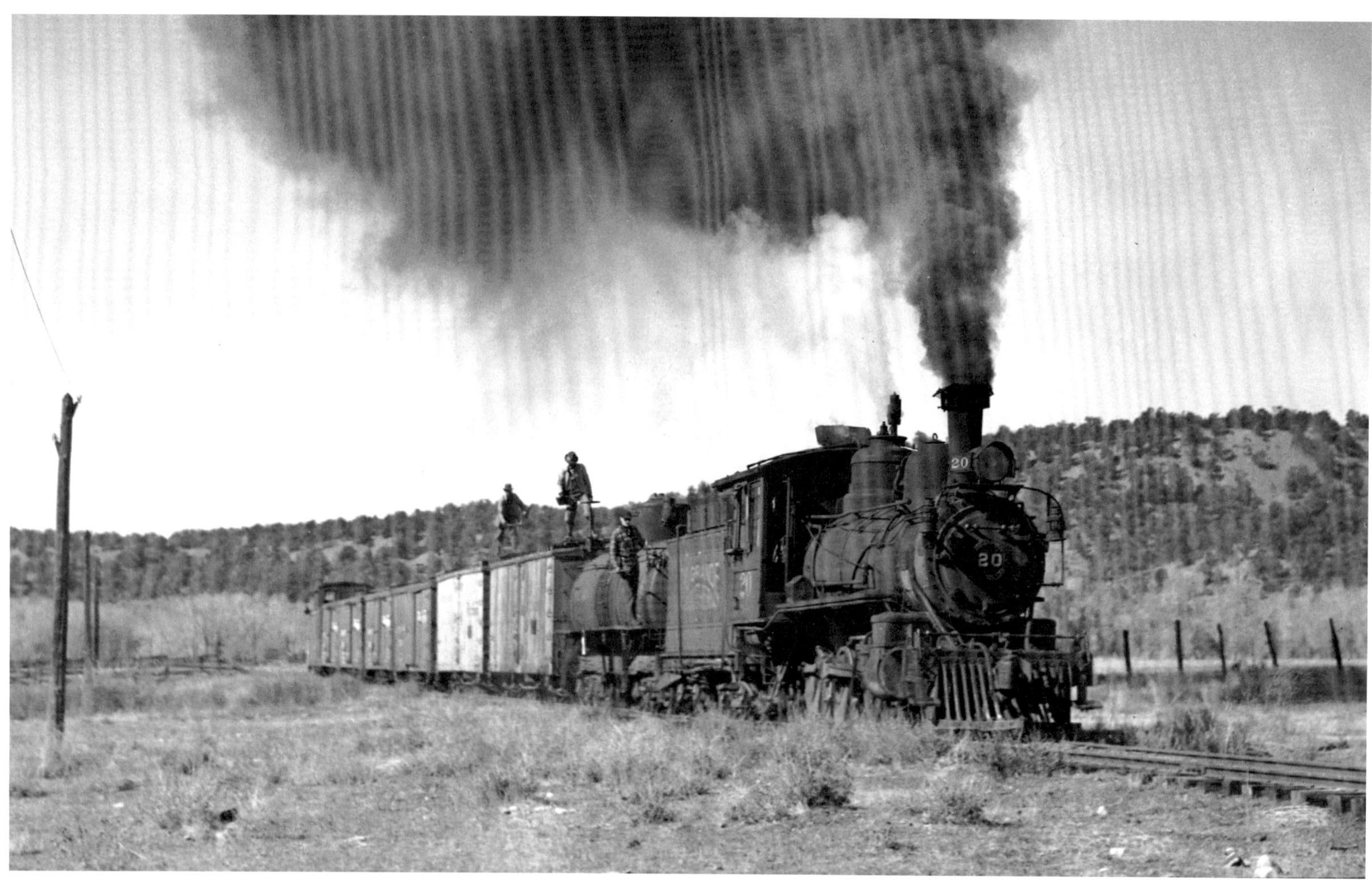

Plate 88. Rio Grande Southern No. 20, today a survivor of the narrow-gauge era based at the Colorado Railroad Museum, leads a Rio Grande Southern freight at Mancos, Colorado. Note the three crew members decorating the cars and applying brakes. One of them appears to be the same brakeman featured in plates 86 and 87. Lucius Beebe or Charles Clegg. Beebe-Clegg negative 3053.

Courtesy of the California State Railroad Museum.

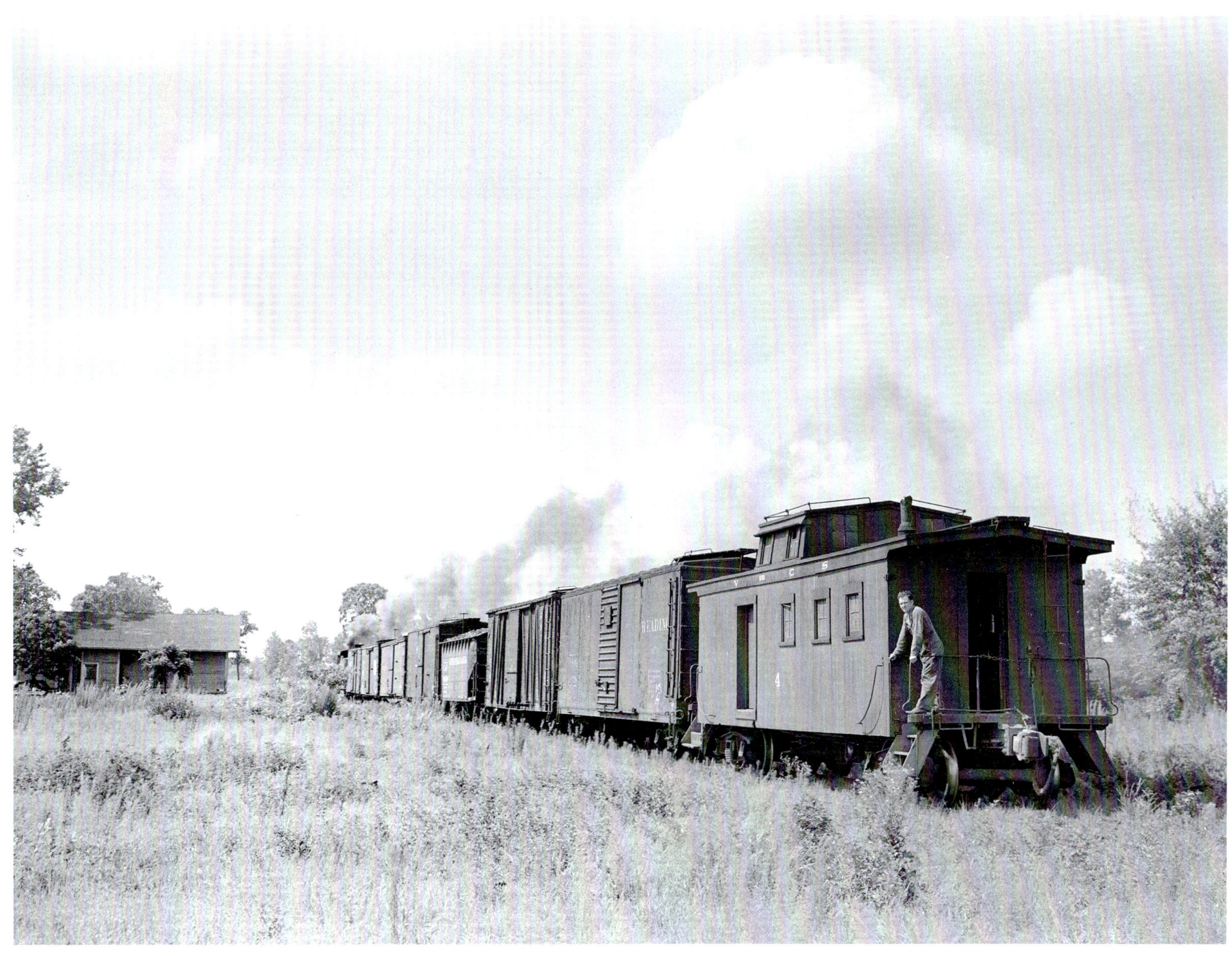

Plate 89. A Virginia & Carolina Southern Railroad freight wanders through the weed-choked landscape of the North Carolina coastal plain while a crewman watches the photographer from the caboose. Charles Clegg. Beebe-Clegg negative 629.

Courtesy of the California State Railroad Museum.

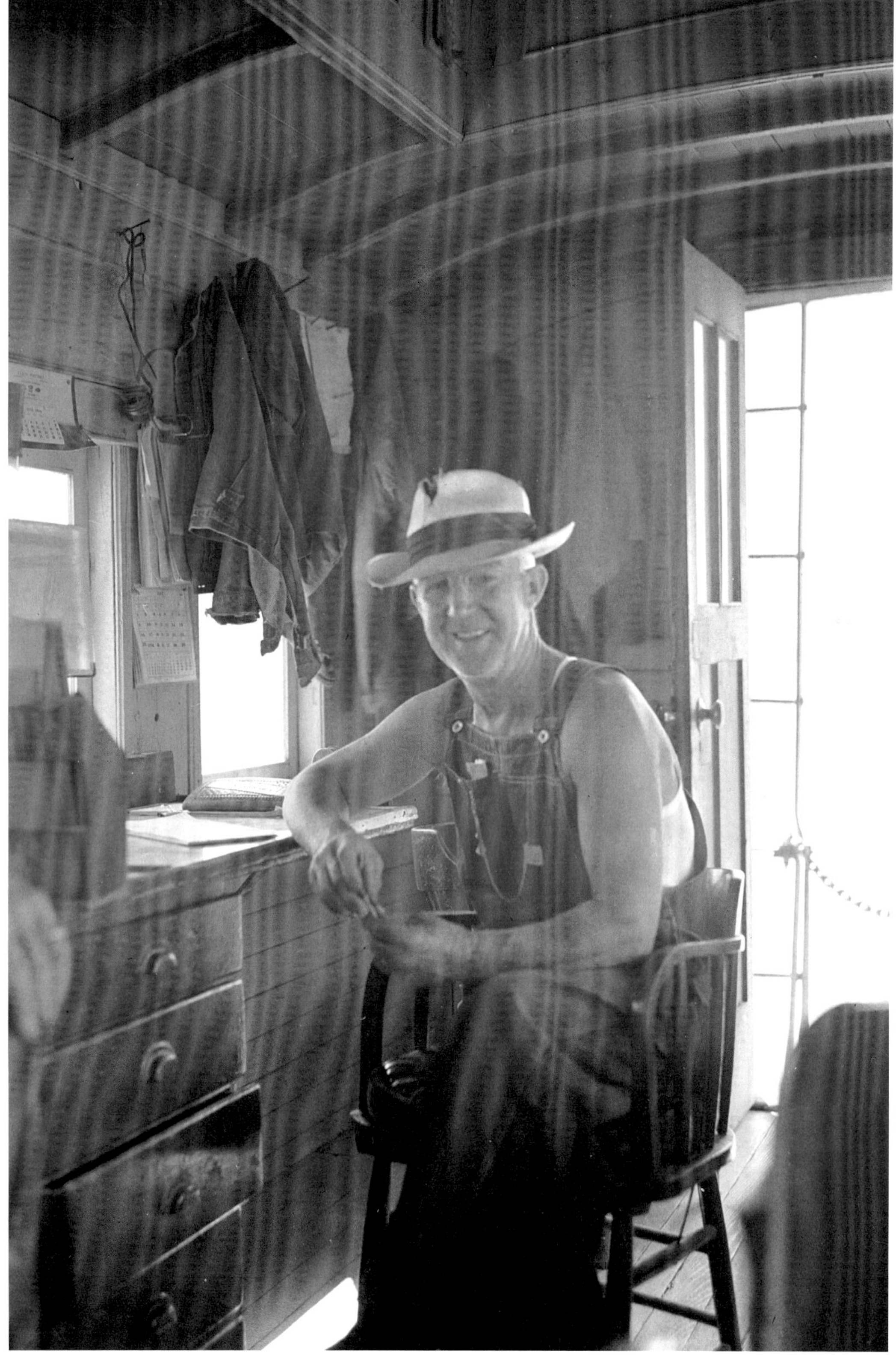

Plate 90. "Train Captain at Work." Charles Clegg's wonderful portrait of. J. A. Brennan, a conductor on the Southern Pacific's narrow-gage freight between Laws and Keeler, California. Brennan is shown at his desk in a former Carson & Colorado Railroad combine, which served as the train's caboose, filling out his daily wheel report. Charles Clegg. Beebe-Clegg negative 1196.

Courtesy of the California State Railroad Museum.

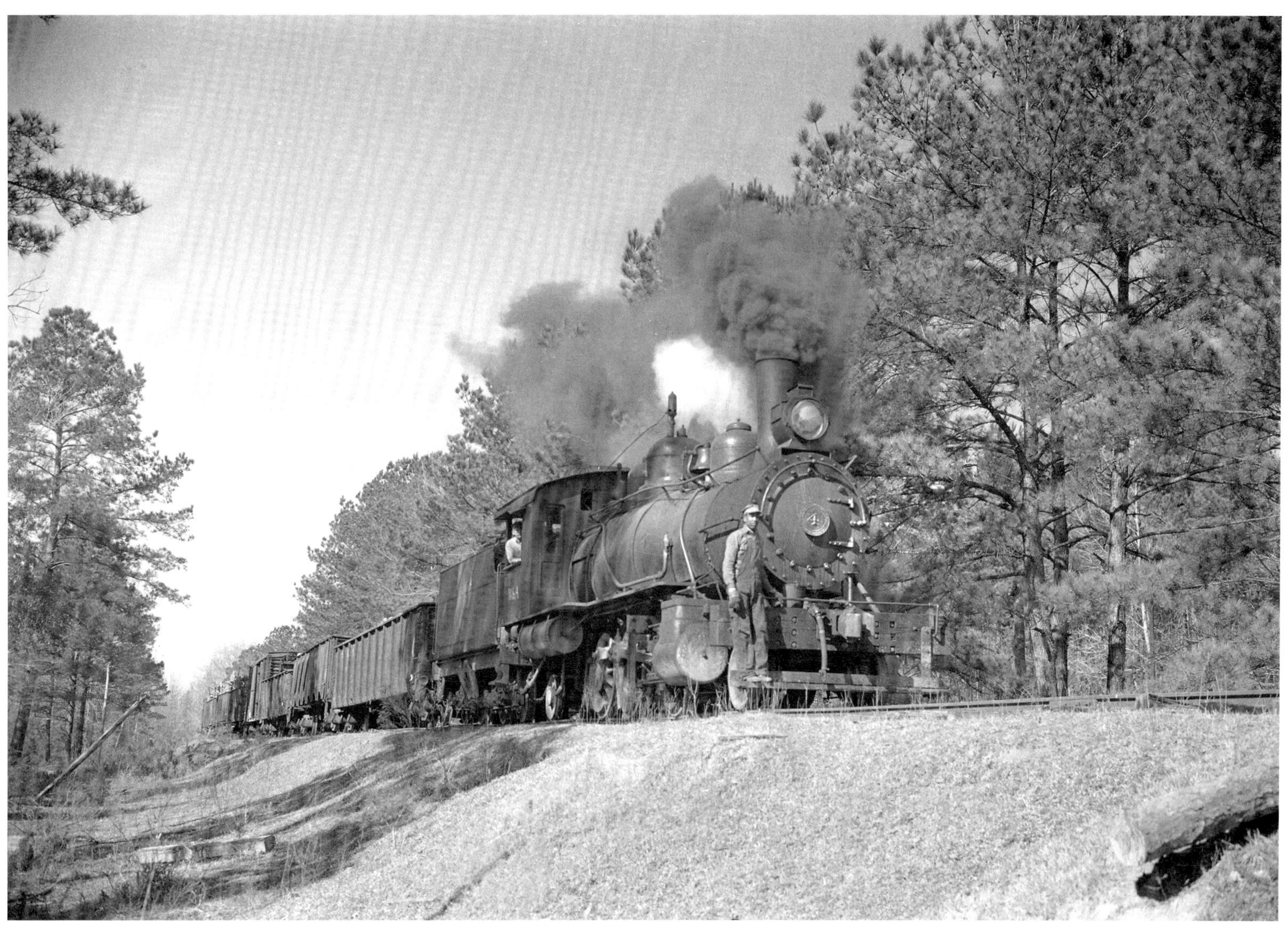

Plate 91. An African American brakeman rides the footboard of his train's locomotive, Mississippi & Alabama Railroad No. 4. The Mississippi & Alabama was noted for its very late use of wood as fuel for its steam engines. Charles Clegg. Beebe-Clegg negative 2354.

Courtesy of the California State Railroad Museum.

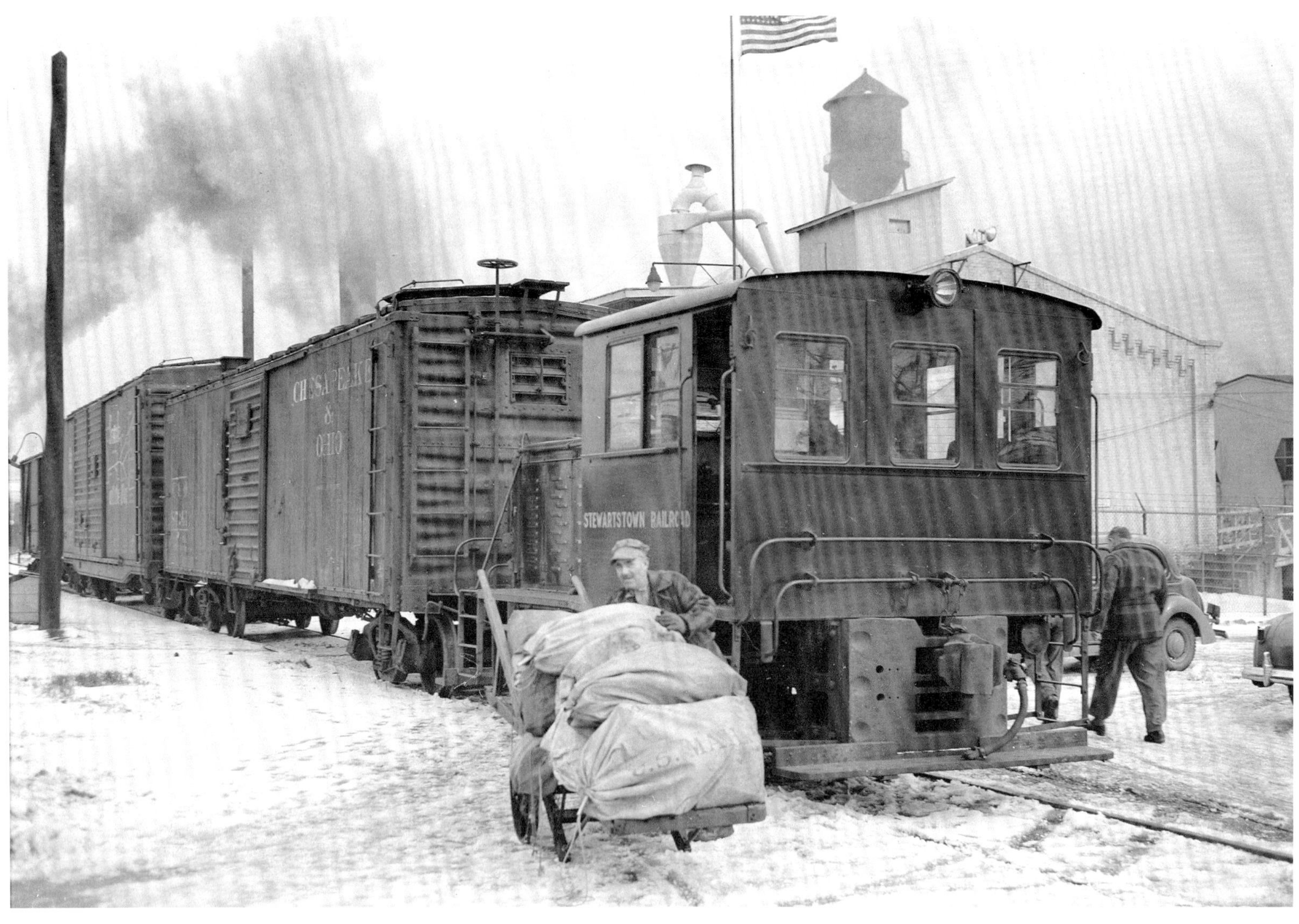

Plate 92. A crew member moves mail bags on a snowy day on the still-existent Stewartstown Railroad. Charles Clegg. Beebe-Clegg negative 1763.

Courtesy of the California State Railroad Museum.

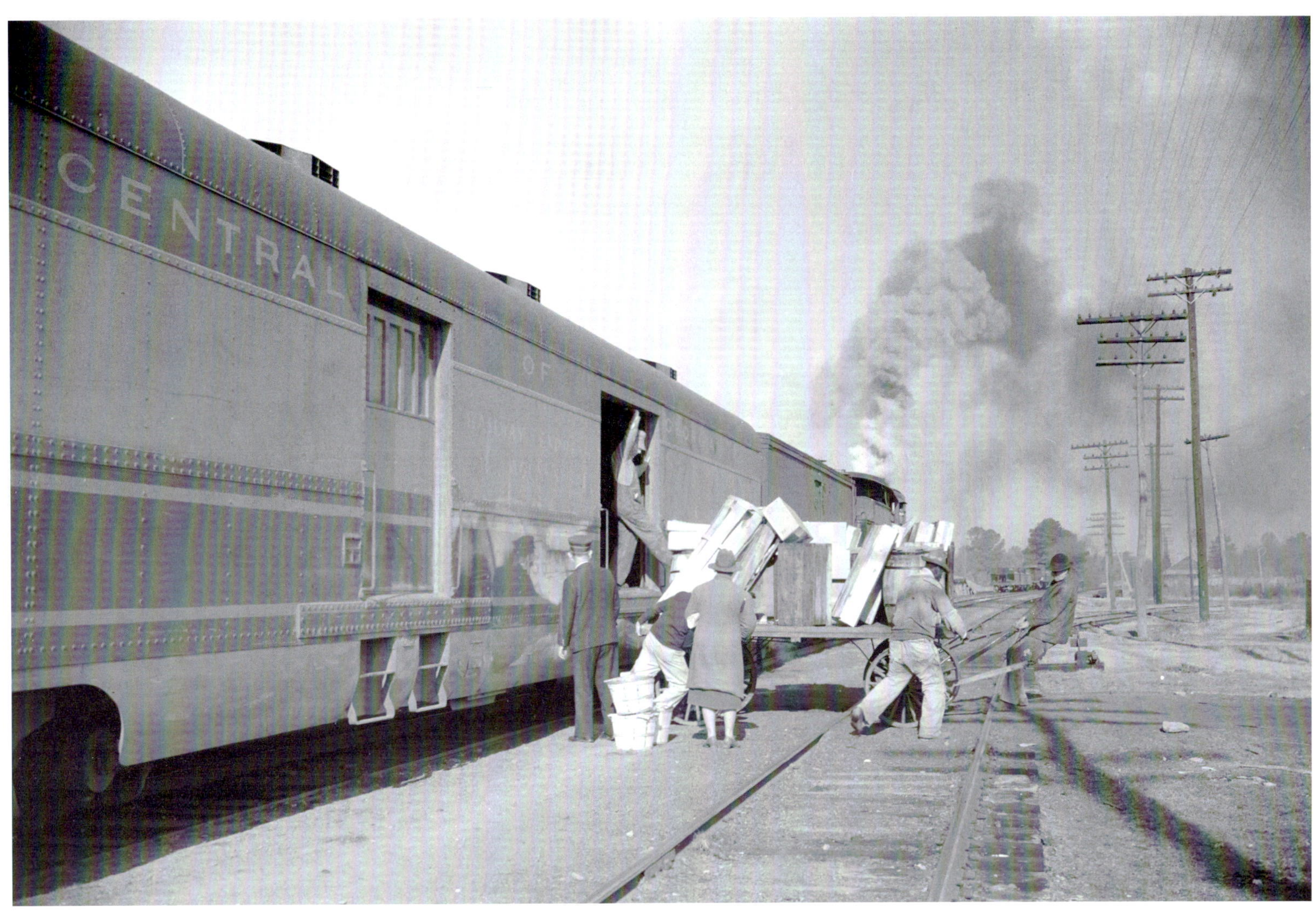

Plate 93. "Mullet for the Tables of Sylvania." The owner of a Sylvania, Georgia, fish market watches as her mullet, fresh from the Georgia coast, is unloaded from a Central of Georgia baggage car at Rocky Ford, Georgia. No fewer than five workers are visible in this image. Charles Clegg. Beebe-Clegg negative 1788.

Courtesy of the California State Railroad Museum.

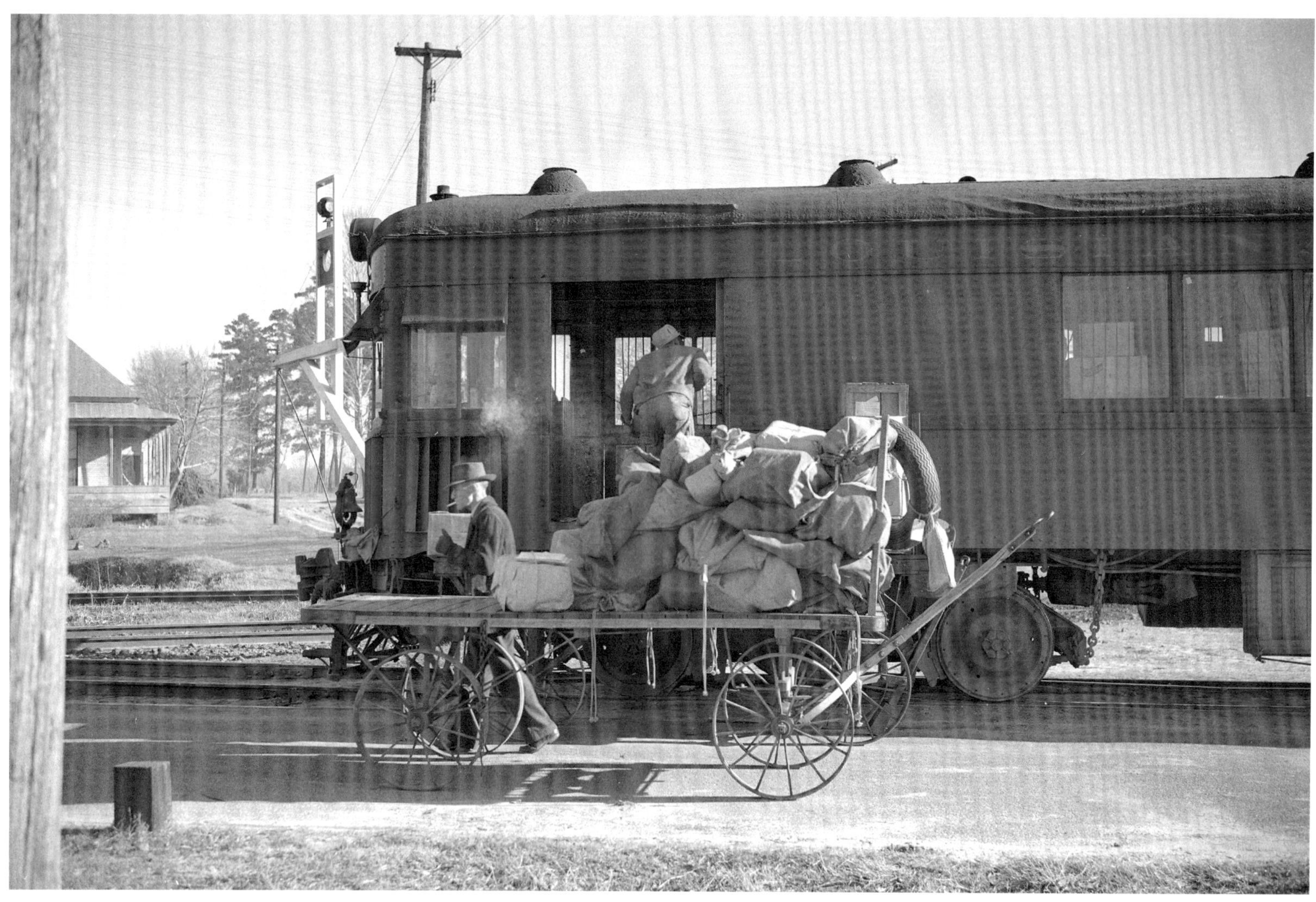

Plate 94. Mail and express are unloaded from a Louisiana & North West Railroad motorcar. Lucius Beebe or Charles Clegg. Beebe-Clegg negative 2765.

Courtesy of the California State Railroad Museum.

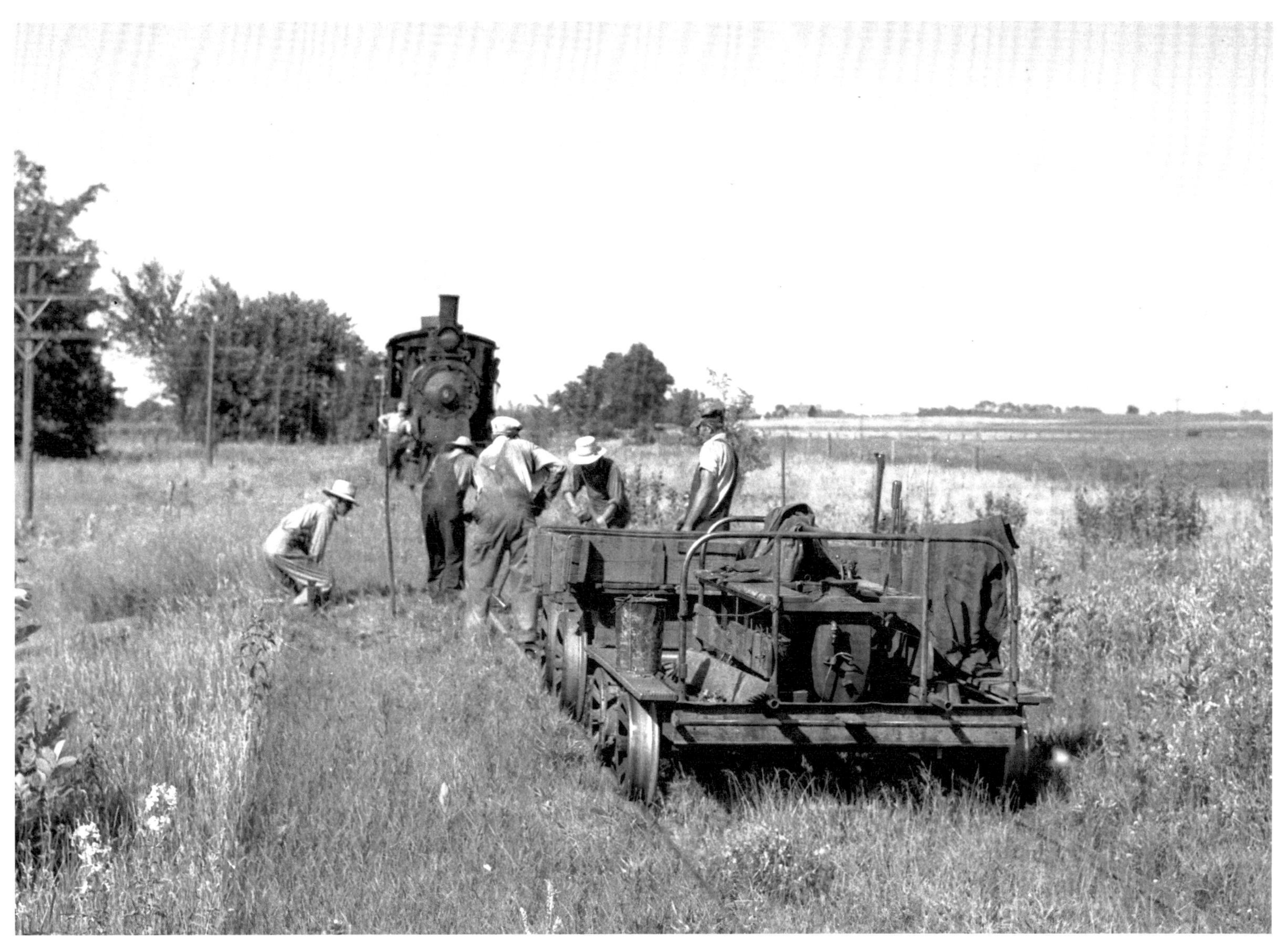

Plate 95. In a wonderful image, a Manchester & Oneida Railway section gang, with their speeder, works on the track while a train waits, July 1946. Note the weed-grown right-of-way, the foreman inspecting the work, and the crew member waiting, leg up, at the front of his train's steam engine. Charles Clegg. Beebe-Clegg negative 2959.

Courtesy of the California State Railroad Museum.

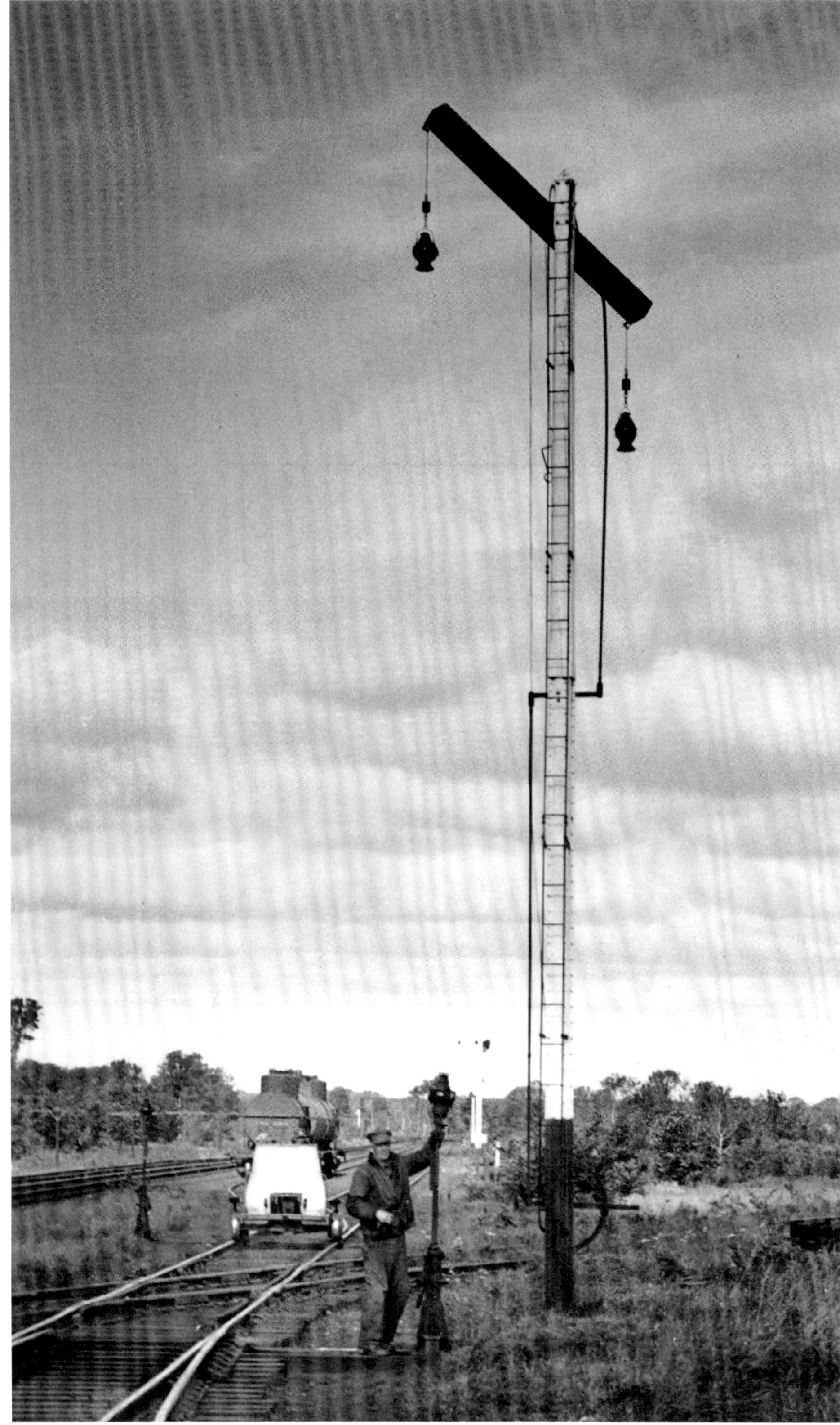

Plate 96. A worker maintains a switch lamp on the Maine Central Railroad, 1945. Note how Charles Clegg framed the worker, switch stand, and switch lamp under the traditional highball railroad crossing signal. Note also how the worker and his speeder are framed between the two switch stands. Charles Clegg.
Beebe-Clegg negative 4014.

Courtesy of the California State Railroad Museum.

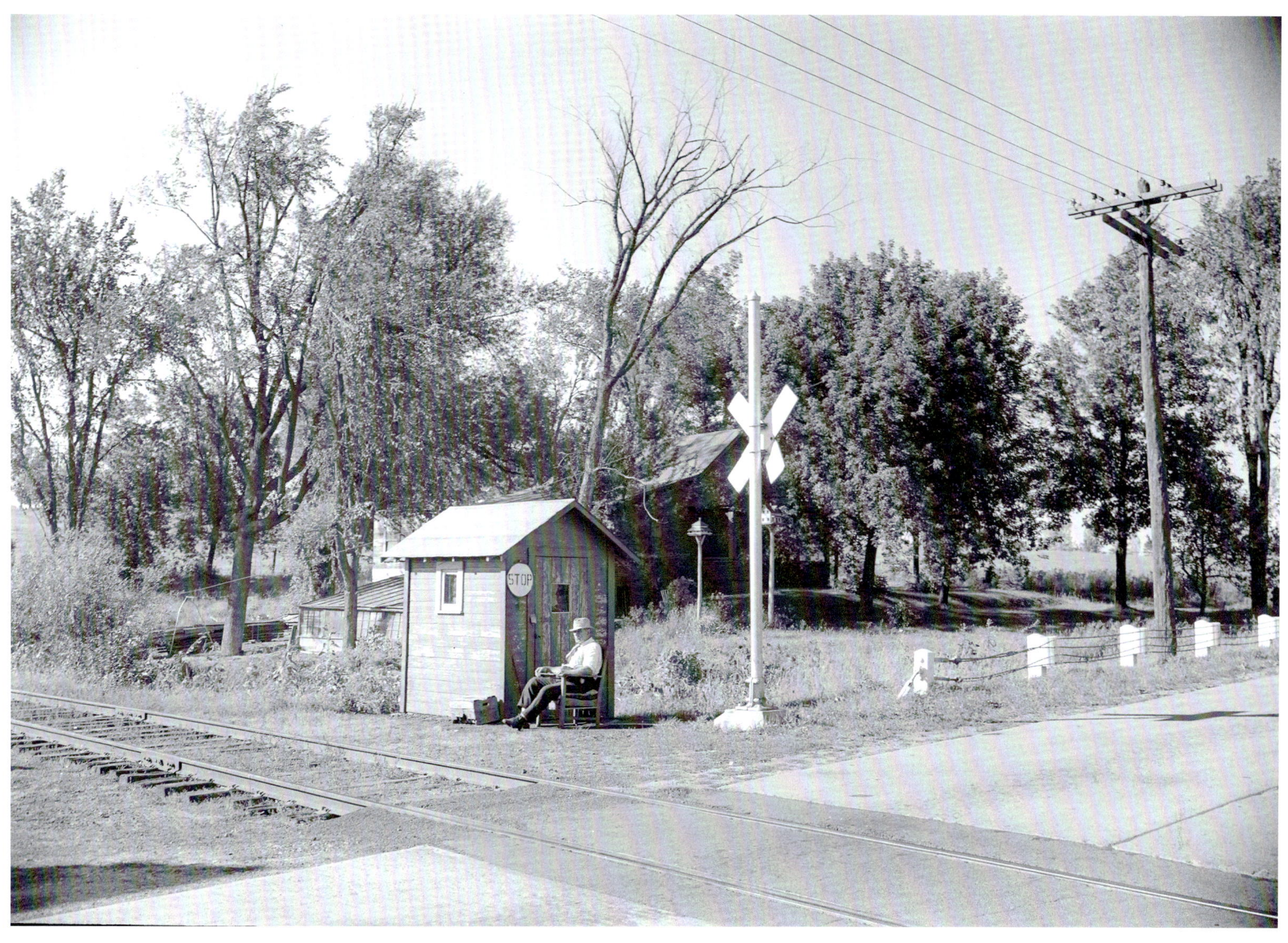

Plate 97. A crossing guard waits at his shack on the Norwood & St. Lawrence Railroad. This was an occupation often offered to elderly and/or disabled railroad workers. Note the guard's comfortable chair and his stock-in-trade, a stop sign, hanging on the side of his shack. Charles Clegg. Beebe-Clegg negative 2673.

Courtesy of the California State Railroad Museum.

4 THE RAILROAD IN ITS ENVIRONMENT

In 1940, Lucius Beebe met the much-younger Charles Clegg. By then, Beebe had already founded the railroad photo-book genre as we know it today and had taken many of his best railroad-subject images, be they wedge shots, modernist views, or portraits of railroaders.

Clegg, born in 1916, was fascinated with electronics, railroads, and photography. Unlike Beebe, who was self-taught as a photographer, Clegg studied photography with J. Ghislain Lootens. Lootens, best known as the author of *Lootens on Photographic Enlarging and Print Quality,* studied with Adolf Fassbender, a well-known pictorialist at the Brooklyn Institute of Arts and Sciences.[1] Lootens taught privately and through the Brooklyn YMCA. His pictorialist influence is clearly reflected in Clegg's work, which tends to show railroad-subject images in the context of the surrounding environment. Clegg, in turn, was a significant influence on railroad-subject photographers such as Phil Hastings, Richard "Dick" Steinheimer, and Jim Shaughnessy, who were to follow him just a few years later.

Another probable influence on Clegg is the artist A. Sheldon Pennoyer, who was known for paintings of trains in the context of historic landscapes. Pennoyer often took photos to use as grounding images for his paintings. In Pennoyer's book, *Locomotives in Our Lives,* he said, "I had a constant desire to film trains in action and in settings that would be useful and attractive, even if not really beautiful from my point of view. It struck me that, rather than photograph just a dead broadside view of a locomotive, the picture would be infinitely more vital and desirable if the whole composition included some action and incidentals that would make it a living image."[2] In this narrative, Pennoyer discusses the desirability of presenting railroad-subject images in a five-by-eight, rather than square, format and showing locomotives in the "rods-down position" while producing "a great cloud of smoke." Pennoyer's comments could serve as Clegg's railroad-subject artistic statement as a photographer. Although Pennoyer's book did not come out until 1954, his paintings were well known at the time and would have been familiar to Beebe and Clegg.[3]

Clegg's influence on Beebe and on American railroad-subject photography first came to the fore in *Highball: A Pageant of Trains,* published in 1945. In many ways, *Highball* is a transitional work, spanning the Beebe-only early books (*High Iron, Highliners,* and *Trains in Transition*) and the Beebe-Clegg masterpiece, *Mixed Train Daily.*

Including more than three hundred images, *Mixed Train Daily* was largely illustrated with photographs by Beebe and

Clegg, with Clegg accounting for about two-thirds of the total. *Mixed Train Daily* is an exceptionally influential book in the area of American railroad-subject photography and deserves to be more widely known. In it Clegg's pictorialism, restrained compared to that of Fassbender and Lootens and often similar in style to Pennoyer's paintings, broadens our view of the American railroad to include its surroundings and therefore produces images that show the railroad's place in American society at the time. We also see Beebe's work, although declining in quantity of photographic output, broadening in response to his partner's lead. *Mixed Train Daily* represents an important moment in railroad-subject photography, forever expanding its view from roster and three-quarters images into an oeuvre with more artistic and social content.

Just three years after *Mixed Train Daily* was published, Beebe and Clegg moved permanently from New York to the West Coast, at first settling in Virginia City, Nevada. Until it was abandoned, they often photographed their local short line, the famous Virginia & Truckee Railroad. From that point on, Beebe and Clegg turned largely to writing and spent little time on photography.

This portfolio presents notable images by Beebe and Clegg depicting the railroad in its environment. Plate 98, Clegg's image of "Railroad Street," which ran through hundreds of American communities, opens the portfolio. Plates 99 and 100 show Beebe and Clegg's broad views, respectively, of the railroad landscape. Beebe's stark image of Sherman Summit shows the influence of one of the most famous railroad-subject images of all time: Alfred Stieglitz's "The Hand of Man." Clegg's image of the Unadilla Valley Railroad, plate 100, which shows the train as a relatively small and integrated part of the surrounding landscape, resembles a medieval tapestry. Plate 101 shows a similar Clegg view, but in vertical rather than horizontal format, of the St. Johnsbury & Lake Champlain Railroad. The similarity between this image and Phil Hastings's many roughly contemporaneous photographs of the same Vermont railroad is obvious.

Plates 102 to 104 are Clegg photographic tableaux that in many ways presage the work of photographers such as O. Winston Link and David Plowden. Plate 102, a little-known but delightful image of the Wood River Branch Railroad, reflects the influence of Walker Evans and presages the similarly detail-filled work of photographers such as Link and, more recently, Gregory Crewdson and Jeff Wall. Plate 103 depicts an entire and humorously short Huntington & Broad Top Mountain train and its watchful, if bored, fireman. Plate 104, another tableau reminiscent of Evans's work, contrasts the signs and rails in the foreground with the covered bridge behind.

Beebe and Clegg took a number of photographs of the Fonda, Johnstown & Gloversville Railroad in upstate New York. In plate 105, Clegg's eye detected a humorous contrast between the stub end of a train, its locomotive running backwards, and the seemingly over-large Gloversville station in the background. At the small Broadalbin depot, plate 106, Beebe captured a timeless tableau of a small-town station stop, including the bicycles and baggage cart in the foreground, the railroad worker climbing up the steps in the middle ground, and the column of smoke in the background. Clegg's influence on Beebe is clearly evident here. Plate 107 is a similar view of the Nelson & Albemarle, one of Archie Robertson's favorite short lines, at Schuyler, Virginia.

As with the Virginia & Truckee and the narrow-gauge railroads of Colorado, Beebe and Clegg had a special fondness for short lines of the US South and developed a sense of the place that shows through in their images. Plates 108 to 120 show their depiction of the railroad in the environment of the South. Plate 108, taken by Clegg in the border-state region of southern Indiana, shows an entire Louisville, New Albany & Corydon train—just a steam engine, box car, and side-door caboose. Passengers and, as shown by the type of caboose used here, express, small freight shipments, and possibly even mail all traveled with the rear-end crew in the caboose. Plate 109, a side view by Clegg of North Carolina's Virginia & Carolina Southern, typifies the swamplands of the southern coastal plain. Plates 110 to 113, all by Clegg, show unusual stations served by short lines of the South: Broadway, North Carolina, on the Atlantic & Western; a gent straight out of a Faulkner novel walking up to a haunted-looking station on North Carolina's Moore Central Railroad; the much-photographed Cranberry, North Carolina, Tweetsie (East Tennessee & Western North Carolina) station; and a station on the Ferdinand Railroad, also in southern Indiana, that could serve as a company house in a textile-mill town.

Plates 114 to 116 continue the theme of unusual stations of the South but with more of the surrounding environment in view. Plate 114 shows the Frankfort & Cincinnati Railroad's stop at Burberry's General Store in Centerville, Kentucky. Characteristic of Clegg's best work, the more you look at this image, the more interesting details you find. In plate 115, the Morehead & North Fork Railroad station, on a logging railroad in the Kentucky mountains, is a structure that would not appear out of place in a restored company town such as Cass, West Virginia, today. Plate 116 shows a post office along the Tallulah Falls Railroad that seems too overgrown with vines for the door to open all the way.

In plates 117 to 120, Clegg takes a broad view of short-line trains in the South. Plate 117 shows a relatively long mixed train plying the undulating right-of-way of the Sandersville Railroad, its passenger accommodations provided by a Jim Crow (segregated) coach. In plate 118, Clegg paired a streamlined Gulf, Mobile & Ohio diesel with a similarly styled automobile at the GM&O's junction with the Mississippi & Alabama Railroad in Vinegar Bend, Alabama. One of the six onlookers watches the New York–based photographer with unconcealed curiosity. In plate 119, a feral hog is spooked by a Tremont & Gulf train at a water tank. This image bespeaks a Louisiana or Arkansas location; the Tremont & Gulf ran from Tremont to Winnfield, Louisiana. Finally, plate 120 depicts the "haunted" water tower on the Wichita Falls & Southern at Ranger, Texas, on the western edge of the US South.

Plates 121 to 133 demonstrate Beebe and Clegg's love for the narrow-gauge railroads of Colorado and northern New Mexico. One of the most striking images in *Highball*, plate 121, by Beebe, shows that Clegg influenced his partner early on. The drama of this image partly derives from how it was cropped and then presented in *Highball*. Plate 122 shows a Rio Grande Southern train under the watchful eye of its engineer as it passes the station in Dolores, Colorado.

Clegg delighted in over and under views of trains. Locations amenable to a view from below a train's level are limited, but Clegg, in plate 123, captured a memorable one taken from under a trestle on the Rio Grande Southern near Durango, Colorado. Plate 124 demonstrates, again, the role of the US mail in keeping the American railroad system of the time alive, as a Rio Grande "Galloping Goose" meets a mail truck at Vance Junction, Colorado. In plate 125, a crowd of local people is shown at a station on the Rio Grande Southern. A small dog marks the foreground.

Beebe and Clegg occasionally took images of the railroad environment without a train. Plate 126 is Beebe's view of an archaic harp switch stand at Mears Junction, Colorado. Plate 127, another of Clegg's masterful tapestries, is a panoramic view of the Rio Grande Southern right-of-way in the Colorado Rockies.

Plate 128, taken in 1940, is Beebe's early environmental view of a train on the narrow-gauge Denver & Rio Grande Western "Chili Line," which ran from Antonito, Colorado, to Santa Fe, New Mexico. The cold of the Christmas season in northern New Mexico permeates the image. In plate 129, Clegg steps back so that two trees, right and left in the photo, provide a grand, natural frame for a narrow-gauge Denver & Rio Grande Western passenger train, the famed *San Juan*, which ran from Alamosa to Durango, Colorado. In plate 130, Beebe shows Denver & Rio Grande Western 478 sitting behind a freight train and another engine. The 478's fireman, as often happened in Beebe-Clegg images, looks back at the photographer, his curiosity obvious.

Plates 131 to 134 show the famed Denver & Rio Grande "Silverton train," then operating as a mixed train and today a noted tourist attraction, and the branch line on which it ran. Plate 131, by Clegg, is a view taken from an open coach platform high above Animas Gorge. In plate 132, Beebe shows the train at its most noted location: the highline, a rocky shelf above the Animas River and its gorge. In plate 133, Clegg shows the Silverton mixed train at its terminal, the D & RGW station in Silverton, Colorado. Plate 134, another pastoral, is Beebe's view of the D & RGW Silverton branch crossing a cattle guard near Rockwood, Colorado.

In plates 135 to 137, we see Beebe and Clegg's views of other parts of the US West. Plate 135, by Beebe, shows narrow-gauge Southern Pacific No. 18 with a train at Laws, California. Plates 136 and 137 show the archetypical railroad of the West, the Santa Fe (Atchison, Topeka & Santa Fe Railway): a diesel-hauled freight by Beebe in plate 136 and Clegg's view of a Santa Fe locomotive enshrouded by smoke and steam in plate 137.

Plates 138 to 140, all by Clegg, a master of this type of photograph, end our view of the American railroad in the landscape.

Plate 138, an image without a train in sight, depicts a homemade signal on the Chestnut Ridge Railroad in Pennsylvania—an image that also lives in the worlds of folk art and industrial archeology. Plate 139 shows the weathered and visually intricate "Cirrhosis Club," the homemade passenger car of New York's Grasse River Railroad that carried lumberjacks back to camp after their Saturday night carouses. And, finally, plate 140 is Clegg's much-published view of the primevally simple end-of-track on Colorado's San Luis Valley Southern Railroad. The clean lines of the photo, the utility poles (two of them in the photo's third points), and the sky and mountains backing the image, all mark this as a Clegg image. Its finality makes this photo a fitting end stop to our survey of Beebe and Clegg's best work.

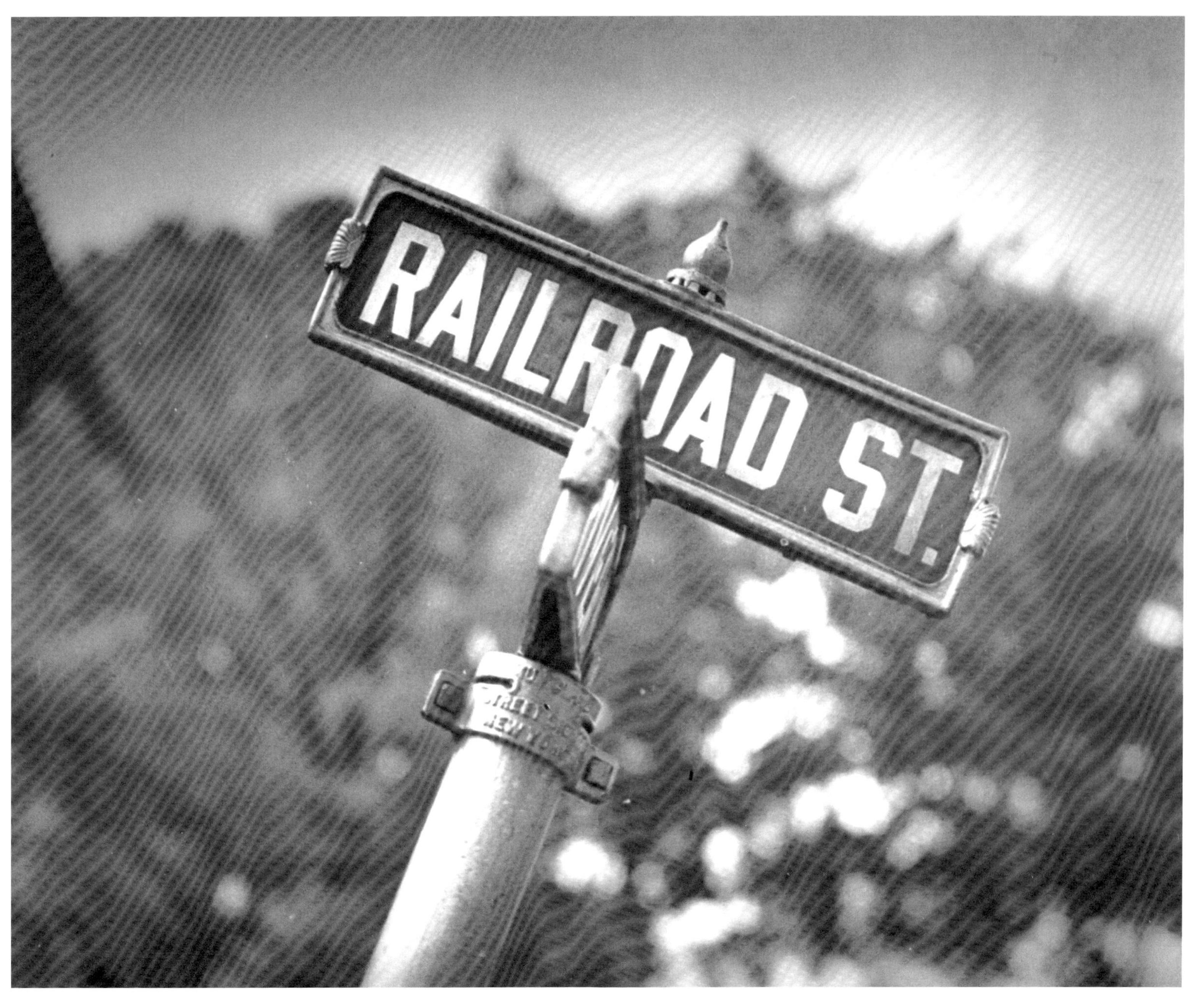

Plate 98. Railroad Street, Otego, New York. Charles Clegg. Beebe-Clegg negative 4015.

Courtesy of the California State Railroad Museum.

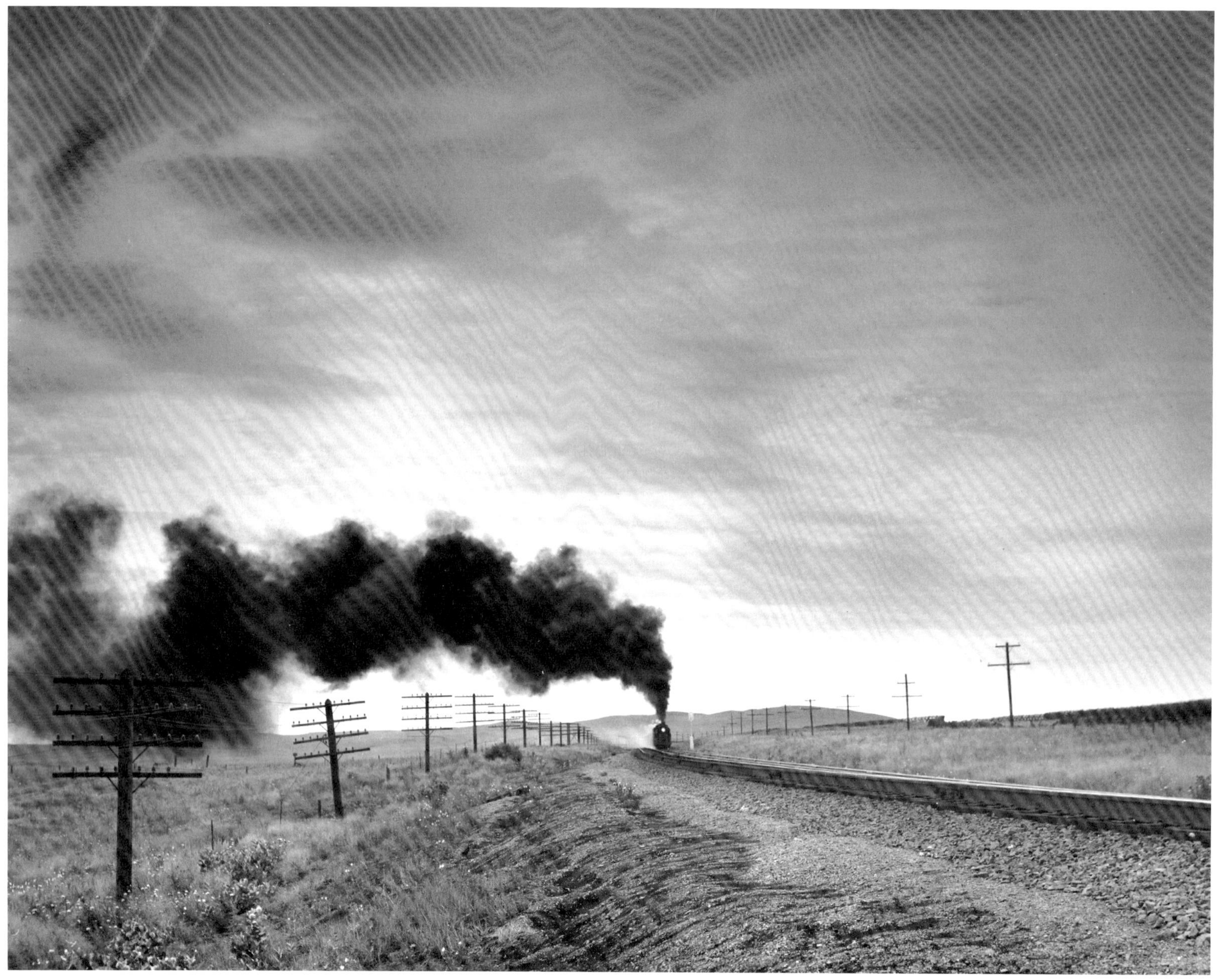

Plate 99. Lucius Beebe's noted evocative photo of a Union Pacific freight train near Sherman Summit. Beebe identified the subject several different ways in his books. Despite Beebe's carelessness with facts, this is a stunning image of American railroading. Lucius Beebe. Beebe-Clegg negative 4016.

Courtesy of the California State Railroad Museum.

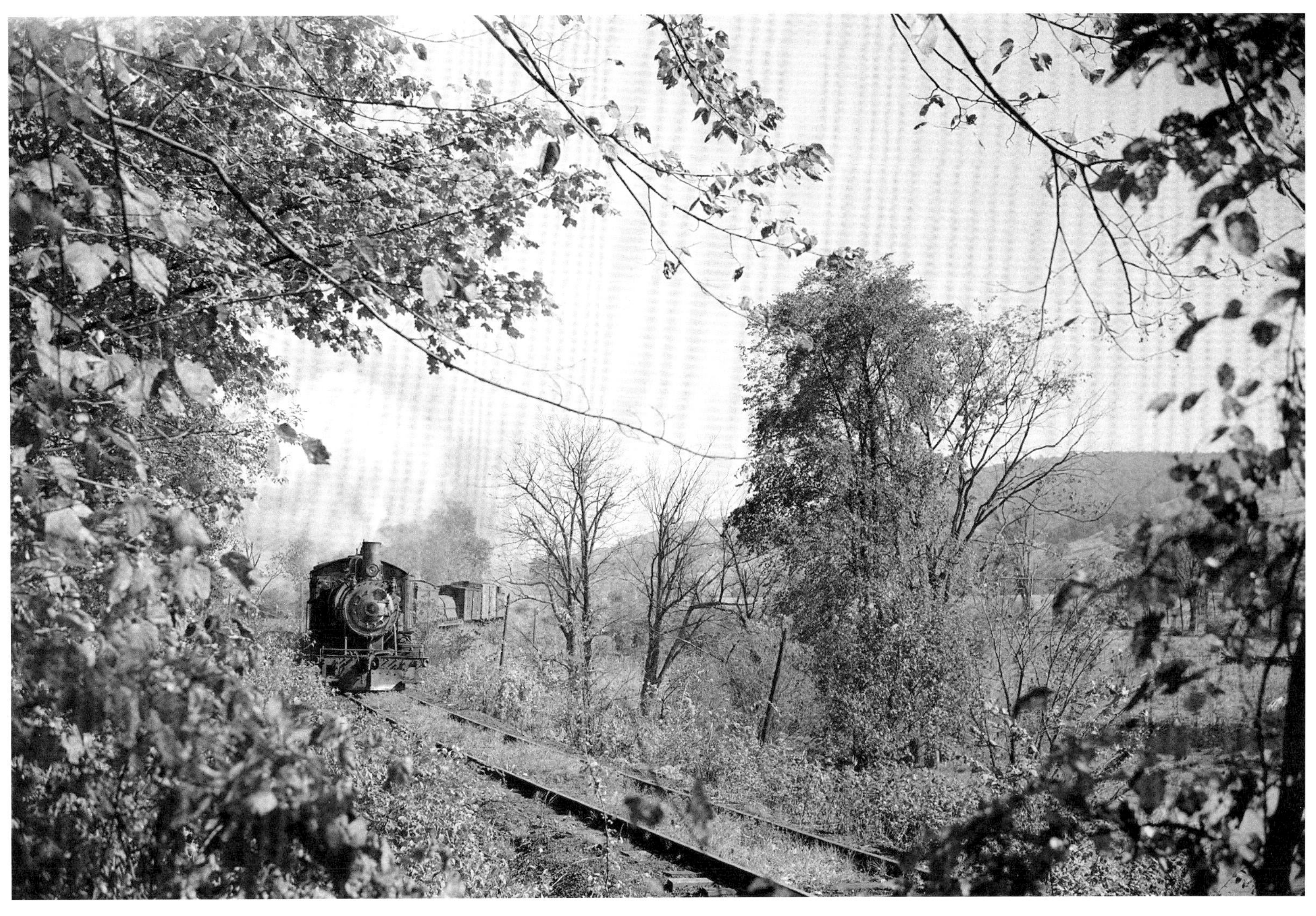

Plate 100. The morning milk train of the Unadilla Valley Railroad approaching New Berlin, New York. Charles Clegg. Beebe-Clegg negative 658.

Courtesy of the California State Railroad Museum.

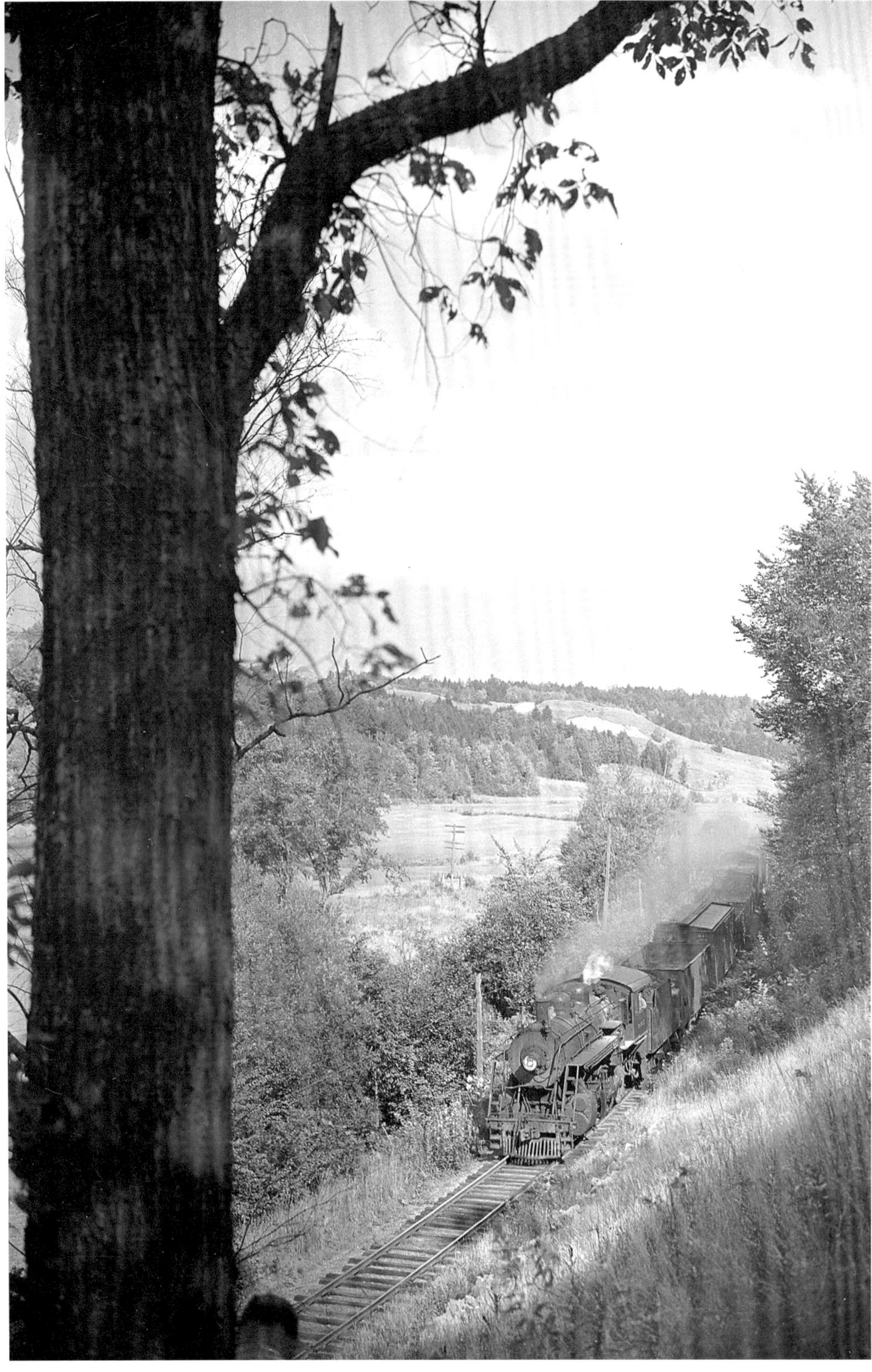

Plate 101. Charles Clegg's evocative portrait of the St. Johnsbury & Lake Champlain Railroad in rural Vermont. Charles Clegg. Beebe-Clegg negative 3175.

Courtesy of the California State Railroad Museum.

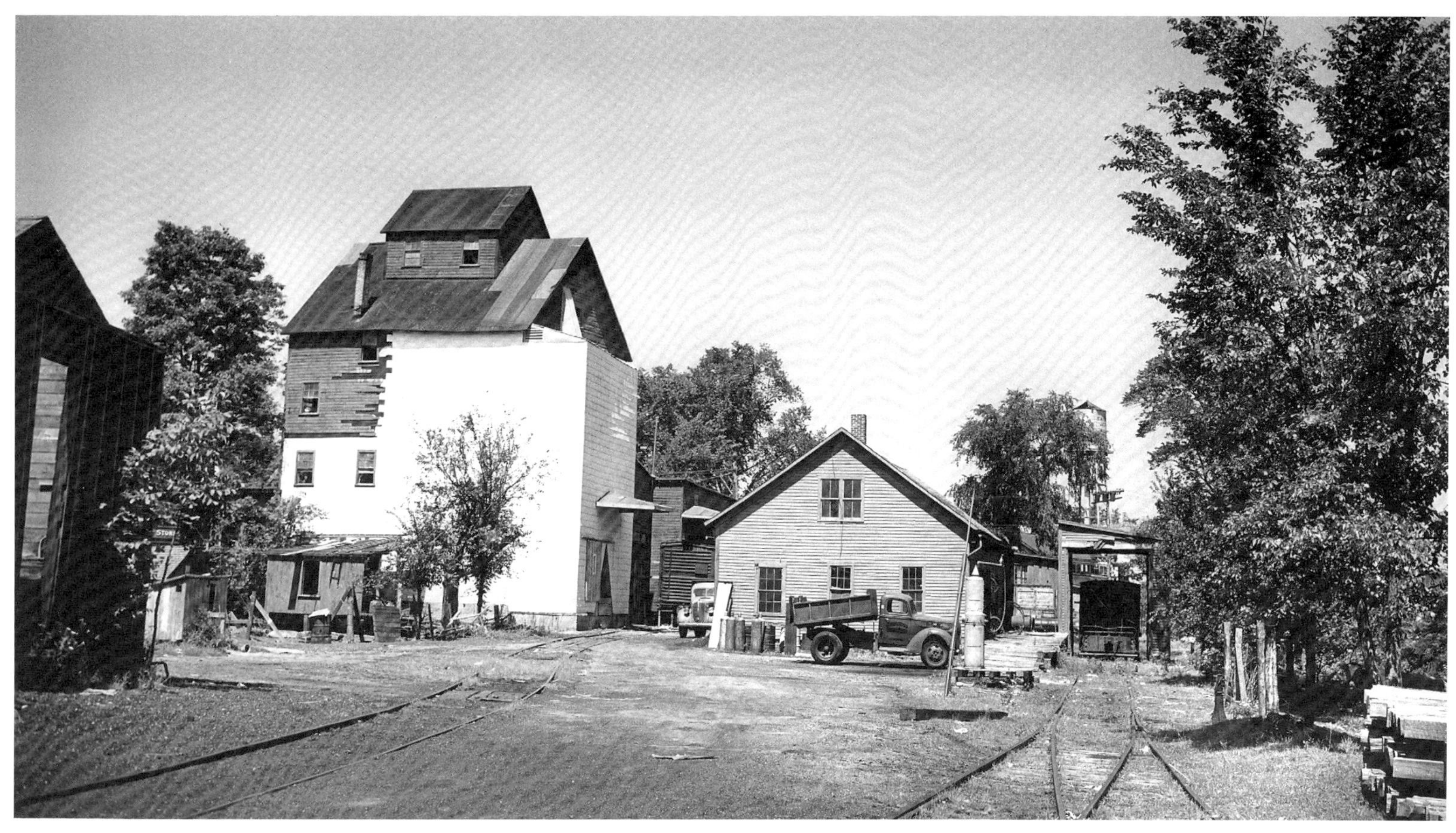

Plate 102. A delightful Charles Clegg image of a terminal area on the Wood River Branch Railroad. Note the mill with two types of siding on the left; the two trucks, one with a partially tilted bed; the railroad structure on the right crowned by a distant water tower; and the ill-maintained tracks wandering over both sides of the image. Walker Evans's influence seems present here. Charles Clegg. Beebe-Clegg negative 3999.

Courtesy of the California State Railroad Museum.

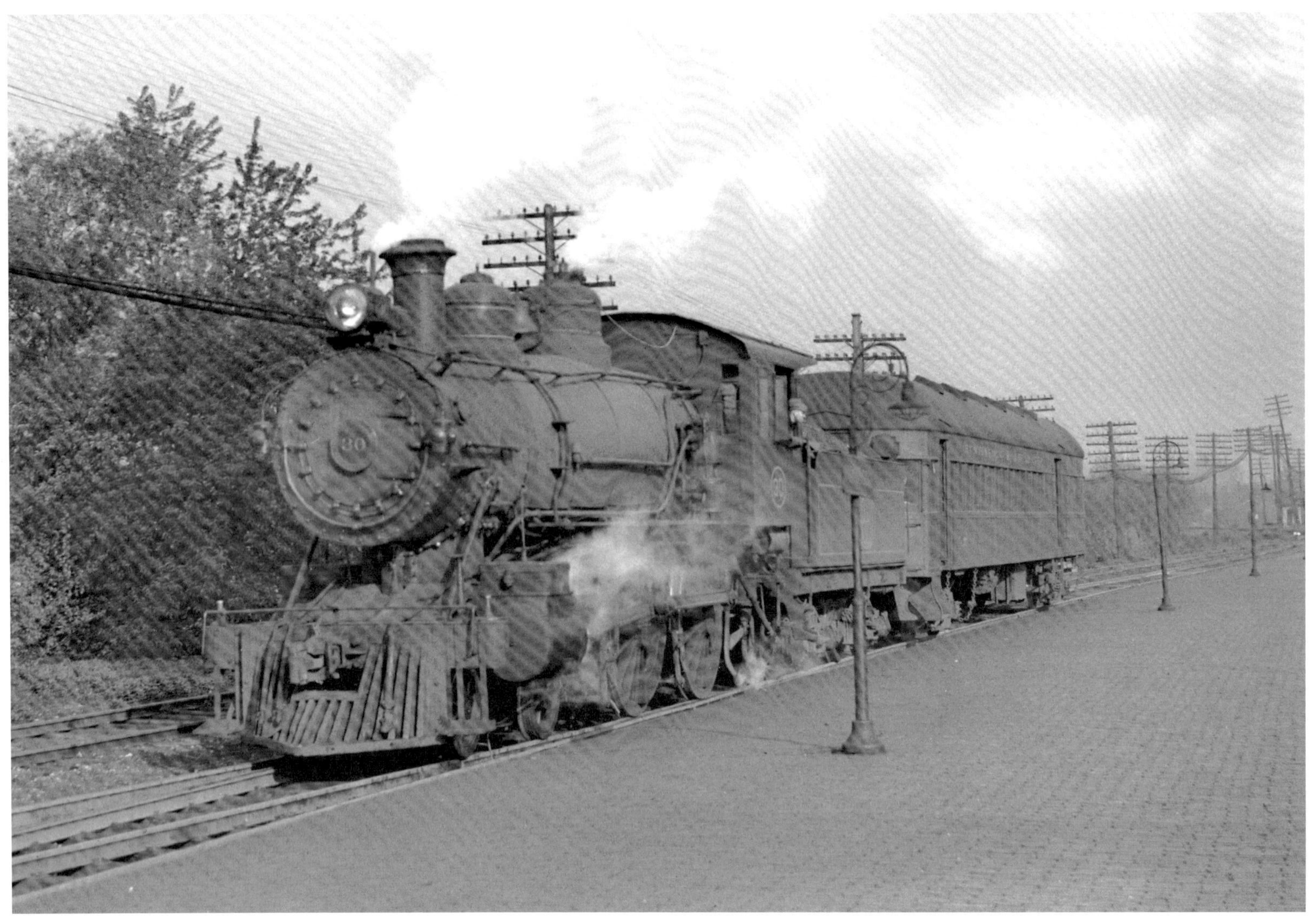

Plate 103. A Huntington & Broad Top Mountain passenger train, led by engine No. 30, waits at the platform in Huntington, Pennsylvania. The neat platform and lineside poles with many cross arms reflect the Pennsylvania Railroad's main-line presence in Huntington. The fireman looks out his cab window. Charles Clegg. Beebe-Clegg negative 2482.

Courtesy of the California State Railroad Museum.

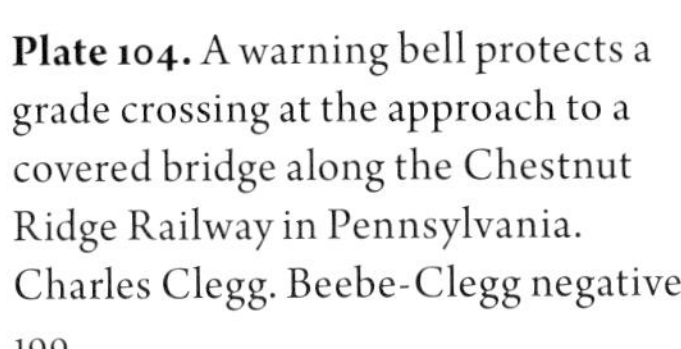

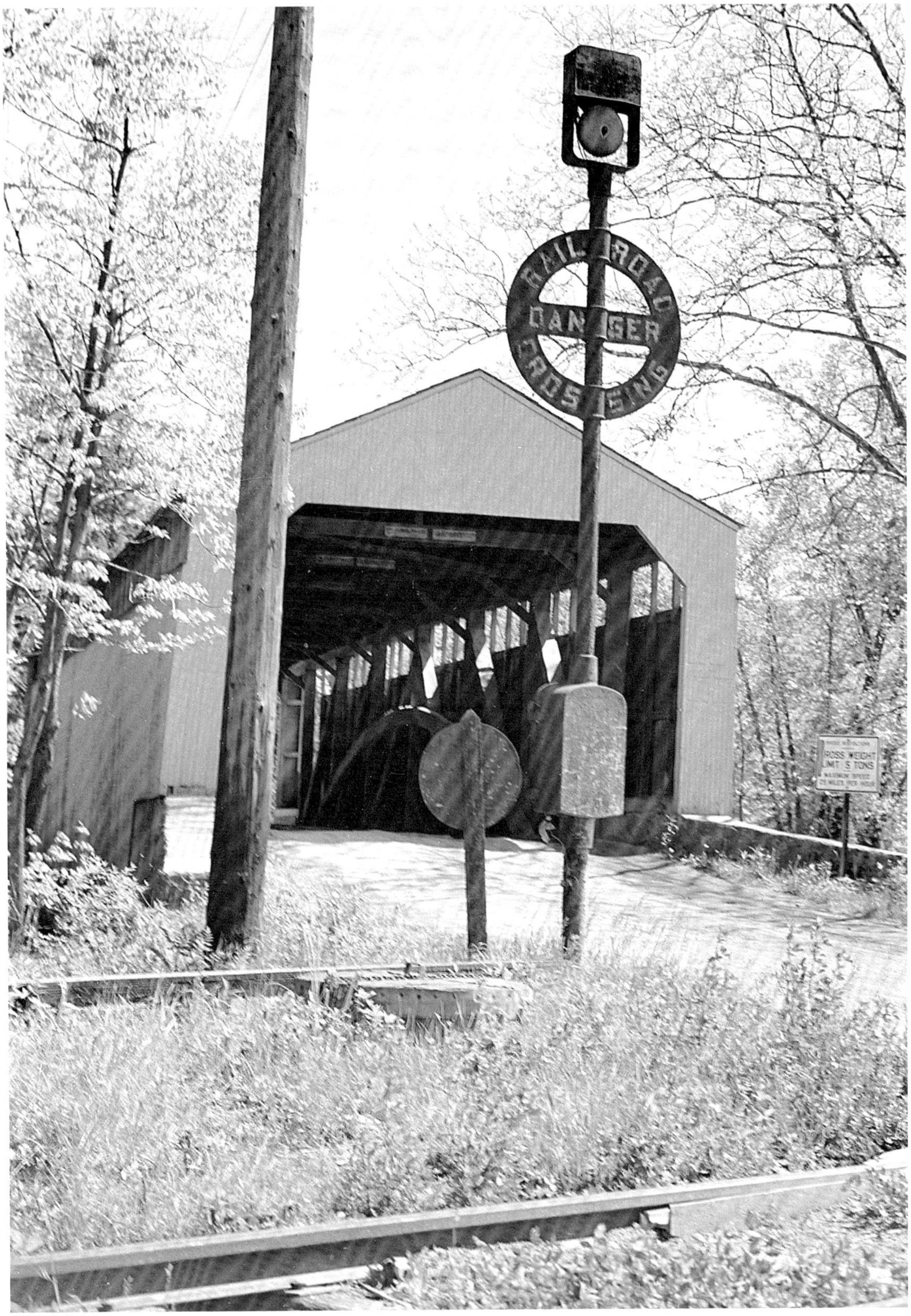

Plate 104. A warning bell protects a grade crossing at the approach to a covered bridge along the Chestnut Ridge Railway in Pennsylvania. Charles Clegg. Beebe-Clegg negative 199.

Courtesy of the California State Railroad Museum.

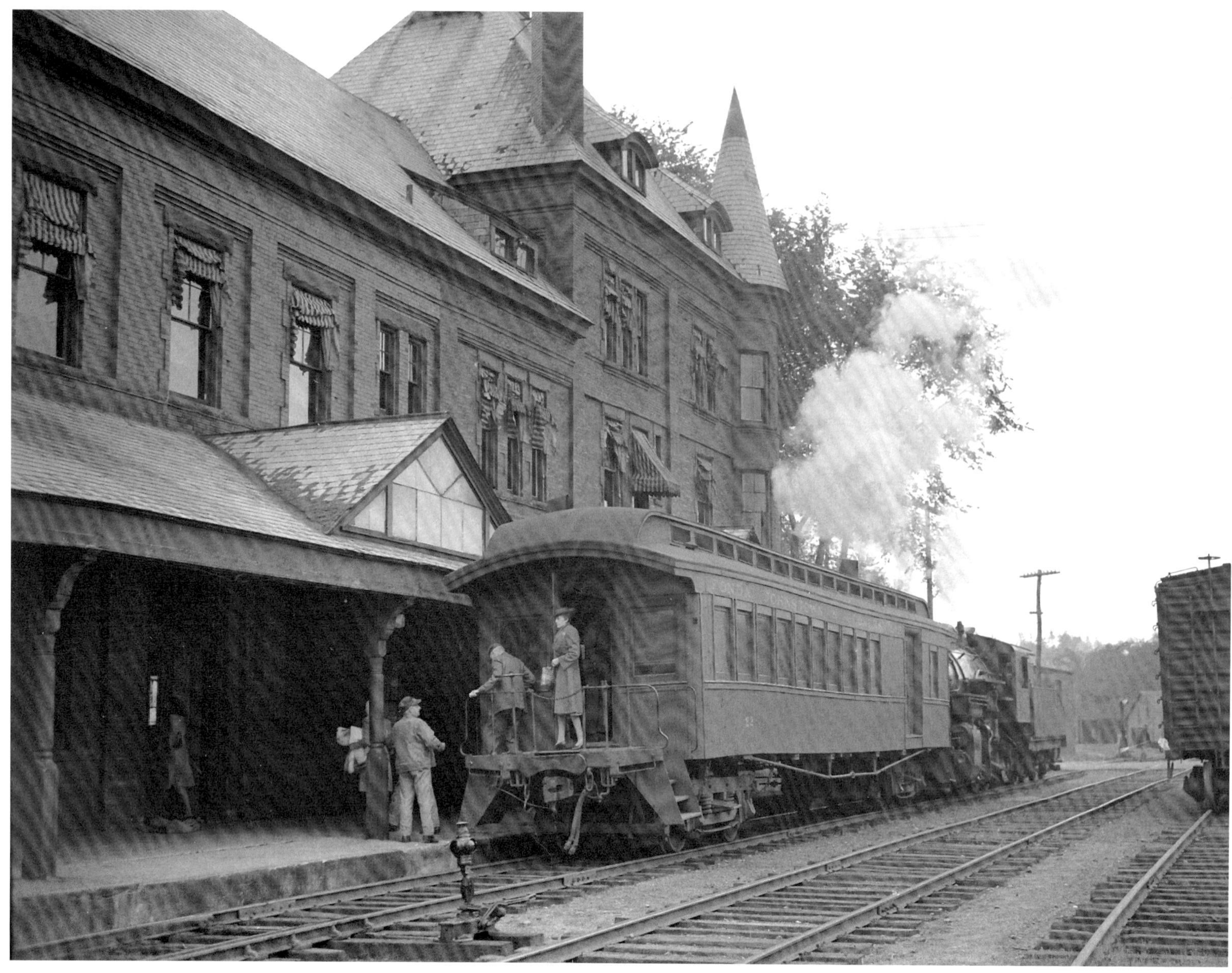

Plate 105. A Fonda, Johnstown & Gloversville Railroad passenger train unloads at the classic station and railroad office building in Gloversville, New York. Charles Clegg. Beebe-Clegg negative 2113.

Courtesy of the California State Railroad Museum.

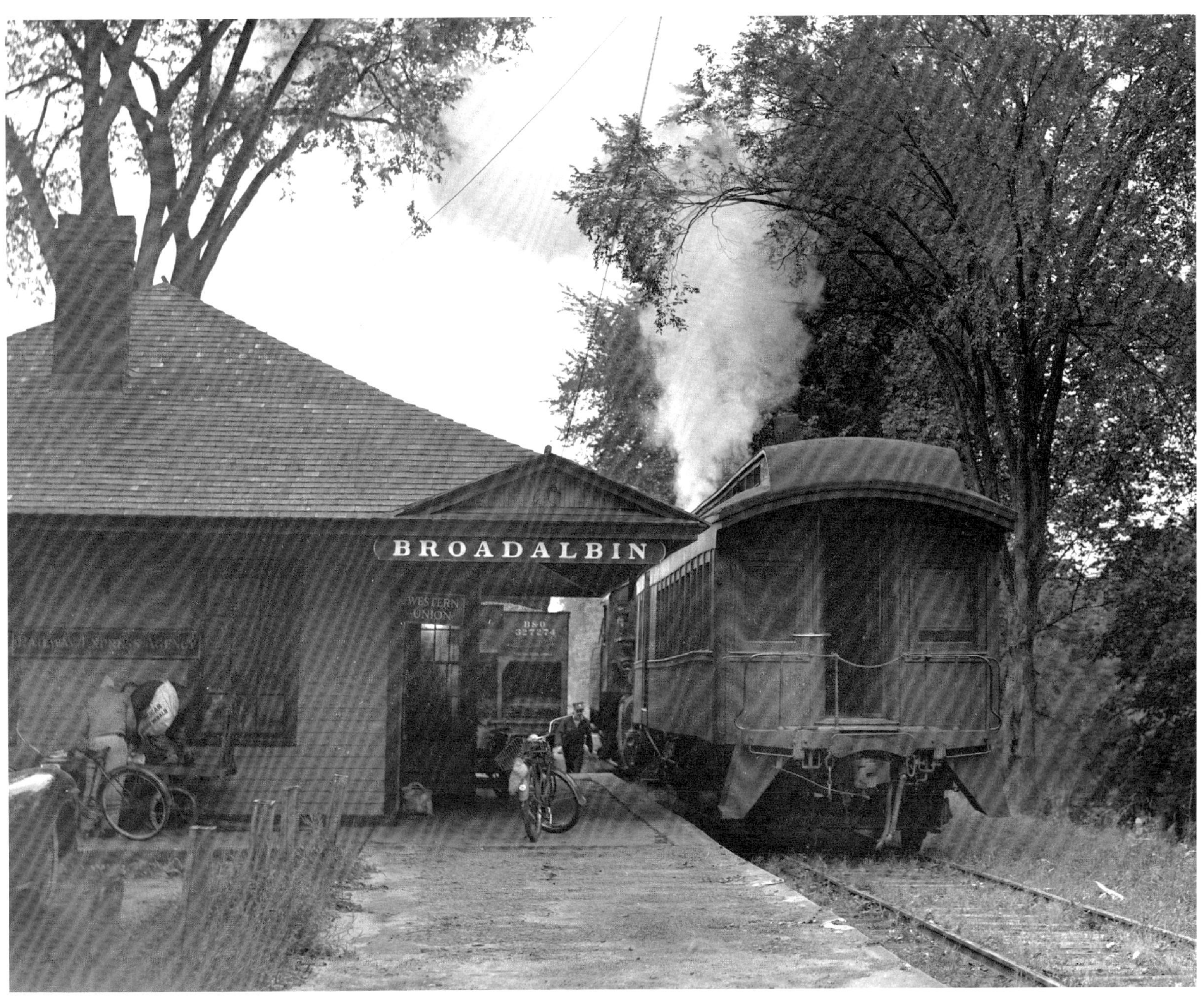

Plate 106. What may be the same train as shown in plate 105 stops at the Fonda, Johnstown, & Gloversville station in Broadalbin, New York. Bicycles seem to be another important transport mode in Broadalbin on this day. Lucius Beebe. Beebe-Clegg negative 2136.

Courtesy of the California State Railroad Museum.

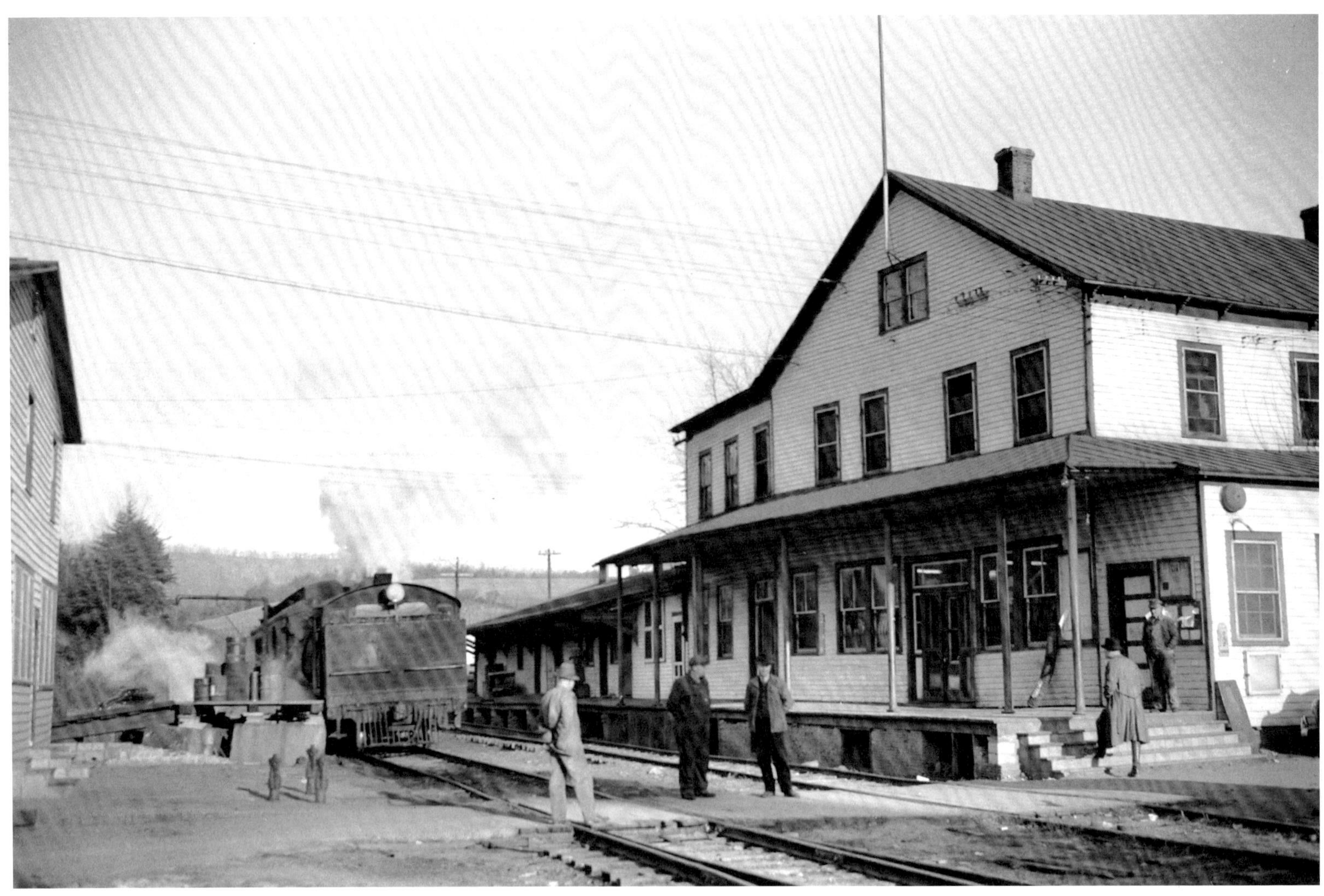

Plate 107. A scene along the Nelson & Albemarle Railroad at Schuyler, Virginia, January 1946. Lucius Beebe or Charles Clegg. Beebe-Clegg negative 2824.

Courtesy of the California State Railroad Museum.

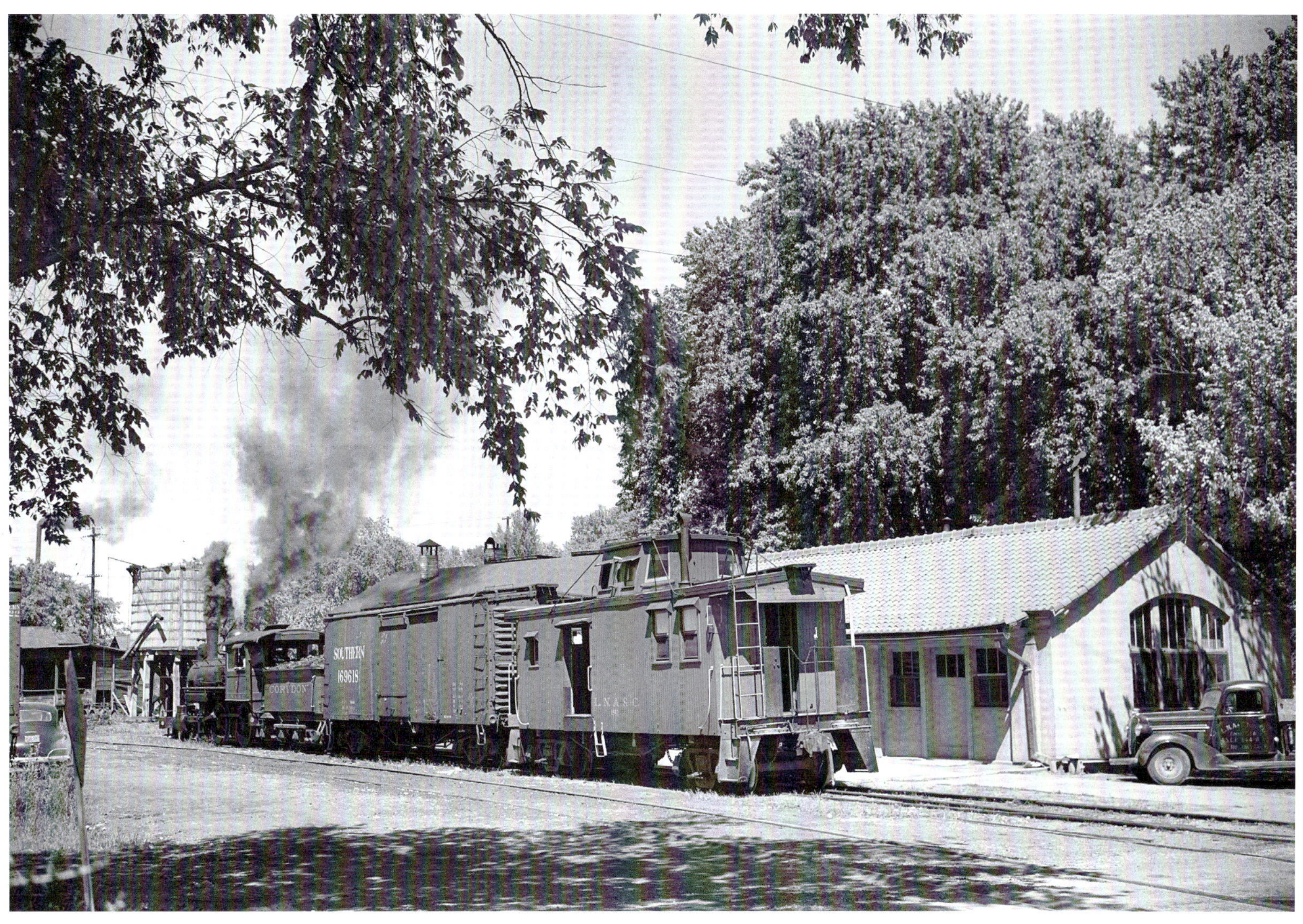

Plate 108. A Louisville, New Albany & Corydon Railroad train with its passenger-carrying caboose. A caboose ride on the Louisville, New Albany & Corydon was described feelingly by Archie Robertson in his *Slow Train to Yesterday,* a major influence on Beebe and Clegg's *Mixed Train Daily.* Charles Clegg. Beebe-Clegg 2801.

Courtesy of the California State Railroad Museum.

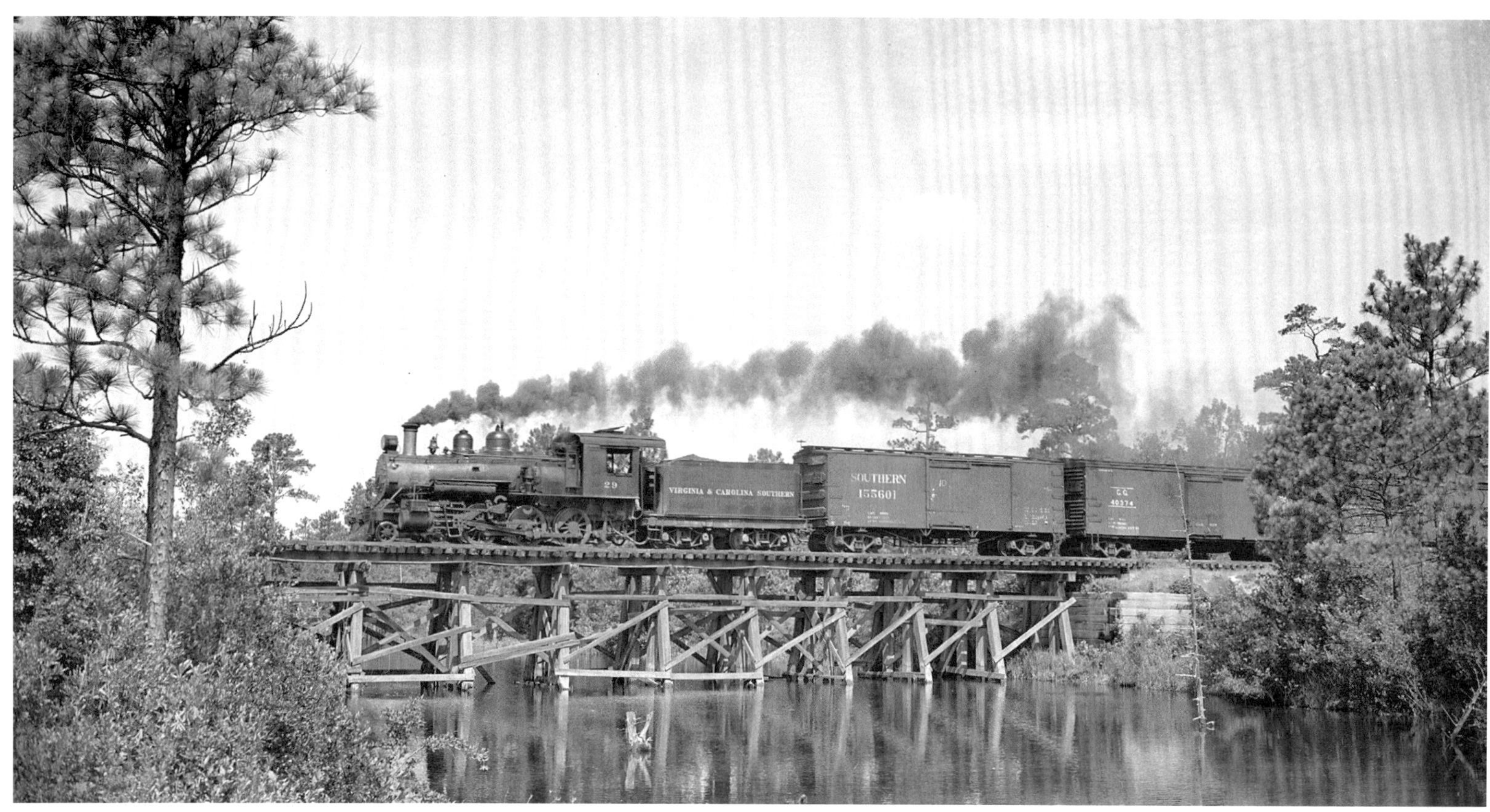

Plate 109. A Virginia & Carolina Southern train crosses a low pile trestle in the North Carolina swamplands. Charles Clegg. Beebe-Clegg negative 628.

Courtesy of the California State Railroad Museum.

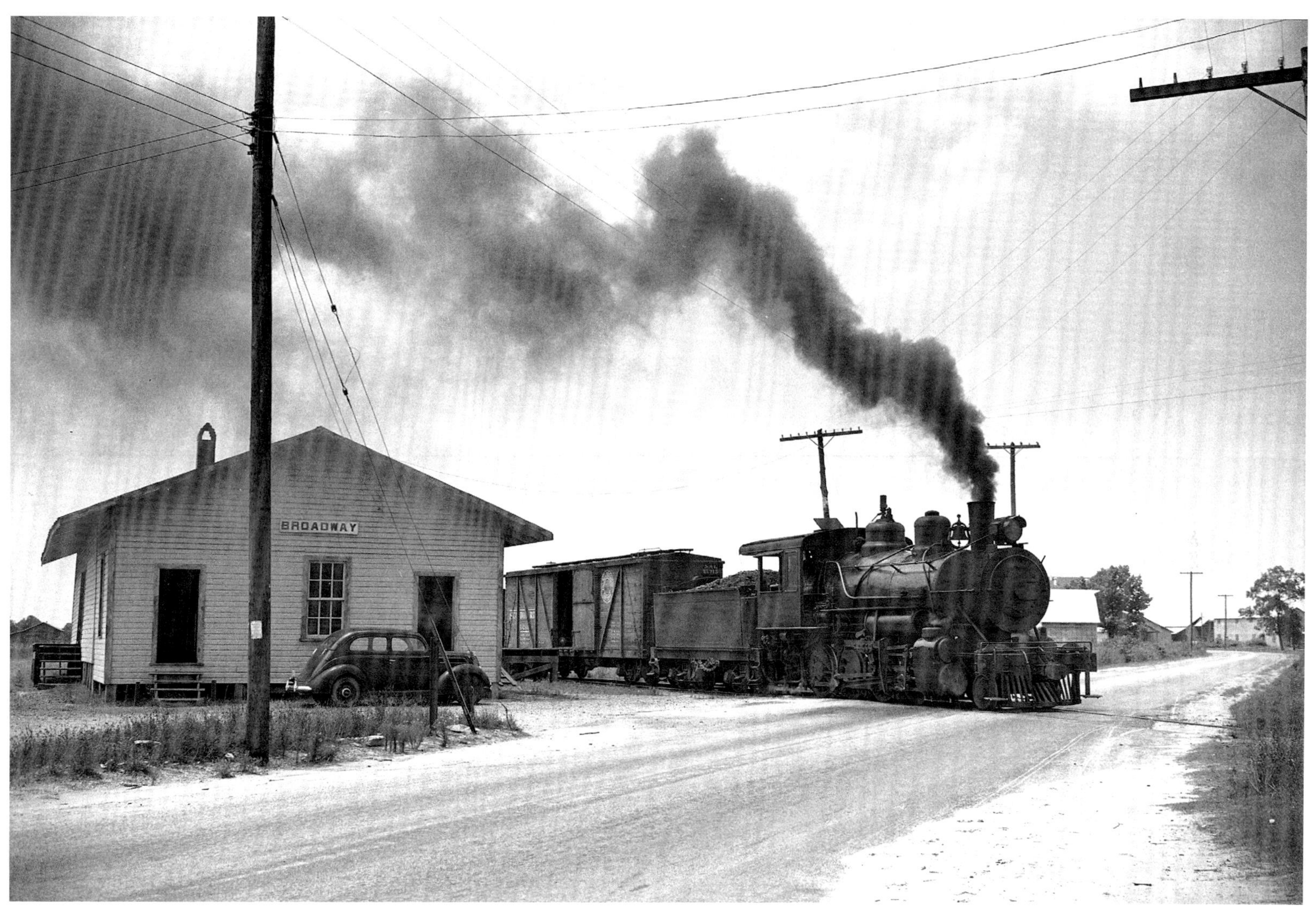

Plate 110. An Atlantic & Western Railway train at the station in Broadway, North Carolina. Charles Clegg. Beebe-Clegg negative 1350.

Courtesy of the California State Railroad Museum.

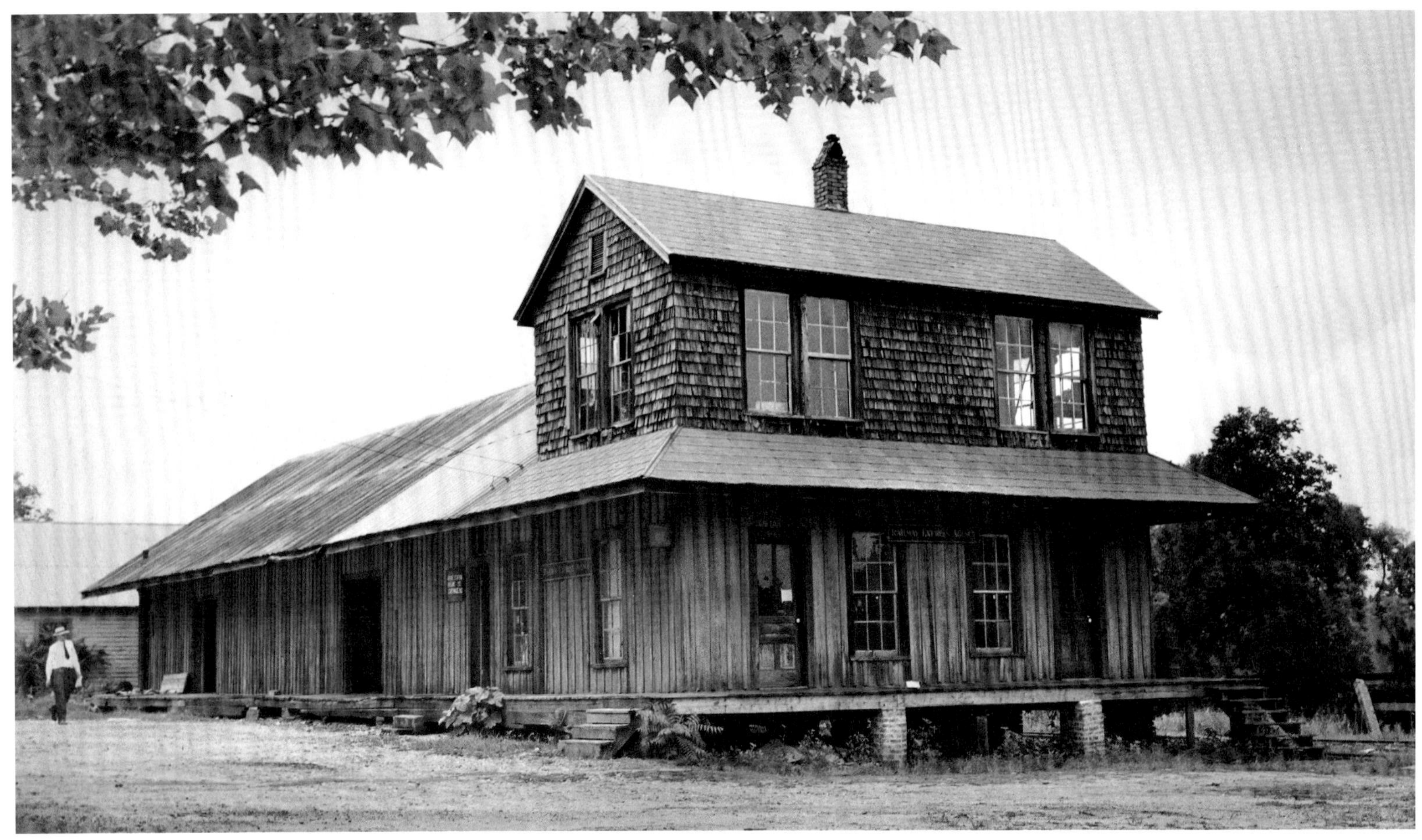

Plate 111. A lonely station on the Moore Central Railroad, in the North Carolina sand hills. The look of the man on the far left indicates that this is the US South. Charles Clegg. Beebe-Clegg negative 4018.

Courtesy of the California State Railroad Museum.

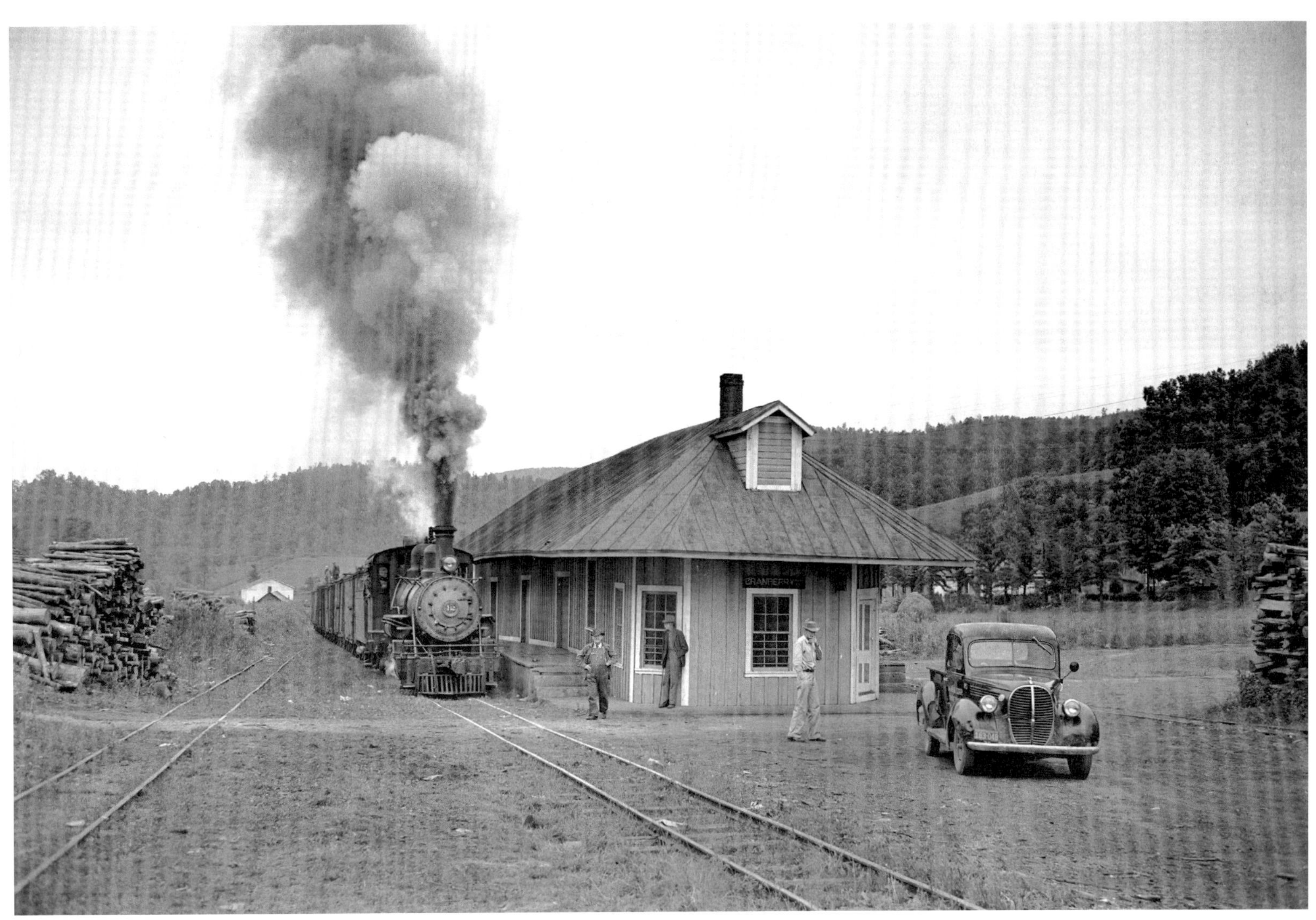

Plate 112. A Tweetsie (East Tennessee & Western North Carolina Railroad) train at the station in Cranberry, North Carolina, June 1946. Cranberry is the site of a now-closed iron mine, one of the reasons for the railroad's existence. Charles Clegg. Beebe-Clegg negative 2240.

Courtesy of the California State Railroad Museum.

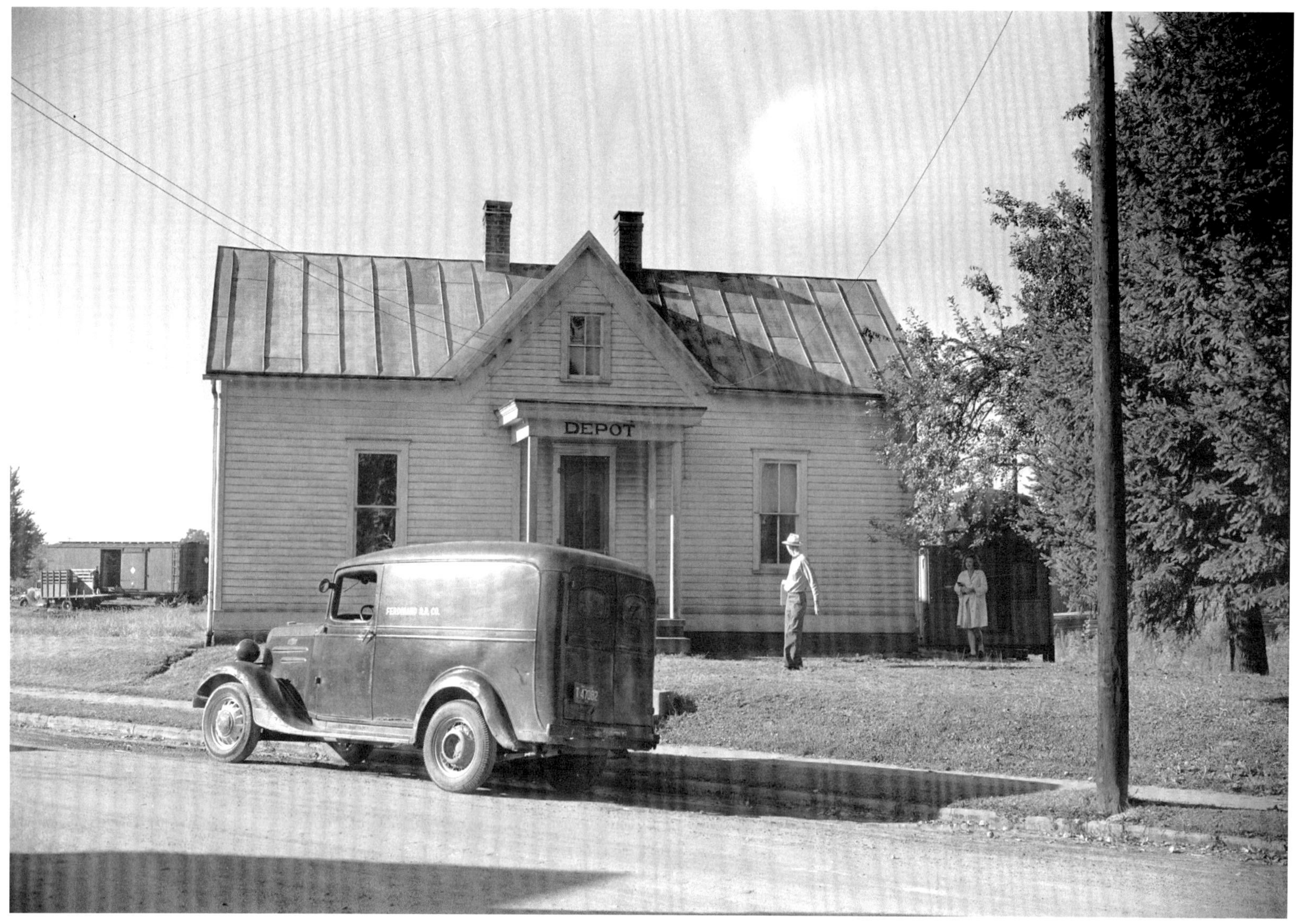

Plate 113. This depot on the Ferdinand Railroad, in Indiana, looks like a mill house. A railroad delivery truck waits at the curb. Walker Evans's influence seems to be visible in this photo. Charles Clegg. Beebe-Clegg negative 424.

Courtesy of the California State Railroad Museum.

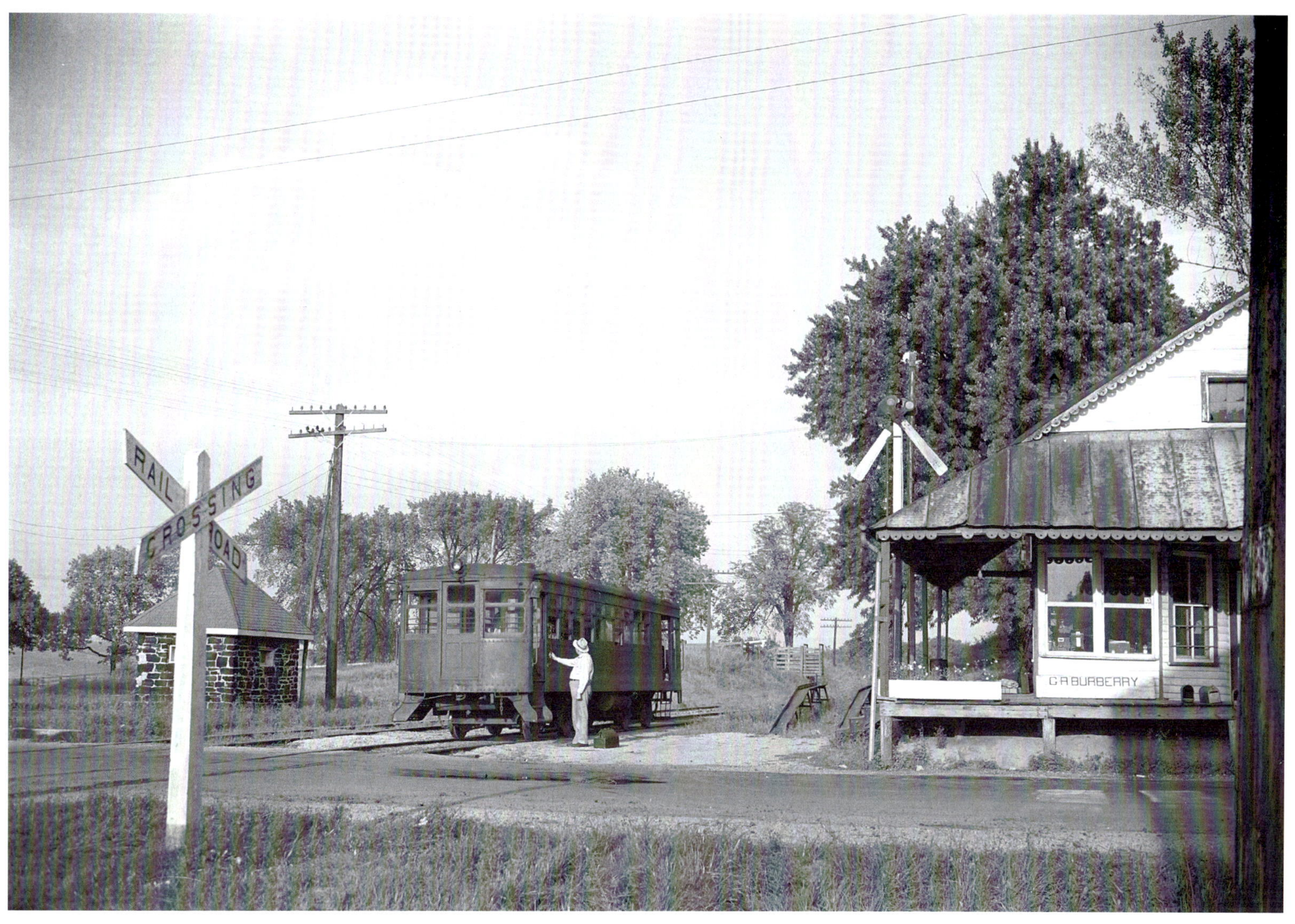

Plate 114. "Along the Whiskey Railroad." A Frankfort & Cincinnati Railroad motorcar, M55-1, the eastbound afternoon *Cardinal*, stops for a passenger at Burberry's General Store and post office, Centerville, Kentucky. This motorcar is now at the Kentucky Railway Museum. Charles Clegg. Beebe-Clegg negative 2142.

Courtesy of the California State Railroad Museum.

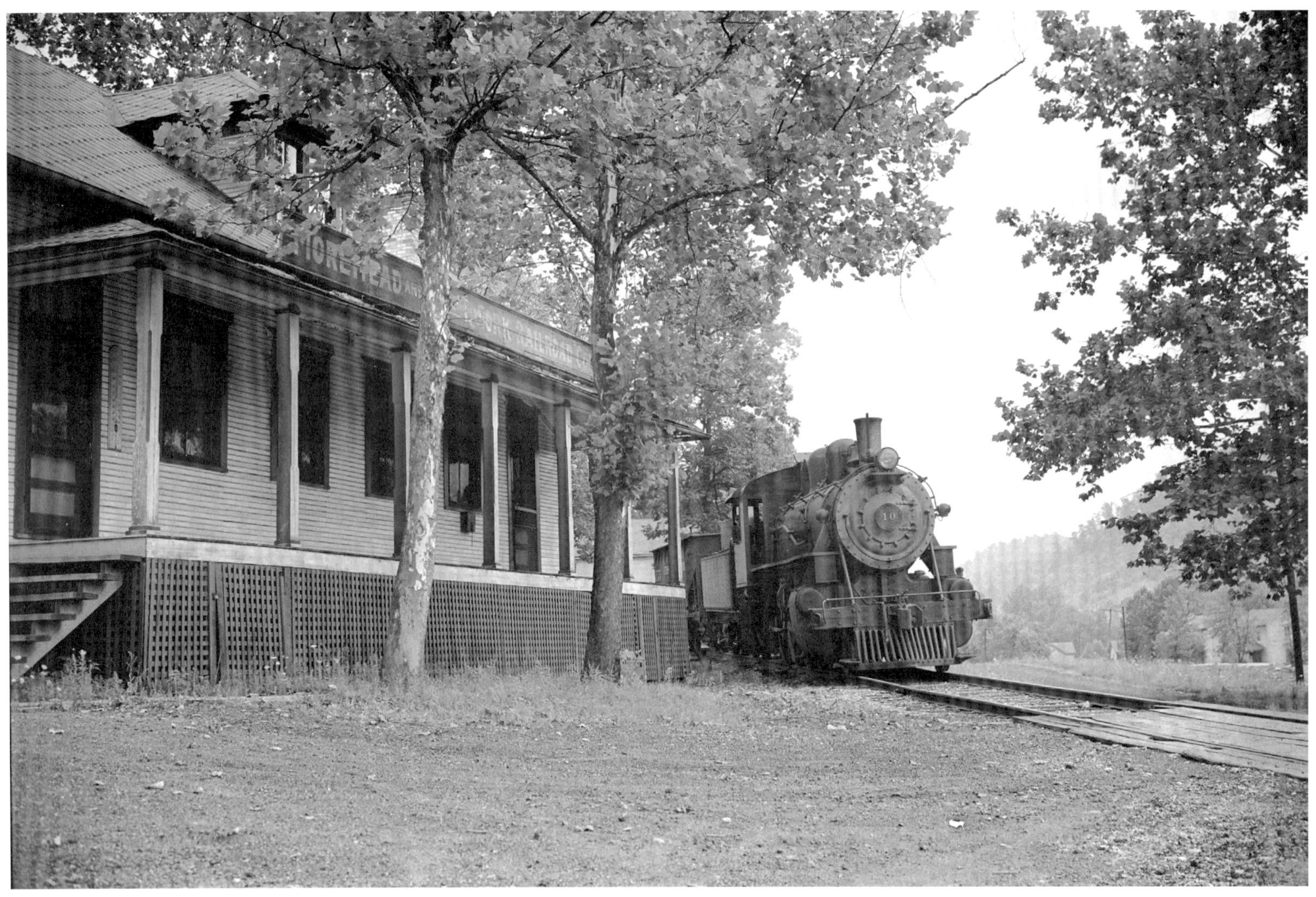

Plate 115. Morehead & North Fork Railroad No. 10 at another railroad station, which looks like a company house, Clearfield, Kentucky. Charles Clegg. Beebe-Clegg negative 2968.

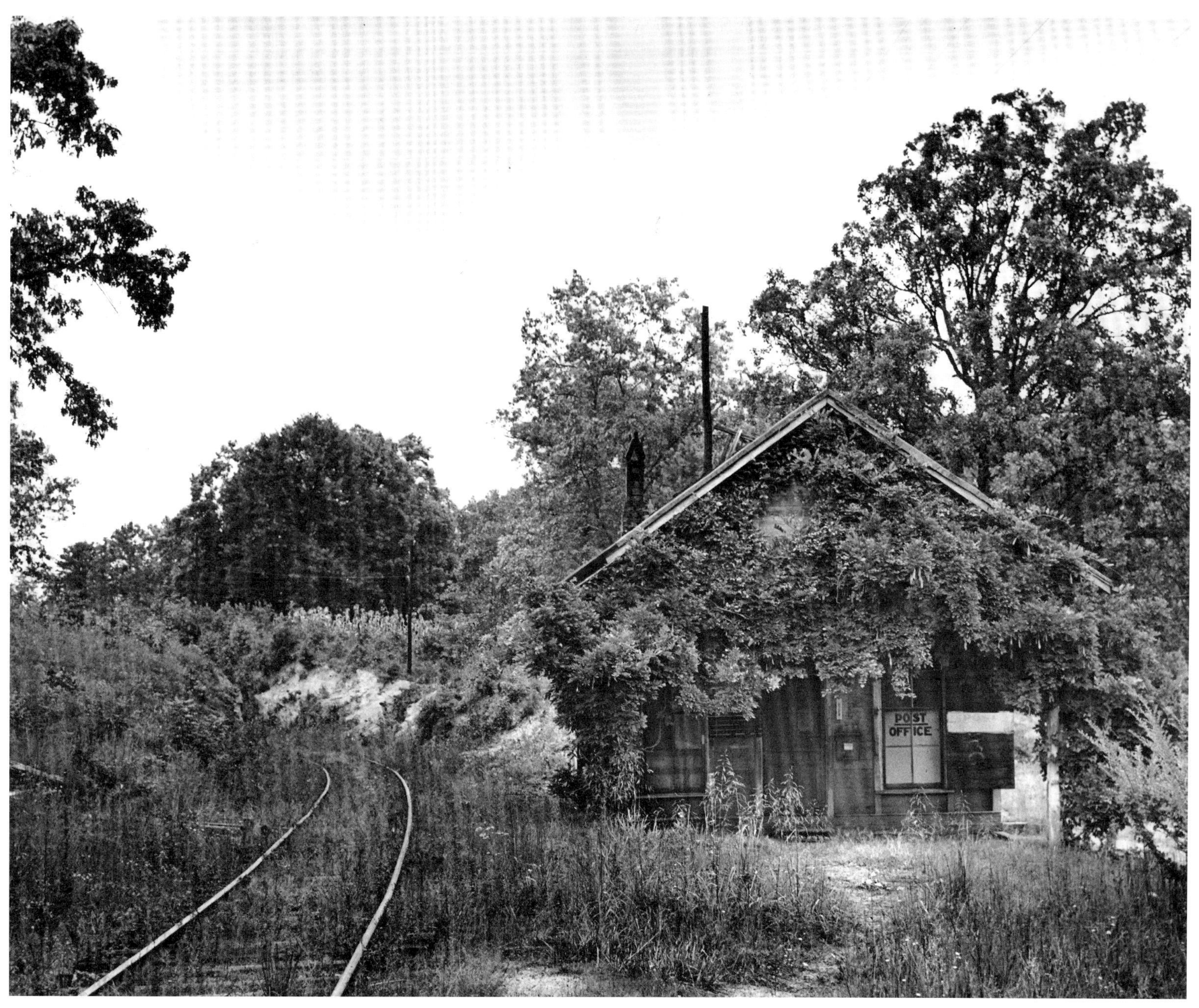

Plate 116. A singularly run-down and vine-covered post office along the Tallulah Falls Railroad in northern Georgia. Charles Clegg. Beebe-Clegg negative 4017.

Courtesy of the California State Railroad Museum.

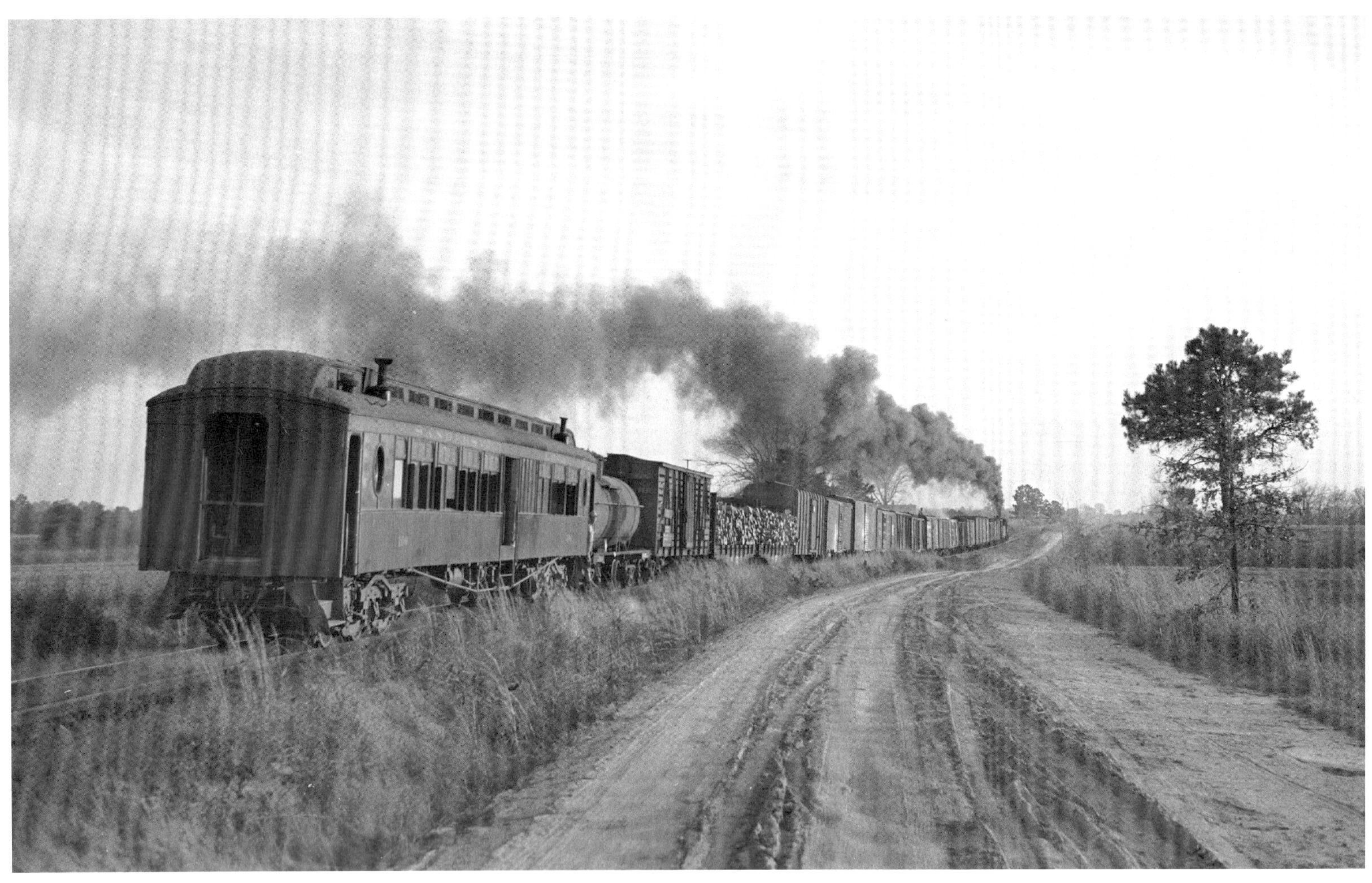

Plate 117. A mixed train on the Sandersville Railroad. Note the Jim Crow coach at the end of the train. Charles Clegg. Beebe-Clegg negative 1757.

Courtesy of the California State Railroad Museum.

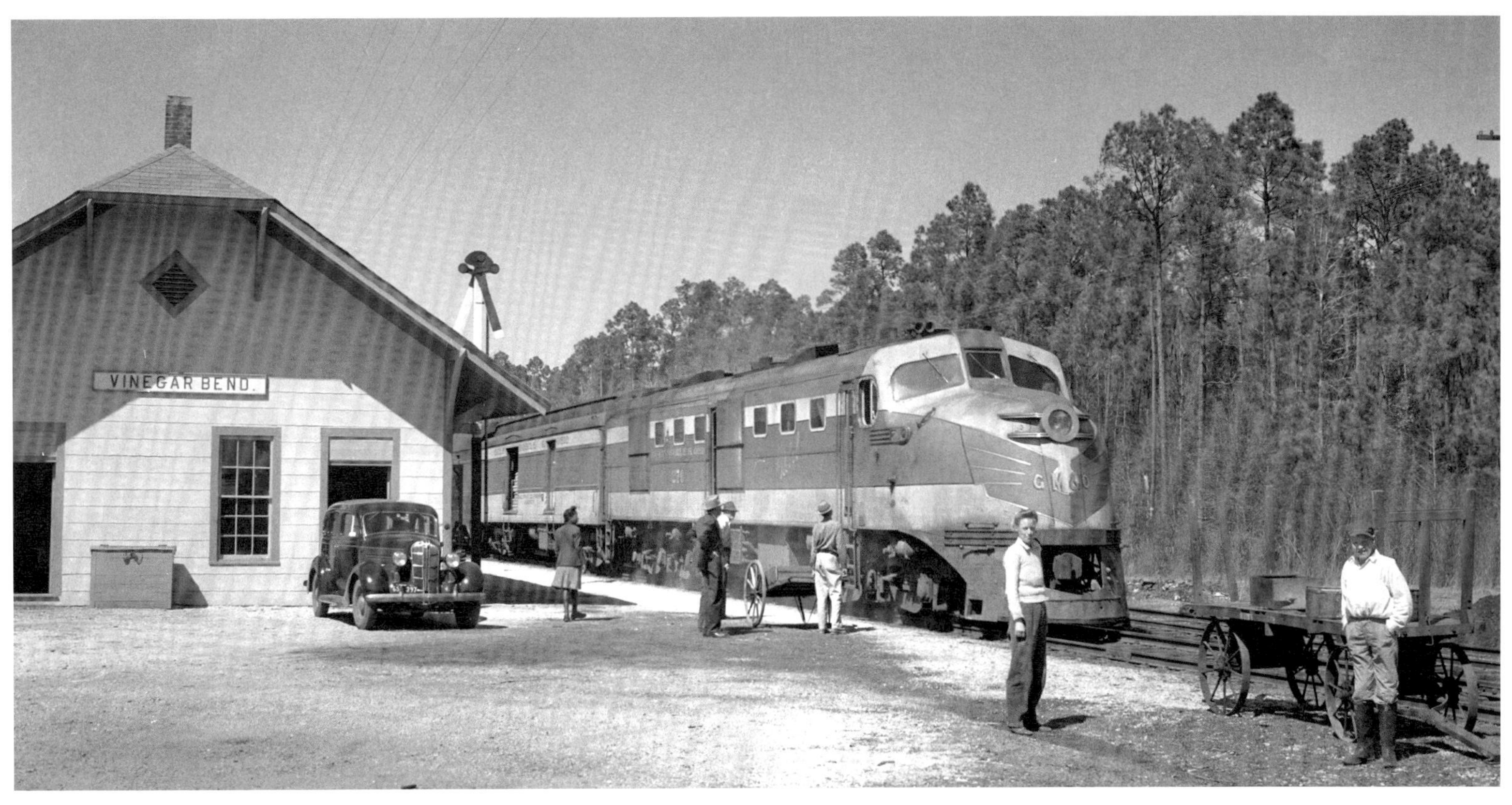

Plate 118. A diesel-hauled train, a rarity in the Charles Clegg oeuvre. This Gulf, Mobile & Ohio passenger train is at the station in Vinegar Bend, Alabama, the junction point with the Mississippi & Alabama Railroad. Charles Clegg. Beebe-Clegg negative 2346.

Courtesy of the California State Railroad Museum.

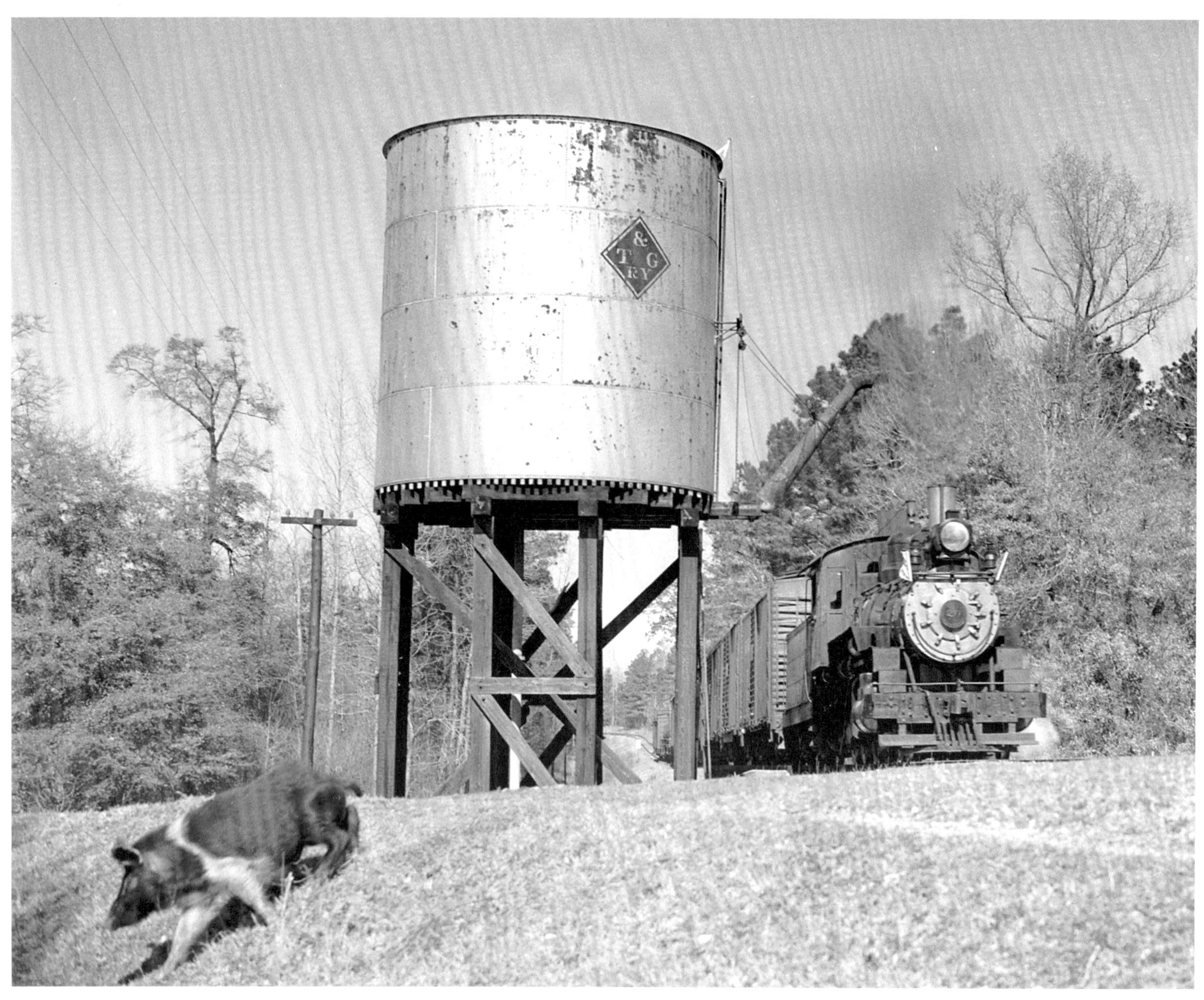

Plate 119. Portrait of the Tremont & Gulf Railway, in Louisiana. *Left to right,* a hog, a water tank, and a train. The location is Grandstaff, Louisiana. Charles Clegg. Beebe-Clegg negative 621.

Courtesy of the California State Railroad Museum.

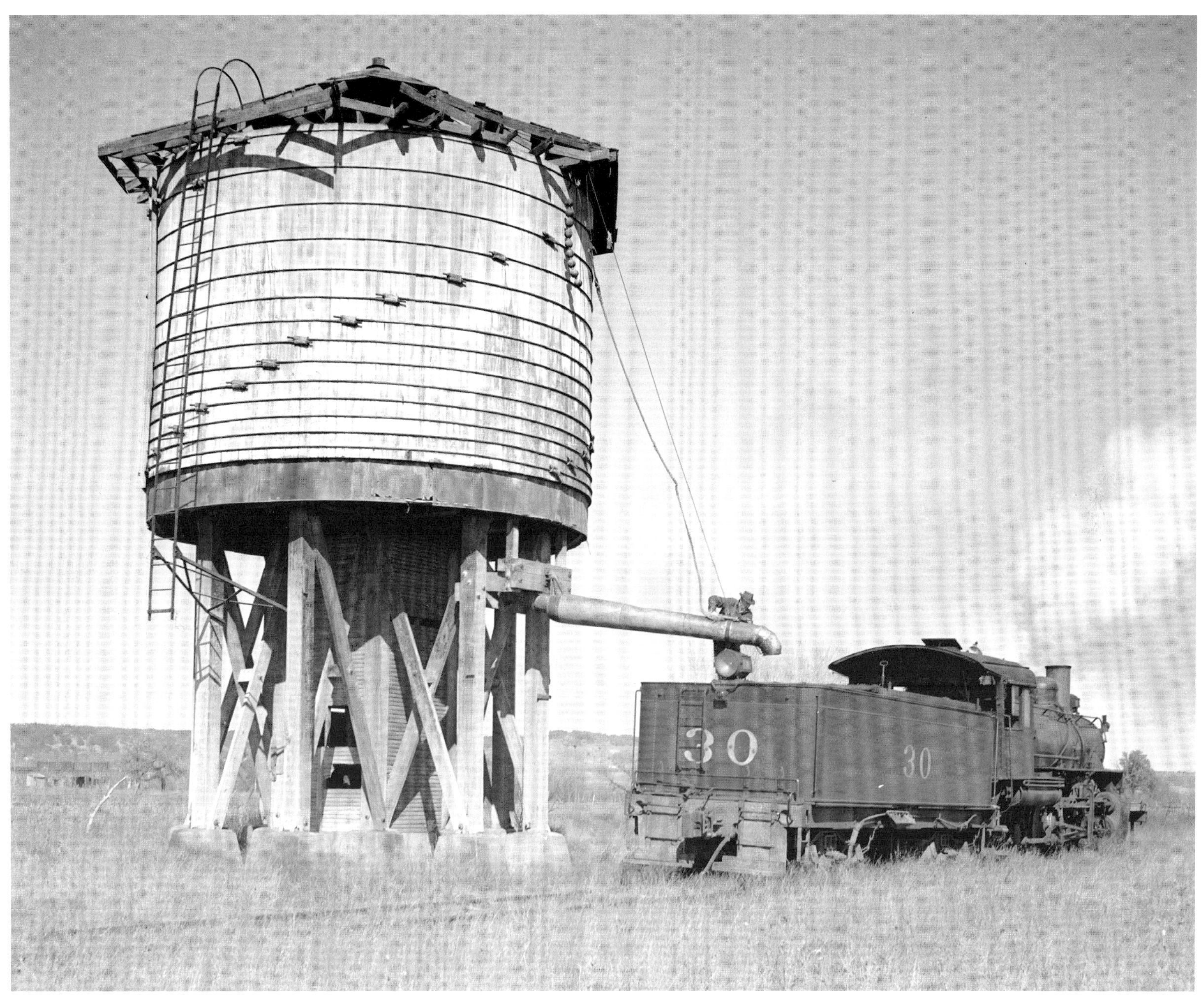

Plate 120. "At the Haunted Water Tower." Wichita Falls & Southern No. 30 stops for water at the tank in Ranger, Texas. Charles Clegg. Beebe-Clegg negative 801.

Courtesy of the California State Railroad Museum.

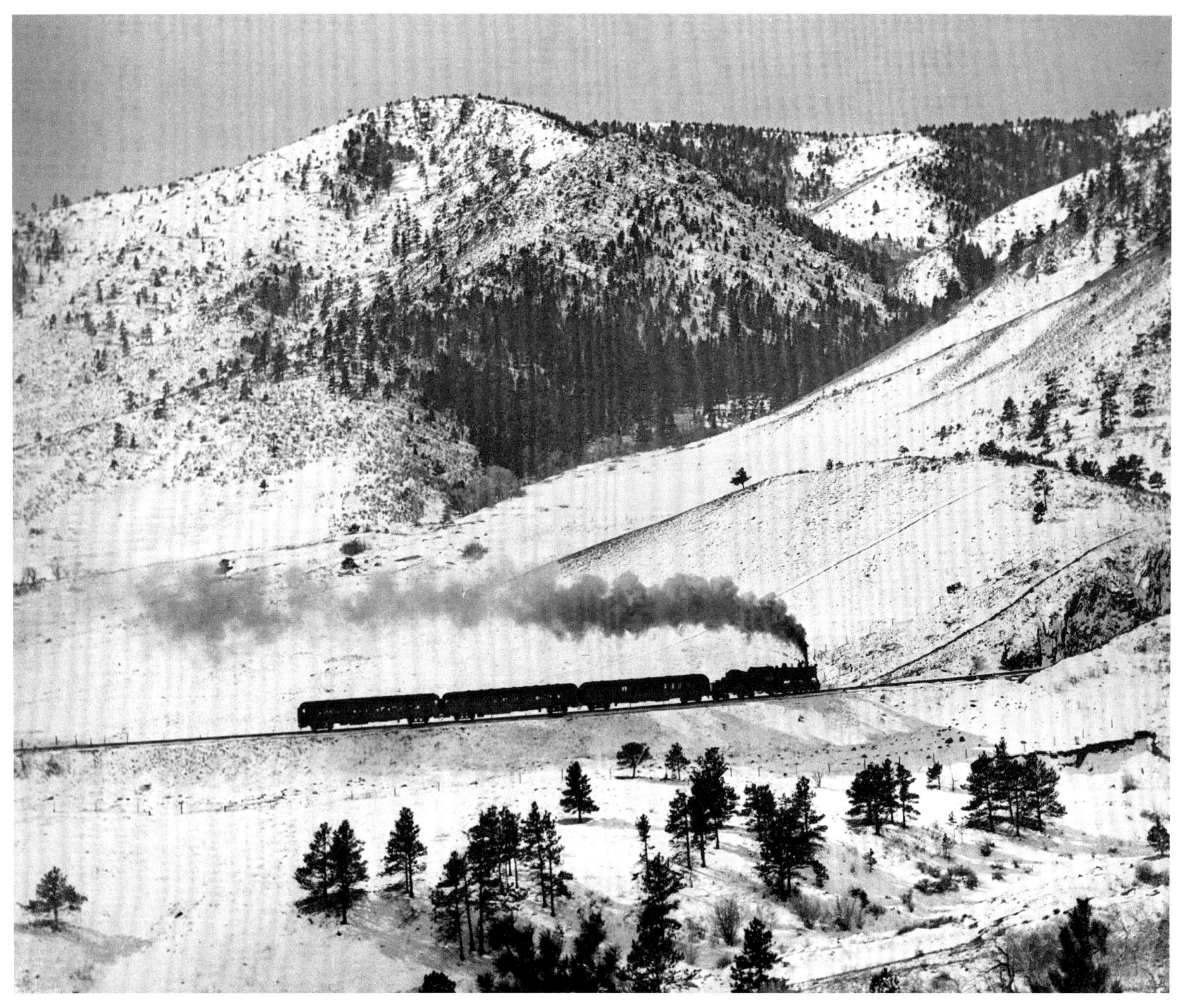

Plate 121. A passenger train on the Denver & Salt Lake in the Colorado Rockies in winter. Lucius Beebe. Beebe-Clegg negative 1118.

Courtesy of the California State Railroad Museum.

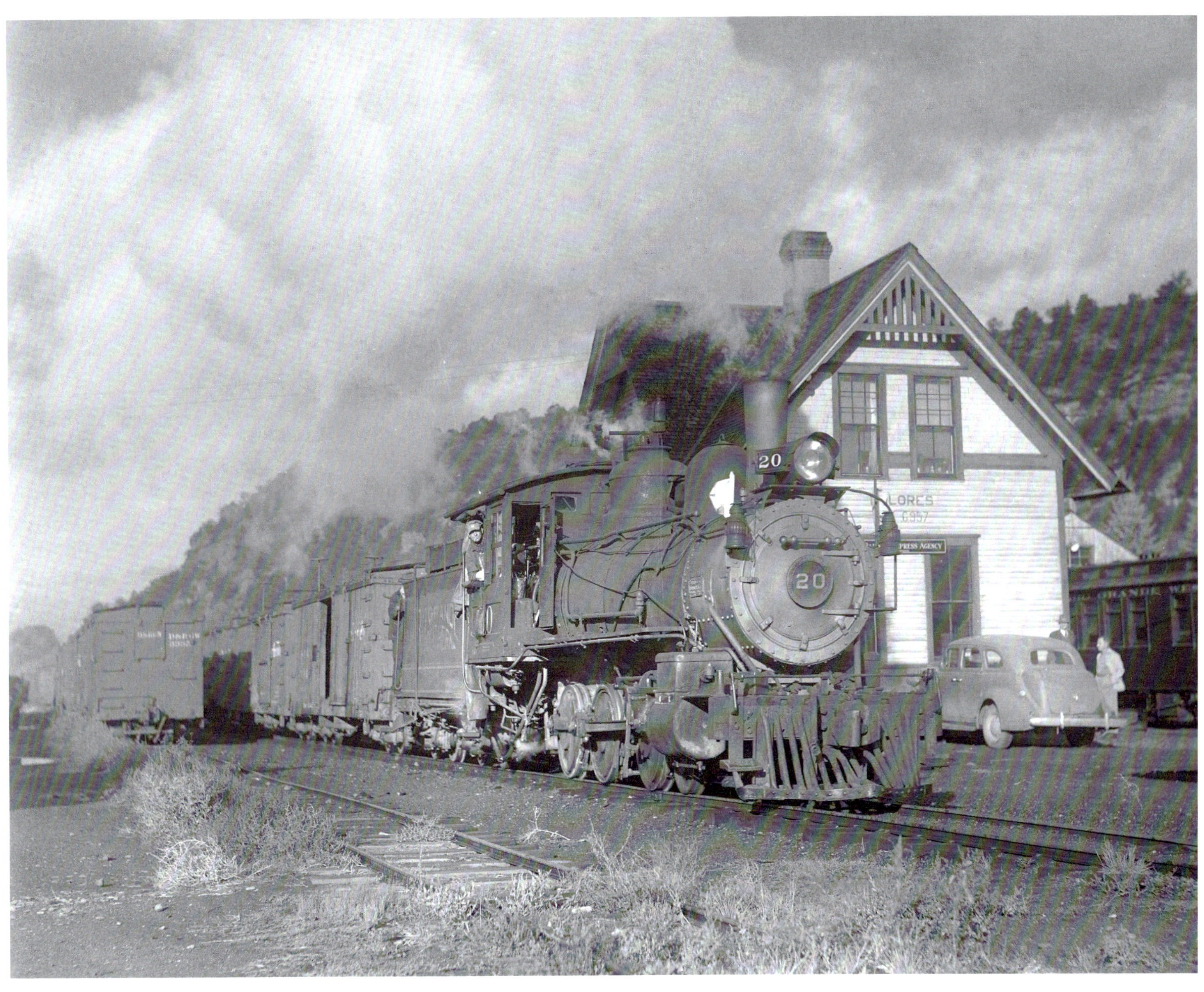

Plate 122. Rio Grande Southern No. 20 with a train at the depot in Dolores, Colorado. The engineer looks out his cab window, and bystanders talk next to a car in the station's parking lot. Lucius Beebe or Charles Clegg. Beebe-Clegg negative 3063.

Courtesy of the California State Railroad Museum.

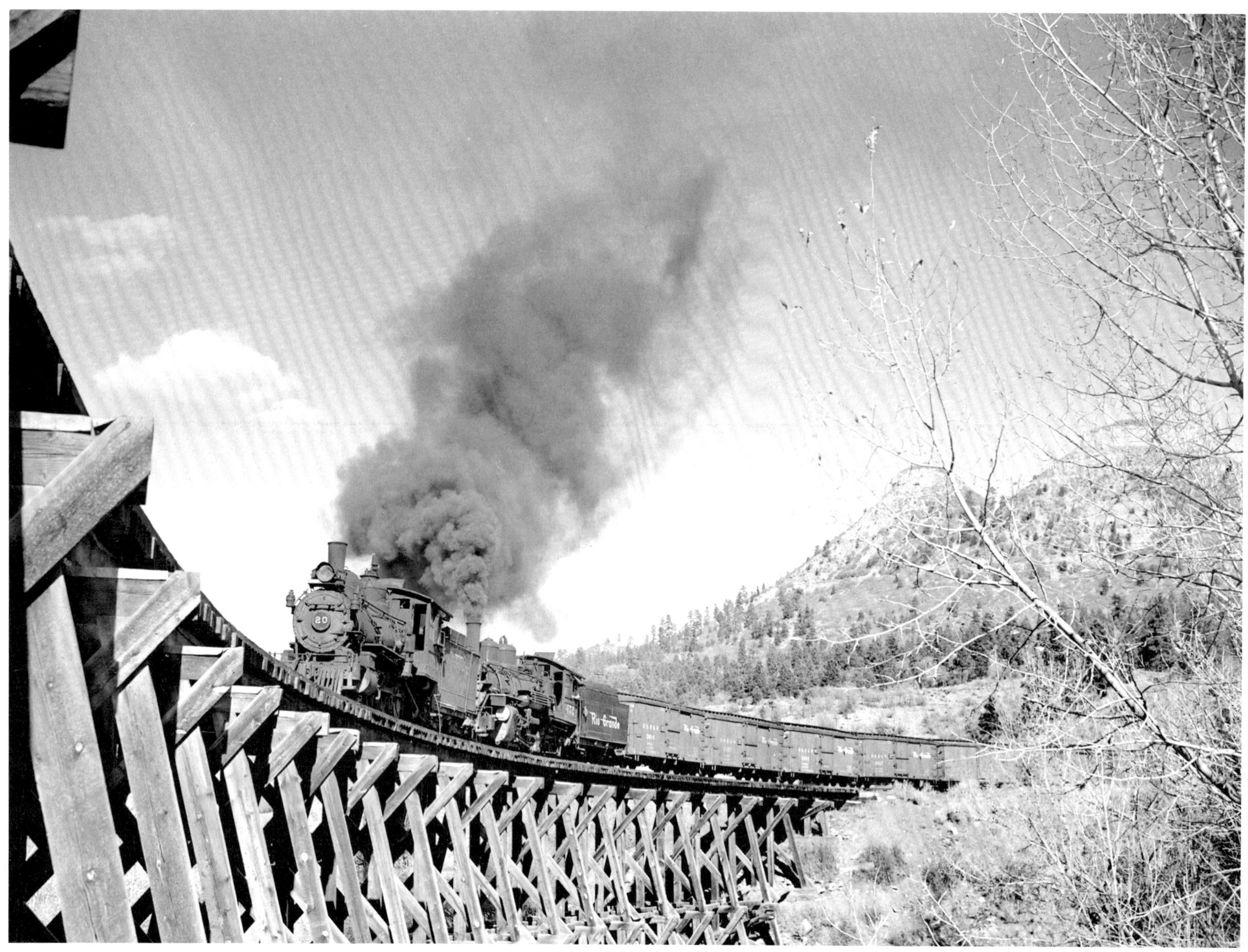

Plate 123. "Symphony in the San Juan." A westbound Rio Grande Southern freight, a doubleheader with RGS No. 20 and a leased Denver & Rio Grande locomotive, crosses Lightner Creek Trestle west of Durango, Colorado. Charles Clegg. Beebe-Clegg negative 1170.

Courtesy of the California State Railroad Museum.

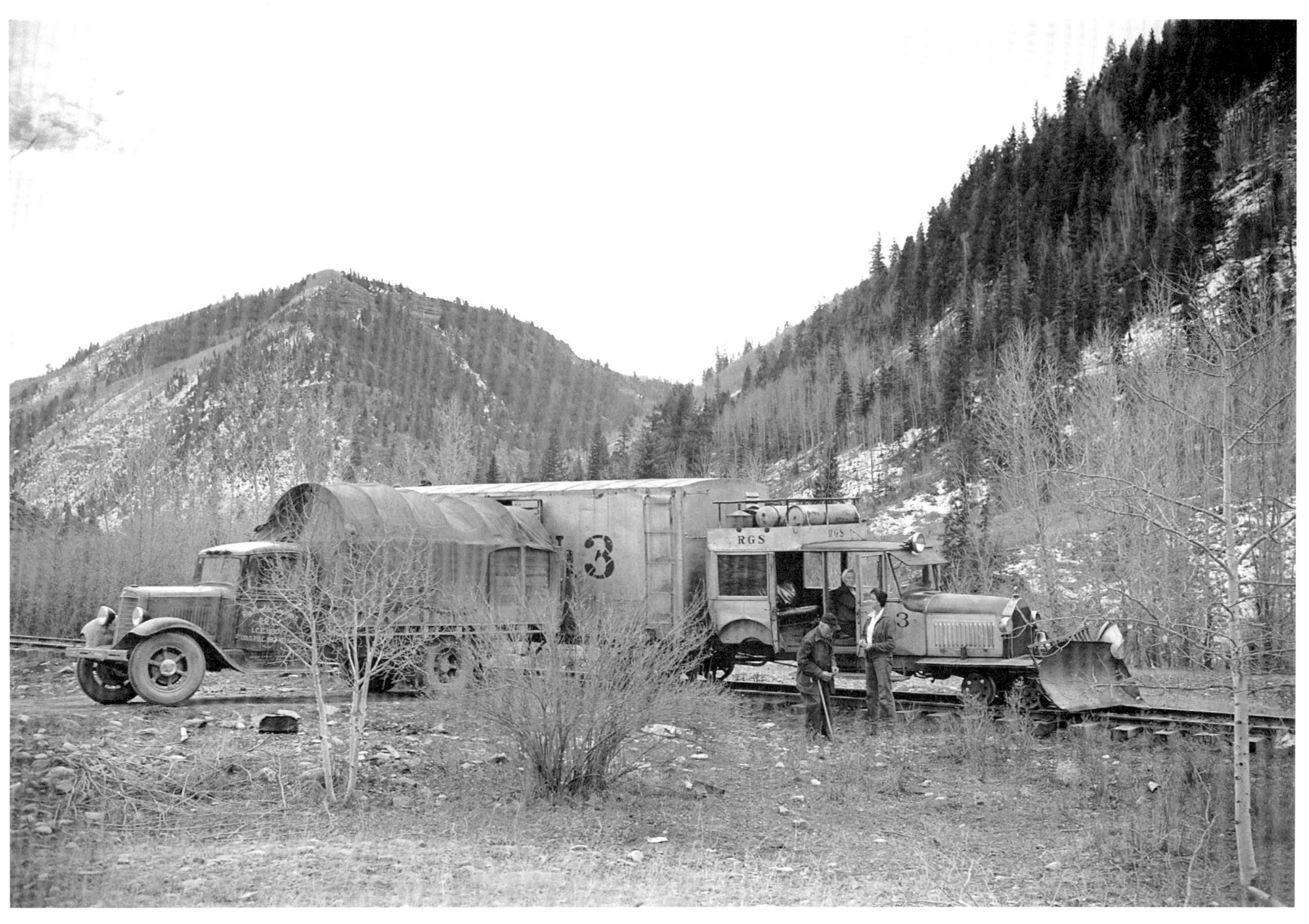

Plate 124. A mail truck meeting a Rio Grande Southern "Galloping Goose" at Vance Junction, Colorado, in October 1945. Vance Junction was where the Telluride branch left the Rio Grande Southern main line. Lucius Beebe or Charles Clegg. Beebe-Clegg negative 3069.

Courtesy of the California State Railroad Museum.

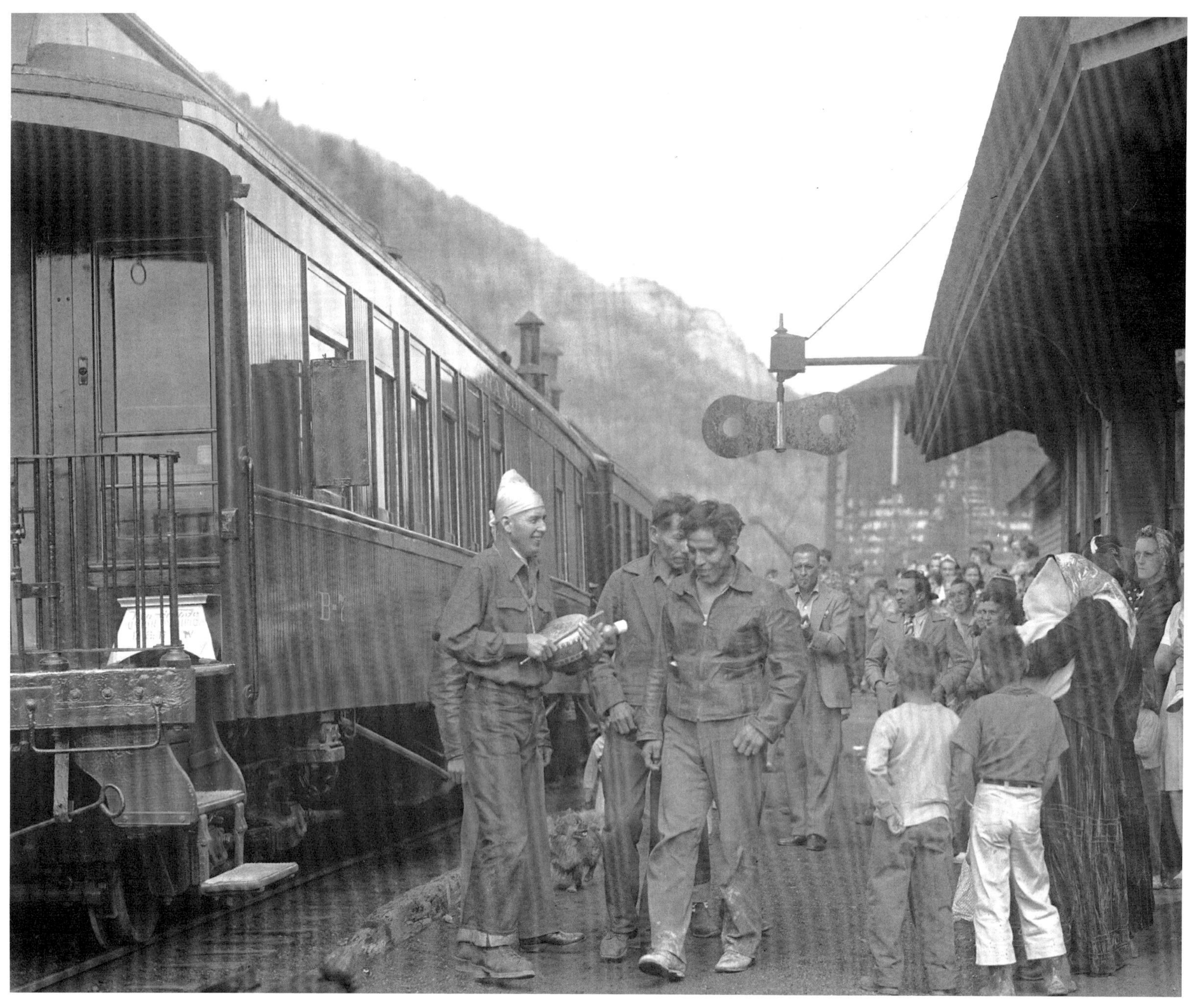

Plate 125. "Our Troops." On the Rio Grande Southern at Rico, Colorado. Charles Clegg. Beebe-Clegg negative 3258.

Courtesy of the California State Railroad Museum.

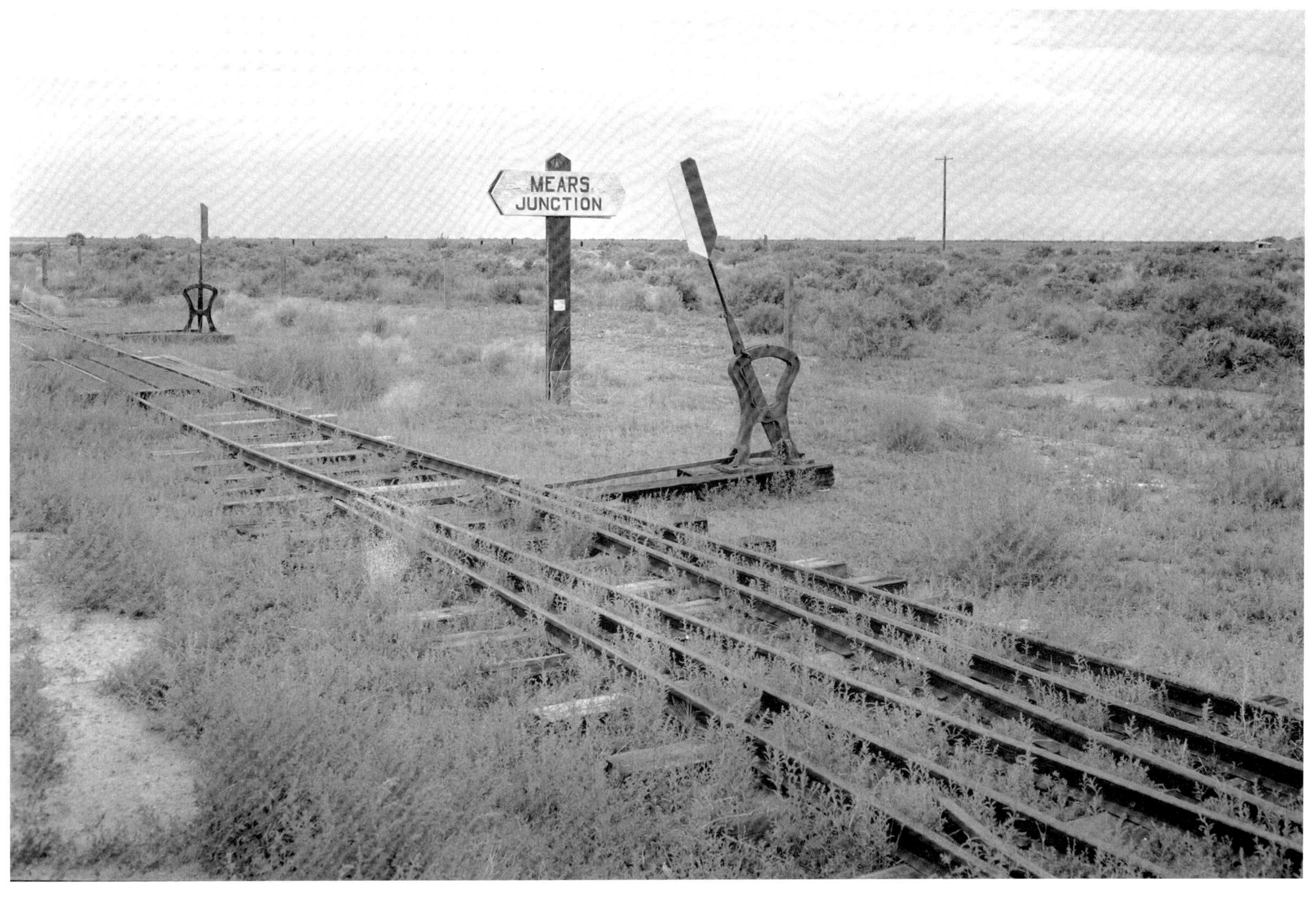

Plate 126. A harp switch stand at Mears Junction, Colorado. Lucius Beebe. Beebe-Clegg negative 3217.

Courtesy of the California State Railroad Museum.

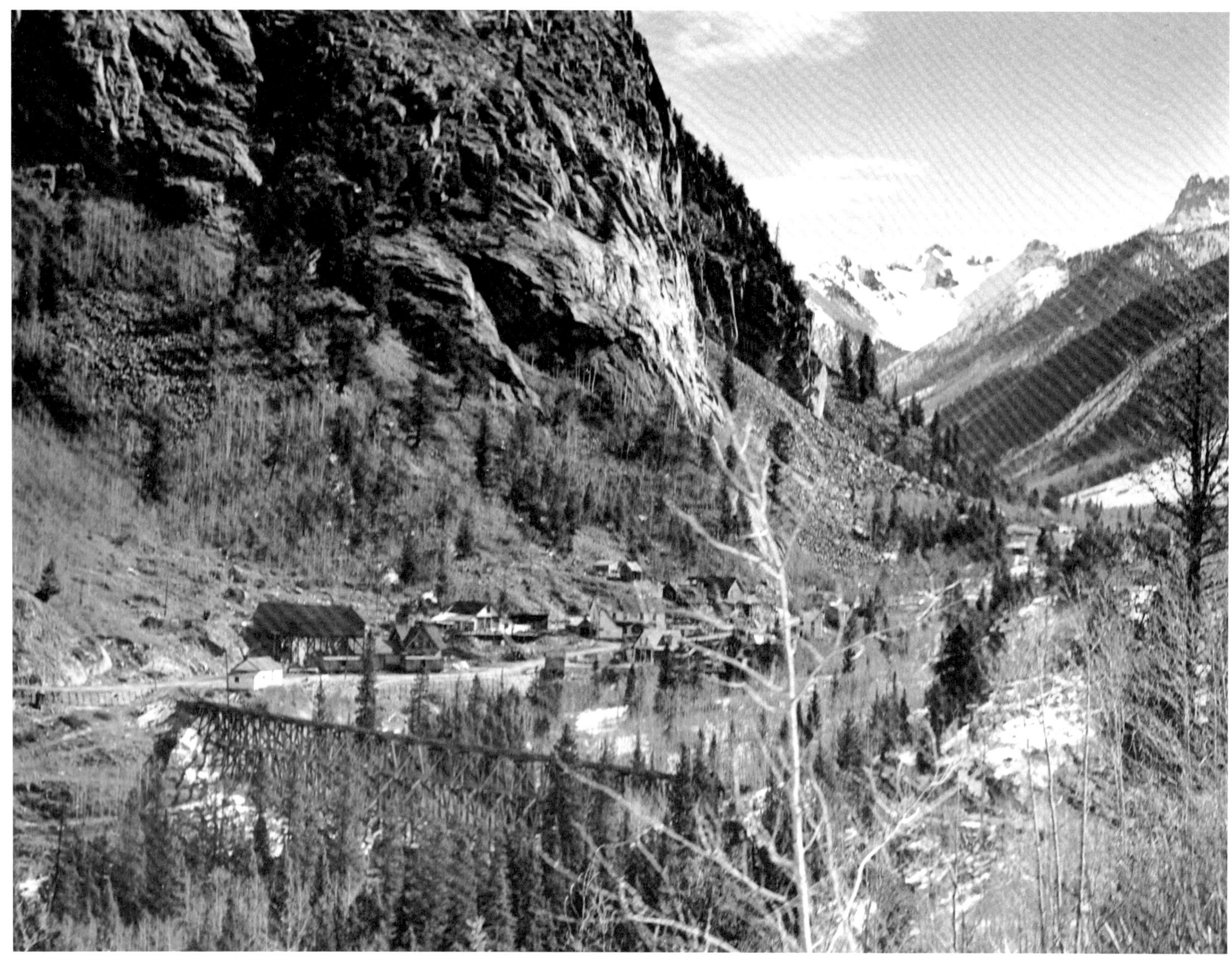

Plate 127. A beautiful landscape view of the Rio Grande Southern at Ophir, Colorado. Charles Clegg. Beebe-Clegg negative 4020.

Courtesy of the California State Railroad Museum.

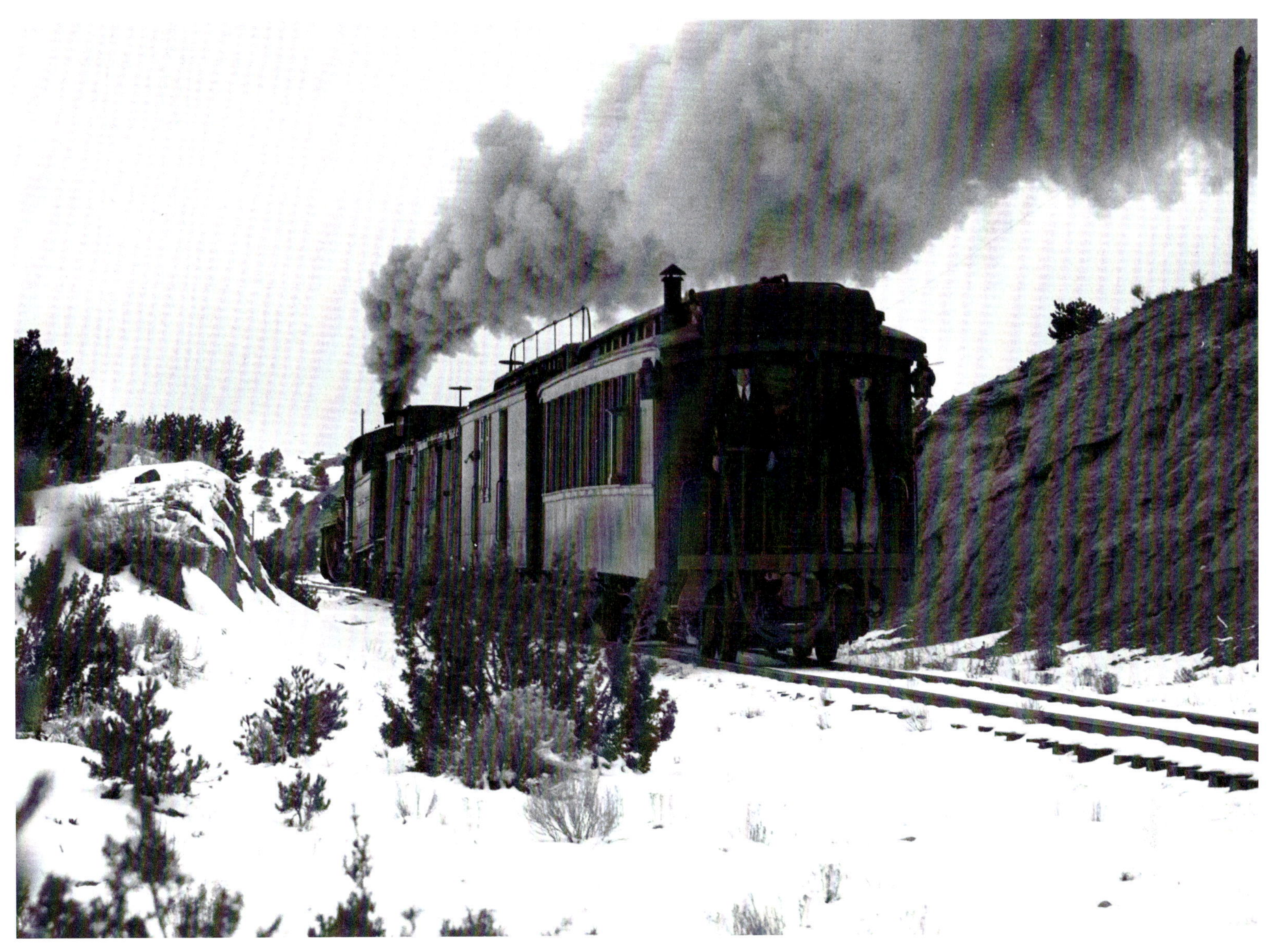

Plate 128. Time is running out for the famed narrow-gauge Denver & Rio Grande Western "Chili Line" branch from Antonito, Colorado, to Santa Fe, New Mexico, on Christmas Eve, 1940. Lucius Beebe. Beebe-Clegg negative 2094.

Courtesy of the California State Railroad Museum.

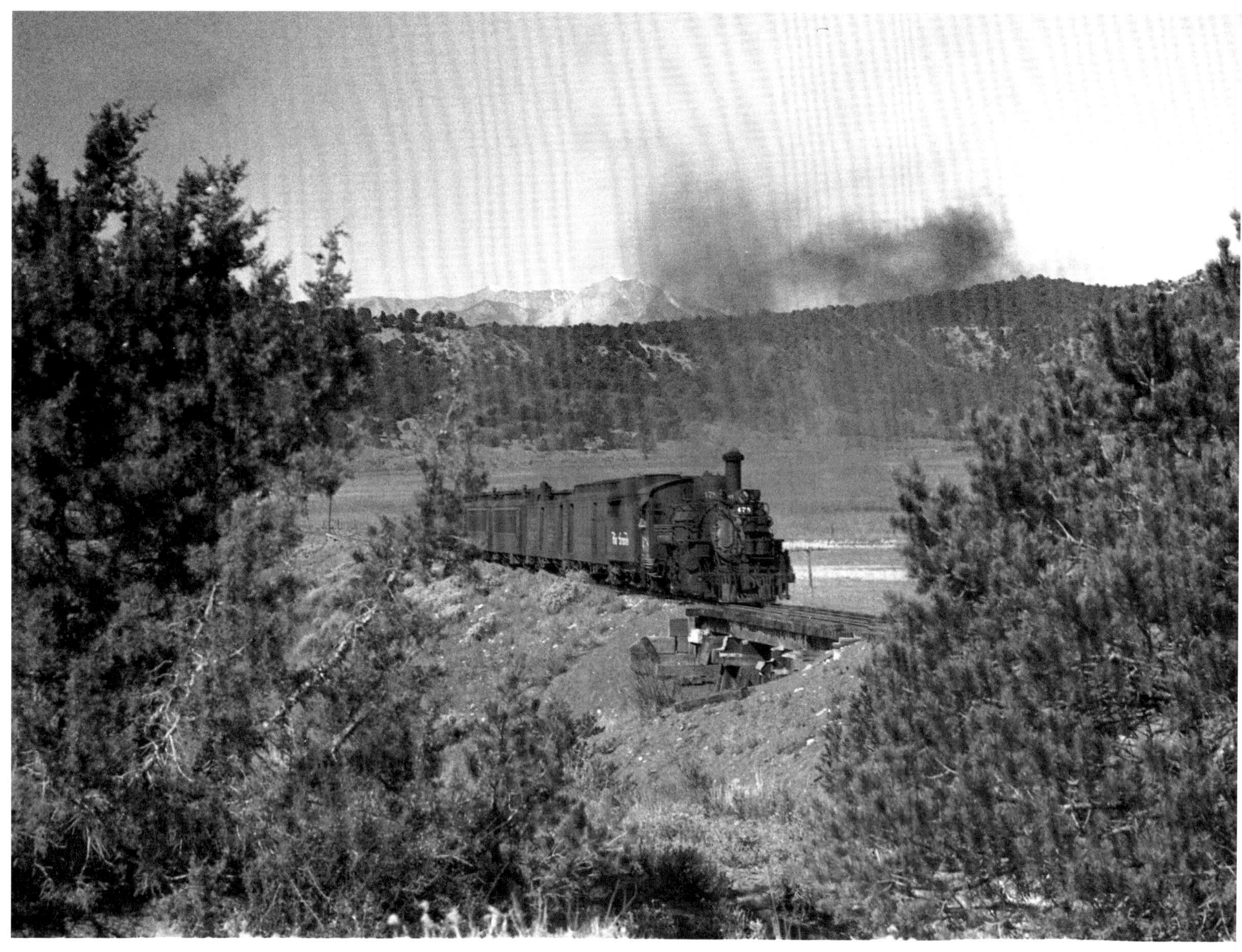

Plate 129. The narrow-gauge Denver & Rio Grande Western's *San Juan* between Alamosa and Durango, Colorado. Charles Clegg. Beebe-Clegg negative 1545.

Courtesy of the California State Railroad Museum.

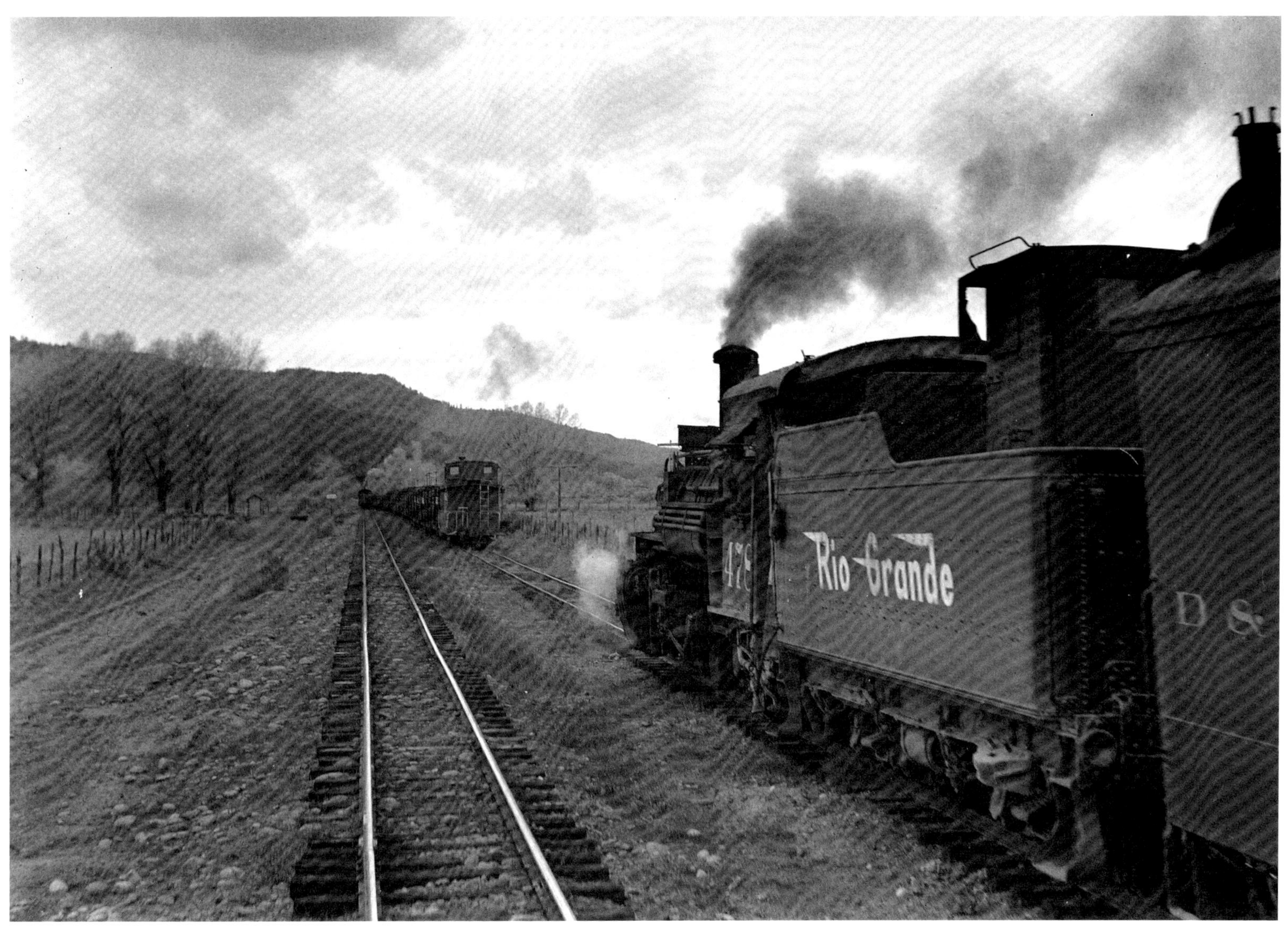

Plate 130. A triple meet on the Denver & Rio Grande narrow gauge, with the westbound *San Juan* and a freight train visible in the photo. The image is taken from the back platform of the eastbound *San Juan*. Lucius Beebe. Beebe-Clegg negative 1570.

Courtesy of the California State Railroad Museum.

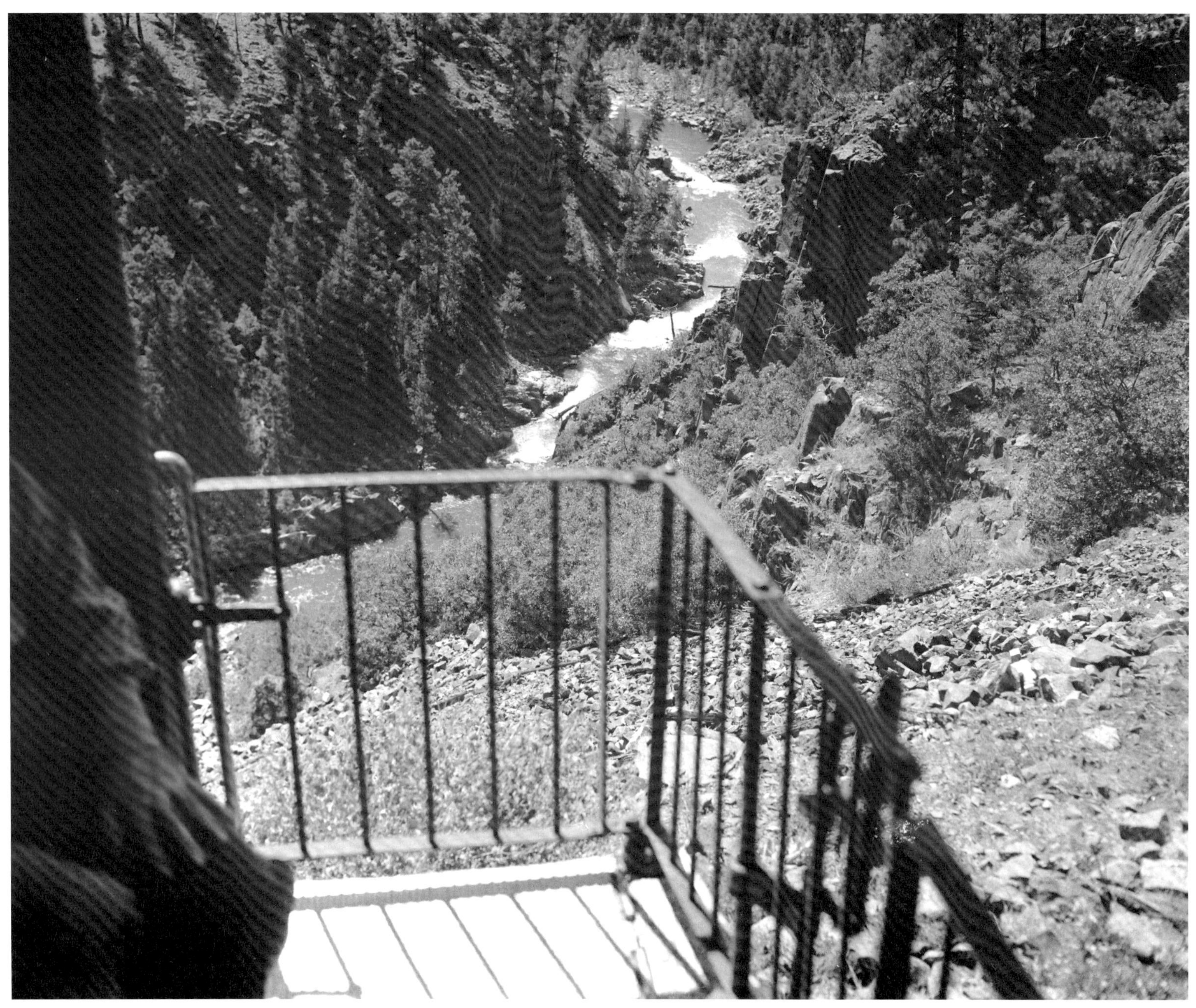

Plate 131. A view of Animas Gorge from the platform of a Denver & Rio Grande Western narrow-gauge train. Charles Clegg. Beebe-Clegg negative 2088.

Courtesy of the California State Railroad Museum.

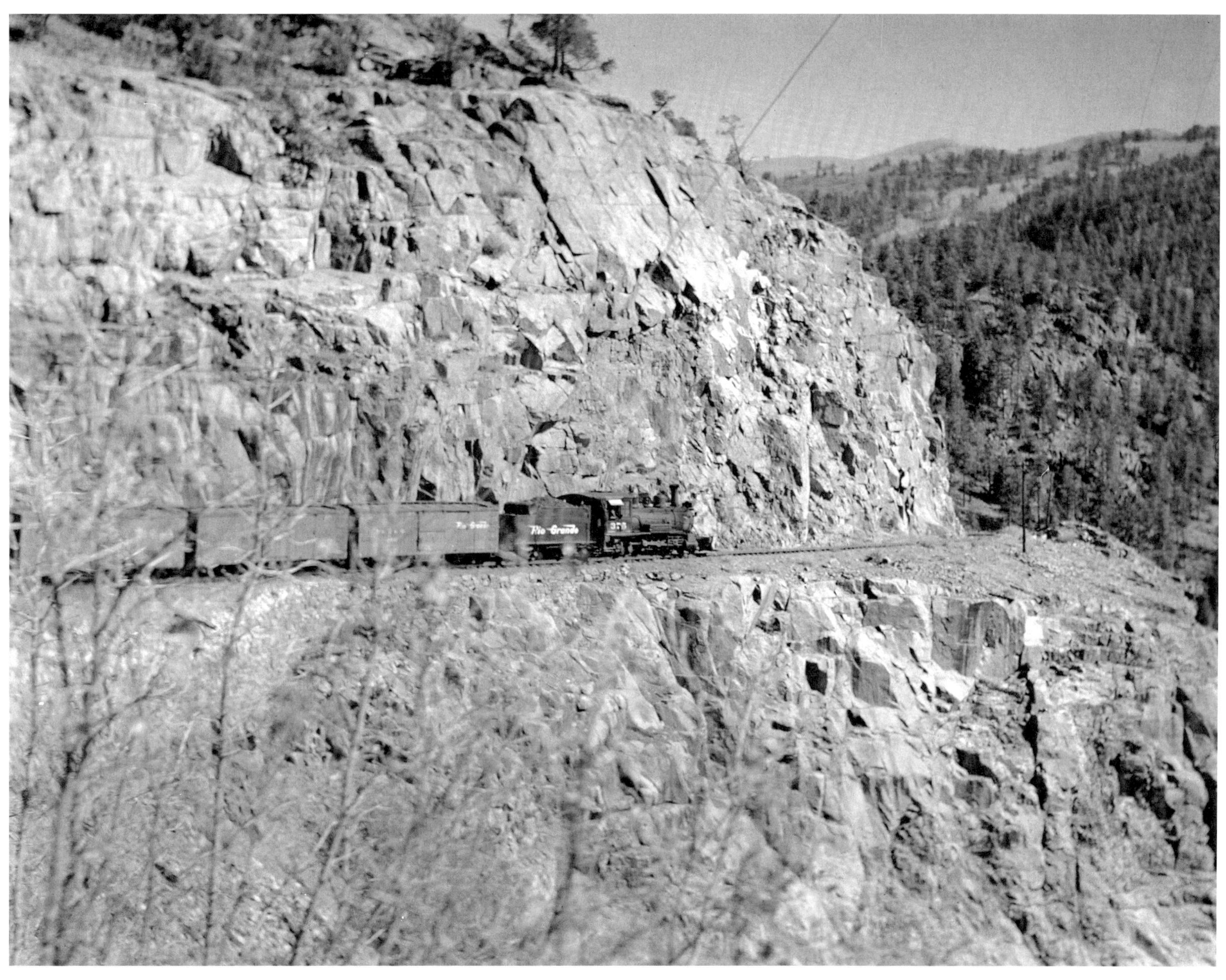

Plate 132. A Denver & Rio Grande "Silverton train" above the Animas River on "The High Line." Lucius Beebe. Beebe-Clegg negative 1533.

Courtesy of the California State Railroad Museum.

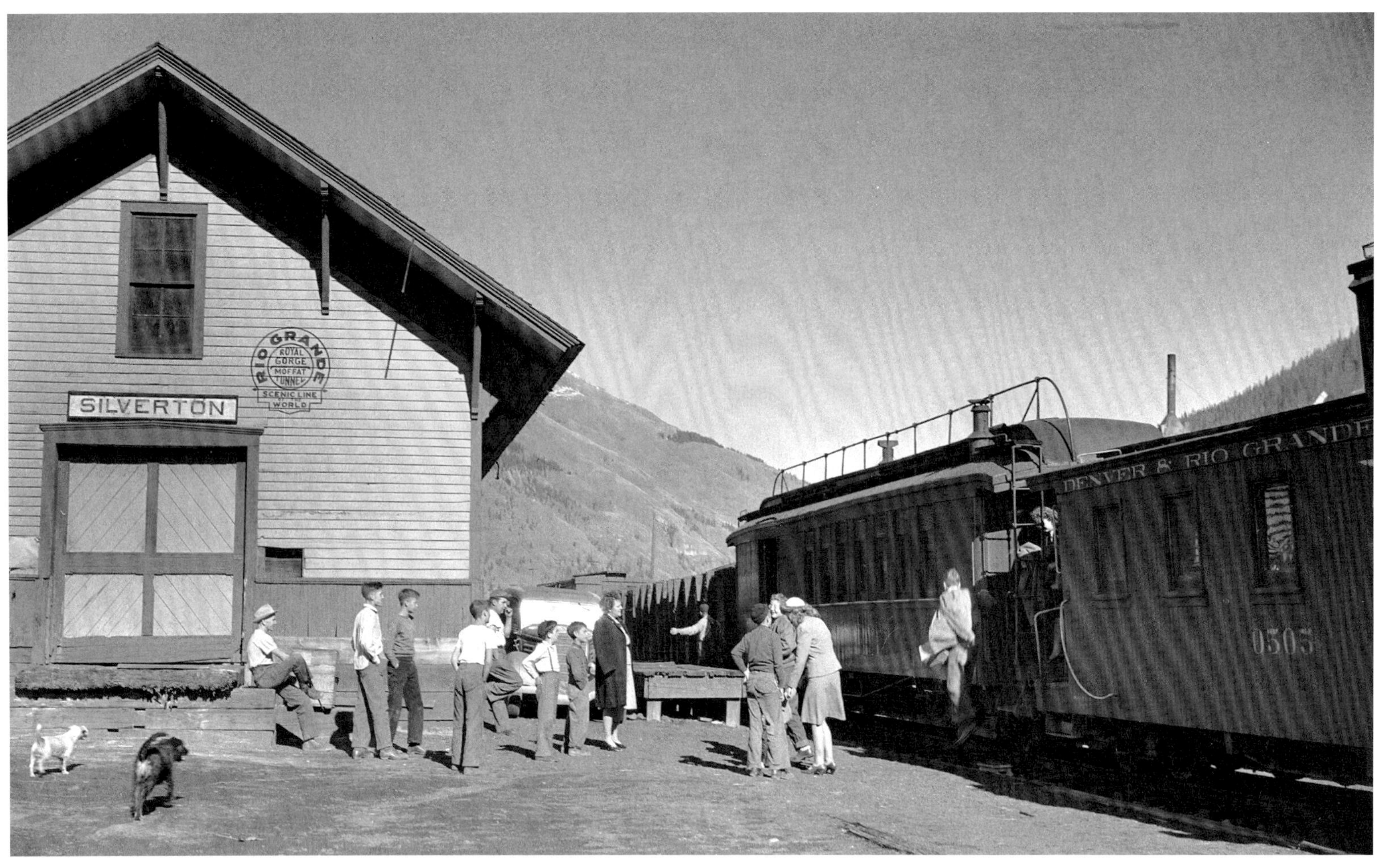

Plate 133. The twice-a-week Denver & Rio Grande Western "Silverton train," a mixed train during this period, arrives at the D & RGW station in Silverton, Colorado. Even the village's dogs came down to meet the train. Charles Clegg. Beebe-Clegg negative 2176.

Courtesy of the California State Railroad Museum.

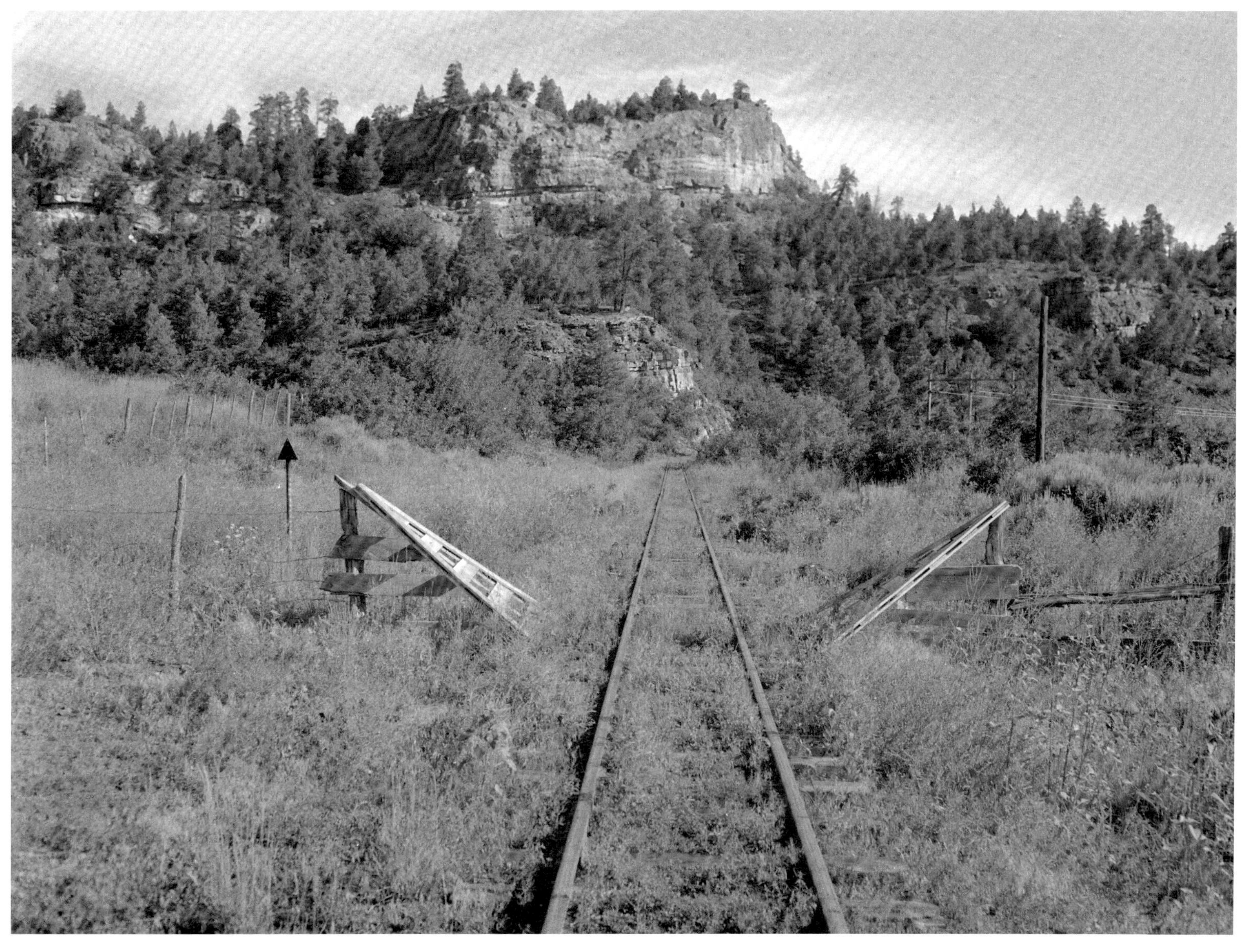

Plate 134. Cattle guards where the Denver & Rio Grande Western's narrow-gauge branch from Durango to Silverton, Colorado, crosses a pasture fence. Taken near Rockwood, Colorado. Lucius Beebe. Beebe-Clegg negative 2719.

Courtesy of the California State Railroad Museum.

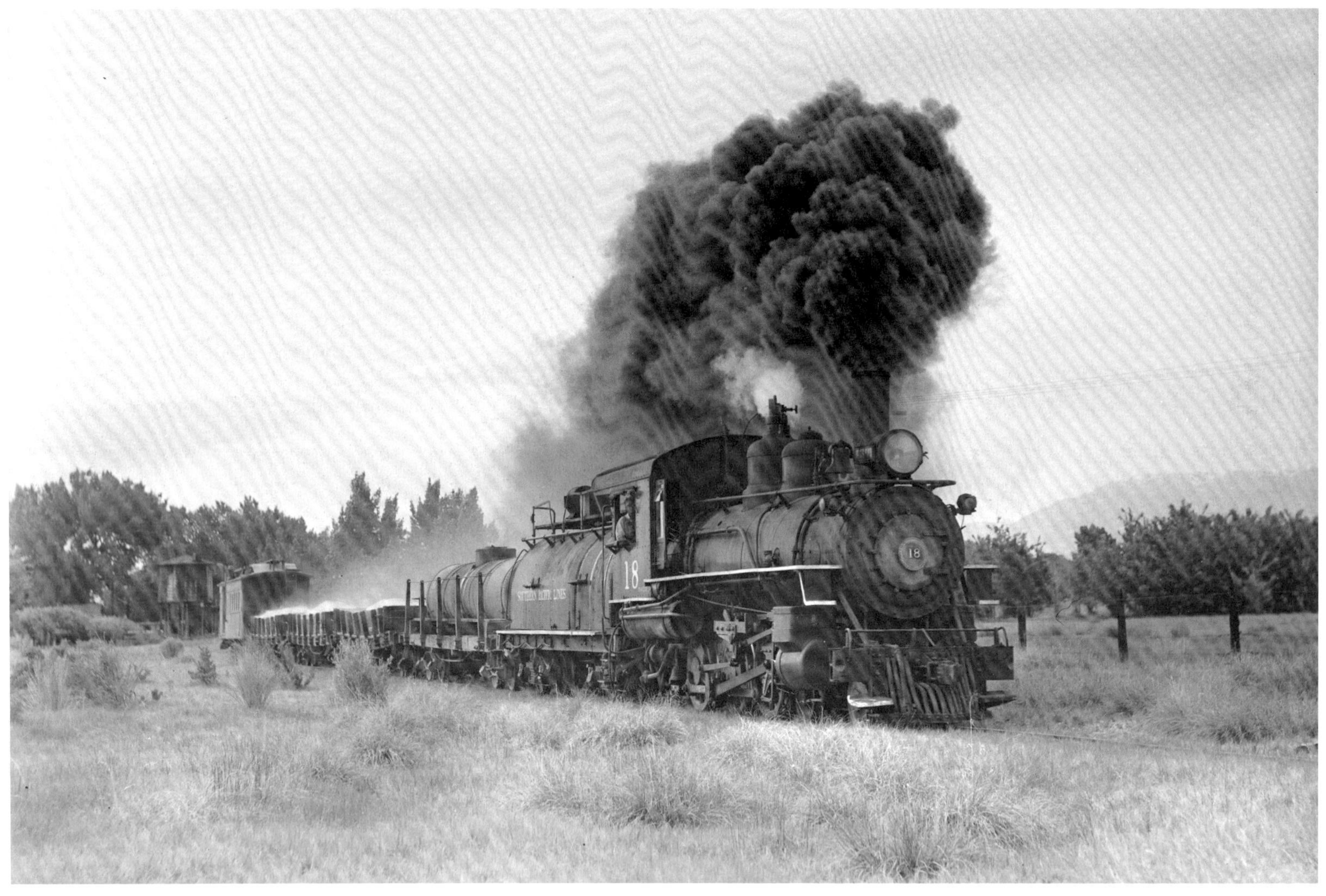

Plate 135. Southern Pacific narrow-gauge steam locomotive No. 18 with a train at Laws, California. Dust rising from loads drifts off the gondola cars. Lucius Beebe. Beebe-Clegg negative 1260.

Courtesy of the California State Railroad Museum.

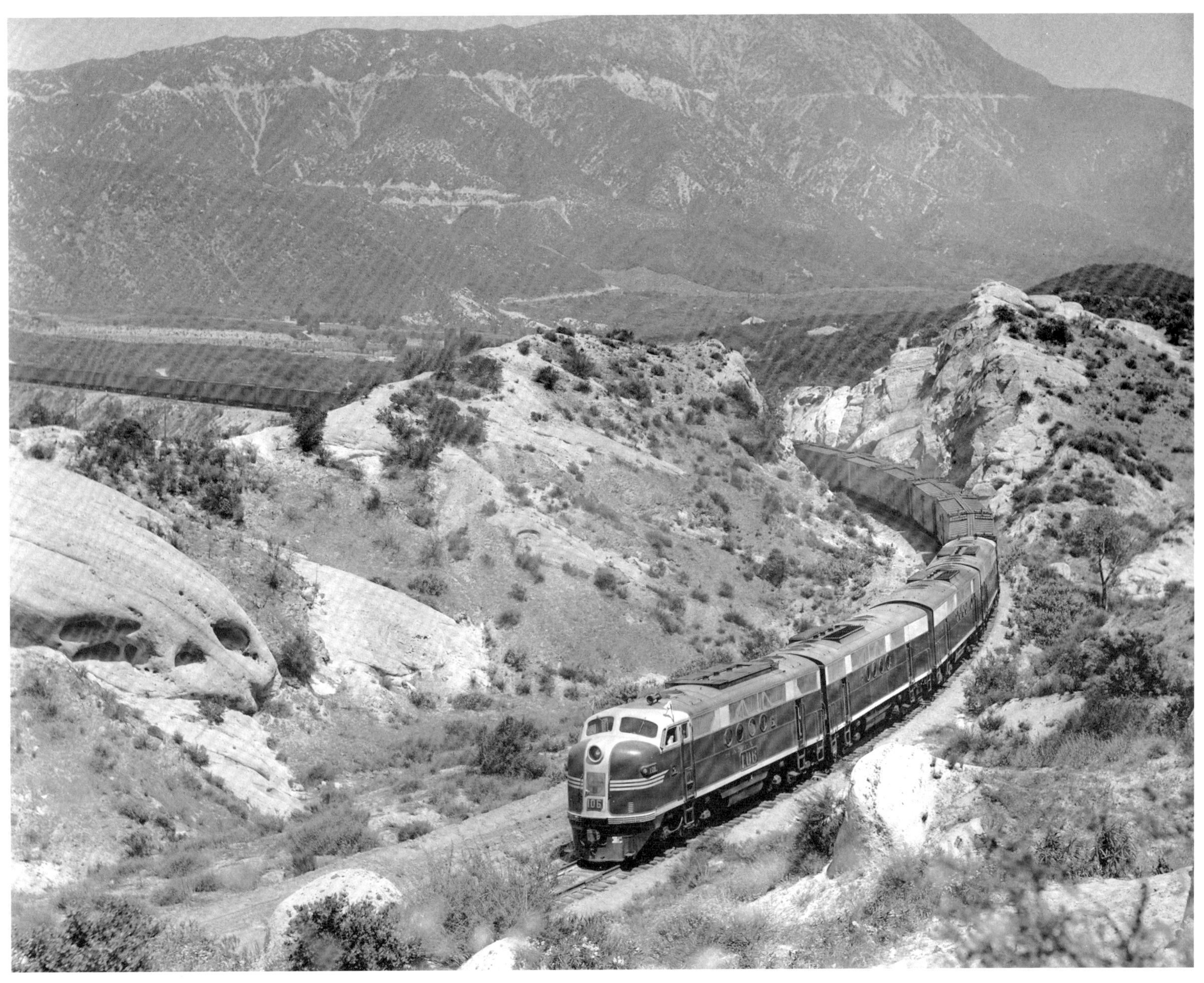

Plate 136. An Atchison, Topeka & Santa Fe Railway freight led by early diesel locomotive No. 106, at Sullivan's Curve on Cajon Pass in California. Lucius Beebe. Beebe-Clegg negative 1093.

Courtesy of the California State Railroad Museum.

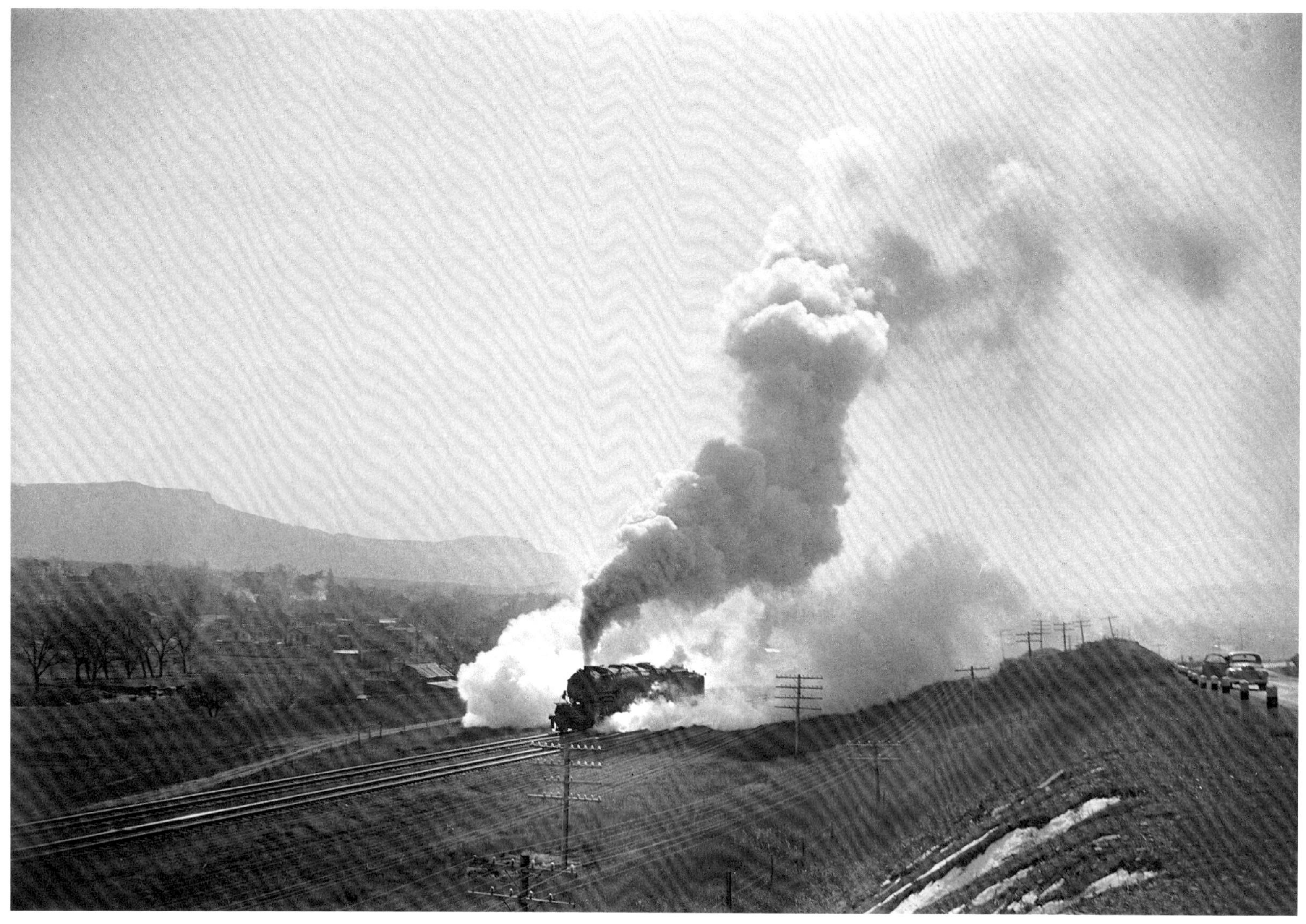

Plate 137. An Atchison, Topeka & Santa Fe Railway locomotive wrapped in smoke and steam, Raton, New Mexico. Charles Clegg. Beebe-Clegg negative 1619.

Courtesy of the California State Railroad Museum.

Plate 138. A primitive signal at Little Gap, near Kunkletown, Pennsylvania, on the Chestnut Ridge Railroad. Charles Clegg. Beebe-Clegg negative 197.

Courtesy of the California State Railroad Museum.

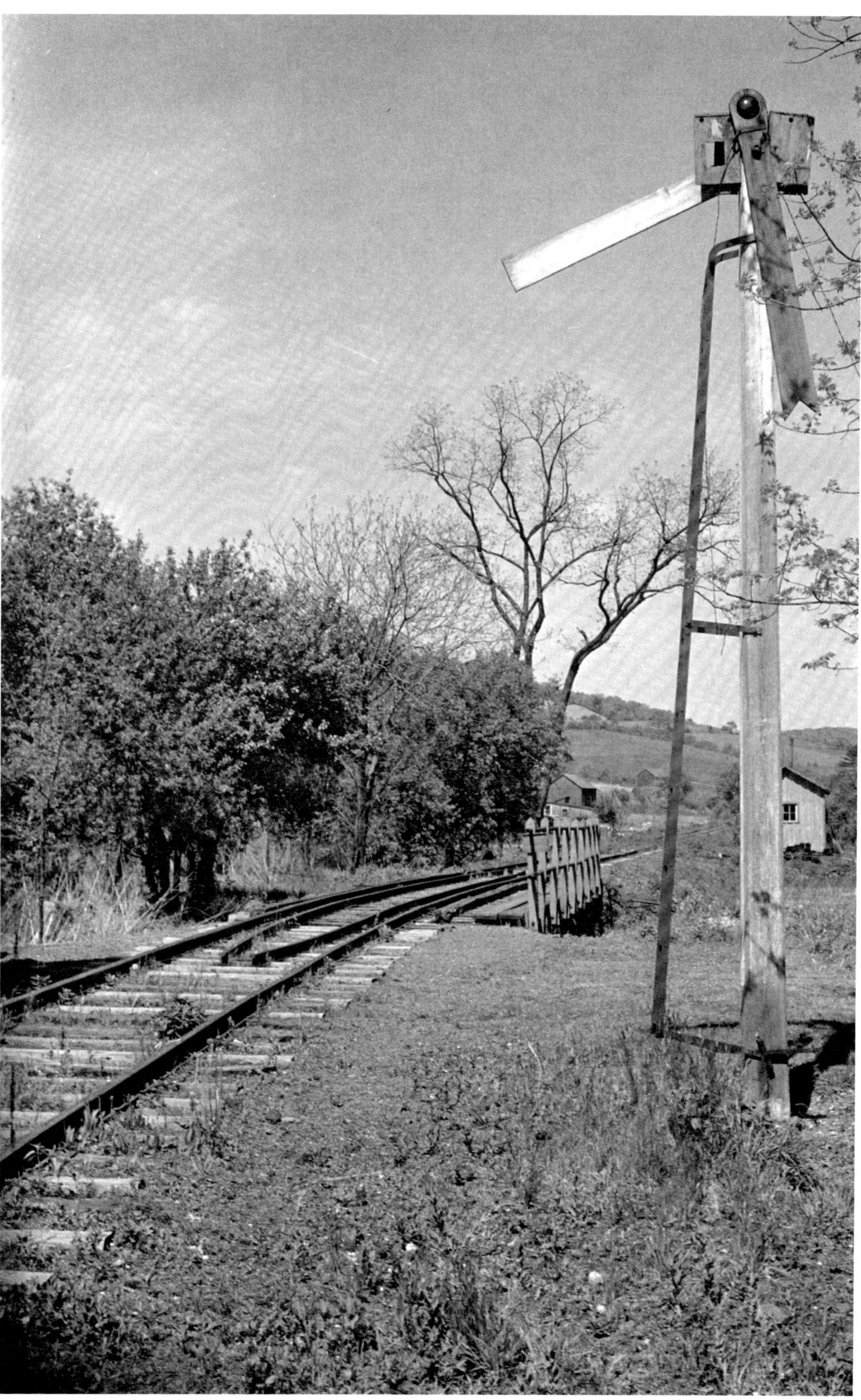

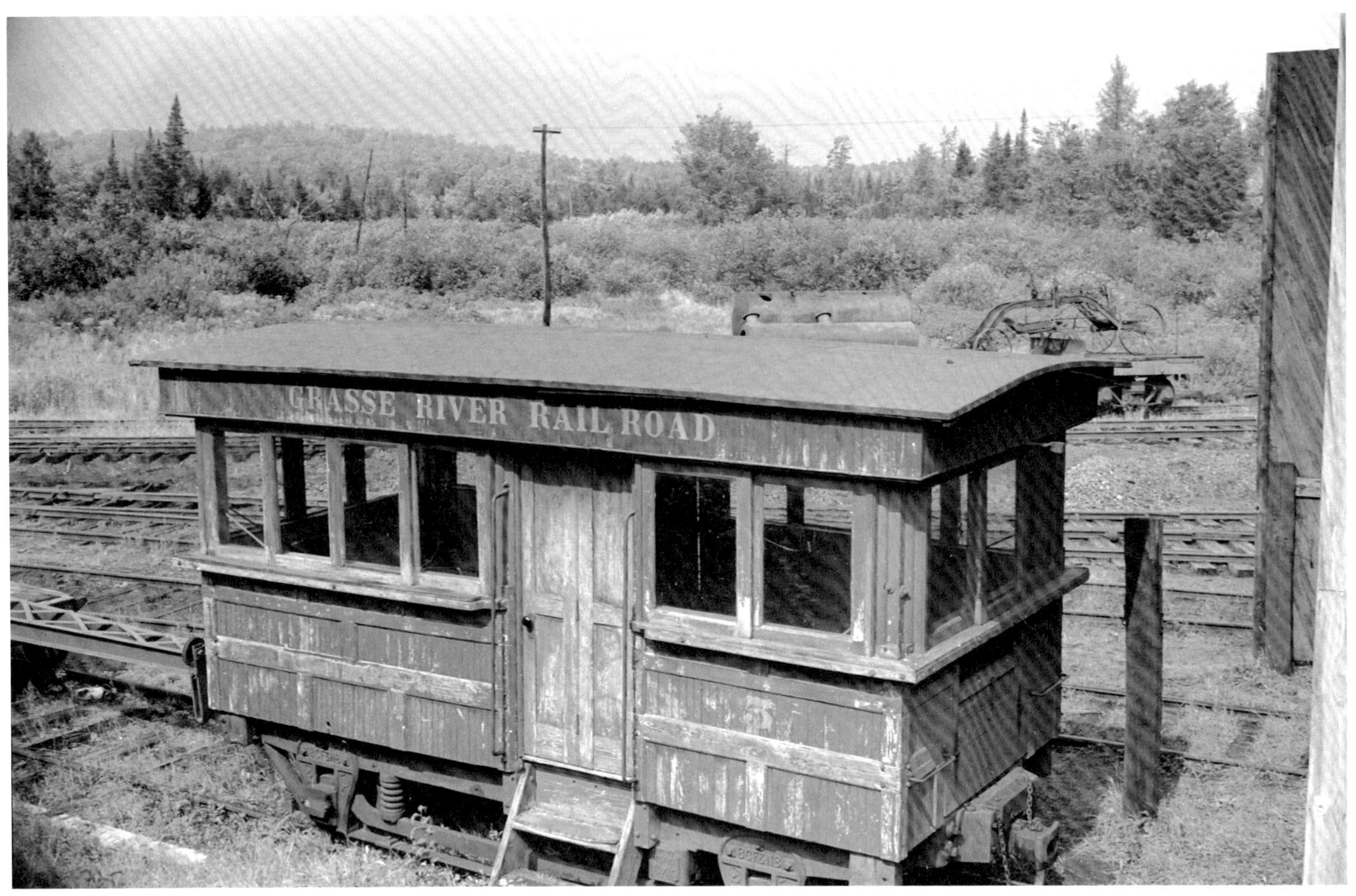

Plate 139. The Grasse River Railroad's homemade passenger car. The Grasse River was a lumber railroad in upstate New York. According to Beebe, this car was called the "Cirrhosis Club," as it carried loggers to and from the town saloons on Saturday nights. Charles Clegg. Beebe-Clegg negative 2317.

Courtesy of the California State Railroad Museum.

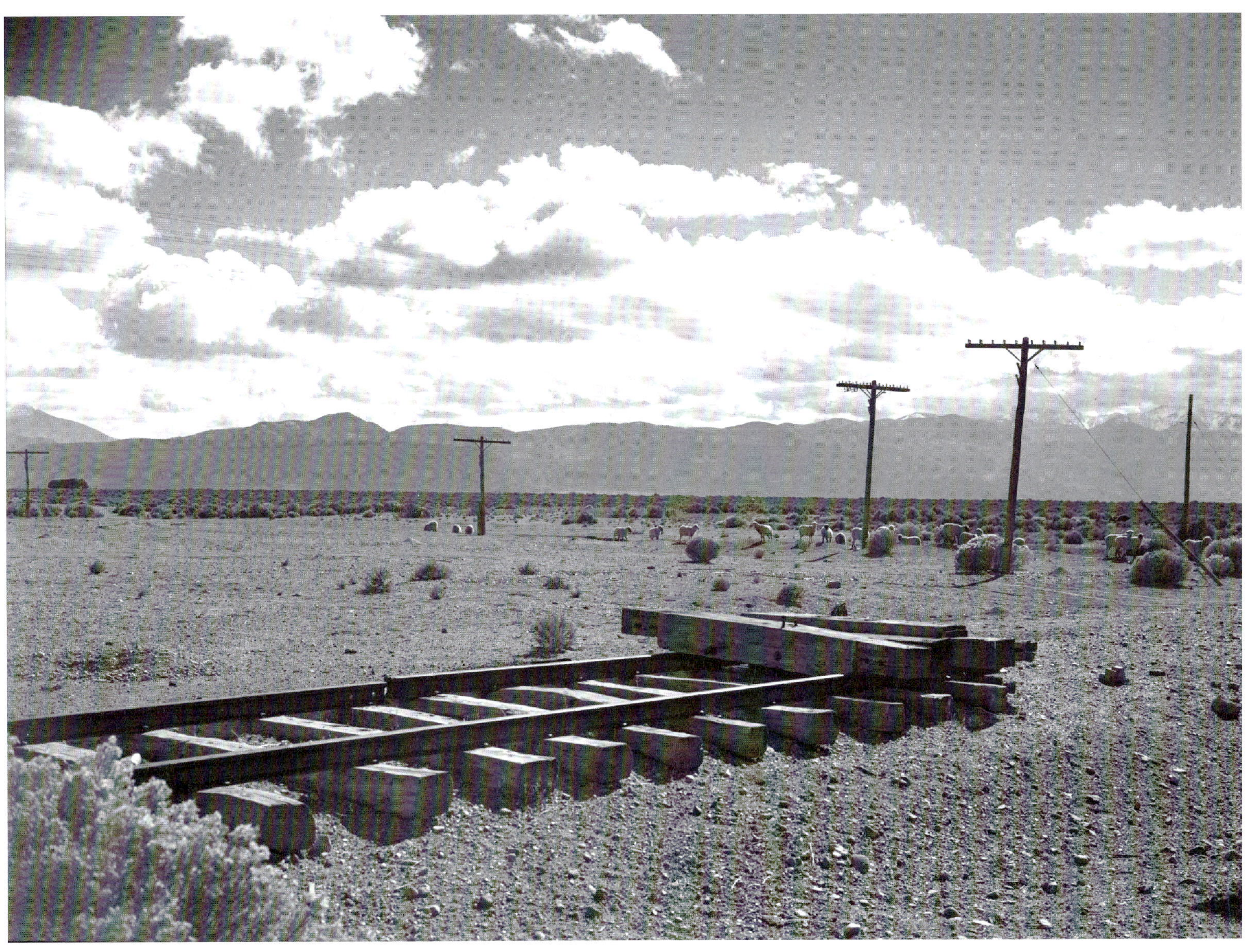

Plate 140. The lonely end-of-track of the San Luis Valley Southern Railway, at Jaroso. Colorado. This is one of Charles Clegg's most noted images. In the photo, Clegg demonstrates his pictorialist influences. As seen here, he often used utility poles to frame his work. Charles Clegg. Beebe-Clegg negative 1404.

Courtesy of the California State Railroad Museum.

APPENDIX

TECHNICAL DETAILS OF THE PHOTOGRAPHY

Lucius Beebe: According to a technical note in Beebe's groundbreaking 1940 article in *Trains,* at the time Beebe used a four-by-five-inch Graflex Model D camera with Zeiss f/3.5 lens, Super XX film packs, Weston exposure meter, and shutter speeds from 1/110 to 1/825.[1] He also used Panchro-Press film packs.[2] Beebe continued to use a similar camera (he also used a Model B and a Speed Graphic) until he stopped taking photographs in about 1950. His negatives in the collection held at the California State Railroad Museum are generally four-by-five-inch black-and-white sheet film images.[3] An interested, contemporary photographer must try the Graflex to experience the complexity of using the camera compared to our present film and digital cameras and cell phones with cameras.

Charles Clegg: Unlike Beebe, Clegg was trained as a photographer. Clegg generally used a Kodak Medalist, a 620-size camera, with shutter speeds of up to 1/400.[4] Photographing for the *Territorial Enterprise* during the 1950s Clegg used a four-by-five-inch Speed Graphic camera.[5]

A note on the plates: In all of my previous work, I have been reluctant to crop other photographers' images, which is the accepted approach for art-photography images. This philosophy worked well for images by photographers such as Jack Delano, Walker Evans, and O. Winston Link. However, many of Lucius Beebe's images and some of Charles Clegg's are cropped, sometimes extensively, in their books. This cropping sometimes transformed somewhat pedestrian "fat" photographs into exceptional images. For examples, see plates 76 and 86. In the uncropped negatives for these plates, the portraits of the railroaders featured are centered without enough emphasis. As published, these images were cropped to focus attention on the fireman in plate 76 and the brakeman in plate 86. In both cases, the result is a classic Lucius Beebe image. In such cases, I have copied the cropping Beebe or Clegg used in presenting the photos for publication. Otherwise, I have left the images uncropped.

NOTES

PREFACE

1. John Gruber, *Focus on Rails* (North Freedom, WI: Mid-Continent Railway Historical Society, 1989), 28.

2. Gruber, *Focus on Rails*, 37.

3. Richard Steinheimer, *Backwoods Railroads of the West* (Milwaukee, WI: Kalmbach, 1963), 174.

4. David P. Morgan, "Lucius Morris Beebe, 1902–1966," *Trains*, April 1966, 4.

5. Herb Caen, "Beebe on Beebe," *San Francisco Chronicle*, February 13, 1966.

THE RAILROAD PHOTOGRAPHY OF LUCIUS BEEBE AND CHARLES CLEGG

1. Unless otherwise indicated, the facts about Beebe and Clegg's lives given in the introduction come from an unpublished doctoral dissertation, Y. Jean Stephens, "Lucius Morris Beebe, Seeing the Elephant" (PhD diss., University of Iowa, 1972); from the two-part profile, Wolcott Gibbs, "The Diamond Gardenia," *New Yorker*, November 20, 1937, 24–29 and Wolcott Gibbs, "The Diamond Gardenia," *New Yorker*, November 27, 1937, 25–29; and from Duncan Emrich, "Lucius Beebe, a Biographical Sketch," in *The Lucius Beebe Reader*, eds. Charles Clegg and Duncan Emrich (Garden City, NY: Doubleday, 1967), 389–93. Beebe lost his surviving brother, Junius Oliver Beebe, to an airplane accident in Boston in 1933 and lost his father, Junius Beebe, in 1934. Ironically, given the younger Beebe's obsession with railroads, Junius Beebe died of a heart attack in New York's Pennsylvania Station. See "Junius Beebe Dies in Penn Station," *New York Times*, March 31, 1943. Beebe's mother, Eleanor Harriet Beebe, died in 1939; see "Mrs. Junius Beebe, Mother of Lucius Beebe, Dies in Her Boston Home at 74," *New York Times*, June 22, 1939.

2. The Tidewater Railroad was a corporate ancestor of the Virginian Railway, as was the Piney River & Paint Creek Railroad.

3. Stephens, "Lucius Morris Beebe," 7. Stephens's unpublished dissertation is the closest thing we have to a biography of Beebe; it devotes most of its attention to Beebe and Charles Clegg's association with the Virginia City, Nevada, newspaper the *Territorial Enterprise*. Beebe discusses his father's career in relationship to railroads in the caption on page 228 of his book *Mansions on Rails: The Folklore of the Private Railway Car* (Berkeley, CA: Howell-North, 1959).

4. Austin Woodward, "Virginia City Remembrances," *Journal of the West* 37, no. 1 (January 1998): 84. Beebe then co-owned the *Territorial Enterprise* with Charles Clegg.

5. Gibbs, "The Diamond Gardenia," November 20, 25.

6. So, in about December 1923. If these dates, which are indefinite in available sources, are correct, Beebe could not have met Jerome Zerbe at the university, as Zerbe started at Yale in 1924.

7. Or 1928. Sources differ. Stephens states that Beebe's graduation year was 1928. For a discussion of Beebe's hiring and tenure at the *Boston Telegram*, see Lucius Beebe, "The 'Boston Telegram,'" in Clegg and Emrich, *The Lucius Beebe Reader*, 53–70.

8. Andria Daley Taylor, "Authors Celebrate Glory of Steam Era," *Vintage Rails*, Fall 1997, 42. Beebe was hired at the *New York Herald Tribune* by legendary editor Stanley Walker, who committed suicide in 1962.

9. Gibbs, "The Diamond Gardenia," November 27, 25.

10. David P. Morgan, "Lucius Morris Beebe, 1902–1966," *Trains*, April 1966, 4.

11. John H. White Jr. (retired Smithsonian Institution executive and author), in discussion with author, December 2004.

12. Cornelius Hauck (financial advisor and railroad historian), in discussion with author, June 2005.

13. Lucius Beebe, "His Own Life in His Own Words," *New York Herald Tribune*, February 5, 1966.

14. Gibbs, "The Diamond Gardenia," November 27, 25.

15. He does not seem to have originated the term, but he certainly had a major role in popularizing it. So, many coffee houses across the United States owe their names, usually unknowingly, to Beebe.

16. Gibbs, "The Diamond Gardenia," November 27, 26.

17. See *Life*, January 16, 1939. In later years, Charles Clegg called Beebe "Lukie." John Gruber and John Ryan [*Beebe & Clegg: Their Enduring Photographic Legacy* (Madison, WI: Center for Railroad Photography and Art, 2018)], state this was spelled "Lukey" (13). Beebe's voice was compared to that of Franklin Delano Roosevelt's.

18. Robert Sacheli, "Steppin' Out with My Beebe: Luscious Lucius Part Two," *Dandyism.net* (blog), April 26, 2008, accessed January 9, 2017, http://www.dandyism.net/2008/04/26/steppin-out-with-my-beebe-luscious-lucius-part-two/.

19. The term *gay* was not yet in use at the time.

20. The facts about Zerbe's life come from Jerome Zerbe and Brendan Gill, *Happy Times* (New York: Harcourt Brace Jovanovich, 1973). Zerbe also authored or coauthored *People on Parade*; *John Perona's El Morocco Family Album*; *Les Pavillions: French Pavilions of the Eighteenth Century*; *Small Castles and Pavilions of Europe*; and *The Art of Social Climbing*.

21. Zerbe and Gill, *Happy Times*, 16.

22. Facts such as this are difficult to find in the written record of the day, as homosexuality (the term *gay* was not used at the time) was not mentioned in mainstream media. Nuanced clues were all that were typically provided in print.

23. See Zerbe's *New York Times* obituary, Wolfgang Saxon, "Jerome Zerbe, 85, Photographer of Café Society and a Columnist," *New York Times*, August 23, 1988.

24. For a finding aid to the collection, see http://drs.library.yale.edu/HLTransformer/HLTransServlet?stylename=yul.ead2002.xhtml.xsl&pid=beinecke:zerbe&clear-stylesheet-cache=yes, accessed June 9, 2018.

25. Jerome Zerbe, *People on Parade* (New York: D. Kemp, 1934), 9.

26. See "'Luscious' Lucius Beebe," Michael L. Grace, *New York Social Diary*, December 15, 2009, http://www.newyorksocialdiary.com/social-history/2009/luscious-lucius-beebe.

27. Beebe's encounter with Haskell, which led to the founding of the railroad picture book genre as we know it, is mentioned in many sources. For the most informative discussion of this event, see Freeman Hubbard (attributed), "Interesting Railfans: No. 3 Lucius Beebe," *Railroad*, August 1961, 17–18. Beebe was involved with D. Appleton Century as the author of *Boston and the Boston Legend*, which was released by the publisher in 1935. This book includes Beebe's first significant railroad-subject publication, a chapter entitled "Highball and Johnson Bar."

28. Gibbs, "The Diamond Gardenia," November 27, 28.

29. Daley, "Authors Celebrate Glory," 44.

30. Here we see another advantage of Beebe's wealth. In the midst of the Great Depression, Beebe was able to simply decide to purchase a suite of expensive camera equipment and then travel thousands of miles. Most people at the time would not have been able to do so. Clegg's family wealth also came into play in the area of his photography; he owned expensive camera equipment and was able to afford photography classes with J. Ghislain Lootens while working as a retail clerk. Many contemporaries, such as Jack Delano, could not afford a large suite of their own equipment and had to use the equipment provided by their employers (in Delano's case, the WPA, then the FSA/OWI).

31. "Railroad Camera Club," *Railroad*, August 1938, 138.

32. For more on Beebe as the originator of the railroad picture book genre, see H. Roger Grant, *Railroads and the American People* (Bloomington: Indiana University Press, 2012), 262–63; Carl Condit, "The Literature of the Railroad Buff: A Historian's View," *Railroad History* 142 (Spring 1980): 7–26; David P. Morgan, "Lucius Morris Beebe, 1902–1966," *Trains*, April 1966, 4; and Walter P. Gray III, "The Last Edwardian Gentleman," *Trains*, February 2000, 80–81.

33. "Transport: Lacey Jones," *Time*, October 31, 1938, 39–40.

34. Daley, "Authors Celebrate Glory," 44–45. Beebe also had at least one script engagement in Hollywood, probably in connection with Edward H. Griffith's *Café Society* (Paramount Pictures, 1939), which starred Fred MacMurray and Madeleine Carroll. The MacMurray character seems to be based, in part, on Beebe, and the Bells Browne character, played by Shirley Ross, in part on Libby Holman.

35. Some sources say Beebe and Clegg met in 1940.

36. John Gruber and John Ryan, assisted by Mel Patrick, *Beebe & Clegg: Their Enduring Photographic Legacy* (Madison, WI: Center for Railroad Photography and Art, 2018), 11.

37. Clegg and Emrich, *Lucius Beebe Reader*, 11–12.

38. Ann Clegg Holloway would later play a significant role in securing the Beebe-Clegg legacy by placing their collection at the California State Railroad Museum, one of the world's most noted railroad history institutions. It was a combined purchase and donation. See "Picture This: CSRM Acquires Beebe and Clegg Photo Collection," *On Track* 1 (Spring 2001): 12–14. Part of the Beebe-Clegg collection at the museum was donated by the family of publisher Grahame H. Hardy, and it also contains letters donated by Arthur Dubin.

39. Gruber and Ryan, *Beebe & Clegg*, 14.

40. Facts about Clegg's life in the introduction, unless otherwise indicated, come from Daley, "Authors Celebrate Glory," 41–48, 50–51, 88, 90, 92, 94, 96, 98; and from Gruber and Ryan, *Beebe & Clegg*.

41. Gruber and Ryan, *Beebe & Clegg*, 14. As Gruber and Ryan note, Clegg was dishonorably discharged from the navy on January 5, 1944. Like many sailors, Clegg got a tattoo while in the navy, and Beebe had an identical tattoo (Gruber and Ryan, 15–17).

42. Grace, "'Luscious' Lucius Beebe."

43. John H. White Jr. (retired Smithsonian Institution executive and author), discussions with author, December 2004 and April 2005. One of the interview sources for the article that preceded this book, who did not wish to be identified, noted that a figure in the railroad industry was reluctant to attend Beebe's funeral because of rumors that Beebe was gay, saying he wasn't sure he wanted to be seen there. Beebe was an imposing figure; he was six foot three or four (sources differ) at a time when the average height for men was shorter than is the case now.

44. Andria Daley [Andria Daley Taylor], "Boardwalk Bons Vivants," *Nevada*, November–December 1992, 35.

45. "The Diamond Gardenia," November 27, 26.

46. Lucius Beebe, *Snoot If You Must* (D. Appleton-Century, 1943), 230–44.

47. To say that Beebe was a drinker is not to imply that he was an alcoholic. Instead, he was a connoisseur of fine spirits and wines, and of gourmet dining; in fact, he was a recognized authority on the subject.

48. "The Diamond Gardenia," November 20, 26.

49. This source did not wish to be named. This wish shows that the opprobrium faced by gay men in Beebe's day lived on, in his surviving friends and acquaintances, long after his death. The interview in question was conducted in 2004.

50. "The Diamond Gardenia," November 27, 29.

51. John H. White Jr. (retired Smithsonian Institution executive and author), in discussions with author, December 2004 and April 2005.

52. Arthur Dubin (architect and author, now deceased), in discussion with author, December 2004.

53. In Beebe, *Snoot If You Must*, 230–44.

54. Archie Robertson, *Slow Train to Yesterday* (Boston: Houghton-Mifflin, 1945). For a short biography of Robertson, see Tony Reevy, "Elegy for Archie," *Railroad History* 187 (Fall–Winter 2002): 109–15.

55. In his review of *Slow Train to Yesterday*, "About Little Railroads," published in the *New York Herald Tribune* on August 26, 1945, Beebe says, "The field [U.S. short line railroads] can stand a great deal more exploitation. In some happy future the reviewer himself would like to undertake a short lines book, but any writer would be hard put to it to produce a volume one-half so appealing, good-humored and perceptive as 'Short [*sic*] Train to Yesterday.'"

56. According to Beebe, it took three years and seventy-five thousand miles of travel. See Lucius Beebe, "Railroads Are Americana," *American Photography*, October 1947, 30–32. Beebe and Clegg reportedly carried their own stock of bourbon on these trips.

57. Beebe, "Railroads Are Americana," 30.

58. See Lucius Beebe, *The Age of Steam* (New York: Rinehart, 1957), 87, for an example of an Associated Press photograph.

59. "Life Goes to a Party on the 'Ma and Pa' Railroad," *Life*, October 13, 1947, 160–62, 164.

60. Lucius Beebe, letter to Haug, no date.

61. Lucius Beebe, letter to Grahame Hardy, no date.

62. This number is often given incorrectly. Twenty-one books counts the two-volume *The Trains We Rode* (Berkeley, CA: Howell-North, 1965–66) as one book and includes *Cable Car Carnival* (Oakland, CA: Grahame Hardy, 1951) as a railroad book. Until he was apparently overcome by depression in later life Clegg's work habits were similar to Beebe's. He once learned conversational French in only six weeks; see Daley, "Boardwalk Bons Vivants," 23.

63. Austin Woodward, "Virginia City Remembrances," *Journal of the West* 37, no. 1 (January 1998): 83.

64. Gruber and Ryan, *Beebe & Clegg*, 18–20. For more on the house, see National Park Service, "Piper-Beebe House," accessed December 28, 2016, https://www.nps.gov/nr/travel/nevada/bee.htm.

65. Daley, "Authors Celebrate Glory of Steam Era," 51. For Beebe's fascinating farewell to New York, see Lucius Beebe, "I Saw the Elephant," in *The Lucius Beebe Reader*, 145–154.

66. Part of it had been abandoned earlier, in 1938. Much of it has been rebuilt in recent years as a tourist railroad. Beebe and Clegg are credited with popularizing the former Denver & Rio Grande Western "Silverton train" and saving it from abandonment. See Hubbard, "Interesting Railfans: No. 3 Lucius Beebe," 18.

67. See Nevada Writers Hall of Fame: "Lucius Beebe," accessed January 10, 2017, http://guides.library.unr.edu/nvwriters-hall-of-fame/beebe-1992. This online resource contains an excellent bibliography of works by and about Beebe.

68. Hubbard, "Interesting Railfans: No. 3 Lucius Beebe," 18.

69. See California State Railroad Museum Docent Roundhouse, "Gold Coast Summary," accessed December 28, 2016, http://portal.parks.ca.gov/CapitalDistrict/csrmdocentroundhouse/SitePages/Gold%20Coast%20Summary.aspx.

70. See Virginia City Rail Car, "Virginia City," accessed December 28, 2016, http://www.vcrail.com/vchistory_railcars.htm and John H. Kuehl, "Welcome back Virginia City," *Private Varnish* 7, no. 5 (1985): 18–21.

71. Beebe, *Mansions on Rails*, 211–12.

72. Gruber and Ryan, in *Beebe & Clegg*, state that Beebe and Clegg sold only a third of their interest in the *Territorial Enterprise* at this time (23).

73. Daley, "Boardwalk Bons Vivants," 35. The notes on the prints in the Beebe-Clegg collection at the California State Railroad Museum are Clegg's. See John Gruber, "Lucius Beebe and Charles Clegg: Railroading Journeys, A Special Retrospective Devoted to Their Life and Times," *Railroad Heritage* 18 (2007): 8.

74. Buzz Eggleston, "Suicides: One Man Blamed the Lack of Good Servants," *Peninsula Times-Tribune*, September 20, 1979.

75. For information about Holloway's family, see "John 'Jack' Ennis Holloway Dies," *Virginia City News*, September 16, 2011, http://virginiacitynews.com/john-jack-ennis-holloway-dies-p4153-96.htm.

76. "MS 61: Lucius Morris Beebe Collection," California State Railroad Museum Library, accessed January 2, 2017, http://csrrm.crewnoble.com/dbtw-wpd/exec/dbtwpub.dll.

77. Tony Reevy and Dan Cupper, "Writers of the Rail: Mixed Legacy," *Railroad History* 193 (Fall–Winter 2005): 36.

78. Gruber, "Lucius Beebe and Charles Clegg," 2–31. Ann Clegg Holloway and Michael Zega also contributed to this special issue.

79. For simplicity's sake, books by Beebe and books by Beebe and Clegg are not differentiated here; the bibliography of all of Lucius Beebe's books included in this volume includes this information.

80. *Great Railroad Photographs* received significant support from noted railroad executive John W. Barriger III who, like railroad executive Alfred "Al" Perlman, was a friend of Beebe and Clegg's. See Gruber and Ryan, 209-210.

81. Daley, "Authors Celebrate Glory of Steam Era," 96.

82. For a discussion of *Mixed Train Daily* and *Slow Train to Yesterday*, see Grant, *Railroads and the American People*, 263.

83. For this review of *Mixed Train Daily*, see Horace Reynolds, "Short Line Railroads," *New York Times*, October 5, 1947, BR14.

84. Dubin, discussion with author, December 2004.

85. Possible examples of this can be found in Beebe and Clegg, *Trains We Rode*, 67, 73, 267, and the bottom of 409. For a proven example, see the top of page 409. Arthur Dubin substantiated the fabrication in this image, the addition of the *Twentieth Century Limited* drumhead on the passenger car depicted at the top of page 409, by finding the unretouched image, Smithsonian Institution P (photo) 8782 L (lot) 3388 (date) 8/27/06 (initials of photographer) JPVV. The observation car type depicted here with drawing room and smoking room was represented by cars *Beaverdale* and *Barnesboro*, which were originally assigned to general service on the Pennsylvania Railroad, more than a decade before the *Twentieth Century Limited* first carried a so-called "named drumhead" in about 1925.

86. In Jeff Brouws and Richard Steinheimer, *A Passion for Trains: The Railroad Photography of Richard Steinheimer* (New York: W. W. Norton, 2004), unpaginated.

87. Lucius Beebe and Charles M. Clegg Jr., *Great Railroad Photographs, U.S.A.* (Howell-North Books, 1964), 10. The book was authored by Beebe and Clegg, but the words are probably Beebe's. Like Beebe, Morgan died relatively young, at the age of sixty-two, in 1990. Morgan's lifestyle, which reportedly included excessive consumption of alcohol, probably hastened his death. See Don Phillips, "I Miss You, David, but Thank You," *Trains* 77, no. 7 (July 2017): 11.

88. Jukes's surviving photos are held by the Western History Collection, Denver Public Library, as part of the Lucius Morris Beebe Papers. Part of the collection was donated by Beebe in 1961, and the remainder by Clegg in 1970. According to the relevant finding aid, the collection includes 650 photographic prints originally acquired by Beebe from Fred Jukes. See "Lucius Morris Beebe Papers, WH33," Western History Collection, Denver Public Library, accessed January 8, 2017, http://eadsrv.denverlibrary.org/sdx/pl/doc-tdm.xsp?id=WH33_doe34&fmt=text.

89. These histories include books on California; Wells Fargo; Virginia City and the Comstock Lode region; and San Francisco as well as *The American West: The Pictorial Epic of a Continent*, a pictorial survey very similar in treatment to *Hear the Train Blow*, and the book *The Big Spenders*, an idiosyncratic survey of the greats of the Gilded Age. The monographs Beebe wrote on great hotels and restaurants include works on the Plaza (New York), the Ritz, the Seeley Diner, the Savoy (London) and, reportedly, the Palace Hotel (San Francisco).

90. Charleston, Durham, Memphis, New Orleans, New York, San Francisco, and Santa Fe are now generally recognized as national centers of US gastronomy. Beebe highlighted the food culture of New Orleans, New York, and San Francisco, and he was dramatically ahead of his time in doing so. Beebe also admired restaurants in Boston, Chicago, Philadelphia, and Washington, DC.

91. Lucius Beebe, quoted in John Mariani, *America Eats Out* (New York: William Morrow, 1991), 137.

92. Lucius Beebe and Charles M. Clegg Jr., *Mixed Train Daily: A Book of Short Line Railroads* (New York: E. P. Dutton, 1947), 7.

1. THE THREE-QUARTERS SHOT

1. For a full discussion of this progression, see John Gruber, *Focus on Rails* (North Freedom, WI: Mid-Continent Railway Historical Society, 1989), 4–9. A. F. Bishop is highlighted as a pioneer of railroad action photography in Lucius Beebe, "Railroads Are Americana," *American Photography*, October 1947, 32.

2. This magazine is one ancestor of *Railfan & Railroad* magazine, which is still in print. The club was later renamed the Railroad Camera Club.

3. For a further discussion of the roster shot, see Gruber, *Focus on Rails*, 10–13. A review of any period issue of *Railroad Magazine* or its predecessors also helps one understand the roster shot genre and movement.

4. In the few railroad books featuring images that were published before *High Iron*, photos were often included in sets of photo pages interleaved between long sections of text-only pages. The major exception that preceded *High Iron* is Robert Selph Henry's *Trains* (Indianapolis: Bobbs-Merrill, 1934), which is discussed in the introduction. Today, many books published with the railfan market in mind set two or more photos on each page, a design approach that can make the pages seem overly busy to the general reader.

5. Lucius Beebe, *Highliners: A Railroad Album* (New York: D. Appleton-Century, 1940) ix, x, xi.

6. A mixed train is a train that includes both freight and passenger cars and that therefore offers both freight and passenger service. Mixed trains were usually found on branch lines and on short lines (small, local railroads). No regularly scheduled mixed trains survive in the United States; two survive "in North America's contiguous rail network" as of 2017. See Bob Johnston, "Mixed Train Outpost," *Trains*, June 2017, 22. The Archie Robertson book mentioned here is *Slow Train to Yesterday* (Boston: Houghton-Mifflin, 1945).

7. See especially *The Central Pacific and the Southern Pacific Railroads* (Berkeley, CA: Howell-North, 1963). For information on the publishing history of Link's work, see Tony Reevy, *O. Winston Link: Life Along the Line* (New York: Abrams, 2012).

2. A MODERNIST VIEW OF THE AMERICAN RAILROAD

1. Lucius Beebe, "Keeping up with the Casey Joneses." *Town & Country*, June 1936, 50–55, 94, 118. An excellent source for examples of Dmitri's innovative (for the time) color images is Ivan Dmitri [Levon West], *Kodachrome and How to Use It* (New York: Simon and Schuster, 1940). Despite Dmitri's importance as a pioneer of color photography, verified biographic sources about him are rare. Unverified sources state that he was born Levon Assadoorian. See "Ivan Dmitri," North Dakota Office of the Governor, accessed December 10, 2016, https://www.governor.nd.gov/rough-rider/ivan-dmitri. Another verifiable source about Dmitri's life is "Levon West/Ivan Dmitri (1900–1968)," Mandan Historical Society, accessed December 10, 2016, http://www.mandanhistory.org/biographieslz/levonwest.html.

2. See Tony Reevy's *O. Winston Link: Life Along the Line* (New York: Abrams, 2012) and "Walker Evans, American Communities, and the Railroad," *Railroad Heritage* 20 (2009): 12–19.

3. For information on this crucial exhibit, see James Polchin, "American or Artist?," *The Smart Set*, November 27, 2012, http://thesmartset.com/article11271201/.

4. Jeff Brouws and Richard Steinheimer, *A Passion for Trains: The Railroad Photography of Richard Steinheimer* (New York: W. W. Norton, 2004). Unfortunately for scholars, this otherwise excellent book is completely unpaginated.

5. See "Charles Sheeler, 1883–1965," Metropolitan Museum of Art, accessed December 10, 2016, http://metmuseum.org/toah/hd/shee/hd_shee.htm. A Sheeler image is featured in Lucius Beebe and Charles M. Clegg Jr., *Great Railroad Photographs, USA* (Berkeley, CA: Howell-North, 1964), 181.

6. See John Stilgoe, *Metropolitan Corridor* (New Haven: Yale, 1983), 164–65, for Stilgoe's noted photograph of this type and Michael Flanagan, *Stations: An Imagined Journey* (New York: Pantheon, 1994), 33, 35, 54, 65, and 79. Fictionalized as "Luther Lincoln," O. Winston Link is a minor character in *Stations*; see page 30.

7. See Tony Reevy, *The Railroad Photography of Jack Delano* (Bloomington: Indiana University Press, 2015), 155, 157 and Walker Evans, "Before they Disappear," *Fortune*, March 1957, 141–45.

8. Lucius Beebe, *Mixed Train Daily: A Book of Short Line Railroads* (New York: E. P. Dutton, 1947), 301.

9. For a classic discussion of monikers (or monicas), see B. A. Botkin and Alvin F. Harlow, eds, *A Treasury of Railroad Folklore* (New York: Crown, 1953), 239–40.

3. RAILROADERS

1. Lewis Hine, *Men at Work: Photographic Studies of Modern Men and Machines* (New York: Macmillan, 1932).

2. For more on Hine's portraits of railroaders, see Tony Reevy, "Men at Work: Lewis Hine's Photographs of Railroad Workers," *Railroad History* 204 (Spring–Summer 2011): 42–51.

3. A camelback locomotive is also known as a Mother Hubbard. These locomotives had large fireboxes. The engineer sat alone in a cab perched on the boiler, while the fireman labored in a separate cab at the rear of the locomotive. This configuration was dangerous, for a number of reasons.

4. Archie Robertson, often cited as a source by Beebe in *Mixed Train Daily*, covered the Louisville, New Albany & Corydon in his

groundbreaking *Slow Train to Yesterday* (Boston: Houghton Mifflin, 1945). Robertson's photograph of the same scene appears between pages 146 and 147 in the book; his narrative about the railroad falls on pages 54 and 55.

5. John Gruber, "Lucius Beebe and Charles Clegg: Railroading Journeys, a Special Retrospective Devoted to Their Life and Times," *Railroad Heritage* 18 (2007): 23.

6. Lucius Beebe and Charles M. Clegg Jr., *Narrow Gauge in the Rockies* (Berkeley, CA: Howell-North, 1958), 216.

7. Almost miraculously, the Stewartstown Railroad survives today and was recently reopened by a group of dedicated volunteers, contributors, and stockholders.

4. THE RAILROAD IN ITS ENVIRONMENT

1. See "Approved Biography for Ghislain J. Lootens (Courtesy of Christian Peterson)," Luminous-Lint, accessed December 17, 2016, http://www.luminous-lint.com/app/photographer/Ghislain_J__Lootens/A/.

2. A. Sheldon Pennoyer, *Locomotives in Our Lives* (New York: Hastings House, 1954), 54–55.

3. Information available on Pennoyer is limited. For a short biography, see "The Monuments Men: Albert Sheldon Pennoyer (1888–1957)," Monuments Men Foundation, accessed December 17, 2016, http://www.monumentsmenfoundation.org/the-heroes/the-monuments-men/pennoyer-capt.-albert-sheldon. Like Beebe and Clegg, Pennoyer's career was divided between time spent in the New York City area and in California. Beebe mentions Pennoyer in his 1945 *New York Herald Tribune* review of Archie Robertson's *Slow Train to Yesterday*, "About Little Railroads."

APPENDIX

1. Lucius Beebe, "Railroad Photography," *Trains*, November 1940, 5.

2. "Railroad Camera Club," *Railroad*, August 1938, 138.

3. "Picture This: CSRM Acquires Beebe and Clegg Photo Collection," *On Track* 1 (Spring 2001): 14.

4. Jeff Brouws and Richard Steinheimer, *A Passion for Trains: The Railroad Photography of Richard Steinheimer* (New York: W. W. Norton, 2004), unpaginated.

5. Austin Woodward, "Virginia City Remembrances," *Journal of the West* 37, no. 1 (January 1998): 83.

CHRONOLOGICAL BIBLIOGRAPHY OF THE BOOKS OF LUCIUS BEEBE

Fallen Stars. Boston: Cornhill, 1921.

Corydon and Other Poems. Boston: B. J. Brimmer, 1924.

Francois Villon: Certain Aspects. Cambridge, MA: privately printed, 1925.

Edwin Arlington Robinson and the Arthurian Legend. Cambridge, MA: privately printed, 1927.

Aspects of the Poetry of Edwin Arlington Robinson. Cambridge, MA: privately printed, 1928.

A Bibliography of the Works of Edwin Arlington Robinson (with R. J. Bulkley). Cambridge, MA: Dunster House, 1931.

Boston and the Boston Legend. New York: D. Appleton-Century, 1935.

High Iron: A Book of Trains. New York: D. Appleton-Century, 1938.

Highliners: A Railroad Album. New York: D. Appleton-Century, 1940.

Trains in Transition. New York: D. Appleton-Century, 1941.

Snoot if You Must. New York: D. Appleton-Century, 1943.

Highball, a Pageant of Trains. New York: D. Appleton-Century, 1945.

The Stork Club Bar Book. New York: Rinehart, 1946.

Mixed Train Daily: A Book of Short Line Railroads (with photographs by Charles M. Clegg Jr.). New York: E. P. Dutton, 1947.

Dreadful California, by Hinton Rowan Helper (edited by Lucius Beebe and Charles M. Clegg Jr.). Indianapolis, IN: Bobbs-Merrill, 1948.

US West: The Saga of Wells Fargo (with Charles M. Clegg Jr.). New York: E. P. Dutton, 1949.

Virginia and Truckee: A Story of Virginia City and Comstock Times (with Charles M. Clegg Jr.). Oakland, CA: G. H. Hardy, 1949.

Legends of the Comstock Lode (with Charles M. Clegg Jr.). Oakland, CA: G. H. Hardy, 1950.

Cable Car Carnival (with Charles M. Clegg Jr.). Oakland, CA: Grahame Hardy, 1951.

Hear the Train Blow: A Pictorial Epic of America in the Railroad Age (with Charles M. Clegg Jr.). New York: E. P. Dutton, 1952.

Comstock Commotion: The Story of the Territorial Enterprise and Virginia City News. Stanford, CA: Stanford, 1954.

The American West: The Pictorial Epic of a Continent (with Charles M. Clegg Jr.). New York: E. P. Dutton, 1955.

Steamcars to the Comstock: The Virginia and Truckee Railroad, the Carson and Colorado Railroad (with Charles M. Clegg Jr.). Berkeley, CA: Howell-North, 1957.

The Age of Steam: A Classic Album of American Railroading (with Charles M. Clegg Jr.). New York: Rinehart, 1957.

Narrow Gauge in the Rockies (with Charles M. Clegg Jr.). Berkeley, CA: Howell-North, 1958.

Mansions on Rails: The Folklore of the Private Railway Car. Berkeley, CA: Howell-North, 1959.

San Francisco's Golden Era: A Picture Story of San Francisco Before the Fire (with Charles M. Clegg Jr.). Berkeley, CA: Howell-North, 1960.

Mr. Pullman's Elegant Palace Car: The Railway Carriage That Established a New Dimension of Luxury and Entered the National Lexicon as a Symbol of Splendor. Garden City, NY: Doubleday, 1961.

Rio Grande: Mainline of the Rockies (with Charles M. Clegg Jr.). Berkeley, CA: Howell-North, 1962.

Twentieth Century: The Greatest Train in the World. Berkeley, CA: Howell-North, 1962.

When Beauty Rode the Rails: An Album of Railroad Yesterdays (with Charles M. Clegg Jr.). Garden City, NY: Doubleday, 1962.

The Central Pacific and the Southern Pacific Railroads (with photographs by Richard Steinheimer). Berkeley, CA: Howell-North, 1963.

The Overland Limited. Berkeley, CA: Howell-North, 1963.

Great Railroad Photographs, U.S.A. (with Charles M. Clegg Jr.). Berkeley, CA: Howell-North, 1964.

Two Trains to Remember: The New England Limited, the Air Line Limited. Virginia City, NV: privately printed, 1965.

The Trains We Rode (with Charles M. Clegg Jr.). 2 vols. Berkeley, CA: Howell-North, 1965–66.

The Big Spenders. Garden City, NY: Doubleday, 1966.

The Provocative Pen of Lucius Beebe, Esq. (edited by Gordon Pates). San Francisco: Chronicle, 1966.

The Lucius Beebe Reader (edited by Charles Clegg and Duncan Emrich). Garden City, NY: Doubleday, 1967.

BIBLIOGRAPHY OF OTHER WORKS

Beebe, Lucius. "About Little Railroads." *New York Herald Tribune,* August 26, 1945.

———. *The Awful Seeley Diner.* New York: F. R. Publishing, 1932.

———. Foreword to *The Iron Horse in Art*. Fort Worth, TX: The Fort Worth Art Center, 1958 [unpaginated].

———. "Keeping up with the Casey Joneses." *Town & Country,* June 1936, 50–55, 94, 118.

———. "Luxury on Wheels." *Scribners,* May 1938, 96–98.

———. "Narrow Gauge Holiday." *Holiday,* March 1947, 81–83, 130, 132.

———. *The Plaza: Fortieth Anniversary, 1907–1947.* New York: Hilton Hotels, 1947.

———. "Railroads Are Americana." *American Photography,* October 1947, 30–32.

———. "Railroad Photography." *Trains,* November 1940, 4–5.

———. *The Ritz Idea: The Story of a Great Hotel.* New York: privately printed, 1936.

———. *The Savoy of London.* London: Lund Humphries, 1964.

Blumenthal, Ralph. *Stork Club: America's Most Famous Nightspot and the Lost World of Café Society.* Boston: Little, Brown, 2000.

Botkin, B. A., and Alvin F. Harlow, eds. *A Treasury of Railroad Folklore.* New York: Crown, 1953.

Brouws, Jeff. "On Railroad Photography and Cultural Geography." *Railway & Locomotive Historical Society Quarterly* (Spring 2008): 8–20.

Brouws, Jeff (text), and Jim Shaughnessy (photographs). *The Call of Trains: Railroad Photographs by Jim Shaughnessy.* New York: W. W. Norton, 2008.

Brouws, Jeff (text), and Richard Steinheimer (photographs). *A Passion for Trains: The Railroad Photography of Richard Steinheimer.* New York: W. W. Norton, 2004.

Condit, Carl. "The Literature of the Railroad Buff: A Historian's View." *Railroad History* 142 (Spring 1980): 7–26.

Daley, Andria [Andria Daley Taylor]. "Authors Celebrate Glory of Steam Era." *Vintage Rails,* Fall 1997, 41–48, 50–51, 88, 90, 92, 94, 96, 98.

———. "Boardwalk Bons Vivants." *Nevada,* November–December 1992, 20–24, 35.

Dmitri, Ivan [Levon West]. *Kodachrome and How to Use It.* New York: Simon and Schuster, 1940.

Eggleston, Buzz. "Suicides: One Man Blamed the Lack of Good Servants." *Peninsula Times Tribune,* September 20, 1979.

Evans, Walker. *American Photographs.* New York: Museum of Modern Art, 1938.

———. "Before They Disappear." *Fortune,* March 1957, 141–45.

Ferrell, Mallory Hope. *Silver San Juan: The Rio Grande Southern.* Boulder, CO: Pruett Publishing, 1973.

Flanagan, Michael. *Stations: An Imagined Journey.* New York: Pantheon, 1994.

Gibbs, Wolcott. "The Diamond Gardenia," *New Yorker,* November 20, 1937, 24–29.

———. "The Diamond Gardenia," *New Yorker,* November 27, 1937, 25–29.

———. "One with Nineveh." *New Yorker,* March 24, 1956, 28–32.

Grant, H. Roger. *Railroads and the American People*. Bloomington, IN: Indiana University Press, 2012.

Gray, Walter P. III. "The Last Edwardian Gentleman." *Trains*, February 2000, 80–81.

Gruber, John. *Focus on Rails*. North Freedom, WI: Mid-Continent Railway Historical Society, 1989.

———. "Lucius Beebe and Charles Clegg: Railroading Journeys, a Special Retrospective Devoted to Their Life and Times." *Railroad Heritage* 18 (2007): 2–31.

Gruber, John, and John Ryan, assisted by Mel Patrick. *Beebe & Clegg: Their Enduring Photographic Legacy*. Madison, WI: Center for Railroad Photography and Art, 2018.

Henry, Robert Selph. *This Fascinating Railroad Business*. Indianapolis: Bobbs-Merrill, 1942.

———. *Trains*. Indianapolis: Bobbs-Merrill, 1934.

Hilton, George W. Jr. *The Ma & Pa: A History of the Maryland & Pennsylvania Railroad*. Berkeley, CA: Howell-North, 1963.

———. "The Trains Were in Transition, and It *Was* a Fascinating Railroad Business." *Trains*, November 1990, 82–83.

Hine, Lewis. *Men at Work: Photographic Studies of Modern Men and Machines*. New York: Macmillan, 1932.

Holbrook, Stewart. *The Story of American Railroads*. New York: Bonanza, 1947.

Hubbard, Freeman (attributed). "Interesting Railfans: No. 3 Lucius Beebe." *Railroad*, August 1961, 17–18.

———. *Railroad Avenue*. New York: Whittlesey House, 1945.

Keefe, Kevin. "Lucius & David." *Trains*, January 2011, 50–55.

Kuehl, John H. "Welcome back *Virginia City*." *Private Varnish* 7, no. 5 (1985): 18–21.

"Life Goes to a Party on the 'Ma and Pa' Railroad." *Life*, October 13, 1947, 160–62, 164.

Link, O. Winston (photographs), and Tim Hensley (text). *Steam, Steel & Stars: America's Last Steam Railroad*. New York: Harry N. Abrams, 1987.

Link, O. Winston (photographs), and Thomas H. Garver (text). *The Last Steam Railroad in America*. New York: Harry N. Abrams, 1995.

Lootens, J. Ghislain. *Lootens on Photographic Enlarging and Print Quality*. Baltimore: The Camera, 1944.

"Lucius Beebe." *Current Biography*, 1940, 66–67.

"Lucius Beebe, Newspaper Columnist, Author and Bon Vivant, Dies at 63." *New York Times*, February 5, 1966.

Lyden, Anne M. *Railroad Vision: Photography, Travel, and Perception*. Los Angeles: J. Paul Getty Museum, 2003.

Mariani, John. *America Eats Out*. New York: William Morrow, 1991.

Morgan, David P. "Lucius Morris Beebe, 1902–1966." *Trains*, April 1966, 4.

Parker, Dorothy. "The Trough of Plenty." *Saturday Review of Literature*, December 11, 1942, 11.

Pennoyer, A. Sheldon. *Locomotives in Our Lives*. New York: Hastings House, 1954.

Phillips, Don. "I Miss You, David, but Thank You." *Trains* 77, no. 7 (July 2017): 11.

"Picture This: CSRM Acquires Beebe and Clegg Photo Collection." *On Track* 1 (Spring 2001): 12–14.

Plotnikoff, David. "One-Man Show." *Saveur* 117 (January–February 2009): 26–28.

Plowden, David. *Requiem for Steam: The Railroad Photographs of David Plowden*. New York: W. W. Norton, 2010.

Reevy, Tony. "Artist of the Rails: David Plowden." *NRHS Bulletin* 71 (Winter 2006): 4–23.

———. "Artist of the Rails: Jim Shaughnessy." *NRHS Bulletin* 70 (Spring 2005): 4–23.

———. "Artist of the Rails: Phil Hastings." *Railroad History* 198 (Spring–Summer 2008): 66–78.

———. "Elegy for Archie." *Railroad History* 187 (Fall–Winter 2002): 109–115.

———. "Men at Work: Lewis Hine's Photographs of Railroad Workers." *Railroad History* 204 (Spring–Summer 2011): 42–51.

———. *O. Winston Link: Life Along the Line*. New York: Abrams, 2012.

———. *The Railroad Photography of Jack Delano*. Bloomington, IN: Indiana University Press, 2015.

———. "Walker Evans, American Communities and the Railroad." *Railroad Heritage* 20 (2009): 12–19.

Reevy, Tony, and Dan Cupper. "Writers of the Rail: Mixed Legacy." *Railroad History* 193 (Fall–Winter 2005): 28–39.

"Railroad Camera Club." *Railroad*, August 1938, 138.

Reynolds, Horace. "Highballing Down the Track." *New York Times*, September 28, 1952.

———. "Short-Line Railroads." *New York Times*, October 5, 1947.

Robertson, Archie. *Slow Train to Yesterday*. Boston: Houghton-Mifflin, 1945.

Ross, Don. "Legendary Lucius Beebe Dies—Olden Elegance at Any Cost." *New York Herald Tribune*, February 5, 1966.

Saxon, Wolfgang. "Jerome Zerbe, 85, Photographer of Café Society and a Columnist." *New York Times*, August 23, 1988.

Steinheimer, Richard. *Backwoods Railroads of the West*. Milwaukee, WI: Kalmbach, 1963.
Stephens, Y. Jean. "Lucius Morris Beebe: Seeing the Elephant." PhD diss., University of Iowa, 1972.
Stilgoe, John. *Metropolitan Corridor*. New Haven: Yale, 1983.
"Transport: Lacy Jones," *Time*, October 31, 1938, 39–40.
Villas, James. "Legends: Lucius Beebe, the Last Magnifico." *Gourmet*, February 1998, 82–85.
Woodward, Austin. "Virginia City Remembrances." *Journal of the West* 37, no. 1 (January 1998): 80–85.
Wrinn, Jim, and Ed Lewis. *The Road of Personal Service: A Centennial History*. Aberdeen, NC: Aberdeen & Rockfish Railroad, 1992.
Zerbe, Jerome. *John Perona's El Morocco Family Album*. New York: privately printed, 1937.
———. *People on Parade*. New York: D. Kemp, 1934.
Zerbe, Jerome, and Brendan Gill. *Happy Times*. New York: Harcourt Brace Jovanovich, 1973.

INDEX

Page numbers in *italics* refer to illustrations.

Aberdeen & Rockfish Railroad, *45*, *78*
Adams, J. Foster, 23
African Americans: brakemen, *121*; Jim Crow coaches, *11*, 96, *111*, 131, *152*
Age of Steam, The (Beebe and Clegg, 1957), 18–19
Alabama (places): Vinegar Bend, 131, *153*
Amador Central Railroad, 24, *60*, 96, *104*, 130
Amtrak, 66
Apache Railway, 66, *92*
Art Deco, 19, 65–66, *67–73*
Atchison, Topeka and Santa Fe Railway, *38*, *70*, *75*, *93*, 131, *171–72*
Atlantic & Western Railway, 130, *145*
Atlantic & Yadkin Railway, *46*

baggage services, 97, *123*, 130
Baltimore & Ohio Railroad, 24, *32*
Banner Blue, The, *26*
Beard, James, 14, 22
Beebe, Lucius: biographical sketch, xiii, 3–4, 16; as café society figure, 6–9, 19, 22, 65; class status, 95, 180n30; Clegg collaboration, xiii–xiv; Clegg romantic partnership, 8–10, 22; as journalist, 4–6, 16, 18–19, 22; marketing savvy, 10–11, 13–14; photography technical details, xiii, 8, 177; as photo subject, *2*, *4*, *7*, *11*, *12*, *13*, *17*, *19*; political views, 65; portraiture of, 95–96; railroad writings, 16; train photography career, 7–9; *Union Pacific* involvement, 7, *7*; writing style, 4, 9, 14, 18–19, 65; Zerbe romantic partnership, 6–9, 22, 65
Beebe & Clegg: Their Enduring Photographic Legacy (Gruber, Ryan, and Patrick, 2018), 16
Bellefonte Central Railroad, *40*
Best, Gerald M., 16
bicycles, 130, *141*
Big Spenders, The (Beebe, 1966), 16
Bishop, Albert F., 23
Boston and the Boston Legend (Beebe, 1935), 22, 180n27
"Bozo Texino" moniker, 66, *93*
brake clubs, *116*
brakemen, 96–97, *115–17*
brake wheels, *112*, *117–18*
Brennan, J. A., 97, *120*
Brill Railcars, *48*
Brouws, Jeff, 19

cable cars, 13–14
cabooses, *42*, *52*, 96–97, *113*, *119*, *120*, *143*
Caen, Herb, 16
café society, 6–9, 19, 22, 65
California: Amador Central Railroad, 24, *60*, 96, *104*, 130; California State Railroad Museum, 14, 16, 181n38; Henry E. Huntington

Library, 16; narrow-gauge tracks, *82*; "This Wild West" (*San Francisco Chronicle*), 16, 65. **PLACES**: Cajon Pass, *171*; Hillsborough, xiv, 16, *21*; Laws, *64*, 131, *170*; Owenyo, *82*; San Bernardino, *93*; Surf, *34*; Truckee, *35*
camelback locomotives, 96, *106–107*, 183n3 (Chap. 3)
cameras. *See* photography
Camino, Placerville & Lake Tahoe Railroad, 96, *100*
Cardinal (Frankfort & Cincinnati Railroad), *149*
Carolina & Northwestern Railway, *88*
Carson & Colorado Railway, 25, *120*
cattle guards, 131, *169*
Center for Railroad Photography and Art, 16
Central America, 10–11
Central of Georgia Railway, 33, 97
Central Pacific and Southern Pacific Railroads, The (Beebe, 1963), 18
Central Railroad of New Jersey, *106*
Chestnut Ridge Railway, 132, *173*
Chicago, Burlington & Quincy Railroad, 66, *71*
Chicago, Rock Island & Pacific Railway, 66, *71*
Child, Julia, 22
"Chili Line" (Denver & Rio Grande Western), 131, *163*
Clark, Walter Van Tilburg, 14
class status, 95, 180n30
Clegg, Charles "Chuck": as Beebe collaborator, xiii–xiv; Beebe first meeting, 7, 8; as Beebe romantic partner, 8–10, 22; biographical sketch, 8–9, 16; class status, 180n30; close-cropped composition, 66, *83*, *92*; completion of Beebe writings, 16; diesel train photographs, *153*; environmental photography and, 25, 65; military service, 9–10; as photographer, 19, 129, 177; as photo subject, *13*, *17*, *19*; Piper-Beebe House restoration, 14; portraiture of, 95–97; railroad writings, 16
club cars, *62*
Colorado: Colorado Railroad Museum, 16, *118*; Denver Public Library, 16; "High Line" route, *167*; mountain backdrop images, 24, *53*, *56*, *58*, 131–32, *156*, *162*, *164*; narrow-gauge railroads, 24, *53–59*, 131; San Luis Valley Southern Railway, *89*, 132, *175*. **PLACES**: Animas Canyon, *55*, *56*, *166*, *167*; Blanca, *89*; Coal Creek, *53*; Dolores, 131, *157*; Durango, *57*, *86*, 131, *158*; Idaho Springs, *79*; Jaroso, *175*; La Junta, *70*; Mancos, *116*, *118*; Mears Junction, 131, *161*; Midland, *54*; Ophir, *162*; Rico, *114*, *160*; Rockwood, *56*, 131, *169*; Silverton, *55*, 131, *168*; Vanadium, *58*; Vance Junction, 131, *159*
Colorado & Southern Railway, *79*
color photography, 65, 183n1 (chap. 2)
Columbus & Greenville Railway, *87*
combines, *11*, *82*, *120*
commuter trains, *49*
Comstock mining area, 13
conductors, 96–97, *112–13*, *120*
consolidations, *39*, *54*
Copper Range Railroad, 96, *112*
Cornwall Railroad, *115*
Crewdson, Gregory, 22, 130
crossings, *85*, *87*, *127*, *139*
crossing tenders, 97, *127*

Daley, Andria, 8
Daylight, *34*
"decorating" car tops, 97, *117–18*
Delano, Jack, 95
Delaware & Hudson Railway, *31*
Denver & Rio Grande Western Railway, 24, *55–57*, 66, *72–73*, *117*, 131, *158*, *164–69*
Denver & Salt Lake Railway, *53*, *156*
DeVoto, Bernard, 14
diesel railroading: Art Deco locomotive design, 66; Atchison, Topeka, and Santa Fe diesel, *171*; diesel locomotives, 24, *36*, 97, 131; diesel logos, *70*
dining cars, *2*
Dixie (Tidewater business car), 3
Dmitri, Ivan (Levon West), 7, 65, 183n1 (chap. 2)
double headers, *63*
draft gears, *83*
Dreyfuss, Henry, 65–66, *68*
driving wheels, *76*
Dubin, Arthur, 16, 18–19, 182n85

East Tennessee & Western North Carolina Railroad (Tweetsie), *91*, 96, *108*, 130, *147*
elderly and disabled workers, 96–97, *109*, *127*
Emrich, Duncan, 14, 16
engineers, *107–108*, *157*, 183n3 (chap. 3)
environmental photography: as Clegg specialty, 25, 65; emergence of, 25, 130; environmental pictorialism, 24, *33–35*; environmental portraits, 24, *42*; narrow-gauge mountain tracks, 24, *53–59*
Evans, Walker, 65, 130, *137*, *148*

Fassbender, Adolf, 129–30
Ferdinand Railroad, 66, *81*, 130, *148*
firemen, *35*, 96, *101–104*, *106*, *138*, 183n3 (chap. 3)
flagmen, 96
Flanagan, Michael, 66

folk art photography, 66, *78*, *93*, *108*
Fonda, Johnstown & Gloversville Railroad, 130, *140*, *141*
food writing, 22
footboards, *121*
Fortune magazine, 65
Frankfort & Cincinnati Railroad, *48*, 131, *149*
freight train operations: freight cars, *117*; freight train cabooses, 97; Santa Fe diesel-hauled freight train, 131

Gainesville Midland Railway, 96, *105*
"Galloping Goose" railcars, 96, 131, *159*
Georgia: post offices, *151*. **PLACES**: Albany, *33*; Cornelia, *47*; Rocky Ford, *123*; Swainsboro, *43*; Sylvania, *123*
Georgia & Florida Railway, 96, *111*
Gibbs, Wolcott, 4, *7*, 9
Gold Coast (Beebe-Clegg railroad car), xiv, 14, *17*
gondola cars, *111*, *170*
Gourmet, 16
graffiti, 66, *93*
Grasse River Railroad, *83*, 132, *174*
Great Depression, ix, 6, 22
Great Railroad Photographs U.S.A. (Beebe and Clegg, 1964), 18, 19, 25
Gruber, John, 16, 19, 96
Gulf, Mobile & Ohio Railroad, 131, *153*

"Hand of Man, The" (Stieglitz), 130
Hanley, Robert, 14
Happy Times (Zerbe and Gill, 1973), 7
harp switches, 131, *161*
Haskell, Elizabeth, 7–8, 180n27
Hastings, Philip R. "Phil," 16, 18–19, 25, 95, 129, 130
Hauck, Cornelius, 4, 8
hazardous cargo, *58*
Hear the Train Blow (Beebe and Clegg, 1952), 18
Henry, Robert Selph, 8, 183n4 (chap. 1)
Highball: A Pageant of Trains (Beebe, 1945): Clegg influence in, 129; close-cropped composition, *74*, 131; composite images, *27*; modernist photography in, *69*, *94*; as pictorial album, 18; whistling and whistle codes, *94*; writing and publication, 10
highball signals, 97, *126*
High Iron (Beebe, 1938): close-cropped composition, *71*, *76*; photographic style in, 23, 25, 65, *67*; portraiture in, 96; significance of, 8, 18, 19; writing and publication, xiii, 8
Highliners (Beebe, 1940), 19, 24, *70*
Hine, Lewis, 96
hobo moniker, 66
Holbrook, Stewart, 11, 14
Holiday, 16
Holloway, Ann Clegg, 16, 181n38
Holman, Libby, 6–7
homebuilt cars, *83*, 132, *174*
Hopper, Edward, 65
Hubbard, Freeman, 14
"Hudson" locomotives, *68*
Hungerford, Edward, 11
Huntington & Broad Top Mountain Railroad, 130, *138*

Illinois (places): Dearborn Station (Chicago), *26*
Illinois Central Railroad, *69*
Indiana: Ferdinand Railroad, 66, *81*, 130, *148*; Louisville, New Albany & Corydon Railroad, 130. **PLACES**: Corydon, *113*
industrial railroads, 96
insignia, 66
inspection cars, 96, *110*
International Engine Picture Club, 19, 23
International Great Northern Railroad, *93*

Jeffersonian, The, *27*
Jim Crow coaches, *11*, 96, *111*, 131, *152*
Jones, Casey, 10, *13*
Jukes, Fred, 19, 22, 23
Julia Bulette, *62*

"Katy" (Missouri-Kansas-Texas Railroad), 96, *110*
"Keeping up with the Casey Joneses" (Beebe *Town & Country* article, 1936), 65
Kelly's Creek & Northwestern Railway, *49*
Kentucky: Kentucky Railway Museum, *149*. **PLACES**: Centerville, 131, *149*; Clearfield, *150*
Kindig, Dick, 8

landscapes, 130
Laurentian, *31*
Laurinburg & Southern Railroad, *44*
Lehigh & New England Railroad, *39*
LGBTQ relationships, 8–10, 22
Life magazine, 65
Link, O. Winston, 18–19, 22, 25, 65, 95, 130
link and pin couplers, 66, *83–84*
Live Oak, Perry & Gulf Railroad, *4*
Locomotives in Our Lives (Pennoyer, 1954), 129
logging railroads, 131

logos, 66, *73*, *78*, *92–93*
Lootens, J. Ghislain, 19, 129–30
Louisiana: Tremont & Gulf Railway, *154*. **PLACES**: Grandstaff, *154*; Rochelle, *42*
Louisiana & North West Railroad, 97, *124*
Louisville, New Albany & Corydon Railroad, *52*, 96, *113*, 130, *143*
lubricating work, 96, *98*, *100*
Lucius Beebe Reader, The (Clegg and Emrich, eds., 1967), 16
lumber industry, 96, 132, *174*
luxury rail travel, 18. *See also* private railroad cars

mail service, *47*, 97, *122*, *124*, 130, 131, *151*, *159*
Maine Central Railroad, *126*
"Mallet" steam locomotives, 96
Manchester & Oneida Railway, 97, *125*
Manhatta (Sheeler and Strand film, 1921), 66
Manistee & North-Eastern Railway, *41*
Mansions on Rails (Beebe, 1959), 16, 18
Maryland, *National Limited* in, *32*
Maryland & Pennsylvania Railroad, 10
Massachusetts (places): Wakefield, 16
McKinley, J. H., *93*
Men at Work (Hine, 1932), 96
Metropolitan Corridor (Stilgoe, 1983), 66
Mexico, 10–11
Midland Terminal Railway, 24, *54*
milk trains, *135*
Mills, Ogden, 4
mining, *54*, *58*, *147*
Mississippi & Alabama Railroad, 97, *121*, *153*
Missouri-Kansas-Texas Railroad ("Katy"), 96, *110*
Missouri Pacific Railroad, *42*, *93*
Mixed Train Daily (Beebe, 1947): engineers and firemen, *108*; photographic style, 10, *53*; Robertson influence, *143*; significance of, 18–19, 25, 66, 129–30; writing and publication, 8, 10–11
mixed trains: defined, 183n6 (chap. 1); Jim Crow coaches, 96, 131; as tourist trains, 131. **PARTICULAR TRAINS**: Bellefonte Central, *40*; Denver & Rio Grande Western, *55*, *56*, 131, *168*; Georgia & Florida, *111*; Prescott & Northwestern, *50*; Sandersville, 131, *152*; Tremont & Gulf, *42*; Wadley Southern, 24
modernism, 65–66
Moore Central Railway, 130, *146*
Morehead & North Fork Railroad, 131, *150*
Morgan, David P., 4, 19, 22, 25
Morristown & Erie Railroad, 96, *103*
Moscow, Camden & San Augustine Railroad, *84*
Moser, Emily, 19
"Mother Hubbard" locomotives, 183n3 (chap. 3)
motorcars, 24, *45*, *48*, *124*, *149*
Mr. Pullman's Elegant Palace Car (Beebe, 1961), 18

nameplates, *67–72*
narrow-gauge railroads: Beebe-Clegg fondness for, 130, 131. **PARTICULAR TRAINS**: Colorado & Southern, *79*; Denver & Rio Grande Western, 24, *57*, *86*, *117*, 131, *163*, *164*, *165*, *169*; Rio Grande Southern, *58*, *118*; Southern Pacific, 25, *64*, *82*, *120*, 131, *170*; Sumpter Valley, 96
National Limited, *32*
Nelson & Albemarle Railway, 130, *142*
Nevada: Nevada Historical Society, 16. **PLACES**: Carson City, 14, 24, *61*, *82*, *90*; Minden, *61*, *62*; Reno, 24; Sparks, 14; Tonopah, *63*; Virginia City, xiii, 9, 14, *15*, 16, 24, 130
New Jersey (places): Hainesburg Junction, *39*; Whippany, *103*
New Mexico: narrow-gauge railroads, 131. **PLACES**: Lordsburg, *98*; Raton, *172*
New York: Grasse River Railroad, *83*, 132, *174*; New York Public Library, 16. **PLACES**: Broadalbin, 130, *141*; Childwold, *83*; Gloversville, 130; New Berlin, *135*; Otego, *133*
New York, New Haven & Hartford Railroad, *30*
New York Central Railroad, *29*, *68*
New York Herald Tribune, xiii, 4, 6, 10, 14
North Carolina: coastal plain tracks, *119*; Moore Central Railway, 130, *146*; trestles, *144*; Tweetsie, 130. **PLACES**: Blowing Rock, *108*; Boone, *91*; Broadway, 130, *145*; Cranberry, 130, *147*; Franklin, *47*
"Northern" passenger locomotive, *75*
Norwood & St. Lawrence Railroad, 97, *127*
nostalgia, 10, 14

observation cars, 182n85
Oklahoma (places): Staley Tower, *110*
"One-Man U.S.O." (Beebe, 1943), 9
order boards, *89*
ore cars, *54*, *58*
outsider art, 66, *77–81*
Overland Limited, *98*

painting (train paintings), 129
paparazzi photography, 6–7, 65
passenger train operations: Beebe fondness for, 13; commuter trains, *49*; diesel passenger trains, *36*; homemade passenger cars, 132, *174*; Jim Crow coaches, *11*, 96, *111*, 131, *152*; local passenger trains, *33*; luxury passenger trains, xiv; passenger shelters, *111*;

passenger train services, 97; Virginia & Truckee passenger trains, *61*. *See also* stations, terminals, and depots
pastoralism, *39–41*
Patrick, Mel, 16, 19
Pennoyer, A. Sheldon, 129–30
Pennsylvania: Chestnut Ridge Railway, 132, *139*, *173*. **PLACES**: Horseshoe Curve, *40*; Huntington, *138*; Kunkletown, *173*
Pennsylvania Railroad, *27–28*
People on Parade (Zerbe, 1934; introduction by Beebe), 7
Pere Marquette Railway, *41*
photography: Art Deco influences, 19, 65–66, *67–73*; Beebe career in, xiii, 7–8, 24, 177, 180n30; Clegg career in, 19, 177, 180n30; color photography, 7, 65; composite images, *27*, 182n85; cropped images, *67*, *70*, 96, 131; New York Depression-era photography, 65; night train photography, 19; over/under train views, 131; paparazzi photography, 6–7, 65; photojournalism, 65; photomontage, 19; pictorialism influences, 19; posed roster shot, xiii, 19, 23; railroad photo books, 16, 129, 180n27; tableau photography, 22, 130; tightly-framed images, 66, *68*, *71*, *74–80*, *82–84*. *See also* environmental photography; pictorialism; portraits; wedge/wedgie
pictorialism, 19, 24, *33–35*, 130, *175*
Piney River & Paint Creek Railroad, 3
Plowden, David, 19, 130
portraits: baggagemen, 97, *123*; Beebe class status and, 95; brakemen, 96–97; conductors, 96–97, *112–13*, *120*; crossing tenders, 97, *127*; elderly and disabled workers, 96–97, *109*, *127*; engineers, *107–108*, *157*; environmental portraits, 24, *42*; firemen, *35*, 96, *101–104*, *106*, *138*; flagmen, 96; history of railroad portraiture, 95–96; J. A. Brennan as subject, 97, *120*; lubricating work, 96, *98*, *100*; section workers, 97, *125*; signalmen, 97; speeders, *125*; supervisors and managers, 96; trainmen, 96–97
Prescott & Northwestern Railroad, *50*
private railroad cars, 14, 16, 18. *See also Gold Coast*; luxury rail travel; *Virginia City*
Prohibition, ix
Prospector, 66, *72–73*
Pullman Company, 18

Ragan, Leslie, 65
railcars, *48*, 96
railfan hobby, 16, 23, 66
Railroad Magazine, 19, 23
Railroad Man's Magazine, 23
railroad picture books, 16, 129, 180n27
Railroad Stories, 23
"Railroad Street," 130
Raritan River Railroad, *77*
Reading Railroad, *107*
Reid, H., 18, 25
Reid, Ogden, 4, 14
Reynolds, Horace, 18
Rio Grande Southern Railroad: brakemen, 96–97, *116*; Colorado Railroad Museum holdings, *118*; "decorating" car tops, *117*; derailed trains, *12*; engineers, 131, *157*; "Galloping Goose" railcars, *12*, 96; hazardous cargo, *58*; mail service, *159*; mountain backdrop images, *12*, 24, *58–59*, 131, *162*; as narrow-gauge railroad, 24, *118*; passenger train operations, *160*; stations, terminals, and depots, 131, *157*; trestles, 131, *158*
Rio Grand: Mainline of the Rockies (Beebe and Clegg, 1962), *53*
Robertson, Archie, 10, 18, 96, 130, *143*
rod assemblies, *75*, 129
running gears, 66, *74–76*
Ryan, John, 16

Sam Houston Zephyr, 66, *71*
sand domes, *105*
Sandersville Railroad, 131, *152*
sand houses, *86*
San Francisco Chronicle, 16
San Juan (Denver & Rio Grande Western), *164*, *165*
San Luis Valley Southern Railway, *89*, 132, *175*
Santa Fe Railway. *See* Atchison, Topeka and Santa Fe Railway
section workers, 97, *125*
service equipment, 66
Shaughnessy, Jim, 18–19, 22, 25, 129
"Shay" geared locomotive, 96, *100*
Sheeler, Charles, 66, *74–75*
"Shoreliner" Class locomotives, *30*
short-line railroads: Beebe-Clegg fondness for, 10, 130; eccentricity of, 96; as *Mixed Train Daily* subject, 10, 18; mixed trains and, 183n6 (Chap. 1); stations and terminals, 130–31; vernacular trappings in, 66, *77–81*, *109*, 132; Virginia & Truckee project, 14. **PARTICULAR TRAINS**: Amador Central Railroad, 24, *60*, 96, *104*, 130; Atlantic & Western Railway, 130; Ferdinand Railroad, 66, *81*, 130; Gainesville Midland Railway, 96, *105*; Georgia & Florida Railway, 96, *111*; Tweetsie, *91*, 96, *108*, 130; Virginia & Truckee Railroad (*see main heading*); Wadley Southern Railway, 24; Wichita Falls & Southern Railroad, 96, *109*
signals: highball signals, 97, *126*; homemade signals, 132, *173*; signal lamps, 97; warning bells, *139*
signs, *85*, *87–88*, *90*
"Silverton train" (Denver & Rio Grande Western), 131, *167–68*

Slow Train to Yesterday (Robertson, 1945), 10, 18, *143*
Smithsonian Institution, 16
Snoot If You Must (Beebe, 1943), 9, 22
snow plows, *55*
Southern Pacific Railroad: "cab forward" locomotive design, *35*; commercial viability, *64*; *Daylight*, *34*; dining cars, *2*; firemen, *102*; J. A. Brennan as conductor, 97, *120*; as narrow-gauge railroad, 25, *64*, *82*, 131, *170*; overhead views, 25; service crews, *98*; Steinheimer photos of, 18
spark arrestor, *77*
speeders, *125–26*
Spirit of St. Louis, *28*
Stanwyck, Barbara, *7*
stations, terminals, and depots: company houses, *150*; Ferdinand Railroad, *148*; as photo subjects, xiii, 130–31; small-town station stops, 130, *141*; Wood River Branch Railroad, *137*. **PARTICULAR STATIONS**: Broadalbin (New York), 130, *141*; Broadway (North Carolina), *145*; Carson City (Nevada), *90*; Clearfield (Kentucky), *150*; Cranberry (North Carolina), *147*; Dearborn Station (Chicago), *26*; Gloversville (New York), 130, *140*; Huntington (Pennsylvania), *138*; Moore Central Railway (North Carolina), *146*; Schuyler (Virginia), *142*; Silverton (Colorado), 131, *168*. *See also* passenger train operations
Stations: An Imagined Journey (Flanagan, 1994), 66
Steam, Steel & Stars (Link, 1987), 25
steam railroading: Beebe interest in, 14; brakeman archetype, *116*; "cab forward" locomotive design, *35*; camelback locomotives, 96, *106–107*; close-cropped images, *74*, *80*; driving wheels, *76*; fire checking, *35*; "Mallet" steam locomotives, *96*; narrow-gauge locomotives, *170*; rod assemblies, *75*, 129; running gear images, *74–76*; "Shay" geared locomotive, *100*; smoke and steam depictions, 24, *37–38*, 129, 130, 131, *172*; steam locomotives, *4*; water tanks, 96, *99*, *101–104*, 131, *154*, *155*; wood-burning engines, *121*
Steinheimer, Richard "Dick," 18–19, 22, 25, 129
Stephens, Y. Jean, 3
Stewartstown Railroad, 97, *122*
Stieglitz, Alfred, 130
Stilgoe, John, 66
St. Johnsbury & Lake Champlain Railroad, 130, *136*
Stork Club Bar Book, The (Beebe, 1946), 22
Sumpter Valley Railway, 96, *99*
Super Chief, *70*
supervisors and managers, 96
switch-engine pilots, 97
switch keys, *116*
switch lamps, *126*
switch stands, *91*, *97*, *126*, 131, *161*

tableau photography, 22, 130
Tallulah Falls Railway, *47*, 131, *151*
Tennessee (places): Johnson City, *91*
Territorial Enterprise (Beebe-Clegg newspaper), xiii–xiv, 14, *15*, 16, 65
Texas: DeGolyer Collection (Southern Methodist University), 16. **PLACES**: Denison, *110*; Ranger, 131, *155*; San Antonio, *93*
"This New York" (Beebe *Herald Tribune* column), 6, 10
"This Wild West" (Beebe *San Francisco Chronicle* column), 16, 65
"thousand-mile shirt" image, *116*
Tidewater Railway, 3
ties, 96
Tonopah & Goldfield Railroad, 25, *63*
tourist trains, 131
Town & Country, 16
track ends, 175
trainmen, 96–97
Trains (Henry, 1934), 8, 183n4 (chap. 1)
Trains in Transition (Beebe, 1941), *36*, 66, 73, 96, *102*
Trains magazine, ix, 19, 25
Trains We Rode, The (Beebe and Clegg, 1965–66), 16, 19, 25
Tremont & Gulf Railway, *42*, 131, *154*
trestles, *47*, 131, *144*, *158*
triple meets, *165*
trucks, 66, *82*
Twain, Mark, 14
Tweetsie (East Tennessee & Western North Carolina Railroad), *91*, 96, *108*, 130, *147*
Twentieth Century Limited, 65, 182n85

Unadilla Valley Railway, 130, *135*
Union Pacific (1939 film), 7, *7*
Union Pacific Railroad, *36–37*, 96, *98*, *101*, *134*
unions, 95
utility poles, 132, *134*, *138*, *175*

Vermont (railroads): St. Johnsbury & Lake Champlain Railroad, *136*
vertical framing, 24, *53*, *56*, *60*, *126*
Virginia (places): Schuyler, 130, *142*
Virginia & Carolina Southern Railroad, *119*, *144*
Virginia & Truckee: A Story of Virginia City and Comstock Times (Beebe and Clegg, 1949), 11, 18

Virginia & Truckee Railroad: as Beebe-Clegg photo subject, 4, 130; *Gold Coast* private car, xiv, 14, *17*; *Julia Bulette* car, *62*; passenger operations, *61*, *62*; rescue efforts, 4, 14; ticket office sign, *90*; tightly-framed images, *80*, *82*; as tourist train, 13; *Virginia & Truckee* (1949), 11, 18
Virginia City (Beebe-Clegg railroad car), xiv, 14, 16
Virginia City News, 14

Wabash Railroad, *26*
Wadley Southern Railway, *11*, 24, *43*
Wall, Jeff, 22, 130
warning bells, *139*
water tanks, 96, *99*, *101–104*, 131, *154*, *155*
Weatherford, Mineral Wells & Northwestern Railway, *51*
Webb, Clifton, 6
Webb, Sim, *13*
wedge snow plows, *55*
wedge/wedgie (three-quarter) shots: backwards motion shots, 24, *49*; Beebe use of, xiii, 19; diesel wedge shots, *36*; environmental portraits, *42*; examples, *26–31*; overhead wedge shots, 24–25, 32, *64*; pastoralism influences in, *39–41*; "smoking wedges," 18–19; technique for, 23–24
West Virginia (places): Cass, 131
wheel reports, *120*
whistling and whistle codes, *94*
White, John, Jr., 4, 8, 9–10
Wichita Falls & Southern Railroad, 96, *109*, 131, *155*
Wood River Branch Railroad, 130, *137*
World War II, 9–10
Wyoming (places): Laramie, 96, *98*; Sherman Summit, 130, *134*

Zerbe, Jerome, 6–7, 22, 65

TONY REEVY is director of development for the General H. Hugh Shelton Leadership Center and the Institute for Emerging Issues at North Carolina State University, Raleigh, North Carolina. He is a graduate of North Carolina State University, UNC-Chapel Hill, and Miami University. His previous publications include poetry, nonfiction, and short fiction. He resides in Durham, North Carolina, with his wife, Caroline Weaver, and children, Lindley and Ian.

JIM SHAUGHNESSY is one of the most influential forces that reshaped American railroad-subject photography in the 1950s. Shaughnessy's work has appeared in over one hundred books and has been featured in *Trains, Railroad, Railfan,* and *Classic Trains.* He authored the seminal works *Delaware & Hudson* (1967) and *The Rutland Road* (1964). He was honored with a lifetime achievement award for photography from the Railway and Locomotive Historical Society in 1987. He lived with his wife, Carol, in Troy, New York.